Library of
Davidson College

SIMULATED INTERNATIONAL PROCESSES

To **Bud**
    that is, Dr. Wayman J. Crow, Director
                 Western Behavioral Sciences Institute
                 La Jolla, California

and to **Tom**
    that is, Dr. Thomas W. Milburn, former Director
                 Project Michelson
                 Naval Ordnance Station
                 China Lake, California

and to **Thane**
    that is, Colonel William Thane Minor, USAF, retired
                 Joint War Games Agency/Studies, Analysis and Gaming Agency
                 The Joint Chiefs of Staff
                 U.S. Department of Defense
                 Washington, D.C.

and to **Dick**
    that is, Dr. Richard C. Snyder, former Chair
                 Department of Political Science
                 Northwestern University
                 Evanston, Illinois

Without the intellectual, organizational, and emotional support of these generous colleagues, the outcomes of our Northwestern project on Simulated International Processes would have been fewer and of less import. And without the beneficence of Dr. Gordon Scott Fulcher, completion of the task would have been impossible.

Simulated International Processes

Theories and Research in Global Modeling

edited by
HAROLD GUETZKOW
and **JOSEPH J. VALADEZ**

ⓢ SAGE PUBLICATIONS   Beverly Hills   London

327.07
S614

Copyright © 1981 by Sage Publications, Inc.

All rights reserved. No part of this book may be reproduced or utilized in any form or by any means, electronic or mechanical, including photocopying, recording, or by any information storage and retrieval system, without permission in writing from the publisher.

For information address:

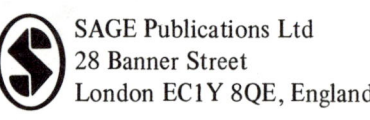

SAGE Publications, Inc.
275 South Beverly Drive
Beverly Hills, California 90212

SAGE Publications Ltd
28 Banner Street
London EC1Y 8QE, England

Printed in the United States of America

Library of Congress Cataloging in Publication Data

Main entry under title:
Simulated international processes.

    Includes bibliographies and index.
    1. International relations—Research.
I. Guetzkow, Harold Steere.   II. Valadez,
Joseph J.

JX1291.S395   327'.0724   80-29047

ISBN 0-8039-1574-8   82-7431

FIRST PRINTING

CONTENTS

Preface	7
Part I. Simulations in International Relations	11
1. Simulated International Processes: An Incomplete History Harold Guetzkow	13
2. The Inter-Nation Simulation Harold Guetzkow	23
3. An Economic Model and Government Stability: Reconstructing the Inter-Nation Simulation Charles D. Elder and Robert E. Pendley	65
4. The International Processes Simulation Paul L. Smoker	101
5. The Simulated International Processer Stuart A. Bremer	135
Part II. Simulated International Processes: Interpretations	179
6. Generational Development in Modeling Joseph J. Valadez and Gary L. Tygesson	181
7. International Relations Theory: Contributions of Simulated International Processes Harold Guetzkow and Joseph J. Valadez	197
8. Simulation and "Reality": Validity Research Harold Guetzkow and Joseph J. Valadez	253

9. Six Continuing Queries for Global Modelers: A Self-Critique
    Harold Guetzkow   331

Appendix A: Core Bibliography on
            Simulated International Processes
    Joseph J. Valadez   359

Appendix B: Guide to Northwestern University
            Simulation Documents
    Joseph J. Valadez   387

Appendix C: The Northwestern Simulation Archives
    Walter E. Busse   393

Index   394

About the Editors   400

PREFACE

We are thankful for Stuart M. Bremer's (1976: 4) complaint about the "relative inaccessibility of many of the studies" from the Simulated International Processes (SIP) project. His gentle proding influenced our decision to turn our energies to this panorama of the past two decades of SIP research.

Our driving goal in developing this volume has been to highlight the research produced by the SIP collaborators. In this way the insights from the three simulation models (Inter-Nation Simulation, International Processes Simulation, Simulated International Processer) may be displayed and compared. We consider this volume to be a relatively complete and final exhibition of SIP research, accumulating its most important substantive products. It examines variables which are of interest to a broad group of scholars. Its analyses may be seminal for social scientists who have encountered difficulties in their investigations of international behavior, either in the laboratory or in the field (but see Hoole, 1979: 1509).

There is a growing excitement in the field of global modeling, as witnessed by the flurry of research produced during the last ten years by projects commissioned by the Club of Rome. At the 1979 World Congress of the International Political Science Association in Moscow, a special meeting was devoted entirely to world modeling. With the heightened interest in simulations for nurturing understanding of global processes both inside and outside of academia, we hope that scholars and policymakers alike will find this volume useful as a source book.

SIMULATIONS IN INTERNATIONAL RELATIONS

The book commences with "an incomplete history" of fifteen years of simulation research at Northwestern University (1957-1972). Harold Guetzkow views the project's three simulation models in terms of philosophical, methodological, educational, and policy issues, and identifies salient influences nurturing the development of SIP. There are two important ways in which enrichment of the substantive contents of the simulations have occurred: (a) Generational changes resulted from overall dissatisfaction with the adequacy of contents of earlier models; and (b) as the simulations were used in problem investigation, their contents were elaborated to enable scholars to mount their research designs.

Following this initial overview, Guetzkow presents in Chapter 1 details about the Inter-Nation Simulation, SIP's widely used prototype person-computer simulation. Through narration and the use of mathematical equations, he exhibits underlying assumptions of the model. He describes national decision-making processes and then delineates relations among the simulated nations.

In "An Economic Model and Government Stability: Reconstructing the Inter-Nation Simulation," Charles D. Elder and Robert E. Pendley propose an alternative interpretation of Guetzkow's equation modeling "officeholding" in the Inter-Nation Simulation (INS). Using contemporary international relations theory and empirical information, they conclude that while the INS equation may represent stability, it refers to the stability of a governmental system rather than to the stability of a particular regime. The programmed relationships of the economic submodel of the INS are also analyzed. Having detected conceptual weaknesses, the authors present empirical material supporting adoption of an alternative set of equations.

Paul L. Smoker's chapter, "International Processes Simulation," describes a second-generation SIP person-computer model. The International Processes Simulation (IPS), while representing decision-making processes among heads of state, as does the Inter-Nation Simulation, adds nongovernmental organizations, international corporations, and citizens' groups. By increasing the complexity of person-computer simulations, Smoker is able to develop political and economic variables previously unstudied by simulation researchers.

In Chapter 5, Stuart A. Bremer presents the Simulated International ProcessER (SIPER), an all-computer SIP model of decision-making in international affairs. Complementing his exposition with detailed flow diagrams, Bremer substitutes "artificial intelligence" programs for the human decision-makers used in the Inter-Nation Simulation and develops algorithms to represent the interactions among nations, encompassing such features as trade, aid, and alliances. (The equations Bremer uses to delineate these processes are modified versions of those he published in his 1977 volume, *Simulated Worlds*.) In addition to moving skillfully from a person-computer to an all-computer format, Bremer's achievement is to ground many of his computer routines conceptually and empirically in the scientific literature of international relations.

SIMULATED INTERNATIONAL PROCESSES: INTERPRETATIONS

Joseph J. Valadez and Gary L. Tygesson begin this section by comparing and contrasting salient characteristics of each of the three simulation constructions (INS, IPS, and SIPER). Using flowcharts for heuristic purposes, the authors highlight distinct features of the SIP models. We recommend their chapter to those who may not want to read the preceding chapters, which are devoted to individual discussion of each simulation. The Valadez and Tygesson piece should give sufficient background for one to distinguish between the three simulations in terms of their underlying structures and the varying uses to which the models may be put.

In "International Relations Theory: Contributions of Simulated International Processes," Guetzkow and Valadez inspect outputs from twenty-one INS studies. Alker and Bock's synthesis of some seventy-five summary articles on international relations from the *International Encyclopedia of the Social Sciences* is used as comparative material for exhibiting the outputs of this simulation research. Guetzkow and Valadez display the capacity of SIP for mounting and clarifying theories prominent in traditional theoretical work. They conclude with an integration of SIP's substantive findings.

This analysis of SIP's outcomes is followed by Guetzkow and Valadez's validity study of outputs from the three SIP constructions. The authors survey over thirty SIP studies comparing SIP outputs (mostly derived from the Inter-Nation Simulation) with empirical materials obtained through political, economic, social, and military studies of international affairs. From these studies more than 130 instances are examined for correspondences between simulations and international "realities." This chapter is the most comprehensive treatment of simulation validity available at this time.

It is hoped that our more graphically minded readers will find our tables and charts of some value as they pursue the intricacies of the simulations and their outputs. Almost always the contents of our visual materials, including the quasi-causal schematics, are presented in the verbal text to accommodate those who usually find graphics confusing rather than helpful (see Ward, 1979: 1114).

The text concludes with an epilog by Guetzkow, "Six Continuing Queries for Global Modelers: A Self-Critique," in which he describes salient questions that continue to haunt those engaged in global modeling.

APPENDICES

The three appendices present the references and descriptions of source materials. Appendix A is a bibliography consisting of titles cited in this book plus the essays and books produced by the SIP project at Northwestern University. The latter (in part developed by Doreen R. Ellis in Hoole and Zinnes, 1976: 497-513) are distinguished from the former by an asterisk preceding the author's name. This list of materials is the most comprehensive consolidation of SIP references available and should be an aid to scholars tracing its roots. Appendix B, a "Core Bibliography on

Simulated International Processes," lists the content of a collection of in-house papers, now in the archives of the Northwestern University Library; the three volumes include discussions of SIP theory, analyses, and mathematical models and methods. These are available through interlibrary loan.

Appendix C is a brief description of Walter E. Busse's (1969) "The Northwestern Simulation Archives: Person-Computer Models of International Relations." These materials consist of a wealth of simulation outputs produced by a series of INS and IPS runs executed during the 1960s. Many of these protocols have not yet been analyzed; they are available for use by all.

By consolidating SIP materials we hope to resolve the "complaint" by our friend and colleague that SIP studies are inaccessible.

The construction of three SIP models was pursued within a diverse research environment (Valadez and Tygesson, 1981: passim) consisting of "super-teams," "sub-teams," and "side-teams" (Guetzkow, 1970: 42). The individuals fulfilling these roles have been inexorably linked to Guetzkow's professional life since 1956. Thus, a short history may be more appropriate than mere enumeration of those who have played a role in the development of SIP. It is quite appropriate, then, that the chapter following this orientation is Guetzkow's brief autobiographical essay, in which he identifies salient influences and individuals in the Simulated International Processes project.

Appreciation is due to the Fulcher Chair of Decision-Making in International Affairs at Northwestern University, under whose auspices many simulators have been nurtured, both in body and mind. We should also like to thank Ted R. Gurr, Chair of the Political Science Department, and Allan Schnaiberg, Chair of Sociology, who extended research facilities to Joseph J. Valadez during his two years of post-doctoral activities at Northwestern. We are grateful to Thomas L. Jacobs of the Vogelback Computing Center for his consultation as we sorted out our computer problems. Finally, we want to give a special word of thanks to Michael Don Ward for his valuable opinions and responses to our numerous requests for feedback on "just one more question" as the essays in this volume were edited and developed. And to Norma L. Wood and Catherine V. Montague: What would we have done without your loyalty and eleventh-hour fortitutde?

–H. G.
Evanston, Illinois
J.J.V.
College Park, Maryland

PART I

Simulations in International Relations

1
Simulated International Processes: An Incomplete History
Harold Guetzkow

Work on simulated international processes began during my year at the Center for Advanced Study in the Behavioral Sciences (1956-1957), while I was involved in a study group with Richard C. Snyder, Karl W. Deutsch, Charles A. McClelland, and Wilbur Schramm. My background of experiences as the director of the Social Science Laboratory at Carnegie-Mellon University (1950-1956) acquainted me with the limitations and potentials of social psychological experimentation, as well as those of all-computer simulations. The latter were pinpointed in the area of my substantive interest (international relations) by "A Simple Diplomatic Game," by Oliver Benson (1961: 504-511). Hans Speier, also at the center that year from the RAND Corporation, shared insights from his use of all-manual games, which usually focused upon crisis situations (Goldhammer and Speier, 1959: 71-83). The goal was to develop a creative, balanced simulation of the overall international scene, using a vehicle that would facilitate both explicitness and cumulative work.

Construction of an inter-nation simulation was begun immediately upon my arrival at Northwestern University in the fall of 1957, within the context of a broad international relations program that had been formulated by Snyder (1962) and sponsored by the Carnegie Corporation of

Author's Note: This essay was originally published under the title "An Incomplete History of Fifteen Short Years in Simulating International Processes," pp. 247-258 in Francis W. Hoole and Dina A. Zinnes (eds.), *Quantitative International Politics: An Appraisal* (New York: Praeger, 1976). Its preparation formed part of my activities as Gordon Fulcher Professor of Decision-Making at Northwestern University.

New York. One of the project's most critical decisions was taken then, which was to utilize a person-machine format for creation of the simulation, hoping thereby to combine the advantages of both all-manual and machine simulations and simultaneously to avoid their peculiar shortcomings, as has been explained elsewhere (Guetzkow, 1970: 31-53). After pilot runs (Noel, 1963c: 69-102), including an as yet exploratory but quite critical demonstration at Asilomar with senior members of the academic community and a number of former foreign service officers, further development of the Inter-Nation Simulation (INS), as it was then labeled, was ready for outside sponsorship. Support was obtained from the Air Force Office of Scientific Research (AFOSR) in 1959. In 1964 the sponsorship shifted from AFOSR to the then newly established Advanced Research Projects Agency (ARPA) of the U.S. Department of Defense.

At this point the project became known as Simulated International Processes (SIP), inasmuch as the Inter-Nation Simulation (INS) was already being considered as only a "first-generation" simulation. The generous support now being received made possible a succession of "in-house" assistant directors, each of whom helped elaborate the ongoing work and gave his own distinction to it. Lloyd Jensen (1965-1966) implemented his interest in comparing the "output" validity of various runs of INS with the outcomes of judgments made by foreign service officers (Guetzkow and Jensen, 1966: 261-274). Paul L. Smoker (1966-1969) emphasized the extension and reformulation of programmed aspects of the Inter-Nation Simulation, while enriching its manual components. His work represented such a quantum change from INS that it seemed wise to rechristen this modified version of the original simulation as the "International Processes Simulation" (IPS), truly a "second-generation" model (see Chapter 4). Throughout the participation of Smoker as well as that of Michael R. Leavitt, there was a growing interest in all-computer simulations of world affairs. As the last assistant director (1966-1971), Leavitt constructed a macro-module known as "A Computer Simulation of International Alliance Behavior" (Leavitt, 1971a). However, it was the initiative of Stuart A. Bremer in taking advantage of a year's student exchange privilege that crowned the effort of SIP with the construction of the Simulated International ProcessER (SIPER), an all-computer specification of a revised and updated version of the Inter-Nation Simulation, the "third-generation" model (Bremer, 1970, 1977).[1]

The Simulated International Processes (SIP) project was funded from both private and public resources, the private money enabling us to complement the public money when federal restriction on certain uses of the latter prevented completion of the task. Full acknowledgments, along with contract and grant numbers, are detailed elsewhere (Guetzkow, 1970:

1-2; 1972). It was a tremendous privilege to participate in the stewardship of these funds. I am most grateful for the intellectual and bureaucratic aid given me in the development of the SIP project, by my government monitors as well as by our foundation aides. May I certify herewith that in no way was there ever interference in our scholarly work by anyone in the organizations from which we received funding. We worked with complete academic freedom.

The intellectual history of SIP to date has been exhibited in two contexts, as an exercise in model development (Guetzkow, 1970) and by the self-assessment of its cumulative characteristics recently prepared for the National Science Foundation (Guetzkow, 1976b). Bremer's evaluation, in Chapter 15 of Hoole and Zinnes's *Quantitative International Politics: An Appraisal,* of the substance of the project accurately develops a chronology of four phases: development of the INS as a person-machine simulation with its many variations, its applications in education and research, the study of its validity, and the forays into all-computer simulation. Another historical record is found in its products, as listed in the project bibliography. Complaint about the "relative inaccessibility of many of the studies" (Bremer, 1977: 14) is well taken; an attempt is being made to remedy this situation by placing some of the studies on microfilm.

Now it is possible to consider the intellectual development of the project from yet another point of view, less chronologically oriented, by noting how it confronted some of its challenges: (1) how it posed and tried to solve its underlying problems in methodology and technique, all within the framework of a day-by-day working philosophy of science; (2) how it attempted to integrate its findings; (3) how it went about meshing its development with contemporary research in the substance of international politics; and (4) how it strove to build a communication net between makers and users for policy purposes. Let us now consider each of these encounters briefly, inasmuch as they give background for the reading of the four essays on SIP that constitute its evaluation. (See Hoole and Zinnes, 1976: Chs. 13-16.)

THE PHILOSOPHICAL AND METHODOLOGICAL CONTEXT OF THE SIMULATED INTERNATIONAL PROCESSES PROJECT

The central question of the project was formulated early: Can one construct a simulation of international relations? The question was answered by constructing a person-machine simulation consisting of both domestic and international components, called the Inter-Nation Simulation (INS). This pragmatic style permeated our approach to problems in the philosophy of science.

The first essay that presented the INS also sketched an overall philosophic viewpoint of the effort to be undertaken, and positioned its working definition of "simulation" (Guetzkow, 1969c: 284-300). The perspective was stated with more insight and fullness in the course of the project; it showed the development of this perspective as follows:

> [It] became increasingly clear, as we went from pilot run to pilot run in 1957 through 1959, that our participants were not serving as human subjects within an experimental situation, as it had been my custom to regard those who took part in the experiments at Michigan and Carnegie Tech. This laboratory situation was different, in that our human participants were acting as surrogates rather than as experimental subjects in their own right. In the development of our national entities it was our intention to use abstract representations, so that all participants, regardless of nationality, could man any of the nations [and] act in terms of the simulated environment within which they would find themselves. . . .
>
> Thus, our simulation was not . . . a laboratory counter-part of field behaviors. As it gradually developed the Inter-Nation Simulation was rather a theoretical construction complemented by the verbal and mathematical formulations [Guetzkow, 1970: 42-43].

In an attempt to check out this phase of the project's posture, a small working conference was developed in the winter of 1964-1965 to tap the philosophic wisdom of Wes Churchman, Herbert Hockberg, and Abraham Kaplan. A dissenting reaction to the conference was prepared at the time by a colleague, Paul Kress, which has been published but without updating its materials, thereby constituting another part of the printed historical record (Kress, 1974: 41-50). Inasmuch as this was the period in which the project was moving from its emanation of the INS simulation as such into checks on its veridicality, problems in validity were considered at the meeting, resulting in the essay by Charles F. Hermann (1967b: 216-231). This helped us recognize the Churchmanian emphasis on the fact that the purposes for the use of the simulation also help determine the selection of the methodology to be employed for the study of validity.

Although I was being rapidly socialized in the scholarship of political science at Northwestern by Richard C. Snyder and Chadwick F. Alger, two colleagues with whom I was in constant and close interaction until their lamented departure from Northwestern, it seems to me that my sociological and psychological backgrounds were important determinants in placing the emphasis of the project upon validation, once a working simulation had been constructed. However, after the findings in validity were integrated (Guetzkow, 1969c), it seemed that little would be gained by continuing such work on the INS. It appeared that strategic advances were more likely to be made through construction of a revised model, as was being done by Smoker (1968) in his International Processes Simulation (IPS).

Another of my colleagues at Northwestern, namely Donald T. Campbell, was important in establishing the context in which we worked, as he became a person of increasing charisma in our seminars and for our graduate students, especially in the application of his notions of "proximal similarity" in support of our "quasi-experiments." The essay by John R. Raser, Donald T. Campbell, and Richard W. Chadwick documents this aspect of our philosophic methodological context (Raser et al., 1970: 183-204).

ATTEMPTS TO INTEGRATE OUTCOMES

There were at least two reasons for me, as the director of the project, to create substantive integrations of our work as we went along. I needed such for summing up where we stood as we developed the guidelines for our work, and I needed ways of placing our project within the field of other simulation efforts as well as more broadly within the net of persons who were making such assessments; but on occasion it was possible to commission efforts with common focus, even though each author usually insisted upon tailoring his essay to his own perspectives. Though they were often disjointed, parallel efforts were being undertaken by others. I tried always to be sensitive to the academic freedoms of my collaborators, especially since I was conducting government-sponsored research.

To make sure that the milieu in which I was operating in the simulation field was well canvassed, Richard Dawson helped me prepare a reader of simulation pieces in other social science disciplines (Guetzkow, 1962c). This review was updated at the conclusion of the project (Guetzkow, Kotler, and Schultz, 1972). Although it would have been desirable for the latter book to have included a piece surveying the overall philosophical-methodological developments in international relations at that time, I failed to identify anyone with such an interest. I myself was by then too fully involved in my long-postponed leaves of absence, gaining life experiences in decision-making in international affairs under Elliot Richardson in the U.S. Department of State (1969-1970) and Ralph Bunche in the United Nations (1970-1971).

Three pieces, focusing on simulation works in international relations as such, analyzed developments in the "manual" or "all-person" game, as exemplified by the RAND-MIT developments of Lincoln Bloomfield and his associates (Fischer, 1969), in the person-computer development (Coplin, 1966: 562-578), and in the all-computer simulation (Gordon, 1968: 222-245). These constituted another attempt at integration in the field. Hayward R. Alker and one of his students worked empirically in an effort to integrate these three simulation approaches, using the same substantive problem (Alker and Brunner, 1969: 70-110). His efforts resulted in three case studies, tightly interwoven, using a scenario revolving around a nuclear explosion in the People's Republic of China.

Based upon this comparative work, Alker then made an appraisal of the decision-makers' environments in the Inter-Nation Simulation (Alker, 1968: 31-58). This important piece had little impact upon developments in the project, however, inasmuch as Smoker had already formulated most of the changes involved in his International Processes Simulation. It was possible to get a critique of the Inter-Nation Simulation from Modelski, too (Modelski, 1970: 111-134). Although it was reassuring to know that Smoker had anticipated almost all of Modelski's creative suggestions, the timing was such that Modelski's essay was not used in the development of Smoker's work.

As an individual I was able to prepare an integration of our findings from some twenty-four different studies on the substantive validity of the person-computer simulations (Guetzkow, 1966a). My inability to correlate the timing of the commissioned pieces, given the previous obligations of those involved, discouraged further attempts to develop consolidations. Perhaps the project's greatest failure was brought about in my attempt to mount a joint effort with a full-time research associate in the "Event Simulation Project," as mentioned elsewhere (Bremer, 1976). This endeavor fell apart after some years of effort, largely because of exogenous factors.

MESHING PROJECT DEVELOPMENTS WITH CONTEMPORARY DEVELOPMENTS

Through the decade and a half of the project's existence, it seemed desirable to keep close contact with the developments in international relations of the more traditional variety, which were continuing apace, as well as to attempt to mesh the activities of SIP with more recent data-grounded research (Jones and Singer, 1972). The funding agreements of the projects made it possible to "contract out" portions of the research for such purposes as integration, as described above. This device was also used to induce Robert L. Pfaltzgraff, Jr. (1972a), to make a check on the extent to which the concepts utilized in the three prototype simulations (RAND-MIT, the political-military exercise [Bloomfield and Whaley, 1965: 854-870]; the Inter-Nation Simulation; and TEMPER, the all-computer simulation developed by Clark C. Abt and Morton Gordon [1969, 245-262]) overlapped with those used by ten prominent scholars in the verbal literature, in some ways coming full circle on the work of Denis G. Sullivan (1963) who had early attempted to spell out concepts found in textbooks for inclusion in the original formulation of the Inter-Nation Simulation.

On the other hand, there were a small number of projects commissioned, in each of which the contracting investigator was asked to apply his own materials to simulation formulations in order to modify the latter conceptually in terms of his frame of reference; he later attempted to use his own empirical work to check out the adequacy of the suggested revisions in the simulation.[2] A stellar example of such work is found in the utilization of data from the 1914 project by Dina A. Zinnes, in which she made an analysis of person-machine runs, using both the designs of her earlier analysis and the data obtained from historical archives on the interchange of communications during the period before World War I (Zinnes, 1966b: 289-293).

BUILDING A COMMUNICATION NET
FOR POLICY PURPOSES

One important motivation of the U.S. government in providing the bulk of the funding for the project derived from the interest of two unusual military officers, both from the Air Force, Colonels William Thane Minor and George L. Draper, who during the existence of SIP were working intermittently within the Joint War Games Agency of the Office of the Joint Chiefs of Staff and the Industrial College of the Armed Forces. These concerned men facilitated within their military complex the use of simulation for gaming purposes, sometimes also providing briefings for audiences on an interagency basis. In this process an extensive network of communications was built between the users of our research and the project researchers. The servicing of the network placed important demands upon our resources. My personal motivations, stemming from my high school debating experience and powerfully reinforced by my five-year period of "alternative service" with like-minded men as a conscientious objector during World War II, spurred my constant attempts to interest personnel from the U.S. Department of State in utilization of the work, but these efforts met with little success. Suggestions for such implementation are described elsewhere (Guetzkow, 1969c: 289-293).

Often the research subcontracts provided for the travel of the contractor to Northwestern as well as for the project director and his associates to consult at the subcontractor's home base, allowing deep exposure of each to the other's work. Field visits to the subcontractor often involved a presentation of details about SIP to colleagues and graduate students who were involved in scholarly work in international relations. In addition, many contacts were made with researchers through programmed panels and informally in the course of corridor contacts.

Our interaction with producers and users was not limited to the United States. In the development of a net among persons interested in simulation in Asia, the six-month visit of Hiroharu Seki to SIP eventuated in laboratory work in Tokyo as well as in a book describing the Inter-Nation Simulation and his realizations thereof (Seki, 1969). On the European scene there was interest by English scholars, such as John W. Burton and his associates (Burton, 1966), as well as by Canadians, through Jerome Laulicht and his colleagues, in the Canadian Peace Research Institute (Laulicht, 1967: 14-18). In these ways the results of SIP were shared overseas, allowing governments of many persuasions to understand the potentials of applying simulations to their foreign policy activities. Although for a while it looked as if the Western Behavioral Sciences Institute would spark a coordinated effort, involving Ruge from Norway, Diaz-Guerrero from Mexico, Mushakoji of Japan, and Raser of the United States, in the end this extremely important project was not executed.

This account is far from a complete history of SIP, although perhaps the foregoing materials have indicated the ways in which four central challenges of the project were met in the course of its development. It was in these efforts that the resources of the project were devoted to creating its meta-methodological postures, to maintaining some integration of its centrifugal tendencies, to reducing its insularity and provinciality, and to centering it in the mainstream of developments in the creation and utilization of knowledge about international affairs.

In the end there were at least two important items on the unfinished agenda of SIP. Early in our project discussions, the notion of executing the INS as a very abstract, highly generalized exercise without substantive international relations content had been suggested by Denis G. Sullivan. Such research would have enabled us to fathom, to some extent at least, the way in which the underlying processes of the INS were influencing the outcomes, and then it would have allowed us to consider the impact of substance-content upon its outcomes, were a comparison to be made between the INS and its abstract formulation, similar to the manner in which Pilisuk and Rapoport explored their prisoner's dilemma games in the Michigan Disarmament series. (Rapoport, 1967: 40-45). Second, it is with regret that a venture in the use of creative persons as decision-makers in the INS was not undertaken, especially in the operation of an IPS. If "social scientists should not only tell it the way it is, but also tell it the way it could be" (Smoker, 1969d: 11), an opportunity for productive, insightful individuals to address the perennial problems of international affairs would not be forgone.

Perhaps this brief history helps one understand why, as director of the project, I thought the fifteen years of its duration formed entirely too short a period in which to build an even somewhat satisfactory simulation of international relations. Little wonder, then, that I cherish the opportunities I hope will be mine during the next fifteen years to work further on the simulation of international processes (Guetzkow, Hollist, and Ward, 1977).

NOTES

1. Professor Bremer was obtaining his doctorate at Michigan State University; he became a visiting research assistant in SIP (1968-1969) through the Traveling Scholar Program of the Big Ten Committee in Inter-Institutional Cooperation. Upon returning to East Lansing, Bremer built SIPER without further communication under a dissertation committee chaired by Rufus P. Browning. Bremer presented a copy of his completed dissertation to the amazed staff of the Simulated International Processes project in the middle of August 1970.

2. This notion of attempting to mesh ongoing research in an articulated way with other researches is argued in the context of studies on disasters in an essay that was prepared by the author for the National Research Council of the National Academy of Sciences (Guetzkow, 1962b: 350-354).

2
The Inter-Nation Simulation
Harold Guetzkow

Snyder (1963a) has located the simulation of relations among nations within the broader context of work in international relations. Brody (1963b) has analyzed the variety of games, exercises, and simulations that have been developed within international relations itself. Guetzkow (1963) has provided an overall description of an inter-nation simulation developed at Northwestern University. Noel (1963b) gives details of how this particular simulation was evolved to meet theoretical needs. In this chapter, it may be helpful to attempt a somewhat rigorous summarization of the assumptions involved in the development of the programs used within the Inter-Nation Simulation. These structured postulates then may be examined as they relate to the emergence of the free activities of the decision-makers operating within the framework of the programmed assumptions. The following analysis presents a summarization of the theoretical model developed in the simulation during 1958 and 1959.

I. GUIDEPOSTS IN THE CONSTRUCTION OF AN INTER-NATION MODEL

The relations among nations are embodied in the simulation by the postulation of programs of operation with respect to the internal function-

Author's Note: This chapter was originally published under the title "Structured Programs and Their Relations to Free Activity Within the Inter-Nation Simulation," pp. 103-149 in Harold Guetzkow et al. (eds.), *Simulation in International Relations: Developments for Research and Teaching* (Englewood Cliffs, NJ: Prentice-Hall, 1963).

ing of the several nations constituting the overall inter-nation system. Using these programs, the decision-makers of each nation then freely develop relations between their states as they deem appropriate, given their unfolding circumstances. It is possible to vary the assumptions made within the programs, as Noel has demonstrated. Such changes in operating postulates should result in variations in the unprogrammed activities, which emerge as the nations relate to each other within the developing overall system.

The simulation is grounded in explicit specification of a basic set of variables and programmed relations among them. But because of the use of human beings as decision-makers in the system, a variety of additional factors—and relations among them—are implicitly incorporated in the representation. Together, these two kinds of factors and their relationships produce an operating environment for the decision-makers which is designed to be isomorphic to the environment in which foreign policy decision-makers operate within the system of world nations.

During the course of our early work on the simulation, an option was available to attempt to program the entire model. Instead, programs were postulated only for limited intranational activities, such as office-holding and revolution. An advantage that we hoped to gain by using human participants rather than computing machines are decision-makers was the former's potential ability to outthink the simulators themselves. Later it may seem fruitful to program more of the system's behavior than has been done in the representations to be described below. However, the development of a completely programmed inter-nation simulation may have to wait until the people behind the computers have further developed the self-programming capability of their machines.

In constructing the simulation, whole sets of variables in the complex of national and international life are represented by simplified, generic factors, supposedly the prototypes of more elaborate realities. For example, the gamut of groups and processes through which decision-makers gain and maintain political office within a nation is represented in the simulation by the relation of the decision-making participants to their validators. This one programmed relationship, which will be described in detail below, provides a condensed version of a gamut of real-life activities, similar to the way in which probability distributions are used by simulators to represent elaborate, underlying mechanisms that are too complicated to detail. Yet these prototypic variables, be they of determinant or stochastic form, constitute the core of the simulation. One important part of the task of this chapter, therefore, is to delineate these core variables. However, no attempt will be made at this time to enumerate the implicit variables—those of personality and of organization expectation—which are carried into the simulation by the persons participating as decision-makers.

Disclosure of such factors awaits experimental work with the simulation (see Guetzkow and Valadez, 1981a).

Once the core variables have been posited, interrelations among them are then programmed through assumptions that assert what happens when the magnitude of one of the variables is changed. For example, when the probability of office-holding reduces to certain levels, validator support is considered as questionable in a program which determines whether or not the decision-makers continue to hold office. These calculations for determination of office-holding are assumptions postulated to simulate processes involved in the "orderly and disorderly transference of political power," as will be displayed below. Another important part of the task of this chapter is to state the assumptions embodied within the programs of the Inter-Nation Simulation. The prescribed programs actually used in making the calculations in the Inter-Nation Simulation are presented after each "programmed assumption."

The core variables and their programmed assumptions constitute the foundations of the simulation. The activities emerging from these postulated conditions, generated as the participants react to their simulated environments, consist of such things as arms races, trade systems, and international organizations. But because this unfolding is not prescribed, it is possible to formulate hypotheses (as contrasted with the programmed assumptions) about these developments. A description of their operation depends on our insight in isolating the important variables that undergird these unprogrammed developments and in hypothesizing the interrelations between them and the core variables. This chapter will provide examples of how the core variables and their programmed interrelations generate free variables, which in turn may be hypothesized as linked to the foundational structure of the simulation.

Although an effort will be made to enumerate all the core variables and all their programmed interrelations, no such coverage can be attempted at this stage in our understanding of the Inter-Nation Simulation for the free activities. Hence, the chapter will have an imbalance, with the free variables and associated hypotheses being described in a fragmentary manner. At some later time it may be possible to present a more complete analysis of the Inter-Nation Simulation in both its programmed and its unprogrammed features. The reader will decide whether it is fruitful at this time, despite the incompleteness, to describe the way in which the programmed characteristics of the simulation—in conjunction with the personal characteristics and organizational expectations of the decision-makers—create the free activities of the Inter-Nation Simulation.

The programs displayed in the following text are usually given with parameters in alphabetic form, indicating that the particular values used in the runs to date might be changed, depending upon the magnitude of the relations one wishes to assert as holding among the nations. It is possible, of course, to vary also the form of the program itself, by simply adding or subtracting or substituting new variables and by changing the relationships asserted within an equation.

II. DECISION-MAKERS AND THEIR NATIONS

Actions within the Inter-Nation Simulation originate through individuals and groups. The human beings participating in the simulation represent the decision-makers within national political systems. A group of two or three to five or six decision-makers, along with their resources and capabilities, operate as the nation. Some or all of these nations, in turn, may combine to form supragroups, such as regional and universal organizations.

Core Unit: Decision-Makers. Humans who develop and choose among alternative policies and actions at the nation or inter-nation levels.

Core Unit: Nations. Groups of validated decision-makers, operating within a political-military-economic system, who are capable of amalgamation and splintering.

Free Unit: Supraunits. Supranational groups of nations, developing and operating various structures, with capabilities derived from national units.

The simulation thus consists of components at three levels: individuals (decision-makers), groups (nations), and supragroups (alliances, international organizations). Some of the following assumptions and hypotheses are concerned with relations within the level of the phenomena being considered; others relate components at one level to those at another.

ORGANIZATIONAL RELATIONS AMONG DECISION-MAKERS

Initially, one individual is designated central decision-maker, who is responsible for overall national policy, both domestic and international. With the central decision-maker are associated other decision-makers, who constitute the nation's government. The central decision-maker possesses final authority in all decisions, within the limits set by the risk of losing his office and the constraints imposed by his associates. The exercise of final authority by the central decision-maker simulates the fact that there is usually a recognized head of state or someone exercising ultimate political power.

Core Variable: Authority. The command of each central decision-maker is honored by the simulation director, even though the decisions of the associated national decision-makers may be at variance in some way with the former's directives.

Free Variable: Delegation of Authority. The central decision-maker may delegate various amounts of authority within particular domains to his associated decision-makers, either informally or formally.

The mechanical reconciliation of conflicts among the decision-makers of a nation by the simulation director attempts to simulate the exercise of actual power within a political system, which by definition resides within the central decision-maker. There is freedom within the delegation of authority for its abuse, if the central decision-maker does not institute adequate controls. A central decision-maker may lose partial control of his decisions until his authority is reestablished by his personal control of the nation's decision forms or by confrontation of disobedient associates so that they are reversed or even disqualified from participation in the exercise by the simulation director. In a run with foreign students, the European nation was divided internally, one of the external decision-makers secretly having joined forces with the decision-makers in the South American state. Advantage was taken of delegated authority to sabotage the effectiveness of the central decision-maker's activities before the perfidy was discovered and accreditation revoked by the latter.

Free Variable: Division of Labor Among Decision-Makers. It is possible for the central decision-maker to use his authority to organize his associates so that each performs different tasks within the nation.

Some participants may become internal decision-makers, specializing in economic or military matters. Others may serve as external decision-makers, focusing upon the international affairs of their nation, regularly conducting negotiations with other nations, and/or operating the international organizations. The lack of prescribed structure among the decision-makers, except for the allocation of prime authority to the central decision-makers, allows freedom for the participants in the evolution of their decision-making roles.

Note how the two free variables are related to the core variable—in this instance, authority. The participants are given definite instructions that the central decision-maker holds the ultimate power within his nation "by definition." But the utilization of this "programmed" authority by the decision-makers depends upon such unprogrammed features of the simulation as their own personalities and developments within their situation. "Delegation" and "division of labor" are but but two of an array of free variables that can be discovered in the operation of the simulation.

In may be that a division of labor gradually develops within the nation, in response to the relations of a country to other nations within the system. In one run, for example, an external decision-maker in Erga[1] became concerned with the economic aspects of his state's relations to two other nations. His counterpart focused his attention upon security affairs, working closely with the central decision-maker concerned with force. In another run of the simulation, the central decision-maker in Omne restricted the role of his external ministers to representing and reporting, allowing them little scope for policy development. In yet another run, the central decision-maker turned over almost all internal functions to a trusted associate so that his full attention could be devoted to foreign affairs.

Unprogrammed Hypothesis. Insufficient delegation of authority within a nation produces inter-nation crises because of lag in the decision-making activities of the nation.

Unprogrammed Hypothesis. The number of decisions demanded of a nation by both internal and external relations is greater than the capability of one decision-maker.

The core variable of authority permits the central decision-maker of any nation to amalgamate his nation with others by agreeing to have his decisions subject to a supranational unit. The core variable of authority also allows for a situation in which the central decision-maker relinquishes control to an antagonistic power. The processes of amalgamation and occupation will be discussed in more detail at a later point in this exposition.

Should the researcher/teacher want to explore the implications of a more complex decision-making organization, the simulation can be so adapted. For example, by restricting direct communications among the national decision-makers to occasional internal conferences interspersed with longer periods of indirect, written communication, significant characteristics of hierarchical organizations can be simulated. Even in the present representation of foreign office operation, the need for coordination among the decision-makers is apparent, especially when they are "abroad" for prolonged periods at international conferences or organizations. Misunderstandings among the decision-makers result from differences in perspective on a particular international problem.

The manner of organization of internal activities also may have external consequences. Specialization among the decision-makers creates coordination problems for other nations. In one run, the senior external decision-maker of Utro specialized in the development of a grand alliance system, which competed with alliances among smaller nations. But the smaller nations had not designated particular decision-makers as opposite numbers to Utro's diplomat, who had great trouble developing a series of bilateral negotiations. To take another example, the management of internal authority within each state creates consequences for the external affairs of all other states. Communications between states have bogged down noticeably in runs characterized by insufficient delegation of authority by the central decision-makers. During one of the 1958-1959 runs, dangerous risks were incurred by Utro because of its slowness in responding to urgent pleas from its allies in a time of crisis.

OFFICE-HOLDING

By definition, the exercise of power in political decision-making situations within a nation depends upon formal or informal office-holding, be it de facto or de jure. Office-holding is a mainspring of the Inter-Nation Simulation. Although no attempt has been made thus far to represent accession to office, an endeavor is made to simulate vital characteristics of the process of remaining in office.

Core Variable: Office-Holding (pOH). The de jure right, as recognized by the simulation director, to make the decisions of the nation with respect to both internal and external affairs.

The retention of office by the central decision-makers depends upon their ability to elicit validation of their office-holding in competition with countermoves by aspiring decision-makers. For purposes of the simulation, this validation process consists in gaining and retaining the support of elites and interest groups within their nation, along with sufficient compliance among all its inhabitants to secure implementation of political decisions. Validation is made operational by a set of mathematical relations between the consequences of the decisions made within nations and the chances of remaining in office.

The validators within such a process may be conceived as individuals and groups in the nation's political system who occupy positions of influence outside the formal governmental structure. Through their situations of power, they influence the chances for office retention by the decision-makers in the nation. In a democracy, the validators might be voters and interest groups. In an autocracy, the validators might be some oligarchic elite or military junta. In all governmental systems, however, it seems there must be some minimal compliance by the peoples as a whole, even if it is only passive acceptance rooted in apathy.

Core Variable: Validator Satisfaction (VSm). The acceptability of the central decision-maker's program to those with power to authenticate his office-holding.

The demands of the validators are postulated to arise from two sources: (1) The nation must satisfy the basic needs of its peoples—and in our "satisfaction with regard to consumption" (VScs) variable, an attempt was made to encompass the whole gamut of living needs of the validators, from bare necessities for the peasant and worker to luxuries for the guardians of the palace or members of the cabinet. (2) The nation also must satisfy the needs of its people with regard to their feelings of national security

(VSns). In later parts of this chapter, details of these validating components will be described. For the moment, overall validation of office-holding may be viewed as a function of the extent to which these prototypic needs are satisfied. The emphases given particular needs may vary over time within a nation, just as they may vary from nation to nation.

Programmed Assumption 1: Relation of Validator Satisfaction to Office-Holding. The probability of continuing in office depends upon the extent to which the decision-makers of the nation satisfy their validators. This assumption is programmed as follows:

$$pOH = a\,(b - DL)\,VSm + c\,(DL - d), \qquad [2.1]$$

where pOH is the probability of continuing office-holding and VSm is mean overall validator satisfaction. When DL or decision latitude is thought of as a constant,[2] equation 2.1 is linear, that is, of the form pOH = a constant × VSm + another constant. The constants were chosen so as to allow use of simpler calculation routines, given the arbitrary scale values assigned to VSm and DL, as follows:

$$a = .01,\ b = 11,\ c = .1,\ \text{and}\ d = 1.$$

The relation between the validating process and office-holding is presented in Figure 2.1. Validation is conceptualized as a two-stage process by which decisions regarding consumption standards and force capability are translated into partial measures of validator satisfaction (Figures 2.1a and 2.1b). These measures are then combined into a single index (VSm), which in turn determines the probability of holding office (pOH; see Figure 2.1c). Undoubtedly the programs represented in these graphs are but approximations of the complex functions which may hold in the national societies of the world.

For operating the simulation, the graphs are not given to the participants, although the general form of the functions is revealed. Each component is described on an eleven-point scale. The two components of validator satisfaction are averaged into a single index on an identical eleven-point scale.

The transformation displayed in Figure 2.1c is explained as the relationship of Table 2.1a to Table 2.1b. When overall validator satisfaction is high, likelihood of retaining office tends to be greater; when overall validator satisfaction is low, the likelihood of retaining office tends to be less.

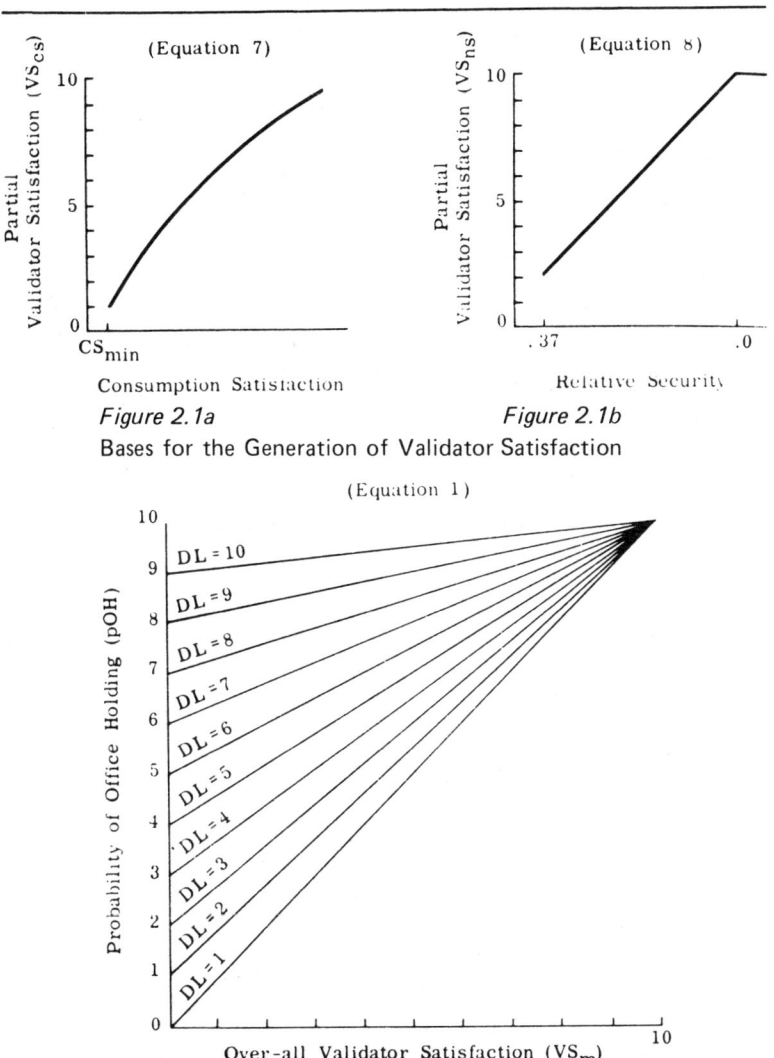

Figure 2.1a

Figure 2.1b

Bases for the Generation of Validator Satisfaction

Figure 2.1c
Relationship Between Overall Satisfaction (VSm) and Chances for Holding Office (pOH) for Varying Levels of Decision Latitude (DL)

Figure 2.1 The Validation of Office-Holding

Programmed Assumption 2: Relations of Overall Validation to Component Validations. The validators are satisfied to the extent to which their national security and standards of living are realized.

Table 2.1
SCALES FOR THE MEASUREMENT OF VALIDATOR SATISFACTION AND PROBABILITY OF OFFICE-HOLDING

(a)
VALIDATOR SATISFACTION (VS)

- 10   maximum satisfaction
- 9, 8, 7   high satisfaction
- 6   moderately high satisfaction
- 5   indifference
- 4   moderately low satisfaction (moderate dissatisfaction) [revolution threshold]
- 3, 2, 1   low satisfaction (high dissatisfaction)
- 0   minimum satisfaction (maximum dissatisfaction)

(Same scale is used for VS_m, VS_{cs}, and VS_{ns})

(b)
PROBABILITY OF OFFICE-HOLDING (pOH)

- 10   certainty of office-holding
- 9, 8, 7   high likelihood of office-holding
- 6   moderately high likelihood of office-holding
- 5   even likelihood of holding or losing office
- 4   moderately low likelihood of office-holding
- 3, 2, 1   low likelihood of office-holding
- 0   certainty of losing office

$$VSm = [e(VScs) + g(VSns)] \qquad [2.2]$$

where VScs represents consumption satisfaction for validators deriving from their living standards, and VSns represents satisfactions deriving from national security. These terms will be defined in more detail below. The parameters e and g were set at .5 in the exploratory runs in 1957-1959.

It is possible to inject some of the effects of an opposition party into the simulation through the use of a participant who makes critiques of the performance of the decision-makers serving as office-holders. In Noel's (1963b) description of the January 1959 runs, he explains how we asked individuals to stand by and be ready to take over when the decision-makers lost office. In his International Organizations course, Alger has worked out procedures to consummate a transfer of power to an opposition group. An aspirant office-holder makes his own decisions, parallel to those made by the office-holders. He functions without the operating responsibilities imposed on the official decision-makers. The extent to which the aspirant's decisions prove to be potentially more adequate in meeting the needs of the validators serves as an indicator of the amount to which validator satisfactions provided by the central decision-makers are diluted because of alternatives provided by an opposition.

The validation process is an example of our endeavor to build essentials into the simulation by the use of so-called prototypic variables. The probability that particular individuals will continue in office in real life is an elaborate, poorly understood process. Yet, it seems that decision-making in domestic and foreign affairs is dependent upon a number of factors, two of which we intuitively assert may be taken as representative of a wider gamut. The decision-makers may endeavor to retain office by favoring one source of validation over another—representing the way in which practical politicians may cater to one validating group rather than another. A running competition with the aspirant decision-maker would make it necessary for those in office not only to satisfy their validators, but to come to decisions which compare favorably with the promises of an opposition that has none of the responsibilities of office-holding. In this way, the simulation creates a conceptual environment for the decision-makers, which typifies variables that are seen as motivating office-holding in political life.

DECISION LATITUDE

In the real world the relationship between validator satisfaction and office-holding varies widely from nation to nation, depending upon the forms of the internal government. In some cases, the decision-makers for certain periods of time have wide latitude in making their decisions, regardless of how their validators respond. In other instances, the decision-makers have little latitude; they find their office-holding is very sensitive to changes in the overall satisfaction of their validators.

These differences in decision latitude are represented in the simulation by varying the functions relating satisfaction and office-holding in Figure 2.1c. The participants are given a scale that indicates the sensitivity of their validators to their decisions, as follows: (10) = complete decision latitude; (9, 8) = high decision latitude; (7, 6, 5, 4) = moderate decision latitude; (3, 2) = low decision latitude; (1) = no decision latitude.

Core Variable: Decision Latitude (DL). The degree to which the probability of office-holding of the decision-makers depends on changes in validator satisfaction.

Programmed Assumption 3: Relation of Office-Holding to Decision Latitude. The higher the decision latitude, the less immediately is office-holding subject to validator satisfaction.

This assumption is incorporated in equation 2.1, when DL now is allowed to vary. This equation is linear with respect to variations in DL, if VSm is considered to be a constant, as the following rearrangement of the terms of equation 2.1 indicates. Multiplying out the constants in equation 2.1 yields pOH = ab(VSm) − a (DL) (VSm) + cDL − cd By regrouping the terms, one obtains the following linear equation:

$$pOH = [c - a\,(VSm)]\,DL + [ab(VSm) - cd] \qquad [2.1']$$

The nation's decision latitude changes slowly, sometimes dependent upon factors quite beyond the control of the office-holders, and at other times responding directly to decisions made by the nation's principals. Changes in the freedom of the decision-makers due to exogenous factors are stochastically developed by the simulator. These are programmed to occur randomly, resulting in a change in the decision latitude of one unit in either an upward or a downward direction. These changes in decision latitude may be thought of as occurring for reasons outside the control of the central decision-makers, such as shifts in leadership among the validators, changes in mass media that allow new ideologies to gain prominence among validating groups, and so forth.

Programmed Assumption 4: Variations in Decision Latitude by Validators. During each period there is random modification in the decision latitude of each nation.

Changes of plus or minus one unit or zero are equally probable. But the central decision-maker himself may attempt to induce changes in decision latitude, never exceeding one unit down or up in a period. Unless he is willing to apply political pressure, a situation to be considered later, conditions generated by the validators predominate.

Programmed Assumption 5: The Predominant Character of the Validators in Producing Changes in Decision Latitude. When pressure is not used to implement changes in decision latitude desired by the central decision-maker, the validators' preferences are effected.

Even when there is agreement between the validators and the decision-makers with respect to the changes in decision latitude, there is no augmentation of the magnitude of the change. By not programming an additive effect, rapid and abrupt changes in decision latitude are avoided, thus representing nonrevolutionary change situations with more adequacy.

The decision to vest authority in an individual rather than a small internal group is dictated by our interest being centered on the interrelations among the nations, rather than on the internal functioning of each of the states. However, an effort was made to represent constraints upon these decision-makers, constraints which seem always to exist in national political systems, whether they be totalitarian or democratic, through the limitations on office-holding as extended by the validators and through restrictions in decision latitude. Thus, the validation and decision latitude functions are designed to represent such constraints as those imposed by courts, legislative bodies, and bureaucratic inflexibilities.

The use of stochastic processes in these programs is analogous to their use by operations research analysts in their simulation of physical systems. Whenever the variables involved in a given consequence are numerous and complicated—and thereby at times little understood—it is possible to represent the resultant by a probability distribution of random numbers. This stochastic representation later may be replaced by a more adequately detailed program which gives rise to the desired consequence by other than random means. Our use of prototypic variables to represent a complex network of poorly delineated variables parallels this employment of stochastic or random determinations in the Inter-Nation Simulation.

ORDERLY AND DISORDERLY TRANSFERENCE OF POWER

The mechanisms of the transference of power from one set of public office-holders to another is of central interest to the political scientist. When overall validator satisfaction is quite low, there would be some chance that disorder might occur, possibly with immediate loss of office. When overall validator satisfaction is high, more orderly and regularized devices for the transfer of power from one set of office-holders to the next would prevail. Yet, even when there is great likelihood of losing office, decision-makers in the real world retain office because of unpredictable circumstances. These hypotheses again are embodied in the simulation by the use of probabilistic devices—this time for the determination of office loss.

Core Variable: Determination of Office-Holding (pOHm). At periodic or intermittent times, a determination of office-holding is made within each nation. This determination may result in continuation of the same decision-makers in office or provide for their replacement.

Core Variable: Determination of Occurrence of Revolution (pR). When a determination of revolution is made, the result may be revolution or no revolution.

Core Variable: Determination of Outcome of Revolution (pSR). When a revolution occurs, the decision-makers may or may not not lose office.

The simulation is divided into periods. To date, we have employed periods ranging from 45 to 75 minutes. At the beginning of each period the office-holders are informed of the likelihood of retaining office. To simulate more routine, orderly shifts in the occupants of positions of power in a nation, regular biperiod or triperiod determinations of office-holding have been employed.

Programmed Assumption 6: Office Retention or Loss Determined by Average of Probabilities of Office-Holding. Whether the central decision-makers of a nation continue in office or lose office at the regular determination periods depends upon the average of the probabilities of office-holding during preceding periods.

The ruling is made on the basis of the average likelihood of office-holding over a given number of periods, as follows:

$$pOHm = \sum_{i}^{j} pOH/(j-i), \qquad [2.3]$$

where the ith period precedes the jth period.

In the runs of the Inter-Nation Simulation during our exploratory work, the average was determined over the last two or three periods.

The span over two or three periods gives the participant the ability to take short-run gambles with his validators, if in the longer run he believes that he can maintain an average of satisfaction high enough to keep his chances for holding office sufficiently great. But even when his chances are high at the times of these regular determinations, there still will be some occasions when office is lost. For example, in a run in 1958, the central decision-maker of P lost office when the random numbers were applied, even though his scale value of 9 indicated nine chances out of ten that he would retain office. Due to the vagaries of politics—"perhaps there was a scandal of political import in his immediate family"—he lost office, even though his decision-making had induced much satisfaction in his validators.

A risk of revolution is encountered within a nation when overall validator satisfaction drops to or below a threshold of three units (see "revolution threshold" in Table 2.1a). The impact of disorder is determined immediately on a probability basis. If there is no revolution, the decision-makers retain office and the orderly process for the transfer of power prevails, despite the low validator satisfaction. If disorder terminates in revolution, then a second stochastic calculation is involved to determine the outcome of the revolution itself.

Programmed Assumption 7: Relation of Regularity in Office Determination to Validator Satisfaction. If the satisfaction of the validators is above the critical threshold of three units, there is periodic determination of office at regular intervals.

Programmed Assumption 8: Relation of Occurrence of Revolution to Validator Satisfaction. If the satisfaction of the validators is below the critical threshold, three units, there is an immediate determination of whether a revolution has occurred.

Note how the combination of programs for the determination of office-holding and revolution imply that although a government in the short run may be threatened by revolution, if it should maintain immediate power during the disorder, its chances for holding office might still be relatively good because of the past satisfactions of its validators. The choice of the levels of probability involved in determining the outcome of revolution will be explained in detail in a later discussion of the use that may be made of force capabilities. It is enough to indicate here that internal controls may be applied by the decision-makers to lessen the chances of the success of the revolution, no matter how immediately dissatisfied their validators are.

If the change in office is induced by orderly or disorderly procedures, once the calculation produces office loss, the central participant yields his decision-making office and is replaced in the simulation by another. Perhaps the greatest impact of the motivational setting of the simulation is felt in this situation. When the office-holders are strangers to each other except for the interaction that occurs in the simulation itself, less than powerful motivations are aroused. But when the simulation consists of adults who make their profession in foreign policy decision-making, their interest in retaining office is keen. Loss of office is loss of face among participant-colleagues with whom they will be in contact during the years ahead. Long-term operation of one's nation was taken as a sign of outstanding decision-making ability in one run of the simulation involving such professionals.

The stochastic determinations in the simulation represent the full scope of causes which may terminate office-holding in real life. The rarer events, such as ill health or death in office from assassination, occur even when there is much overall support for a regime. The common causes of office loss, such as coups d'etat and narrow losses of elections, occur when there is less than full support for a particular set of office-holders. By varying the probabilities of office-holding, these differences in real-world situations are reflected in the Inter-Nation Simulation.

Unprogrammed Hypothesis. Because the associated decision-makers of a government hold office on the authority of the central decision-maker, there is a tendency to replace at least some of the associated decision-makers upon transfer of power from one central decision-maker to another.

In establishing and maintaining the relations of their nation to others, the decision-makers seek to use the results to keep themselves in office.

These efforts may indeed redound to the well-being of the nation's population, as when a comparative advantage arises from foreign trade to increase validator satisfaction. Or the external effort may simply reinforce the leaders' elite position with concomitant decreases in the well-being of their peoples, e.g., through the display of great force which thereby assures an increase in the probability of office-holding. External relations, then, may be motivated by a felt need for office-holding, regardless of the consequences for the external system.

Free Variable: Decisions on External Affairs. A decision with respect to relations of the nation to other nations.

Free Variable: Office-Holding Needs. Considerations thought important by decision-makers in retaining office.

Unprogrammed Hypothesis. The considerations related to office-holding tend to dominate the considerations deriving from external relations in national decision-making.

There is controversy as to the genesis of policy change in foreign affairs, some arguing that basic policy shifts come only through change in the office-holders. The fact that office-holders are transient—often in the short and at least in the long run—is important in the relations among nations. Because the nation's interests and policies implementing them are subject to the interpretations of its office-holders, national goals and strategies are subject to change as the office-holders change. As individuals with different personality needs and different political ideologies take office, the goals and strategies of the nation in its relation to other states reflect such changes.

Free Variable: National Goals. The objectives, implicit or explicit, toward which the decision-makers attempt to direct their nation's behavior.

Free Variable: National Strategies. The plan of means, implicit or explicit, by which the decision-makers attempt to achieve national goals.

Unprogrammed Hypothesis. When different decision-makers take office, national goals and strategies change.

Unprogrammed Hypothesis. When different decision-makers take office, overall satisfaction of the validators may be developed through changed emphasis on the components of validator satisfaction.

Constant flux produces powerful pressures within international systems for "staying" until there are shifts in the office-holders of the other nations, vis-à-vis one's capacity to retain office. Staying tends to induce important limits and potentials in the relations of nations. Because office is often retained by continuation of the same general pattern of external relations that have aided office retention in the past, remaining in office tends to produce conservative, status-quo tendencies. Because change of office-holders often is accompanied by changes in the bases for office retention, it is at this time that rearrangements of the complex relations among states may be attempted.

Free Variable: Continuation in Office. Number of consecutive periods during which a decision-maker holds office.

Free Variable: Similarity of Decisions. The extent to which the substance of decisions is repetitious in content, from time to time.

Unprogrammed Hypothesis. The longer decision-makers continue in office, the greater will be the tendency for similar decisions.

Many consequences of the changes in office-holding flow from uncertainties introduced into complex organizations by personnel changes. Role expectations are generated not only in terms of position demands, but also in terms of the personal characteristics and styles of the nation's representatives in their behavior in bilateral and multilateral contacts. Changes destablilize expectations in the larger system. These uncertainties in expectation make prediction of the behaviors of opposite numbers difficult. Hence, errors in decision-making are more likely.

Free Variable: Stability of Behavior Expectations. The extent of constancy which is expected in the anticipated behaviors of a unit.

Unprogrammed Hypothesis. The longer decision-makers continue in office, the more constant will others expect their behaviors to be.

Unprogrammed Hypothesis. The longer decision-makers continue in office, the greater is their adequacy in achieving their national goals in inter-nation affairs.

Unprogrammed Hypothesis. The more unstable the expected behavior of others, the greater is the chance of error in the nation's decision-making.

NATIONAL CAPABILITIES

All kinds of resources, physical and human, are subsumed in the Inter-Nation Simulation under the concept of "basic capability." The size of a nation's accumulation of basic capabilities reflects the nation's overall ability to produce all goods and services, be they used for consumption or for the exercise of physical force in internal or external affairs.

Units of basic capability at the disposal of the nation's decision-makers may be allocated to the development of further basic capability (e.g., exploration for oil fields, investment in more efficient factories, the training of scientists and engineers) or for research and development. Because of obsolescence, deterioration, and resource exhaustion, all nations must devote parts of their basic capability to regeneration if they desire to maintain constant standards. Growth, stagnation, and retrogression will occur, depending upon the amounts allocated over time to the development and renewal of the nation's basic capabilities.

Core Variable: Basic Capability (BC). The nation's overall ability to produce goods and services, be they used for replacement of or for addition to the basic capability itself, to satisfy consumption needs and wants, or to produce arms.

Core Variable: Generation Rates. The rates at which basic capabilities allocated to different sectors of the economy generate (with a lag of one period) new basic capability units, force capability units, and consumption satisfaction units.

Core Variable: Depreciation of Basic Capability. The rate at which basic capability depreciates each period, due to depletion, obsolescence, and deterioration.

Programmed Assumption 9: Stochastic Variation in Depreciation of Basic Capability. In each period, depreciation may occur in the amount of basic capability. The values 2, 5, and 10 percent used during the exploratory runs for the depreciation rate are equiprobable. The relative magnitude of the depreciation has no relation to the amount of basic capability possessed by the nation.

The nation consumes its own goods and services at varying standards of living. A minimum portion of the nation's basic capability must be devoted each period to the production of goods and services for consumption. This minimum changes from time to time, increasing as the basic capability of the nation increases and decreasing as the nation becomes depressed. The increases, however, are programmed to be a decreasing percentage of the total, as the gross national product increases. The minimum consumption represents that allocated of necessity, to provide for the supply and manning of the nation's productive capability. The minimum requirement further represents the amount of consumption which the peoples of the nation, despite government action, are able to devote to their own maintenance, as in the peasants' hiding of poultry or grains and in the laborers' pilfering of clothes or fuel. These minima are such that they yield little validator satisfaction. For consumption above the minimum the validator satisfaction increases with the ratio of consumption to the minimum consumption standard. The goods created for use in living are conceived in the simulation as entirely expended, with no carryover from period to period.

Core Variable: Consumption Standards (CS). Quantity of goods produced and utilized in the nation for consumption purposes.

Core Variable: Minimum Consumption Standards (CSmin). At least minimal consumption standards for its people must be provided.

Programmed Variable: Maximum Consumption Standards (CSmax). The maximum units of consumption which could be allocated by the nation in a given period to consumption standards; i.e., CSmax = all BCs × generation rate for CSs.

Programmed Assumption 10: Relation of Consumption Satisfaction to Utilization. The goods and services produced through the nation's basic capability are completely expended at the end of any period, without holdover.

In designing the programs involving the consumption standards, an effort was made to include two effects, that (1) as the basic capability of the nation increased, the minimum standards of the nation's population would rise; and (2) simultaneously, the rise of aspirations for increases in the minimum standards would be slow enough that increasingly large amounts of basic capability might be devoted to activities other than consumption.

Programmed Assumption 11: Relation of Minimum Consumption Standards to Basic Capability. The minimum consumption standards of the nation increase as the basic capability of the nation increases in its ability to produce satisfying goods and services.

Programmed Assumption 12: Proportion of Basic Capability Needed to Fulfill Minimum Consumption Standard. The percentage of the realized basic capability required to fulfill minimum living standards decreases as the nation's basic capability increases.

Programmed Assumptions 11 and 12 may be represented simultaneously in a single equation.

$$\text{CSmin} = [1 - (\text{CSmax}/k)]\,\text{CSmax}, \qquad [2.4]$$

where k equals 380,000 CS units.

The constant k was made considerably larger than the values which CSmax reached during the runs before 1960. This constraint assures that equation 2.4 is a monotonically increasing relation between CSmin and CSmax, as asserted in Programmed Assumption 11. When CSmax is quite small compared with k, then CSmin $\cong$ CSmax, for CSmax/k tends to zero. Contrariwise, when CSmax gradually increases, the percentage of basic capability needed for CSmin gradually decreases. This may be seen as follows: Divide both sides of equation 2.4 by CSmax:

$$(\text{CSmin}/\text{CSmax}) = 1 - (\text{CSmax}/k). \qquad [2.4']$$

Note how the ratio CSmin/CSmax decreases with increases in CSmax, thus meeting the assertion of Programmed Assumption 12.

Programmed Variable: Validator Satisfaction with Respect to Consumption Satisfaction (VScs). The satisfactions attained by the nation's validators from the amount and distribution of goods and services.

Programmed Assumption 13: Relation of Validator Satisfaction to Consumption Satisfaction. This assumption consists of three parts:

(1) For consumption near minimum consumption standards, validator satisfaction depends on the relation of consumption satisfaction to minimum consumption standards.

(2) Once minimum consumption standards have been met, larger increases in consumption are necessary to produce corresponding changes in validator satisfaction.

(3) This saturation effect is more prominent for wealthier nations.

The effects of Programmed Assumption 13 are incorporated in a quadratic equation in the Inter-Nation Simulation.

It is conceived that when minimum living standards are but barely met (i.e., when the CS in any period equals CSmin), the validators are minimally satisfied (i.e., VScs = 1). Part 1 of the assumption, then, may be represented as the first term of a quadratic equation, that is:

$$VScs \cong r \frac{CS}{CSmin} + s \qquad [2.5]$$

when consumption is near minimum consumption standards. When VScs = 1, and CS/CSmin = 1 (as CS = CSmin), then equation 2.5 becomes 1 = r + s. By transposing terms, s = 1 - r. Using this value for s and rearranging terms, equation 2.5 for part 1 of Programmed Assumption 13 may be stated as:

$$VScs \cong 1 + r \left(\frac{CS}{CSmin} - 1 \right). \qquad [2.5']$$

As CS increases above CSmin, the saturation effect of part 2 may be represented by subtracting a squared term from equation 2.5' as follows:

$$VScs = 1 + r \left(\frac{CS}{CSmin} - 1 \right) - u \left(\frac{CS}{CSmin} - 1 \right)^2. \qquad [2.6]$$

According to part 3 of our assumption, however, the effect is more prominent for wealthier nations, so that the constant u then should be made to depend upon the relation of CSmin to CSmax. This may be done, so that the final quadratic expression for Programmed Assumption 13, including all three of its parts with appropriate constants, is as follows:

$$VScs = 1 + r \left(\frac{CS}{CSmin} - 1 \right) - u \left(\frac{CSmax}{CSmin} \right) \left(\frac{CS}{CSmin} - 1 \right)^2 \qquad [2.7]$$

where $r = .55$ and $v = .41$ during the exploratory runs.

Although the decision-makers must meet the bare minimum consumption standards for survival of their nation, their allocations of basic capability for strategic purposes may vary from zero to amounts determined by the nation's security needs. The ability of the nation to use force as a threat or for actual warfare depends upon its current level of "strategic capability." Although one's strategic capabilities may be carried over from period to period, the loss in each period is considerable because of high obsolescence and operating costs. The reductions are erratic, depending upon military breakthroughs, weapon developments, and so forth. Because there is lag in the conversion of basic capability to strategic capabilities, preparedness policies demand standing forces, despite their drain on the nation's resources. Validator satisfaction is based on the strength of a nation and its allies in relation to the strength of the nonallies.

Core Variable: Force Capability (FC). Coercion available for the control of external and internal affairs.

Core Variable: Internal Controls (FCic). Force capability which is applied internally for purposes of reducing the chances of revolutions being successful.

Core Variable: Military Costs. The obsolescence and wear (depreciation) as well as the resources consumed and labor involved in operating a military establishment.

Programmed Assumption 14: Relation of Levels of Force Capability to Military Costs. The costs of the force capability of the nation change over a period of time, the percentage amounts varying randomly within given ranges from time to time. The values of 20, 30, and 40 percent for the rate of depreciation of force capability within a period are equiprobable.

Programmed Assumption 15: Time Lag in the Availability of Force Capability. Although there is a period lag involved in the creation of force capability, the force in existence at any time is available for immediate use.

Programmed Variable: Validator Satisfaction with Respect to National Strength (VSns). The extent to which a nation's validators feel secure in their military position in relation to other nations.

Programmed Assumption 16: Relation of Validator Satisfaction to Level of Force Capability. Validator satisfaction is directly related, within limits, to the ratio of the force strength of the nation and its allies vis-à-vis the strongest nation or group of nations not allied with it, as follows:

(1) Top limit: when a nation with its allies is many times stronger than nonally nations or groups.

(2) Bottom limit: when a nation with its allies is insignificant in its strength by comparison to its nonallies.

$$VSns = w \frac{\overset{\text{allies}}{\Sigma} (FC - FCic + a'BC)}{\underset{\text{others}}{\Sigma} (FC - FCic + a'BC)} + b', \qquad [2.8]$$

where $w = 3$ and $b' = 1.3$ are arbitrary constants. The FC units without subscript represent the total coercive power of the nation, from which is subtracted that part which is devoted to internal controls (FCic), a variable already defined above. The force capability available for external use plus a measure of the overall basic capability of the nation are added for the nation and its allies, constituting the numerator of the ratio of strength represented in equation 2.8. The constant a' was set at .5 during the exploratory runs (see Guetzkow et al., 1963: passim). The corresponding sum, which supplies the denominator for the comparison, is gathered for all nonallies. If the nation has no allies, the comparison is made between itself and the total of all the other nations. When the ratio is greater than 3, VSns is considered to have reached its maximum. When the relative level of a nation's FCs is less than .37, the nation is considered disengaged from the armaments race, as is represented by the cutoff in Figure 2.1b. Its VSm, then, is made directly equivalent to VScs rather than to the combination of VScs and VSns assumed in equation 2.2.

The underlying capability decisions made each period by the central decision-maker, therefore, are interdependent. The sum of the allocations made each period to consumption, force, and renewal or improvement of the basic capability is constrained always by the basic capability available from the previous period. In this way, the simulation attempts to represent the allocative choices facing top decision-makers concerned with domestic and foreign affairs.

Unprogrammed Hypothesis. The decision-makers of a nation will allocate their various capabilities so as to increase their chances of retaining office and of implementing their nation's goals.

CONSEQUENCES OF PRESSURED CHANGES IN DECISION LATITUDE

What happens when the validators (through the stochastic process postulated in Programmed Assumption 4) wish to contest the desires of the decision-makers with respect to the nation's decision latitude? Then political pressure may be used to contravene the predominance of their validators. The consequences of the use of such pressure in these circumstances were programmed as follows:

Programmed Assumption 17: Relation of Changes in Decision Latitude to Validator Satisfaction. Increases in decision latitude initiated by the decision-maker induce temporary decreases in validator satisfaction proportional to the difference between the decision-maker's induced change and that desired by the validators.

$$\Delta \text{VSm} = c'(\Delta \text{DL} - \Delta \text{DLv}), \qquad [2.9]$$

with the restriction that $\Delta \text{VSm} \leq 0$.

The delta signs indicate unit changes in the decision latitude, as actually effected by the central decision-maker (DL without suffix) and as proposed by Programmed Assumption 4 for the validators (DLv). The constant c' may take the value of -1 or -2, as given below in Programmed Assumption 20.

Programmed Assumption 17 represents a situation in which the central decision-maker applies pressure for an increase in decision latitude against the wishes of the validators. Such a move, however, incurs a temporary decrease in validator satisfaction, as represented in equation 2.9. The decrease, however, dissipates during the period, as the validators become accustomed to the new state of affairs.

But the pressured change in decision latitude is not without side consequences. Three programmed assumptions were introduced to portray these effects, as follows.

Programmed Assumption 18: The Relation of Pressured Changes in Decision Latitude to Dissipation of Basic Capabilities. Changes in decision latitude effected by central decision-makers against the intention of their validators proportionally decrease the basic capabilities of the nation.

$$\frac{\Delta \text{BC}}{\text{BC}} = c'd'(\Delta \text{DL} - \Delta \text{DLv}), \qquad [2.10]$$

where c' takes values as described in Programmed Assumption 20 and where $d' = .05$.

These losses in the nation's basic capabilities represent the inefficiencies introduced into the economic system by protest movements, work stoppages, and other forms of political activity aroused by the conflicts between validators and decision-makers with respect to decision latitude.

Programmed Assumption 19: The Relation of Pressured Changes in Decision Latitude in Terms of Force Capabilities. Changes in decision latitude effected by central decision-makers against the intention of the validators incur a proportional cost of force capabilities.

$$\frac{\Delta \text{FC}}{\text{FC}} = c'e'(\Delta \text{DL} - \Delta \text{DLv}), \qquad [2.11]$$

where c' again takes values as described in Programmed Assumption 20 and where $e = .10$.

These dissipations in force capabilities of the nations represent the side effects of disagreement between decision-makers and validators, as might be expressed in loss of troop morale as well as in the more tangible forms of reduction in output of munitions factories and inefficiencies of the military support services manned by civilians.

The decreases programmed in equation 2.11 indicate that there is less force capability available for external purposes, as so typically occurs when a nation is preoccupied with internal matters. On the other hand, the side effects of such disagreement are not as severe as during revolution, when force capability must be employed internally to suppress rioting, as is programmed in equation 2.14.

The changes in c' from -1 to -2, depending upon the level of the decision latitude, may be stated as an explicit assumption, as follows.

Programmed Assumption 20: Relation of Decision Latitude to Sensitivity of Validators to Forced Changes in Decision Latitude. The side effects of pressured changes in decision latitude increase when the absolute level of the decision latitude is already very high.

$$c' = -1, \text{ when } 1 \leqslant DL < 8.$$
$$c' = -2, \text{ when } 8 \leqslant DL \leqslant 10. \qquad [2.12]$$

This assumption represents the difficulties governments historically face in gaining complete control over their peoples, even though they may have been able to consolidate their internal powers during the more moderate days of their regimes.

Programmed Assumptions 18, 19, and 20 may be thought of as the costs involved to the decision-makers in imposing their wishes upon their peoples. Note the similarity of forms of the three equations, indicating that all costs are hypothesized as proportional to the magnitude of the differences between the decision latitude effected by the central decision-maker and the intended change generated stochastically by the validation process.

These four Programmed Assumptions (17-20) are complementary to Programmed Assumptions 4 and 5. Taken together, the overall operation of the sources for changes in decision latitude are meshed, so that although the validators generally predominate in controlling their relations to the decision-makers, it is possible for the central decision-makers to contravene when they are willing to pay the costs involved. The elaborateness of the programs illustrates how refined the researcher may become in developing details of the simulation. It seems that these elaborations represent the extreme to which one can usefully go, unless many other components of the simulation are analogously differentiated.

OCCURRENCE AND CONSEQUENCES OF REVOLUTION

Now that capabilities have been described, it is possible to enumerate further details about one of the important political processes within the simulation—revolution. As noted above, when the validator satisfactions descend below the revolution threshold, a two-step program is invoked: First, a determination is made of whether there is or is not a revolution; then, if there is a revolution, its outcome is decided.

The chances of having a revolution, once the critical threshold of validator dissatisfaction is reached, are determined stochastically in the simulation, the probability of revolution varying directly with the insensitivity of the decision-makers to their validators—that is, varying with decision latitude. When the decision-makers are not sensitive to the validators, attempts at revolution are substituted for more orderly political processes. But the likelihood of revolutionaries precipitating upheaval will also depend upon the chances that they might succeed in taking over the government.

Programmed Assumption 21: Relation of Occurrence of Revolution to Decision Latitude and Outcome of a Revolution. The risk of having a revolution, be it eventually successful or unsuccessful, is related directly to the nation's decision latitude and the chances of the revolution being successful.

$$pR = (g'DL + pSR)/h', \qquad [2.13]$$

where $g' = .1$ and $h' = 2$. The programmed variables DL (decision latitude) and pSR (probability of a successful revolution) have been defined above.

The chance of being successful in a revolution, should one occur, is also determined stochastically in the simulation. However, it is possible for the central decision-makers to use the nation's force capability to increase the government's chances of crushing a revolution. The central decision-maker may reserve up to 30 percent of his force capability for application as internal control measures during any period of the simulation. Force units to control the demands of the rebelling validators during periods of upheaval include such devices as riot suppression forces, secret police, and paramilitary activity.

Programmed Assumption 22: Relation of Outcome of Revolution to Internal Controls. The chances for a revolution to be successful, should one occur, are reduced directly by the percentage of force capability applied to internal controls.

$$pSR = 1 - k'(FCic/FC), \quad [2.14]$$

where $k' = 3.3$.

This last hypothesis indicates that although reduction in validator satisfaction may release or trip a revolution, its outcome actually is not dependent upon the level of validator satisfaction. The potential success of the revolution is specified as dependent upon the amount of forceful opposition the government is prepared to give to the revolutionary effort, as defined by FCic above. Because of the tendency of the armed services to participate in revolutions in many parts of the real world, the effectiveness of the forces loyal to the office-holders is expressed as a percentage of the total forces in existence (FCic/FC).

Costs of the force capability, as given in Programmed Assumption 14, remain the same whether the force is applied to internal controls or use for purposes of foreign affairs. Should a revolution occur, the entire allocation of force units is consumed.

Programmed Assumption 23: Utilization of Internal Force During Revolution. When a revolution occurs, the whole force capability devoted to internal controls is expended during the revolution.

Note the flexibility in policy that decision-makers have with respect to their validators, regarding the possibility of revolution within their nation. By keeping validator satisfaction high, the government may almost ensure its perpetuation in office—at most incurring orderly changes. By operating their government so as to ensure themselves sufficient decision latitude, decision-makers can forestall approaches to the revolution threshold (equation 2.1). On the other hand, should revolutionary outbreaks occur, the decision-makers with a nation may apply direct force internally, thereby attempting to suppress the revolt (equation 2.14).

Unprogrammed Hypothesis. Decision-makers will tend to prevent the outbreak of revolutions in the first place, rather than depend upon their suppressive force to control revolution once it has been set in motion.

Still, revolutions are not without cost, even should they be successfully suppressed. Not only is there a loss of the force capability which was applied internally, but the economic life of the nation is disrupted so that its basic capability is reduced.

Programmed Assumption 24: Depletion of Basic Capability Due To Revolution. The basic capability of a nation is depleted by a given amount at the conclusion of each revolution.

$$\Delta BC = r'BC, \quad [2.15]$$

where $r' = 20$ percent during the exploratory runs reported here.

Revolutions also yield benefits. After each revolution, there is an immediate increase in overall validator satisfaction, part of which continues during the subsequent period. In the case of a revolution that has been crushed, the rise in overall satisfaction occurs because the opposition has been silenced and suppressed. In the case of a revolution that has been won, the rise in overall satisfaction occurs because the new government now is operated by individuals of greater popularity. Eventually, however, these revolutionary gains dissipate, as when the decision-makers confront their validators during normal times.

Programmed Assumption 25: Increase in Validator Satisfaction Due To Revolution. At the conclusion of each revolution, there is a rise in validator satisfaction.

$$\Delta\ VS_{mi} = +2 \text{ units}; \Delta\ VS_{m(i+1)} = +1 \text{ unit} \qquad [2.16]$$

During the period i immediately after the revolution, the overall validator satisfaction computed by equation 2.2 for this period (VS_{mi}) was increased by two units during the exploratory runs. During the second period after the revolution (period $i + 1$), only one unit was added to the computed $VS_{m(i+1)}$.

A "silent" revolution already was programmed within the simulation. Consider again the contest between a stochastically induced decrease in decision latitude and the status quo, or even an increase desired by the decision-makers of a nation, as described on pages 46-47. If the stochastic process resulting in decreases in latitude for the decision-makers (Programmed Assumption 4), is considered as an effort by the validators to gain internal freedoms, then the consequences involved in Programmed Assumptions 17 through 20 represent the resistance of the ruled to their rulers. The decision-makers control this silent revolution, however, when they are willing to utilize political pressures other than those force capabilities already allocated for standby against violent revolution. By the application of police measures, resistance to the status quo or to increases in decision latitude may be suppressed.

NATIONALISM

An important ingredient in validator satisfaction within nations is the esteem with which nations are held by the peoples of the world. A constellation of variables is invoked in explaining the role of world opinion, nationalism, and other social processes in building esteem. To date, we have no core variables in the simulation with which to program the feedback of national pride into the validation process. Our two failures in programming feedbacks from the inter-nation system itself into validator satisfactions are described by Noel (1963b).

However, there are unprogrammed feedbacks from the interaction to the decision-makers themselves. The participants become strongly identified with their own nations, feel intense rivalries, and are sensitive to grievances. Among the external decision-makers representing different nations, status hierarchies develop based on such considerations as the nation's capabilities, the skill of the decision-makers in the conduct of their nation's affairs, and the ideological force with which the nation's diplomacy is conducted. These feelings of esteem extend beyond that of friendship, since sometimes a *coup de maître* is the beginning step in a switch of allies.

The following hypotheses suggest the rich isomorphism to reality that has been produced by unprogrammed developments in runs of the simulation.

Unprogrammed Hypothesis. The greater the feeling of identification of the decision-makers with the importance of their states, the greater sensitivity will they feel about their status relations within the inter-nation system.

Unprogrammed Hypothesis. The less secure the decision-makers feel about their tenure in office, the greater sensitivity will they feel about their status relations within the inter-nation system.

Unprogrammed Hypothesis. The greater the esteem with which a nation is regarded in the inter-nation system, the greater are the chances that developments in the inter-nation system may redound indirectly to increase the probability of continuation in office by its decision-makers.

Can one gain perspective on the way in which the model has been constructed to this point by examining the differentiation between the programmed assumptions and the unprogrammed hypotheses? The distinction between the core and free variables discussed above is analogous to the differences between the programmed and unprogrammed relationships among the variables. The programmed assumptions are hypotheses structured into the foundation of the simulation. Although they constitute the basic postulations of the operations forming the simulation, they can be changed from time to time, should they prove at variance with our increased understanding of processes within the real world to which they are supposedly isomorphic. The unprogrammed hypotheses are speculative formulations of the way self-developed features of the simulation operate.

It would be possible to transform some of the unprogrammed hypotheses into the simulation as programmed assumptions. For instance, one might develop a program rule for increasing the nation's decision latitude whenever there is rapid decrease in validator satisfaction—a not unreasonable proposal, in that governments often take self-defense measures that inhibit orderly change procedures when their populations begin creating public disorders. Contrariwise, it would be possible to relax an assumption, allowing the variables involved to operate without a structured program. An instance might be developed by eliminating a program that imposes costs in basic capabilities whenever there is an increase in decision latitude, as now is operative in Programmed Assumption 18. Were this made the case, an unprogrammed relation between basic capabilities and decision latitude could develop, nevertheless. Decision-makers generally might be prone to operate with higher decision standards of living for their people. Such risks might pay off well—or result in impoverishment of the nation's basic capabilities. Thus, even if a programmed assumption were eliminated, the same core variables might still be related to each other through unprogrammed processes.

Is it possible to program a free variable to a core variable, by making an appropriate assumption? For example, could one formally link the esteem variable with the probability of office-holding, as possibly intimated in the last-mentioned unprogrammed hypothesis? It seems the answer is negative. Although one can speculate about the impact of core variables on free variables (and vice versa) by means of unprogrammed hypotheses, one cannot program one's hunches into the simulation unless one already has defined core variables for incorporation into the new assumptions. It will be noted that the programmed assumptions of this chapter consist of relationships only between core variables.

III. RELATIONS AMONG NATIONS

Our effort has been confined so far to a description of the nations and the variables, both core and free, through which the decision-makers operate within the simulation. Now attention may be turned to relations among the nations. At first, focus will be placed upon the interaction processes themselves in the political, economic, and military spheres. Later the development of supranational institutions will be examined. On occasion in the first part of this chapter, the interrelations among nations were incorporated integrally into the operation of the simulation, as in the dependence of satisfaction with one's own national security upon the levels of arms of one's neighbors (Programmed Assumption 16). But in the main, with the exception of the rules for communication and war, interaction between states is generated in unprogrammed ways by the decision-makers themselves, as this section demonstrates.

COMMUNICATIONS

Characteristics of the communications existing between states yield important consequences for their behaviors. Implicit in our description of the simulation to this point has been the existence of communication with and between nations. An attempt has been made within each run to have all the communications between nations, whether oral or written, routed through external decision-makers. Ten to thirty decision-makers send a tremendous number of messages over a period of fifteen to forty-five hours. If the decision-makers do not organize themselves adequately within their nation, the unit becomes paper-bogged and there are consequent failures in communication. Sometimes the neglect of requests by other powers is interpreted as disrespect.

Core Variable: Conferences. Oral communications involving two or more decision-makers within the same nation and between nations.

Core Variable: Messages. Written communications from one decision-maker to another, within the same nation and between nations.

An important difference between sets of inter-nation communication patterns concerns whether they are bilateral or multilateral. In the former, communications are restricted to the two nations involved. When the multilateral exchanges include less than all the nations, as in the case of the trilateral exchanges, decision-makers often are unaware of what is going on in the other parts of the system. This tendency toward ignorance is sometimes strengthened by a division of labor among the two to five decision-makers within the nation, so that even though one of the participants receives a message from another nation, his failure to communicate it internally to others in his government may result in important errors of omission in the actions of the other decision-makers.

These areas of ignorance induced the experimenters to augment the direct exchanges among the decision-makers with a communications system external to the nations themselves—a world newspaper. Journalists were introduced into the simulation to present information about inter-nation events to all decision-makers simultaneously, through a mass medium. Issues of the world newspaper, published every fifteen to thirty minutes during the run, provided communications among the decision-makers which otherwise only the most elaborate and costly intelligence operations could have assembled.

The mass media provide knowledge about the international system, so that most decision-makers know the rough outlines of what is going on within the world. Space is given for the insertion of press releases and communiques by the decision-makers of any nation. The development of nonsecret treaties is publicized through issues of the press, be they concerned with economic, military, or ideological matters. The proceedings of open conferences are reported in summary so that nonattenders may receive dispatches of progress being made or learn of stalemates and conflict. A special statistical supplement is included in the report from time to time, summarizing the information on changes in validator satisfaction and economic well-being, and some statistics on force capability. Extra editions are prepared when there is turnover in government. Although no radio or television apparatus was used in the simulation, the printed media served as a surrogate for the mass media.

Core Variable: Mass Media. Regular reports containing information about states of the inter-nation system, as well as releases issued by the decision-makers; contents are open and circulated to all members of all nations.

During one of the runs, professional editors operated two competing presses. By taking sides with particular blocs, the two papers helped develop propaganda quarrels among the nations. In fact, when one of the blocs was conquered through a devastating war, the deposed decision-makers continued participating in the world complex by starting a rebel newspaper.

Some information circulates in the communication nets among the decision-makers as rumors or secret reports. It is possible for the decision-makers to issue messages which are false or merely speculative. Decision-makers classify some of their messages as restricted. Receivers sometimes find it advantageous to violate the secrecy. At times this creates severe distrust, especially when strategies are divulged in the course of current negotiations. A stochastic leakage of restricted messages is part of the newspaper operation. Without favoring any particular nation, these intelligence reports allow decision-makers to weave a web of conjecture from partial information which is gleaned by tapping one out of every five of the restricted exchanges.

Core Variable: Restricted Messages. Messages whose existence and contents are not known by other than the sender and receiver.

Programmed Assumption 26: Relation of Leakage of Restricted Messages to Volume of Messages. Inasmuch as restricted messages are leaked stochastically, the greater the volume of restricted messages, the greater will be the revelation of secret information to the mass media. The rate of message leakage was set at 20 percent—that is, a leak occurring with every fifth message.

Although no formal espionage operation is included in the simulation, it is fascinating to see how external decision-makers attempt to gain information by posting "observers" at conferences, even when they refuse to have formal representation of their nation at the conference table for reasons of diplomacy. An external decision-maker at times will attempt to ingratiate himself with an ally by communicating supposedly secret information obtained from nonmembers of the alliance.

Because news is communicated in terms of who said what, when, and to whom, the internal and external communication systems help create prestige hierarchies among the decision-makers. These hierarchies of esteem have great import for the operation of influence patterns in the simulation world, as they do within the real world. It is revealing to note how a prestigious nation, once its central decision-maker has spoken, can change the policies of less influential nations.

Unprogrammed Hypothesis. Communication failure due to overload are interpreted by decision-makers as deliberate signs of disrespect and neglect.

Unprogrammed Hypothesis. When there is a preponderant use of bilateral rather than multilateral and mass media channels for communication, there is more distrust and suspicion among the decision-makers of the world.

Unprogrammed Hypothesis. Standards for judgment of national achievement develop in the course of inter-nation communication, thereby defining the "social realities" of the system.

INEQUALITIES AMONG NATIONS

To anyone surveying the more than one hundred independent countries of the real world, an outstanding characteristic of the array is found in their differences. An attempt has been made to incorporate some of this rich variety of the real world in the simulation. The nations may be distinguished from each other by virtue of different weightings of the core factors. Basic differences may be reflected in variations in decision latitude. Authority might be shared instead of centralized in one decision-maker. Some nations might be designated as having higher or lower thresholds for revolution than others. In some, the office-holder's determinations might be made at regular, relatively short intervals, while in others, the determination might be made only after revolutions, following (for example) life-tenured monarchies. It is possible to distinguish one nation from the others through the validation process, by using different weights for the contributions of the components of satisfaction to office-holding (Figure 2.1). One nation, for example, might have a more demanding consumption standard. The validators in another nation might want higher levels of national security.

Different weightings are employed to symbolize inequalities among the nations with respect to their capabilities. Some of the nations are construed as "have-nots" with meager capabilities; others are rich. These differences among the nations are induced in two ways—by starting the nations with different accumulations of basic and force capability, and by assigning differential generation rates for the production of goods and services used for the standard of consumption and for strategic purposes. For example, in one run the initial conditions characterizing nation Erga were designated as 10,000 basic capability units, with an accumulation of 500 force units. The analogous parameters for nation Ingo were 16,000 and 2,400. The rates at which these nations could generate consumption satisfaction units from their basic capability units were 1.0 and 1.5, respectively; the generation rates for force units were .5 and 2.00. In the programmed equations constituting the intra-nation system, some thirty parameters are utilized.

These inequalities among the nations produce important differences in the unprogrammed relations among the nations. Further inequalities, of course, emerge from the ways in which the decision-makers use their resources. In one run, the decision-makers in nation S lost their top position as wealthiest nation. In another run, nation M rose to a position as one of the two nations with the dominant strategic capabilities. It is feasible to go farther by introducing slowly—or suddenly, to correspond to an important technological breakthrough—changes in the generation rates during the course of the historical development of nations. For example, during an exploratory run, a middle-sized nation was allowed to "develop" nuclear power, which increased tenfold its force capabilities.

The employment of differences in the weightings yields important leverage for using the simulation in the study of international relations. By setting the weightings to correspond to the configurations found in today's system of nations, contemporary problems in foreign affairs may be studied. By resetting the weightings, it is possible to represent historical situations. Perhaps as important is the potential development of simulation analyses based on weightings that do not yet exist in the real world. This latter possibility may be the most significant heuristic value to be obtained from the simulation. Research leading to better understanding of the "possible" in the development of world affairs, unbounded by current practices, may lead to unimagined innovations in international relations.

Although at first the participants within a nation feel they are the United States or nineteenth-century Britain or perhaps contemporary Yugoslavia, these identifications with historical or existing nations gradually lose their potency. The simulated nations seem to take on color and characteristics unique in themselves. Then the participants vividly contrast their own nations with those of the real world. Suppose we attempt to set the weightings in our functions as they are found in real nations. Further, suppose each nation is peopled by individuals of the nationality of the nation being represented. Then, if the model simulates adequately, participants of a given nationality should feel themselves conceptually to be operating in their own "home countries" when they serve as decision-makers for their home nations.

ARMAMENTS: DEFENSIVE AND AGGRESSIVE USE OF FORCE

In the exploratory runs undertaken to the first of 1960, the decision-makers tended to make great use of their force capabilities in handling their external problems. As noted earlier, validator satisfaction derives from a given level of strength, because a nation is programmed to depend upon its relation to the strength of its nonallies (Programmed Assumption 16). The relationship, however, is considered to have a ceiling effect, in that validator satisfaction reaches its maximum when the strength of a nation is three or more times that of its strongest potential enemies. Likewise, there is a floor effect, because when the nation's strategic capability is small, its validators become indifferent to the nation's strategic capability in world affairs.

Free Variable: Alliance. Written treaty explicity authorized by central decision-makers to provide military aid and/or support to another nation in case of the latter's involvement in military activity. (There is no enforcement of these treaties by the simulation director.)

The effectiveness of strength as a factor in foreign relations depends on the uses to which it may be put. The simulation provides opportunities for its symbolic employment in both aggressive and defensive ways. The decision-makers within each nation project war plans of an offensive and/or defensive nature, which may be revised from period to period. These plans specify the amounts of force which may be directed against particular nations. The plans provide for target selection, directed toward the basic capability of the other unit and/or toward its military forces.

The attack, counterattack, and defense plans may be kept quite secret or they may be exhibited as part of a deterrent strategy. Sometimes the nations will stage war exercises or make displays of strength. The central decision-makers systematize response plans analogous to the von Schieffen plan; or they may develop automatic response plans, resembling those contemplated for mid-twentieth-century nuclear warfare. The arrangement allows significant variation in the use of force in both limited and more global ways. Since the decision-makers are allowed to ally themselves freely, the possible combinations are great. By building war into its programmed rules, the simulation accommodates a range of use of strength for purposes of threat and intimidation.

The war programs of the Inter-Nation Simulation are still in need of marked revision. However, a general outline of the waging and consequences of war in these exercises can be sketched at this time.

In the making of war, the routines may be phased so that there are opportunities for varying levels of engagement in battle. When a nation goes to war, rallying to the national cause is portrayed through increases in validator satisfaction. The war itself may engage less than the total resources of the system, so that during its conduct there is time for threats and counterthreats, for peace proposals and counterproposals. During these periods, other nations come to decisions on whether they will or will not enter the struggle. Sometimes a "neutral" will attempt to mediate the conflict.

Core Variable: War. The use of force capability by one or more nations against one or more other nations.

Programmed Assumption 27: The Relation of the Making of War to Validator Satisfaction. Whenever a nation makes war against another (or others), its validator satisfaction is temporarily increased.

$$\Delta \text{VSm} = s', \qquad [2.17]$$

where s' was taken as 2 in the exploratory runs.

The hardware intricacies of war itself are abbreviated in the simulation because interest does not center on nonpolitical aspects of violent conflict. The outcomes of the contests of strength depend stochastically upon the relative basic (BC) and force (FC) capabilities of the nations. It is possible to allow consequences to vary in severity, from partial to total destruction. If the nation is not totally destroyed, its decision-makers may surrender, negotiate an armistice, and eventually sign a peace treaty with the victor(s). An occupation may be arranged in which the winning power exercises authority within another nation, through implementation of its decisions with respect to the internal and external functioning of the nation. Included among these decisions is the possibility of reparations and tribute. Of course, there is internal opposition to occupying force, which in time may become acute enough to engage the revolution mechanism against the occupying power, as it sometimes is evoked against an indigenous national government. The rules also permit other nations to throw out the occupying forces through a war of liberation.

Core Variable: Determination of Outcome of War (pOW). When a determination of the outcome of war is made, the result may be victory or defeat.

Programmed Assumption 28: Outcome of War as Related To Relative Strengths. The winning or losing in each phase of a war is determined stochastically, with the chances for winning proportional to the relative strength of one's opponent at the beginning of each phase of the war.

$$pOW = 1 - \left[\frac{(FC - FCic + a'BC)ad}{\sum_{all}(FC - FCic + a'BC)}\right], \quad [2.18]$$

where "ad" is defined as "adversary" and "all" as "all nations in war."

The adversary may be a single nation or a group of allied nations. In the exploratory runs, a' was set again at .5, as in equation 2.9.

Core Variable: War Destruction (WD). The amounts of the basic and force capabilities of a nation which are destroyed during each phase of a war are proportional to the force capabilities applied to one's self by the adversary in the course of each phase.

Programmed Assumption 29: War Destruction as Related to Force Capabilities Applied in Course of War. The war destruction suffered by any nation is proportional to the force capabilities applied by its adversary.

$$\frac{\Delta FC}{FCtar} \text{ and } \frac{\Delta BC}{BC} = \frac{FCad}{\sum_{all} FC}, \quad [2.19]$$

where "tar" is defined as "in-target nation." Whether the percentage destruction is suffered in FCs or BCs or both, depends upon the targeting decision of the adversary.

Unprogrammed Hypothesis. When the members of a coalition are historically unified in terms of ideology, they will come to the defense of one of their members when the latter is attacked by outside forces, either directly through participation in a current war or later through a war of liberation.

The following example of the above unprogrammed hypothesis was found in one run in which three nations operated as tightly reigned states, as reflected in their high decision latitudes. When one of their number clashed with a democratic nation, the other two immediately came to its aid. The decision-makers in the totalitarian bloc simply could not understand why the other nations, which continued to operate with low decision latitudes period after period despite opportunities for increasing those decisional latitudes, wished to remain democratic.

Perhaps the intertwining of the internal and external processes within an inter-nation system is nowhere in the simulation as well represented as in the utilization of the force capabilities of the nations. As has been demonstrated in the history of military aid in the real world, the arms of a country may be used by its decision-makers to control its own peoples, as well as against the peoples of other nations. The intimacy of the reciprocity of domestic and foreign policy is emodied in the Inter-Nation Simulation in the internal control and war programs.

INTERACTION PATTERNS: CONFLICT AND COOPERATION IN WAR AND PEACE

Interest in developing an operating model of inter-nation relations stemmed, in part, from the belief that mathematical and vernacular languages as they exist today seem to limit, for different reasons, our ability to handle abstractions. It was hoped that the central heuristic value of this kind of exercise would reside in its representation of intergroup processes, which we simply are unable to program adequately, given our present state of knowledge.

Enfolded in the capabilities are the sinews of war and peace. Quests for high standards of living, given differential rates of production, may result in trade, loans, or aid. Anxiety about national security may produce alliances and arms races. Although the capabilities seem at first directed only toward fulfillment of validator satisfactions, they too become significant bases for external activity.

There are variations in the degrees to which interactions stabilize in the form of structured organizations. Let us now explore the way in which the interactions involving peace and war yield entanglements in the relations among our simulated nations. In the following section, the more formalized, complex organizations that may evolve in the simulation will be discussed.

The decision-makers can and do make informal and formal agreements on many subjects. Sometimes these agreements are simply de facto working arrangements which develop tacitly in the course of the interactions. For example, in an early exploration run one of the external decision-makers in state P informally helped an external decision-maker of state G arrange a multilateral conference among the nations. Sometimes the agreements are more formal, registered with each nation's signature. Some of the treaties are secret and some are publicized. Some treaties even involve definite commitments of force capability units to other nations, for purposes of aggression against another nation or group of nations or for collective security purposes.

Unprogrammed Hypothesis. When agreements are openly developed and widely publicized throughout the international system, there is less miscalculation of national intentions.

Much interaction is generated among the nations because of the differences in their abilities to transform one capability into another. The economic "law of comparative advantage" induces trade, which is often sporadic but sometimes takes a more stable, long-term form with formal exchange agreements. Because of the impoverishment of some nations, loans are arranged between them and the wealthier countries. These loans may be interest-bearing or free. Agreements may be made to provide that basic capability be sent abroad to generate returns at the rates of the nation within which the investment is made. During our exploratory runs, outright grants of aid were made—sometimes military (in force capability units) or economic (in basic capability units) in form, and sometimes of an emergency nature (in consumption satisfaction units). The aid arrangements at times became part and parcel of security alliances.

Unprogrammed Hypothesis. The more mutual trust among nations, the more likely is the law of comparative advantage to operate. No attempt was made to complicate further the economic features of the simulation by introducing a formal monetary system. With three "commodities" (basic capability, consumption satisfaction, and force capability), transactions by barter seem to be made without awkwardness. In one exploratory run the basic capability units operated for the nation's decision-makers as a gold standard in determining prices used in international transactions. Since there is no explicit private sector of the national economies, the usual need of governmental decision-makers for trade restrictions (tariffs, exchange controls, and quotas) is not present.

Trust and suspicion are generated in these interactions. Some nations become reliable and trustworthy; others are suspect and perceived as crafty. During the course of the simulation runs, it is possible at the end of each period to ask the decision-makers to rate each other nation in terms of its trustworthiness. Mutual trust can be generated, even when the decision-makers are overtly unconcerned with each other's welfare when certain situational conditions hold. One such condition is that in which there is opportunity for each party to know what the other will do before committing itself to irrevocable choice. The entanglements arising from economic and military matters generate ideologies among the nations, which seem to have created in some cases much trust and in others considerable hostility and sense of threat.

Unprogrammed Hypothesis. At any level of congruence or conflict of national goals, the greater knowledge each nation has of the other's action, the greater will be the mutual trust.

INTER-NATION ORGANIZATIONS

When the volume of transactions among the nations becomes stable, sufficiently large, and spread over a long period, the interactions occur through formal inter-nation organizations.

Unprogrammed Hypothesis. Members of an alliance, which exists but for a single purpose under ad hoc conditions, gradually will begin meeting periodically for increasingly broad purposes.

It is intriguing to note how inter-nation collectivities thus evolved tend to develop an autonomy of their own, so that the delegate members no longer act solely in terms of their national reference groups, but develop bases of action within the international organization itself. The organization may be consultative or it may be given decision-making power of its own by delegation of national power from the member states. The evolutions sometimes are followed by devolutions, so that an overall effect of waxing and waning is experienced.

Free Unit: Inter-Nation Organization. A formally chartered supraunit among three or more nations (see p. 26).

Unprogrammed Hypothesis. Inter-nation organizations tend over a period of time to develop an increasing amount of autonomy, to the extent that they are successful in achieving their substantive goals.

In the course of a pair of exploratory runs, two formal inter-nation organizations were created by the external decision-makers acting on behalf of their nations. During one run, an underdeveloped nation induced all but one of the other nations of the world to establish an international bank. Each period the member nations made contributions in basic capabilities to a fund thereafter to be controlled entirely by the bank's board, consisting of external ministers from the contributing states. Before the simulation was terminated, the poorer countries of the world had been given loans, resulting in decided increases in the stability of their governments. During another run, two large powers established an international grants-in-aid corporation to which the dissident smaller powers, flirting with aggressive national policies, might apply for help. The external ministers who manned the corporation, however, squabbled so much among themselves that before the terms of the grants were formulated, the smaller countries experienced internal disorders, with many changes in their decision-makers. The disagreements among the great powers and the disorders within the smaller powers resulted in a world war. It was interesting to note that the subsequent postwar peace treaty provided, among other things, for reestablishment of an international grants-in-aid corporation—this time with a worldwide board membership. During a run in Alger's International Organizations course, the students found themselves unable to build a viable international bank, even though considerable effort was devoted to the enterprise.

Unprogrammed Hypothesis. Basic changes in the international system take place when there are simultaneous changes in office-holders within several of the nations.

Unprogrammed Hypothesis. When there are changes in office-holders within the several nations a short period of time, the decision-makers find the behavior of each other more unpredictable.

Because of the relatively short duration of our runs up to this point in the explorations, there has been little time for the international organizations to consolidate. Each of our nations has needed the opportunity to worry through its internal problems first. Although both the bank and the development corporation began establishing rules for their own internal operation, no attempts have yet been made to erect a court or legislature for the establishment of inter-nation law. When the runs are extended in duration, the nations may develop unifunctional as opposed to multifunctional organizations. It is also possible that regional organizations will emerge to compete with universal complexes. Interrelationships will develop among the various inter-nation organizations themselves. It should even be possible to note how world community norms develop ahead of, or lag behind, the building of legal and political institutions among the nations. Because the central decision-makers may turn over part or even all of their decision-making to supranational groups, it is possible to have federations and/or world governments.

Unprogrammed Hypothesis. When the decision-makers of a nation are intensely involved in meeting internal problems, there is little growth of inter-nation organizations.

Unprogrammed Hypothesis. Inter-nation organizations established for single purposes tend to be less viable than those established for more than one purpose.

Unprogrammed Hypothesis. The norms of conduct of states which develop within an inter-nation organization tend to be applied to relations among all states, whether they are members or not.

The relation of the decision-makers to their own nations plays an important role at the international level. In the simulation runs to date, we have evidence of the problems involved in the relation of the foreign mission to the home foreign office. When the external environment is rich with international activities, how can the external ministers adequately communicate to their internal ministers? One of the external decision-makers for state K had much trouble in a particular run because he acted as a plenipotentiary. The reactions of other states to nation K's inconsistency in policy lost K its membership in a newly forming alliance.

IV. DISCUSSION

One chapter cannot handle all the problems raised by the construction of the simulation. Still, some of these are so pressing that it may be useful to mention them, even if they cannot be solved at present.

Although no explicit reference has been made to the scholarly literature of international relations, the constructors of this operating model have steeped themselves in this body of speculation. Hence, we have borrowed freely from many others for our formulation. Perhaps more attention should have been devoted within the chapter to justification of our decisions, indicating the rationale employed in making each of the choices. As yet, no formalized criteria have emerged to provide guidance for our exploitations of the work of others. For instance, no sampling technique seemed appropriate to guide our selection of core variables. Detailed rationalizations of the choices must be provided eventually. It is important that a firmer embedding of our model within the studies of international relations be attempted, so that an almost total reliance upon an intuitive grasp of this literature may be circumvented.

Has the choice of simulation mixing people with computed programs been sound? An all-computer simulation would obviate the implicit contents introduced into the Inter-Nation Simulation by the use of human decision-makers. An all-person simulation without intra-nation programs, on the other hand, perhaps would make the simulation too much of a face-to-face group. As the simulation stands now, it seems to be a composition of computers and people, so that the inter-group relations emerging from its operation are somewhat isomorphic, from a subjective point of view, to the phenomena one encounters in the interrelations of real nations.

But have not our omissions of important features of the real world developed incapacitating artificialities within the simulation? How can the motivational stress of a game be compared with the deadly struggles for power within and among the governments of the world? For example, has not our positing of authority within the central decision-maker induced an unrealistic security for the holders of power? And how is the impact of geography displayed? Because of the short duration of the simulation, are not the historical factors—especially as they operate through tradition—being short-circuited? Perhaps most puzzling of all, how does the mixture of people and computers distort the time relations? The participants function in terms of biological, or real, time. The machines compress time, so that some seventy minutes of game time are made analogous to a year of life time. These problems certainly need close attention.

If the simulation is to be of heuristic value, as Snyder (1963a) contends, its ability to produce unprogrammed consequences that are isomorphic to reality must be checked thoroughly. For example, Alger unexpectedly found that in several underdeveloped nations in his International Relations course runs, the aspirant decision-makers consolidated their efforts with those of the decision-makers in office, evolving one-party nations. It seems that such nations felt they could not afford the luxury of opposition among their decision-making groups. Work on the validity of the simulation is imperative at this time (see Guetzkow and Valadez, 1981b). When such validity is demonstrated, then one's use of the simulation for exploration in unchartered areas, such as the N-country problem, will be more justifiable.

The task of making explicit the implicit contents generated by the programmed assumptions is a large one. It will be worthwhile only if the simulation demonstrates its potential as a heuristic device in the acquisition and application of reliable knowledge about international relations.

V. SUMMARY

Individual and group components of the Inter-Nation Simulation are meshed into an operating model through both structured programs and free, self-developing interactive processes. In general, programed assumptions are used for setting the foundations of the simulation, serving to provide operating rules for the decision-makers whereby they may handle the political, economic, and military aspects of their nations. On the other hand, with the exception of the rules for the conduct of war, there are no programs prescribing the relations among nations. The basic strategy used in the construction of the simulation has been to allow free development of the inter-nation relations, without restrictions other than those implicit in the characteristics of the nations themselves. Illustrative hypotheses are offered to indicate the richness of the relations of the structures programs to the free activities within the Inter-Nation Simulation.

NOTES

1. It has been our practice in the simulation to designate the nations by fictitious names or by single letters.
2. Definition of decision latitude as a variable is made on p. 34.

3

An Economic Model and Government Stability: Reconstructing the Inter-Nation Simulation

Charles D. Elder and Robert E. Pendley

This chapter reports the results of an investigation undertaken on the Inter-Nation Simulation (INS) as developed by Professor Harold Guetzkow and his colleagues at Northwestern University. In it we delineate a refinement of the INS model through evaluation of certain of its economic and political aspects in terms of internal theoretical consistency, in comparison with other theoretical formulations, and with respect to its empirical viability.

A TEST AND RECONSTRUCTION OF THE ECONOMIC MODEL IN AN INTER-NATION SIMULATION

I. ECONOMIC VARIABLES IN THE INTER-NATION SIMULATION AND THEIR CONTEXT

In the Inter-Nation Simulation, "office-holding is a mainspring" (Guetzkow, 1981b: 29). The probability of holding office (pOH) is dependent

Authors' Note: This study was supported by the JWGA/ARPA/NU Simulated International Processes project at Northwestern University. The authors are indebted to several members of the Northwestern University Department of Political Science for suggestions and criticisms. In particular, we would like to acknowledge the support and encouragement provided by Professor Harold Guetzkow.

upon the ability of the various decision-makers to elicit support from their validators. Support is determined by the level of satisfaction arising largely from the allocation of resources for consumption and for national security (Guetzkow, 1981b: 30).[1] This section of our essay focuses on one determinant of the probability of office-holding, namely, validator satisfaction with respect to consumption standards (VScs).

This is one of four economic variables in the programmed model; the remaining three are determinants of VScs. These latter variables include: (1) consumption standards (CS)—the actual quantity of goods and services produced for consumptive purposes; (2) the maximum consumption standards (CSmax)—the total overall productive capability of the nation; and (3) the minimum consumption standards (CSmin) for a nation.[2] The substantive theory about the relationships between these variables in stated in relatively unambiguous propositions. The task we shall undertake is to examine the mathematical representation of these relationships with the objective of determining whether the model is coherent with respect to these variables. In other words, we are asking whether the formalized relationships behave the way verbal theory says they should. In cases where contradictions exist between verbal and mathematical statements, reformulations will be offered which give the model greater internal consistency. Rather than simply presenting the revised formal relationships, however, we will attempt to show their logical derivation from the verbal hypotheses.

The Relationship Between Minimum and Maximum Consumption Standards

The substantive theory from which the formalized relation between minimum and maximum consumption standards is drawn is found in the following two Programmed Assumptions (Guetzkow, 1981b: 41):

Programmed Assumption 11: Relation of Minimum Consumption Standards to Basic Capability. The minimum consumption standards of the nation increase as the basic capability of the nation increases in its ability to produce satisfying goods and services.

Programmed Assumption 12: Proportion of Basic Capability Needed to Fulfill Minimum Consumption Standard. The percentage of the realized basic capability required to fulfill minimum living standards decreases as the nation's basic capability increases.

Because maximum consumption standards in the INS are a simple linear function of the total realized basic capability of a nation (i.e., the nation's generation rate for consumption units multiplied by its basic capability), these two program assumptions may be combined to read: As maximum

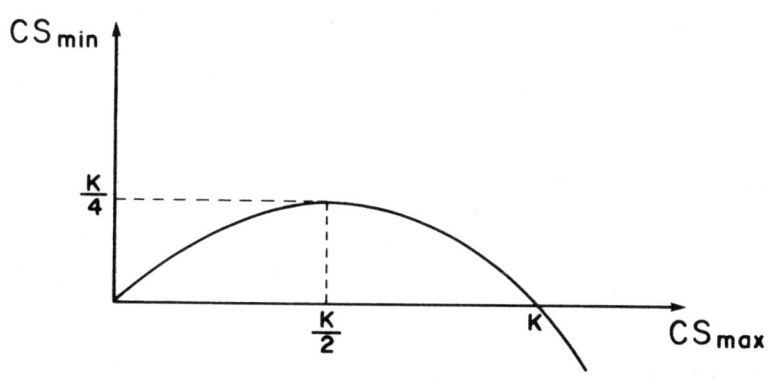

Figure 3.1

consumption standards increase, minimum standards increase but at a diminishing rate. This theoretical statement is represented in the INS by the following equation:

$$CSmin = [1- (CSmax/k)]\, CSmax \qquad [3.1]$$

But from inspection of Figure 3.1 (which shows the behavior of CSmin relative to CSmax as prescribed by the equation), we can see that this equation does not conform to the verbal theory. The values of CSmin produced by the equation will conform to the verbal theory *only* for those values of CSmax which are less than one-half of the parameter k. Thus, there are good theoretical grounds for rejecting the current formulation in the formal model.

As a practical matter, one might ask whether it is reasonable to assume that CSmax might ever become as large as k/2. Note that k is given an arbitrary value of 380,000 units (Guetzkow, 1981b: 41). If a research design called for a simulation which ran for a number of periods, a nation with a beginning CSmax of only 45,000 units and a growth rate of roughly 10 percent per period (not unrealistic figures) would reach a CSmax value of approximately k/2 in about fifteen periods. Thus, we have a practical objection to the current formulation, as well as a purely theoretical one.[3]

Having shown that the current equation relating CSmin and CSmax must be rejected, we have the problem of deriving an equation which will conform to the theory. We resolve this using differential calculus.

Recall that Programmed Assumptions 11 and 12 said that CSmin will increase as CSmax increases, but the proportion (CSmin/CSmax) will decrease as CSmax increases. In other words, CSmin varies directly with *changes* in CSmax but inversely with the *magnitude* of CSmax. This suggests the following differential equation:

$$d(CSmin)/d(CSmax) = a/CSmax \text{ or } d(CSmin) = a[d(CSmax)/CSmax] \qquad [3.2]$$

Integrating this equation yields:

$$CSmin = a \ln(CSmax) + B \qquad [3.3]$$

Because CSmax is not a dimensionless quantity but, rather, has certain units associated with it, we are not permitted in a strictly formal sense to take its natural logarithm. This difficulty could be resolved if CSmax were divided by some theoretically meaningful quantity of the same dimensions, leaving a ratio, which also is unitless. To this end, we offer the following:

> *Axiom I.* There exists, for every nation and/or society, some level of consumption which may be called the "absolute minimum consumption level" (CS_0), beneath which consumption is not adequate to sustain life and bodily health.

The revised equation is:

$$CSmin = a \ln(CSmax/CS_0) + B \qquad [3.4]$$

This auxiliary theoretical assumption does not change the basic theory as contained in the differential equation, but it does provide a way of handling the dimensions of CSmax. It also provides a way of evaluating the parameter B.

Consider those nations where CSmax is *just sufficient to provide the absolute minimum consumption level*. In these cases, CSmin = CSmax = CS_0. Therefore, at absolute minimal levels,

$$CS_0 = a \ln(CS_0/CS_0) + B$$
$$\text{or} \qquad [3.4']$$
$$B = CS_0 - a \ln(CS_0/CS_0)$$

Since $CS_0/CS_0 = 1$ and $\ln(1) = 0$,

$$B = CS_0 \qquad [3.5]$$

Thus,

$$CSmin = \ln(CSmax/CS_0) + CS_0 \qquad [3.6]$$

Given this reformulation, we will now discuss the benefits to be derived from it. This can perhaps be seen best by comparing the reformulated equation (3.6) with the one originally posited in the INS model (equation 3.1).

Comparison of Equations of Minimum Consumption Standards

For comparative purposes the two alternative ways of formulating the equation of CSmin are put side by side:

$$CSmin = a \ln(CSmax/CS_0) + CS_0 \qquad [3.6]$$
$$CSmin = [1 - (CSmax/k)] CSmax \qquad [3.1]$$

The formulation given in equation 3.6 is certainly no more *precise* or *specific* than the form originally suggested by Guetzkow (equation 3.1). Owing to its logical derivation, however, it has the virtue of being *accurate* if the verbal theory is valid, whereas the original form has been shown to be inconsistent with that theory. Figure 3.2 demonstrates that the reformulated equation (which shows the suggested reformulation of CSmin as a function of CSmax) satisfies Programmed Assumptions 11 and 12. The reader may compare this with the graphical representation of the original equation presented in Figure 3.1.

As we turn to the question of parameters we note that the meaning of CS_0 has already been explored. However, does the parameter a in equation 3.6 have an interpretation? The greater a, the more rapidly CSmin increases as CSmax grows larger. Conceptually, this means that a is a measure of the *relative difficulty in satisfying validators with respect to consumption standards*: the larger a, the greater the CSmin demanded by the validators in a nation with a given CSmax capability.[4] Thus, there are good theoretical grounds on which to base an estimation of the value of a; this may be contrasted again to the current formulation (equation 3.1), in which the number "k" has no clear conceptual meaning and is assigned an arbitrary value.

The Relationship Between Validator Satisfaction and Consumption Variables

In the foregoing discussion we have been concerned with the minimum consumption demands which the validators of a nation place upon the

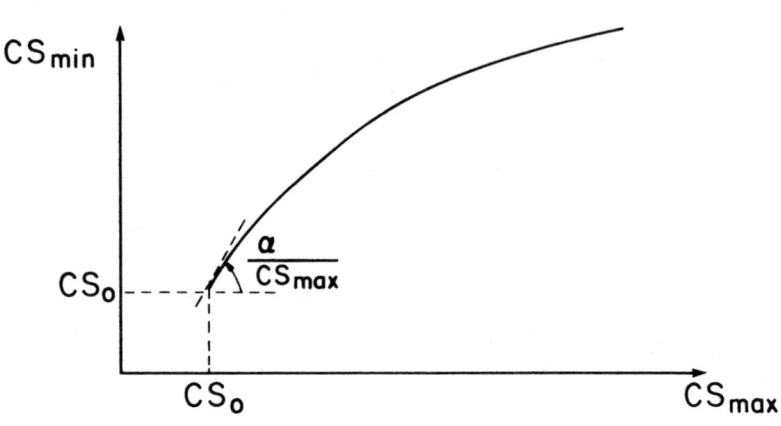

Figure 3.2

decision-makers. In this section we will deal with the process by which actual consumption levels are translated into a degree of support for the regime in power; that is, how actual minimum and maximum consumption levels are related to the satisfaction validators feel from a given level of consumption. As before, we first present the verbal theory on which a mathematical formulation is based.

Programmed Asumption 13: Relation of Validator Satisfaction to Consumption Satisfaction. This assumption consists of three parts:

(1) For consumption near minimum consumption standards, validator satisfaction depends on the relation of consumption to minimum consumption standards.

(2) Once minimum consumption standards have been met, larger and larger increases in consumption are necessary to produce corresponding changes in validator satisfaction.

(3) This saturation effect is more prominent for wealthier nations [Guetzkow, 1981b: 42].

Guetzkow derives a formalization of these propositions by first implementing Programmed Assumption 13.1, which can be paraphrased to read that at consumption near CSmin, the value of VScs will approximate a linear function of the ratio CS/CSmin. Thus, Guetzkow starts with an equation of the form $VScs = A(CS/CSmin) + B$, where A and B are constants. Adding another term to achieve the effect posited in Programmed Assumption 13.2, and still another term for Programmed Asumption 13.3, the following equation results (Guetzkow, 1981b: 42):

$$VS_{cs} = 1 + r[(CS/CS_{min}) - 1] - \frac{V(CS_{max}/CS_{min})}{[(CS/CS_{min}) - 1]^2} \qquad [3.7]$$

This is the formulation which we will examine for internal consistency.

The last term on the right in the above equation—involving the square of a quantity—was added to yield the steadily decreasing marginal *gain* in VScs per CS expenditure. To be consistent with the verbal assumptions, this equation must yield values of VScs which increase for any increase in CS expenditures above CSmin. It is easy to show that in fact this criterion is not met by the equation. Consider the case in which CS is greater than twice CSmin: Here the ratio (CS/CSmin) is greater than 2, and the quantity [(CS/CSmin) - 1] is greater than 1; thus, the bracketed term squared is greater than the term itself. This means that for CS greater than twice CSmin there will actually be a *decrease* in VScs for further expenditures on consumption. Again, it might be asked whether it is possible for CS ever to be greater than twice CSmin. Such a value is indeed possible. Although not presented here, calculations demonstrate that if the current equations are assumed, it is possible for consumption (CS) to exceed twice CSmin whenever CSmax is greater than one-half of the parameter k in equation 3.1. Similarly, such a CS value is possible in the reformulated equation 3.6.

This suggests that another reformulation is in order. Looking again at the programmed assumption on which the mathematical representation is to be based, we notice that 13.1 and 13.3 are *boundary* conditions for the basic relationship: they are statements about the relation for particular values of CS and CSmax, respectively. The functional relationship, stated in Programmed Assumption 13.2, relates *changes* in consumption standards to *changes* in validation satisfaction: as CS increases, VScs increases, but at a diminishing rate as CS/CSmin becomes larger. As was seen in the derivation of equation 3.6 above, such propositions relating changes in variables normally contain the basic theory. Generally, the boundary conditions should be imposed only after the differential form of the theory has been integrated, to give the final formalization.

Programmed Assumption 13.2, analogous to the derivation of equation 3.6, suggests the following differential equation:

$$\frac{dVS_{cs}}{d\frac{CS}{CS_{min}}} = \frac{\gamma}{\frac{CS}{CS_{min}}} \qquad [3.8]$$

By simple integration, this yields[5]

$$VS_{cs} = \gamma \ln CS/CSmin + \delta . \qquad [3.9]$$

Since this equation is derived from Assumption 13.2, we know that the equation is consistent with that assumption. We must now show that it is consistent with the other two. First consider Programmed Assumption 13.1: For values of CS near CSmin, VScs will approximate a linear function of CS/CSmin. The problem is to demonstrate that our equation reduces to this general form for CS approximately equal to CSmin. This can be done as follows. For CS = CSmin, first define

$$Y = CS/CSmin \cong 1. \qquad [3.10]$$

Next define

$$X = Y - 1 \cong 0. \qquad [3.11]$$

Now for values of X near 0, it is true that $e^x \cong 1 + X$. Therefore,

$$e^x \cong 1 + X = 1 + Y - 1 \cong Y. \qquad [3.12]$$

Now, by taking natural logarithms of both sides,

$$X \cong \ln Y. \qquad [3.13]$$

Therefore,

$$Y - 1 \cong \ln Y, \qquad [3.14]$$

which means that for values of CS near CSmin:

$$\ln(CS/CSmin) \cong (CS/CSmin) - 1 \qquad [3.15]$$

We now insert this substitution for the ln(CS/CSmin) in our reformulated equation 3.9:

$$VS(cs \cong csmin) \cong \gamma (CS/CSmin) - \gamma + \delta . \qquad [3.16]$$

This is now of the form

$$VS_{cs} = A(CS/CSmin) + B, \qquad [3.17]$$

which says, verbally, that at consumption near minimum levels, VScs goes up approximately linearly as CS/CSmin goes up. Thus, equation 3.9 satisfies Programmed Assumption 13.1.

The demonstration that the equation satisfies Programmed Assumption 13.1 may be done even more easily. Recall from above that as CSmax grows larger, CSmin also increases. Thus, for nations with larger CSmax, the ratio CS/CSmin will be smaller for the same CS expenditure, and VScs will therefore be smaller for such a nation. The constant may also contribute to this effect.[6]

Comparison of Equations for Validator Satisfaction with Respect to Consumption: The Question of the Parameters

Before proceeding to the question of what conceptual meaning the paramaters δ and γ might have, let us juxtapose the reformulated equation 3.9 with the current INS equation (equation 3.7).

$$VScs = \gamma \ln(CS/CSmin) + \Delta \qquad [3.9]$$

$$VScs = 1 + r\ [(CS/CSmin - 1] - V(CSmax/CSmin)\ [(CS/CSmin) - 1]^2 \qquad [3.7]$$

The reader will note that the logically derived reformulation (equation 3.9) is in this case actually less complex than the current formulation (equation 3.7), at least with respect to the number of terms involved.

Turning now to the parameters, we first allow CS in our reformulated equation to equal CSmin (i.e., expenditures for consumption are at the minimum demanded by the validators). In this case, by making the substitution,

$$VS(cs=CSmin) = \gamma \ln(1.0) + \delta = 0 + \delta,$$
$$VS(cs=CSmin) = \delta. \qquad [3.18]$$

Now notice the interesting result of allowing CS to equal CSmin in the current equation 3.7:

$$VS(cs=CSmin) = 1 + r(0) - v(1)[0]^2$$
$$VS(cs=CSmin) = 1 \qquad [3.19]$$

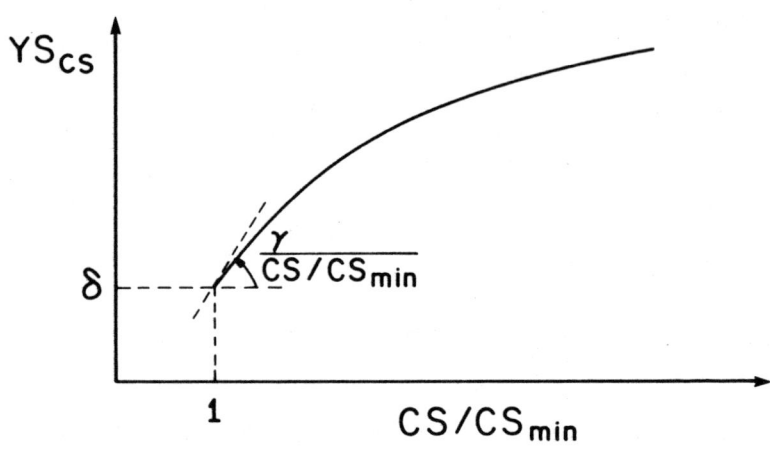

Figure 3.3

The current model apparently was constructed under the following assumption:

> *Axiom II:* When actual consumption standards are at the *minimum* demanded by the validators in a nation, then the satisfaction with respect to consumption standards in that nation is equal to 1; further, this is true for all nations.

The theoretical justification for this axiom is not given in the source of the equation. While the question we raise is in part a scaling problem, the axiom does suggest that a positive increment of satisfaction is accrued from minimal acceptable consumption. Perhaps it might be better to simply leave the value of δ to future work, thus giving theorists an opportunity to investigate the matter. At any rate, the conceptual meaning of the constant δ is clear: It is the validator satisfaction accrued when CS expenditures are at the minimum acceptable level.

The meaning of the second constant, γ, perhaps will be made clearer by inspection of Figure 3.3, which shows graphically the reformulated relationship between VScs and CS/CSmin. From this figure, it can be seen that when CS equals CSmin, the slope of the curve equals γ. This means that holding the relationship between CS and CSmin constant, larger values of γ produce greater validator satisfaction. Thus, it would seem that γ is a measure of the relative ease with which validator satisfaction can be gained from a given level of expenditure for consumption, ceteris paribus. Again, the reader may contrast this conceptually meaningful parameter with the arbitrarily assigned values of those in the current formulation (equation 3.7).[7]

II. COMPARISON OF THE INS ECONOMIC MODEL AND ECONOMIC THEORY

Before attempting to assess the reformulated INS economic model empirically, it would seem appropriate to evaluate the theoretical notions posited there with those of other theorists. Such comparison will perhaps allow us to assess the general credibility of the INS model and perhaps provide guidelines for altering the model should its empirical adequacy be found lacking.

As already mentioned, in the Inter-Nation Simulation, validator satisfaction is determined on the basis of three assumptions which are distinctly economic in nature (Guetzkow, 1981b: 41-42):

(1) "The minimum consumption standards [CSmin] of the nation increase as the basic capability [BC] of the nation increases in its ability to produce satisfying goods and services."

(2) "The percentage of realized basic capability required to fulfill minimum living standards decreases as the nation's basic capability increases.

(3) "[a] For consumption [CS] near minimum consumption standards, validator satisfaction depends on the relation of consumption satisfaction to minimum consumption standards.

[b] Once minimum consumption has been met, larger increases in consumption are necessary to produce corresponding changes in validator satisfaction.

[c] This saturation effect is more prominent for wealthier nations."

We should mention at the outset that these assumptions refer to the behavior of nations, while certain of the economic conceptions which we find relevant are concerned with individual economic actors. Economists have generally assumed, however, that the "reaction of the community will be the aggregate of the reactions of the individuals it comprises" (Galbraith, 1958: 121). Thus, they have used microeconomic theory to build macro theory. Consequently, comparison of INS and economic theories would seem to be justified.

Comparison of Variables

As earlier discussed, validators in the INS provide a generalized measure of political support. This support or validation of office-holding is tendered largely on the basis of satisfaction arising from the allocation of resources for consumption and for national security. Thus, validators in the Inter-Nation Simulation correspond roughly with the voters in Anthony Downs's *Economic Theory of Democracy,* and validator satisfaction is closely analogous to an aggregate measure of what Downs has called "utility income" (1957: 3-50).[8] Here we are concerned only with one source of satisfaction or utility—validator satisfaction with respect to consumption (VScs).

From the assumptions listed above, we have seen that validator satisfaction is dependent upon three variables: (1) the minimum consumption standard (CSmin) or "that allocated of necessity, to provide for the supply and manning of the nation's productive capability" (Guetzkow, 1981b: 40); (2) the current consumption standard (CS); and (3) the realized basic capability of a nation (CSmax).[9] For the latter two, it is quite easy to find corresponding economic conceptions. The realized basic capability (CSmax) might be conceived of as *a nation's per capita gross national product,* or some similar measure of a nation's wealth. The current consumption standard (CS) is analogous to what Keynes called the "propensity to consume," i.e., *the amount of a nation's aggregate income spent for consumption.*

The minimum consumption standard (CSmin) might be compared to concepts in economic theory such as subsistence level or "necessaries" in the traditional division of necessaries, comforts and luxuries. But in the INS (via Programmed Assumption 1), this minimum "changes from time to time, increasing as the basic capability of a nation increases and decreasing as the nation becomes depressed" (Guetzkow, 1981b: 40). If the CSmin simply were descriptive of the necessaries of existence, one would expect it to be relatively stable and markedly influenced only by extreme changes in the population. If we assume that a nation's population is relatively stable (i.e., not subject to sudden and extreme changes), the minimum consumption standard (CSmin) suggested by Guetzkow clearly does not refer solely to the "necessaries," which correspond more closely to the CS_0 we have posited as a boundary condition.

Rather, this minimum standard seems more analogous to what Alfred Marshall called the "standard of comfort." Hypothesizing that the necessaries for existence and the necessaries for efficiency are not the same, Marshall suggested that "every estimate of necessaries must be relative to a given time and place" (Marshall, 1895: 138). The habits of living dictate what he called "conventional necessaries"; these are not necessaries in the strict sense, but to some extent take the place of them.

Comparison of Variable Relationships

Marshall's discussion of the "standard of comfort" seems to imply a relationship consonant with Programmed Assumption 11. A more explicit statement of the relationship between the standard of comfort (or the standard of life) and a nation's basic capability is offered by John Maynard Keynes, a student of Marshall. Keynes argues that "the psychology of the community is such that when aggregate real income is increased, aggregate consumption is increased, but not so much as income" (Keynes, 1936: 27). This is in agreement with not only Programmed Assumption 11, but also Programmed Assumption 12. Keynes (1936: 251) also seems to provide an economic analog for Programmed Assumption 13.1 when he asserts that as "real income increases, both the pressure of present needs diminishes and the margin over the established standard of life is increased; and as real income diminishes the opposite is true." This comparison is, however, somewhat tenuous. Keynes does not go so far as to say that the margin over the established standard of life determines marginal change in satisfaction or utility.

It is even more difficult to find economic counterparts to Programmed Assumptions 13.2 and 13.3. Taken together with 13.1, they suggest that the urgency of wants diminishes as more of them are satisfied, even to the point of saturation. While this may seem intuitively reasonable, the "concept of satiation has little standing in economics" (Galbraith, 1958: 117). A law of satiable wants, or what is commonly called the law of diminishing marginal utility, is employed by economists, but only to explain *prices*. It is assumed that the "total utility of a commodity to a person increases with every increment in his stock of it, but not as fast as his stock of it" (Marshall, 1895: 171). While this would appear to be in agreement with the assumptions being considered, it refers only to a particular commodity. While there may be a limit to a *particular* want, economists have tended to consider the *variety* of wants to be infinite. Consequently, they have not generalized the concept of diminishing marginal utility to the theory of consumer demand.

There has, however, been dissent from this view. John Kenneth Galbraith (1958: 124) asserts that "the notion that wants do not become less urgent the more amply the individual is supplied is repugnant to common sense." Consonant with Programmed Assumptions 13.1, 13.2, and 13.3, he contends that with "increasing per capita real income, men are able to satisfy additional wants . . . which are of a lower order of urgency" (1958: 118). This leads him to conclude that consumption can be carried "to the point where marginal utility is small or even negligible" (1958: 119).

Thus, it would seem that we have successfully identified economic analogs for certain conceptions set forth in the Inter-Nation Simulation. It is, however, somewhat difficult to assess the "goodness of fit" of the concepts compared. There is always a danger of Procrustean distortions, even though we have tried consciously to avoid them. Even in consideration of these problems, we feel that there is real value in comparing the conclusions of independent "judges" assessing similar problems from somewhat different perspectives. Certainly, we feel that such comparisons can aid in the development and refinement of simulation models.[10] Regardless of the usefulness of such comparative efforts in adding credence to the operations of the Inter-Nation Simulation and contributing to its refinement, validation must ultimately be empirical.

III. EMPIRICAL EVALUATION OF ECONOMIC SUBMODEL

In the preceding section we evaluated economic aspects of the INS national political model in terms of economic theories. The task now is to evaluate these conceptions empirically.

The Relationship Between Minimum and Maximum Consumption Standards

Looking first at the relation between minimum consumption standards (CSmin) and the maximum consumption standards possible (CSmax—or, equivalently, the realized basic capability), the derived equation was of the form

$$CSmin = a \ln (CSmax/CS_0) + CS_0, \qquad [3.6]$$

Where CS_0 was postulated as a boundary condition.

In accord with the current INS verbal theory, we will assume that a is constant across all nations.[11] Observe that it is necessary to define operationally only CSmin and CSmax, since CS_0 is a constant and consequently will not influence the results of testing the proposed relationship. As an operational measure of CSmax, we will use gross national product per capita. For CSmin, per capita food expenditure will be used as an operational index. These measures were taken or constructed from selected variables in the Yale Political Data Program (Yale; Russett et al., 1964) and the Dimensionality of Nations project (DON; Rummel, 1972). A discussion of the rationale for these and all subsequent operational definitions and indices is presented in the appendix to this chapter.

Regressing CSmin on CSmax (using the above stated operationalizations) yielded the scatterplot presented in Figure 3.4. By inspection, it can

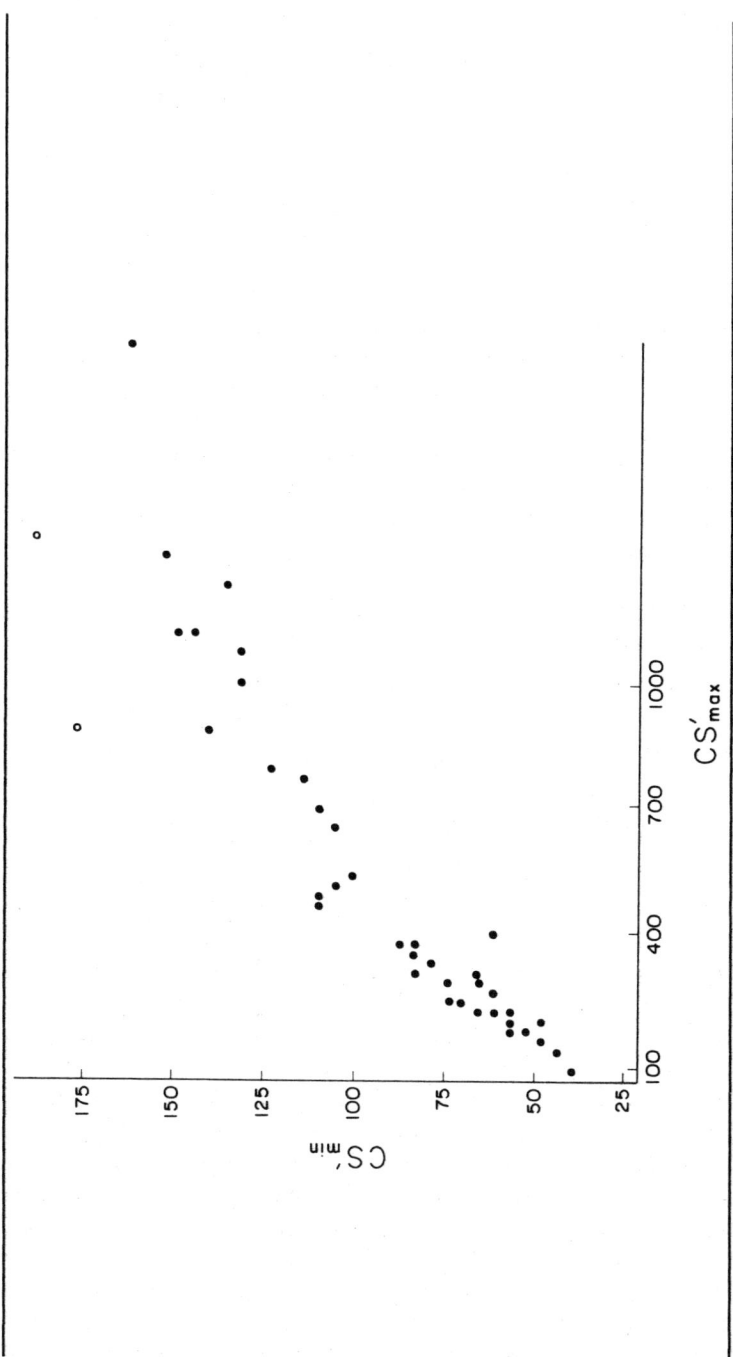

Figure 3.4 Relation of Consumption Standards, Minimum (CSmin) and Maximum (CSmax), for 41 Nations in the Mid-1950s

be seen that a clear relationship exists between these two variables. Note, however, that the observed relationship is *not* linear. If the theoretically posited relationship between CSmin and CSmax is more consistent with the data than a linear relationship, performing the logarithmic transformation of CSmax as indicated by the formalized model and then regressing CSmin on the ln CSmax should straighten the curve to produce roughly a straight line. As can be seen in Figure 3.5, this is exactly what happens. Comparing the two figures, it is clear that the theoretically posited relationship fits the data better than a linear model.[12]

Striking the two extreme outliers indicated in Figure 3.4,[13] the correlation between CSmin (as operationally indexed) and the theoretically predicted value of CSmin is .96 (N = 38). Thus, INS theory allows us to explain 92 percent of the variance in CSmin.[14] Therefore, we conclude that insofar as our operationalizations tap the theoretical concepts involved, the relationship between CSmin and CSmax posited in the INS model is sound.

The Relationship Between Validator Satisfaction and Consumption

Turning now to the relation between validator satisfaction with respect to consumption (VScs), minimum consumption standards (CSmin), and the current consumption standard (CS), the derived equation was

$$\text{VScs} = \gamma \ln(\text{CS}/\text{CSmin}) + \delta , \qquad [3.9]$$

where δ equals the value of VScs when CS equals CSmin.

Again, data from Yale and DON are used as a source for operational measures. As an index of VScs, we will use gross national product per capita percentage literate.[15] Again, food expenditure per capita is used as an index of CSmin. For CS we will use private expenditure per capita as an operational measure. As earlier discussed, it is unnecessary to operationalize δ, since it is assumed to be a constant.

Plotting VScs against CS/CSmin (as operationalized), we obtain the scatterplot presented in Figure 3.6. Note that although the formally hypothesized relationship is logarithmic, the scatterplot reveals no clear curvilinearity in the relationship. In fact, by plotting VScs against the hypothesized logarithmic function, ln(CS/CSmin), we see from Figure 3.7 that *the logarithmic transformation serves only to bias the predictive power of the model.* This bias also can be seen by looking at the correlation between VScs and the hypothesized predictive function in comparison with the correlation between VScs and a simple linear predictive function. The correlation between VScs and the hypothesized

(Text continued p. 84)

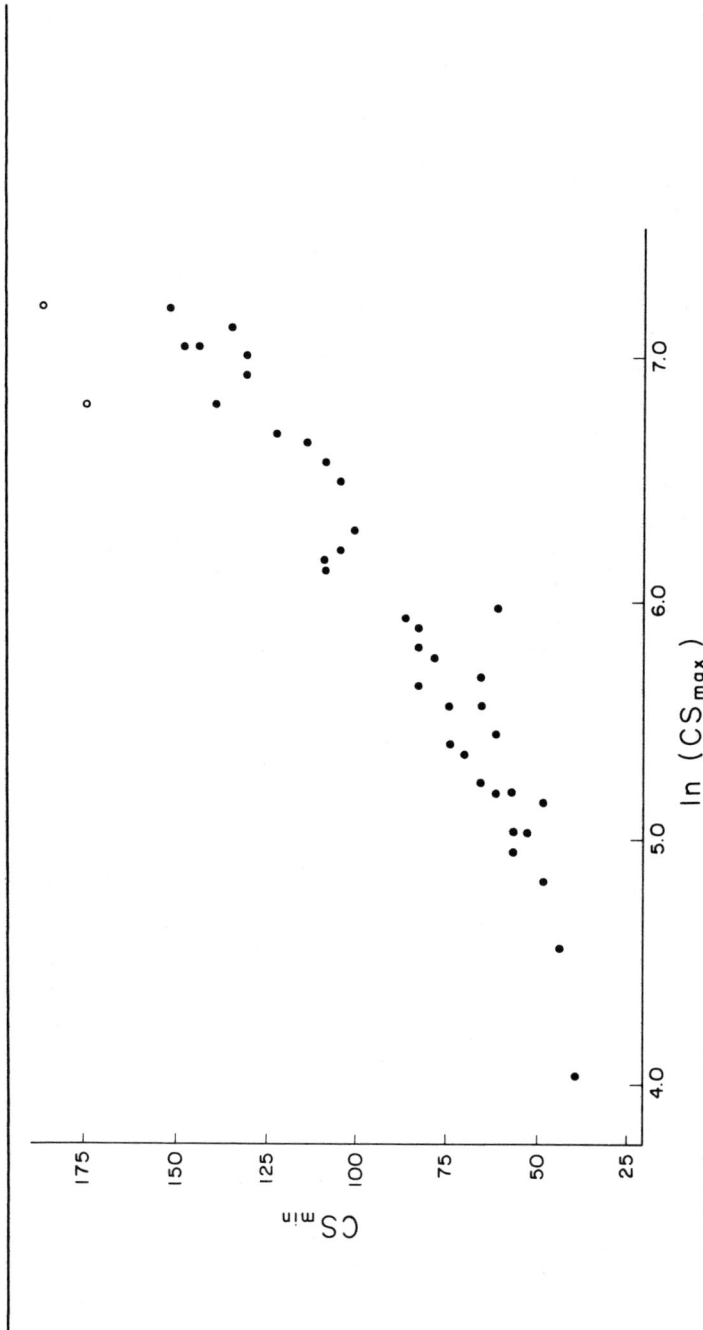

Figure 3.5 Relation of Consumption Standards, Minimum (CSmin) and Maximum (CSmax), When Transformed in Accord with Revised INS Model

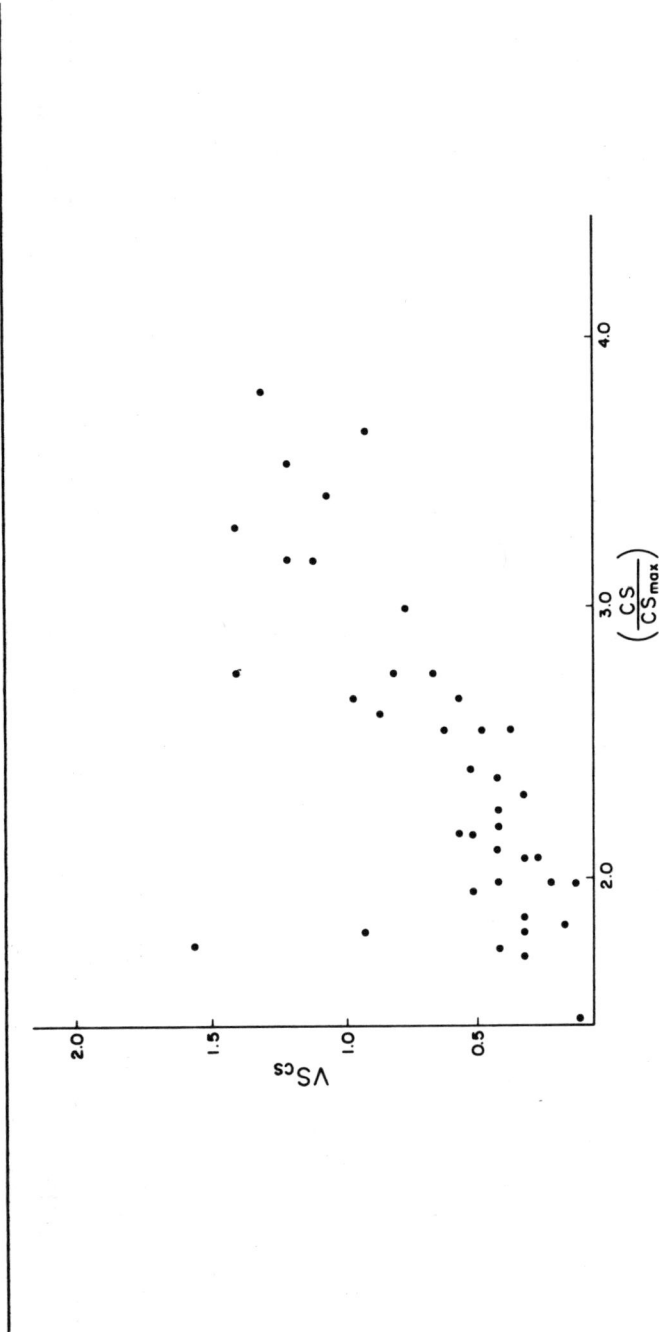

Figure 3.6 Relation of Validator Satisfaction with Respect to Consumption (VScs) and Consumption Standards, Current (CS) over Minimum (CSmin), for 41 Nations in the Mid-1950s

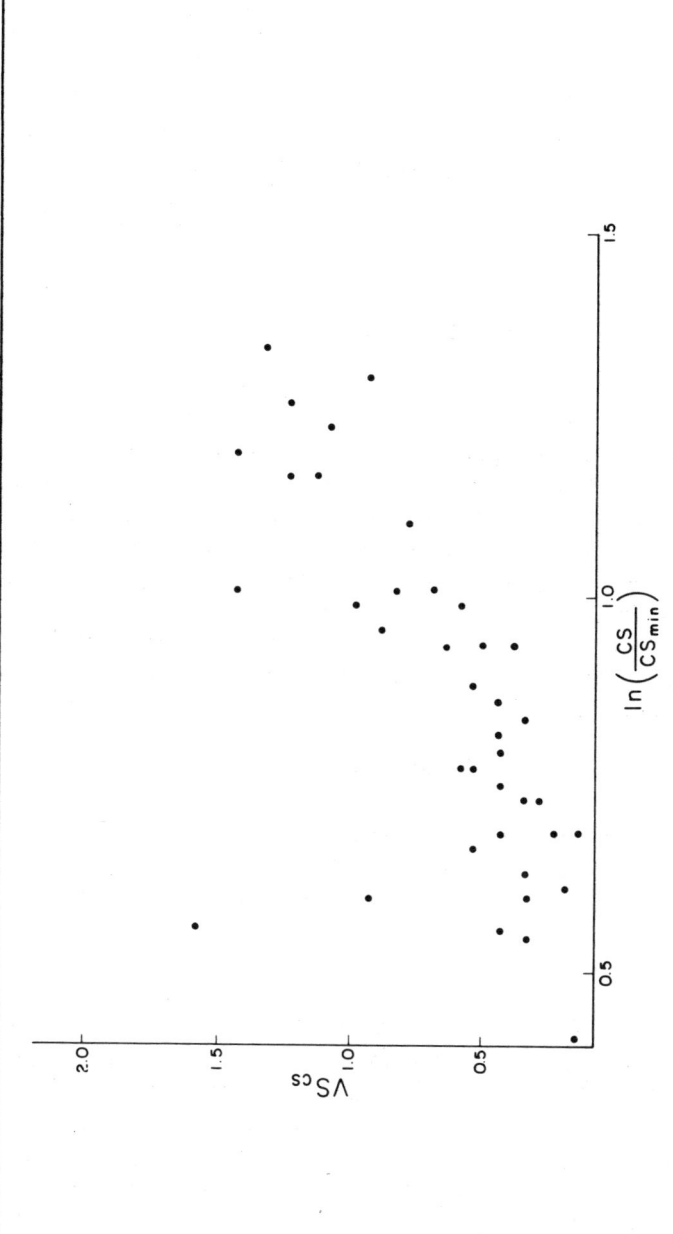

Figure 3.7 Relation of Validator Satisfaction with Respect to Consumption (VScs) and Consumption Standards, Current (CS) over Minimum (CSmin), When Transformed in Accord with Reformalized INS Model

function—i.e., ln(CS/CSmin)—is .71 (N = 41), while the correlation of VScs and CS/CSmin, the latter function, is .75 (N = 41).[16] Although the magnitude of the difference is not impressive, the linear model's production of a larger observed correlation suggests a possible error in the theoretical model. Let us then proceed to isolate the source of the possible error.[17]

As presented earlier, the following differential equation was derived from Programmed Assumption 13:

$$\frac{dVScs}{d\frac{CS}{CSmin}} = \frac{\gamma}{\frac{CS}{CSmin}} \qquad [3.8]$$

This equation, upon integration, yields the logarithmic function we have just examined. Simply stated, this differential equation suggests that changes in VScs are directly proportional to changes in CS/CSmin, but inversely proportional to the magnitude of CS/CSmin. Conceptually, this is comparable to a generalized law of diminishing marginal utility—a notion to which few economic theorists ascribe.

If the model were made consonant with the generally accepted economic assumption that wants are insatiable, the equation would take the following differential form:

$$dVScs/[d(CS/CSmin)] = \gamma \qquad [3.20]$$

Changes in VScs would not be affected by the magnitude of CS/CSmin, but rather would be dependent only upon changes in CS/CSmin. Integration of this differential equation yields the familiar form of a linear model:

$$VScs = \gamma (CS/CSmin) + \delta , \qquad [3.21]$$

where the parameters γ and δ have roughly the same conceptual meaning as discussed previously.[18] Since the data presented above suggest that this model is perhaps more adequate than the model derived from Programmed Assumption 13, it may be useful to reformulate this programmed assumption, accepting the economic assumption that consumption wants are infinite and do not diminish in intensity as more of them are satisfied. The reformulated assumption might read as follows:

Relation of Validator Satisfaction to Consumption Satisfaction. Validator Satisfaction (VScs) depends on the relation of consumption satisfaction (CS) to minimum consumption standards (CSmin). Increases in consumption *over and above minimum standards* produce corresponding changes in validator satisfaction.

The conclusions that may be drawn from our attempt to test the economic aspects of the INS national political model are highly tentative. Many would probably disagree with (or at least question the adequacy of) our operationalization of the various INS concepts. Moreover, the data used, perhaps the best available, are themselves subject to error. Data from only forty-one nations (less than half of the nations of the world) were found to be complete enough for inclusion in this study. Subject to these limitations, we conclude that those aspects of the current INS model relating CSmin to CSmax as stated in Programmed Assumptions 11 and 12 and as reformulated in this chapter are empirically tenable. With respect to the relation of VScs to CS, we suggest that Programmed Assumption 13 perhaps is in need of reformulation. In particular, it would seem that the assumption that diminishing marginal validator satisfaction accrues from increases in consumption above minimum standards is highly questionable. Rather, on the basis of the above analysis, we are inclined to suggest that a simple linear relation exists between VScs and CS above CSmin.

POLITICAL CONSTRAINTS IN AN INTER-NATION SIMULATION: THE STABILITY OF GOVERNMENTS

I. THE PROBABILITY OF OFFICE-HOLDING IN THE INTER-NATION SIMULATION

In the words of William Coplin (1966: 563), "the central assumption of the Inter-Nation Simulation concerning national decision-making is that the desire to remain in office is a prime motivation of foreign policy-makers." On the assumption that retention of office will be a prime drive for those individuals in key decision-making positions in the simulation, office-holding is made contingent upon the ability of these decision-makers (called central decision-makers) to gain and retain the support of politically relevant groups within their nation. Generically, these groups are called validators. "Validation is made operational by a set of mathematical relations between the consequences of the decisions made within nations and the chances of remaining in office" (Guetzkow, 1981b: 29). Thus, the importance of the office-holding variable is clear. Here we want to examine theory relating to that variable and the way this theory is implemented in the simulation. Our first concern is whether the *manner* of implementing the office-holding notions in the formal INS model is consistent with the theory expressed verbally by Guetzkow. Later, we will examine this theory in light of relevant literature and attempt to assess its empirical adequacy.

The Determinants of the Probability of Office-holding

In the Inter-Nation Simulation, office-holding is determined stochastically on the basis of an overall office-holding probability (pOHm) which is the average likelihood of office-holding over a given number of periods (Guetzkow, 1981b: 34).[19] The periodic office-holding probabilities (pOH) are a function of two variables: overall validator satisfaction (VSm) and decision latitude (DL), a measure of the extent to which the actions of decision-makers are constrained by their validators. The theory relating these two variables to pOH is contained in the following two assumptions:

Programmed Assumption 1: Relation of Validator Satisfaction to Office-Holding. The probability of continuing in office depends upon the extent to which the decision-makers of the nations satisfy their validators. ... When overall validator satisfaction is high, likelihood of retaining office tends to be greater; when overall validator satisfaction is low, the likelihood of retaining office tends to be less [Guetzkow, 1981b: 30].

Programmed Assumption 3: Relation of Office-Holding to Decision Latitude. The higher the decision latitude, the less immediately is office-holding subject to validator satisfaction [Guetzkow, 1981b: 34].

These assumptions are formalized in the following equation (Guetzkow, 1981b: 30):

$$pOH = a(b - DL)VSm + c(DL - d) \qquad [3.22]$$

With respect to the four parameters (a, b, c, and d), Guetzkow (1981b: 30) tells us that these are constants, "chosen so as to allow use of simpler calculation routines, given the arbitrary scale values assigned to VSm and DL."

Guetzkow has explained the derivation of this expression (1965c: 32-33). We have no qualms with this derivation. However, because it may mask certain conceptual ambiguities, the existing equation will be put aside for the moment as we return to the verbal theory to derive an independent formalization from the assumptions stated there.

The basic theory relating pOH to decision latitude and validator satisfaction is stated in Programmed Assumptions 1 and 3. Assumption 1 tells us that changes in validator satisfaction produce corresponding changes in the probability of office-holding, ceteris paribus. Assumption 3 provides additional information about this relationship: At higher levels of DL, pOH is "less immediately" subject to the influence of VSm. This may be paraphrased to read: At higher values of DL, changes in pOH with respect to changes in VSm are less. Taken together, the two assumptions constitute a statement about differentials which may be formulated as[20]

$$\partial pOH/\partial VSm = A/DL \qquad [3.23]$$

Following from this equation we need information concerning the variation in pOH due exclusively to variation in DL. Ideally, this entails a programmed assumption or assumptions which tell us what the partial derivative of pOH with respect to DL is, VSm being held constant. Unfortunately, the verbal theory does not explicitly provide such a programmed assumption. What we do have is a statement by Guetzkow (1981: 34) that when VSm is held constant, pOH will vary linearly with DL. This suggests the following partial derivative:

$$\partial pOH/\partial DL = B \qquad [3.24]$$

Assuming that the statement represented by this equation constitutes what is rightly a programmed assumption, our final derivation must be consistent with the restriction indicated in the equation. But as can be readily demonstrated, equation 3.23 is inconsistent with equation 3.24. By integrating equation 3.23 (with respect to VSm), we obtain:

$$pOH = (A/DL)VSm + f(DL) + C \qquad [3.25]$$

Since we are integrating a partial differential equation, f(DL) can be at most a function of DL; it cannot be a function of VSm without violating the differential form of the equation (i.e., equation 3.23). However, we need not specify what the f(DL) is in order to demonstrate that equation 3.25 is incompatible with equation 3.24. Taking the partial derivative of pOH with respect to DL in equation 3.25, we obtain:

$$\partial pOH/\partial DL = -(a/DL^2)VSm + f'(DL), \qquad [3.26]$$

which is clearly inconsistent with equation 3.24. We must therefore reformulate equation 3.23.

It will be recalled that the equation was based on the following assumptions: The greater VSm, the greater the pOH, ceteris paribus; but as

DL increases, pOH becomes less sensitive to changes in VSm. As an alternative to equation 3.23, we represent these assumptions in the form of the following differential equation:

$$\partial \text{pOH}/ \partial \text{VSm} = \gamma (A - DL), \qquad [3.23']$$

with the restriction that $A \geq DL$. The equation states that the change in pOH with respect to VSm is a function of the difference between some number (A) and DL, such that pOH increases as VSm increases but the rate of increase decreases as DL increases. Integrating equation 3.23' with respect to VSm, we obtain:

$$\text{pOH} = \gamma (A - DL)\text{VSm} + f(DL) + C \qquad [3.25']$$

Now taking the partial derivative of pOH with respect to DL in equation 3.25':

$$\partial \text{pOH}/ \partial \text{DL} = - \gamma \text{VSm} + f'(DL) \qquad [3.26']$$

Equation 3.26' is consistent with the restriction represented by equation 3.24, provided that $f'(DL)$ is equal to a constant. In other words, the f(DL) in equation 3.25' must be a linear function of DL. Therefore, we set f(DL) equal to $B(DL) + D$ and combine constant terms to give our final equation:

$$\text{pOH} = \gamma (A - DL)\text{VSm} + B(DL) + \phi \qquad [3.27]$$

To compare this equation with the one formulated by Guetzkow, we place the two equations side by side:

$$\text{pOH} = a(b - DL)\text{VSm} + c(DL - d) \qquad [3.22]$$

$$\text{pOH} = \gamma (A - DL)\text{VSm} + B(DL) + \phi \qquad [3.27]$$

As the reader may confirm for himself, the two expressions are identical with $a = \gamma$, $b = A$, $c = B$, and $cd = \phi$. We therefore conclude that with the explicit identification of a programmed assumption relating DL to pOH when VSm is held constant, the formal model is consistent with INS verbal theory with respect to office-holding.

The Question of Parameters

Having demonstrated the logical consistency of the current equation for determining pOH, we may now inquire into the meaning of the four parameters in equation 3.22. It will be recalled that Guetzkow tells us that these are constants or simply artifacts of the way in which scales of the variables are defined in the Inter-Nation Simulation. This means that the values of a, b, c, and d cannot be arbitrarily specified, but rather are uniquely determined. They are not subject to parametric variation over time or between nations. In other words, it is implicitly assumed that decision latitude, validator satisfaction, and the probability of office-holding form a closed system (meaning that DL and VSm are theorized to be the *only* possible determinants of pOH). Parametric variation of the relationship between pOH and VSm is achieved through the variable DL, which mitigates the influence of the general variable "satisfaction" in determining whether decision-makers remain in power. Any parametric variation between nations or over time in VSm is dependent upon the components of VSm and how these components are parametrically related.

II. THE CONCEPTUAL MEANING OF THE PROBABILITY OF OFFICE-HOLDING

As we have seen in previous sections, the probability of holding office (pOH) within a given simulated nation is dependent upon the ability of the central decision-maker (and his subordinates) to elicit support from relevant validators (VSm) and the decision latitude (DL) which the system accords him. Two factors are assumed to be representative of the number of potentially relevant factors that could give rise to validator satisfaction. These are satisfaction with respect to consumption (VScs) and feelings of national security (VSns). The programmed relation is:

$$VSm = e(VScs) + g(VSns), \qquad [3.28]$$

where e and g are parameters indicating the relative weight given to each factor (Guetzkow, 1981b: 32).[21] Validation within a nation then is largely determined by the satisfaction which arises from "guns or butter" allocative decisions made by that nation's decision-makers.

In an unprogrammed hypothesis, Guetzkow (1981b: 44) suggested that the "decision-makers of a nation will allocate their various capabilities so as to increase their chances of retaining office." Thus, there is a circularity: Governmental actions are dependent in some measure upon considerations of validation, validation is determined largely on the basis of governmental actions.

The fact that in "the real world the relationship between validator satisfaction and officeholding varies widely from nation to nation, depending upon the form of the internal government," is taken into account by the decision latitude variable [DL] (Guetzkow, 1981b: 33) INS theory thus posits a single model of national decision-making processes which is assumed to be representative of all national governments through parametric alteration in one variable, DL.

In his study comparing the INS national political model with the work of other theorists, William Coplin (1966: 562-578) concluded that while many theorists would agree that office-holding is dependent upon something like overall validator satisfaction, few would support the INS contention that this satisfaction accrues solely from consumption satisfaction and feelings of national security.[22]

Perhaps part of the disconsonance between the INS theory and the work of other theorists arises from the conceptual ambiguity of the office-holding variable (pOH). Rather than reviewing the literature relevant to the INS political model, we will concentrate here on elucidating certain of these conceptual problems. In particular, we will focus on the meaning of pOH and the processes through which validator satisfaction with respect to consumption (VScs) via VSm contributes to it.[23] Later, we will focus more closely on DL and VSm per se.

In the Inter-Nation Simulation, office-holding is simply the "de jure right, as recognized by the simulation director, to make the decisions of the nation with respect to both internal and external affairs" (Guetzkow, 1981b: 29). The retention of office by a central decision-maker (and consequently his regime) is, as we have seen, dependent upon validator support. Concerning validators, we are told:

> In a democracy, the validators might be voters and interest groups. In an autocracy, the validators might be some oligarchic elite or military junta. In all governmental systems, however, it seems there must be some minimal compliance by the peoples as a whole, even if it is only passive acceptance rooted in apathy [Guetzkow, 1981b: 29].

From Guetzkow's statement, officeholding in the Inter-Nation Simulation clearly refers to the stability of a regime headed by a particular individual who in the simulation is called the central decision-maker. But is the central decision-maker in the simulation analogous to, say, the chief executive or the head of state in some referent system? Although it may initially appear so, the group of decision-makers, headed by the central decision-maker and sanctioned by validators constitutes a "political-military-economic system" (Guetzkow, 1981b: 26). Could it then not be that *office-holding in the Inter-Nation Simulation refers to the stability of the governmental system rather than the stability of a given regime?*[24]

These two types of stability are distinctly different, as can be demonstrated by comparing the histories of four nations since World War II: South Vietnam, Argentina, the United States, and England. While these four nations' political systems have had several different heads of government, the latter two systems have been markedly more stable than the former two.

The proposition that office-holding in the Inter-Nation Simulation should be interpreted as "system" stability rather than "regime" stability is strengthened by comparing the simulation determinants of revolution with those of office-holding. *Both* are dependent upon overall validator satisfaction (when VSm reaches a critically low level, the probability of revolution is automatically calculated) and upon decision latitude [DL] (Guetzkow, 1981b: 47).

The relationship of pOH and VScs, the economic component of VSm, also supports the system stability interpretation of pOH. As earlier discussed, VScs is dependent upon consumption allocations made by the decision-makers of a simulated nation. VScs is one of the two independent contributors to VSm, a direct determinant of pOH. Presumably then, validation is a direct function of allocative decisions. However, as Murray Edelman pointed out (1964: 42-43), in democratic systems "the factors which explain voting behavior (validation?) can be quite different from the factors that explain resource allocation."[25] Campbell and his associates (1960: 399), in their study, *The American Voter,* find that the economic outlook in specific elections is of little importance. This suggests that perhaps economic outlook provides an *antecedent condition* rather than a primary influence on the outcome of a particular election. If we can generalize from these findings, we are led to doubt the adequacy of the current INS formulation as a predictor to the stability of a *particular* regime. Thus, the problem of interpreting pOH can be reduced to an empirical one: Does the current INS formulation predict better to regime or to system stability?[26]

III. SOME EMPIRICAL TESTS OF THE OFFICE-HOLDING EQUATION

In the previous section, a theoretical tension was posed between two possible interpretations of office-holding in the Inter-Nation Simulation. The question centered on whether pOH as currently formulated was indicative of the stability of a certain *regime* within a given political system or the stability of the *system* per se. Alternative definitional criteria will be helpful in the following empirical analysis; thus, we not only will report the correlations between pOH and its supposed determinants, but also be able to make *comparative* statements about the relative fit of the programmed assumptions with measures of regime and system stability.

The relevant concepts were operationalized using selected variables from the Yale Political Data Program (Yale; Russett et al., 1964), the Dimesionality of Nations (DON) project (Rummel, 1972), and the Banks and Textor Cross-Polity Survey (1963). Two separate measures of regime stability (denoted as pOH1 and pOH2), one measure of system stability, three measures of decision latitude (DL1, DL2, and DL3), and one composite index of validator satisfaction were used in the analysis. The specific operational definitions were as follows:

pOH1 = average tenure of last two governments (DON)

pOH2 = executive stability (Yale)

system stability = governmental stability (Banks and Textor)

VSm = (GNP per cap)/(percentage literate) [Yale]

DL1 = 10 − (3.33)(freedom of opposition) [DON]

DL2 = 11 − (number of political parties) [DON]

DL3 = (DL1)(DL2)/10

The numbers in these definitions were inserted so that the maximum values of the various measures of DL would approximate 10 and thus conform roughly with the scaling requirements of the INS equation. A discussion of the rationale for these operational definitions and indices is presented in the appendix to this chapter.

Intercorrelating these variables yielded the results shown in Table 3.1. There are several points of interest in this table. First, the two measures of regime stability (pOH1 and pOH2) have a sizable intercorrelation (.62), while the correlation between these two measures and that of system stability are considerably smaller (.26 and .41). This tends to indicate *operational* difference between regime and system stability that we posited at a *conceptual* level.

Second, the question of primary interest is the degree of correlation between the various measures of stability and the programmed function of VSm and DL. In *all three cases* the programmed relation *correlates more highly with system stability than with either measure of regime stability.* Third and last, there is almost no correlation between the measures of regime stability and VSm, but VSm correlates significantly with system stability. Thus, we would tentatively assert that the programmed assumptions in the Inter-Nation Simulation tend to express relationships between *system stability* and its determinants, rather than regime stability and its determinants.

Table 3.1
CORRELATIONS OF pOH_1 pOH_2, and SYSTEM STABILITY WITH VARIOUS VARIABLES[a]

	pOH_1	pOH_2	system stability
pOH_1	–	.62	.26
pOH_2	.62	–	.41
system stability	.26	.41	–
$a(b - DL_1)VS_m + c(DL_1 - d)$	.20	.15	.36
$a(b - DL_2)VS_m + d(DL_2 - d)$	.18	.23	.46
$a(b - DL_3)VS_m + c(DL_3 - d)$	.21	.20	.46
VS_m	-.05	-.04	.39
DL_1	.26	.16	-.09
DL_2	.30	.24	.24
DL_3	.33	.26	.06

a. The sample size in all cases was 62. $r = .250, p < .05; r = .325, p < .01$.

In a further test, stepwise regressions were carried out, using the two pOH measures and system stability as dependent variables. In each case, independent variables were entered so that a maximum percentage of the variance in the dependent variable was accounted for.[27] The results of this analysis are presented in Table 3.2. In addition to the multiple correlation coefficient (R) for the various combinations, the table shows in parentheses the squares of these coefficients multiplied by 100–this being the accepted value of the variance accounted for the dependent variable, expressed as a percentage.

The results are so uniform that little discussion of them is required. The most astounding feature of this set of correlations is that *in every case the correlation with system stability is higher than either correlation with the measures of regime stability.* Thus, we feel justified in making even stronger our assertion that the programmed relation is oriented toward system, as opposed to regime, stability.

Further, there does seem to be a significant interaction between VSm and DL of the type indicated in the verbal theory of the Inter-Nation Simulation. Focusing on the system stability column, note the rise in correlation when the interaction terms (VS) (DL) are added to the independent contributions of VS and the three DL measures: The correlation rises from .48 to .63, with a corresponding increase in explained variance from 23 to 29 percent.

Our most important conclusion, in this exposition, is that INS theory is in fact a fairly good predictor of stability, but that it is the stability of the

Table 3.2

MULTIPLE REGRESSION ANALYSES WITH REGIME AND SYSTEM STABILITY MEASURES AS THE DEPENDENT VARIABLES[a]

Independent Variables in the Regression	Correlations with:				System Stability	
	pOH_1		pOH_2			
1. $VS + DL_1$	.26	(7)	.16	(3)	.39	(15)
2. $VS + DL_1 + (VS)(DL_1)$	.33	(11)	.30	(9)	.54	(29)
3. $VS + DL_2$	.30	(9)	.24	(6)	.45	(20)
4. $VS + DL_2 + (VS)(DL_2)$	.31	(10)	.33	(11)	.50	(25)
5. $VS + DL_3$	.33	(11)	.26	(7)	.41	(17)
6. $VS + DL_3 + (VS)(DL_3)$	.37	(14)	.39	(15)	.56	(31)
7. $VS + DL_1 + DL_2 + DL_3$	.36	(13)	.30	(9)	.48	(23)
8. $VS + DL_1 + DL_2 + DL_3 + (VS)(DL_1) + (VS)(DL_2) + (VS)(DL_3)$	.43	(18)	.42	(18)	.63	(39)
9. $a(b-DL_1)VS + c(DL_1-d)$	.27	(7)	.18	(3)	.49	(24)
10. $a(b-DL_2)VS + c(DL_2-d)$	.31	(10)	.25	(6)	.50	(25)
11. $a(b-DL_3)VS + c(DL_3-d)$	.34	(11)	.27	(7)	.50	(25)
12. $AB_1+AB_2+AB_3+DL_1+DL_2+DL_3$[b]	.40	(16)	.32	(10)	.60	(36)
13. $ABCD_1 + ABCD_2 + ABCD_3$[b]	.22	(5)	.23	(5)	.50	(25)

a. The symbol "+" here means that each of the variables was entered separately, not that they were added together numberically.
b. The following abbreviations are used: $AB_1 = a(b - DL_1)VS$; $ABCD_1 = a(b - DL_1) VS + c(DL_1 + d)$; and so on.

governmental system rather than the stability of particular office-holders that is explained.

While we recognize that our findings are subject to the limitations inherent in the data analyzed and dependent upon the adequacy of our operationalizations, they nonetheless remain sufficiently compelling to warrant some serious rethinking of the political constraints in the INS model. Certainly, it would seem that if the object is to "provide an operating environment" for surrogate decision-makers which attempts "to simulate vital characteristics of the process of remaining in office" (Guetzkow, 1981b: 29), considerable reformulation of the simulation model is in order.

NOTES

1. Satisfaction arising from feelings of national security is also dependent upon success in external relations, although operationally this means a simple comparison of military capabilities.

2. For a more detailed description of these variables and their conceptual meanings, see Guetzkow (1981b: 39-43).

3. From discussions with Paul Smoker at Lancaster University in England (July 1966), we learned that the objection we are raising has in fact created problems in actual simulation runs.

4. In terms of the actual behavior of nations, the parameter a is subject to at least two operational interpretations: It might be a universal *constant*, describing a cross-sectional relationship between the variables holding across many nations (all other things being equal); or it might be a *parameter*, being constant for any one nation, but varying from nation to nation and distinguishing differing levels of ease in satisfying validators with respect to consumption. If the first alternative is true, then we expect cross-sectional data for one point in time to bear the relationship in the final equation (3.1). This will be explored empirically in a later section. If the second alternative is true, then we would expect that data for any one nation would conform to the equation as the value of CSmax for that nation varies *over time*. And if the relationship holds for any one nation but the value of a varies from nation to nation, then we would have in a the leverage to describe individual differences within the framework of a general theoretical proposition.

5. Note that the problem of having a dimensionless quantity for our logarithm function is solved by measuring CS expenditures as the ratio of CS to CSmin.

6. This comment is prompted by the same sort of considerations raised with respect to a in equation 3.6 (see note 4 above). The question hinges on whether γ is a universal constant applicable to all nations or a parameter constant for one nation but varying relative to others.

7. The current model demands that the value of VScs be bounded such that it ranges from 1 to 10. The reader will note that our reformulation allows, at present, a maximum value of infinity, since this is the limit of the logarithm function. This issue is one concerning the scale the theorist wishes to impose on the concept of VScs; we can easily impose the original maximum value of 10 on our reformulation by

asserting that the functional relationship is as we describe it until VScs reaches 10, and that it then stays at that value even for further increases in CS. Further discussion of whether theoretical grounds can be given for placing *any* upper bound on the VScs function certainly would be useful in a complete evaluation of the INS model, but is unnecessary for the present inquiry.

8. The similarity between Downs's model and the national political model posited in the INS is striking. The variables Downs considers to be representative of a government are essentially the same as those considered prototypic of a nation in the simulation. Moreover, the same general propositions seem to be contained in both. While Downs's model is clearly limited to democratic systems, he seems to anticipate something like the INS model when he asserts that comparable models are needed for differently constituted political systems and further contends that in such models the core assumptions would remain essentially the same (Downs, 1957: 290-294). Davis and Hinich (1966, 1967) offer a similar conception of validation processes in their model of policy formation in a democratic society. Rather than focusing on the utility accrued from governmental policies, they construct a loss function and assume that support will be based on the extent to which the average loss is minimized. Although their model is designed to illuminate candidate strategies for winning support in democratic systems, they show that it is also useful in understanding validation processes in nondemocratic systems (1966: 180). The empirical viability of an extended version of the Davis and Hinich model has been demonstrated by Shapiro (1969: 1106-1119).

9. Recall that CSmax is the maximum consumption standard *theoretically possible* for a nation at a given time, and thus is a linear function of the total realized basic capability of a nation.

10. As we have argued elsewhere (Elder and Pendley, 1966), the present lack of adequate data and empirical techniques need not stifle the development and refinement of the simulation. The social sciences are rich in relevant theoretical conceptions which can be used to facilitate the development of simulations like the INS. In like manner, simulation can contribute to the refinement of theory as well as to the development of more adequate empirical techniques.

11. Whether or not a is a constant or a variable is an empirical question that can be resolved only by longitudinal study of several nations. Here we use only cross-sectional data and assume they are constant.

12. If this had not been found to be the case, we would be obliged to alter our theoretical propositions, or at least be exceedingly skeptical of them. In particular, we would have questioned, if it were *not disavowed*, the notion of decreasing marginal changes in CSmin with increasing CSmax.

13. There was a total of 41 nations for which the data required for our operational measures were available. Of these, 40 are shown in Figure 3.4. The United States departed so radically from the pattern that it was impossible to place it in the figure. Thus, there were actually three nations struck as outliers: the United States, West Germany, and Switzerland. The assumption in doing this was that in these three cases extraneous factors caused these nations to depart from the general pattern and consequently they could not legitimately be used without further exploration of what these confounding factors might be.

14. This may be compared with 86 percent of the variance in CSmin ($r = .93$) explained by a linear model. Thus, the INS model here explains 6 percent more variance than does a linear model. While this difference is not striking, it does indicate that the INS model may be more adequate. The predictions of the two

models will diverge more, the greater the CSmax. Since the basic capabilities of most nations are increasing, both the descriptive and predictive differences in the two models may become increasingly important in the future.

15. We assume that validator satisfaction can be indexed as a linear function of the ratio of GNP/capita to percentage literate. Our argument is that more and more consumptive wants are satisfied as a nation becomes wealthier (GNP/capita), but whether or not this is translated into political support (validator satisfaction) is dependent upon the aspiration level of the validators. It seems that the level of aspiration of a nation's validators will be directly related to their general awareness of a larger environment which can provide multiple standards of comparison and which can, in effect, create new wants. Literacy, we suggest, fosters such awareness. Thus, as an index of aspiration level we use percentage literate.

16. The hypothesized function explains 50 percent of the variance in VScs, whereas a linear function would allow us to explain 56 percent of the variance in VScs. This difference in the two models could have important predictive implications.

17. For present purposes, we will assume that our operational measures are adequate. This is not, however, to deny that they may be in error.

18. The only difference is that the rate of change in VScs is now dependent only upon γ, whereas before it was dependent upon both some γ and the magnitude of CS/CSmin. Thus, γ is here the marginal satisfaction accruing from changes in CS/CSmin.

19. The referent time span represented by a simulation period is unclear and varies with the simulator's purposes, although the processes programmed for each period are the same, regardless of the temporal referent. Even if this problem is ignored, it is interesting that the overall probability of office-holding is computed as a simple average of the periodic probabilities over a given number of periods. Intuitively, it is more reasonable to make the overall probability a decaying function of the discrete probabilities of previous periods. In the World Politics Simulation, an offshoot of the INS, the probability of a change in government, which is analogous to the overall probability of office-holding in the INS, is determined on the basis of such a decay function. See *World Politics Simulation: Description of the Model* (1969).

20. We are using the *partial* derivative, rather than the total derivative, because pOH is assumed to be a function of at least two variables, and we are considering changes in pOH due to changes in only one of the two, the other being held constant.

21. A value of .5 is usually assigned to both e and g. Thus, the two demands, consumption and national security, are usually coequal in their effect upon pOH. However, if a nation's VSns falls below .37, VSm is made directly equivalent to VScs (Guetzkow, 1981b: 44). Donald Skinner and Robert Wells (1965), at the University of Michigan, have made alterations in these parametric values, but to our knowledge this was done only on an intuitive basis. For a brief discussion of the effects of altering these two parameters, see Alker (1968: 45).

22. Because Coplin did not cite the work of Anthony Downs (1957), we would reiterate the striking similarity between Downs's model and the INS national model noted earlier. Downs, in fact, anticipates something like the INS model by suggesting that his democratic model might be generalized by means of some parametric alteration which would take into account different governmental structures.

23. Consideration of the national security component of VSm, and of the relative weightings of VScs and VSns, poses particular thorny problems which we have

skirted. It is hoped that the present analysis will contribute greater clarity to the concept of pOH which will, in turn, facilitate the handling of these other problem areas.

24. By "regime" we mean a particular set of persons occupying authoritative decision-making positions at a particular time. By "system of government" we mean a particular structure of authority and the norms and values associated with that structure. The same sorts of distinctions are made by Easton in differentiating the total political system, though he uses different terms. He identifies three basic political objects: the authorities, regime, and political community. His "authorities" correspond to what we are calling a regime, and his "regime" is analogous to what we are here calling a system of government. See Easton (1965b: 153-219).

25. The generalizability of this notion that actual resource allocation is not necessarily the primary determinant of the stability of a regime is reinforced by the work of Merelman (1966).

26. Of course, for the simulator the *conceptual* problem remains: What *referent phenomena* are to be simulated? Until this conceptual problem is resolved, the political model cannot be developed further.

27. In some of the problems all the independent measures of DL were allowed to enter the regression equation if they could contribute to the explained variance. The reason for doing this was that it could be that some linear combination of various measures will be the best composite index of decision latitude; the stepwise procedure will yield that linear combination which maximizes the explained variance in the dependent variable.

APPENDIX: OPERATIONAL MEASURES AND INDICES OF INS VARIABLES

Minimum Consumption Standards (CSmin)

Definition: The standard of consumption which must be provided by a nation for its people. It roughly corresponds to what Marshall has called "conventional necessaries," as opposed to strict necessaries (Guetzkow, 1981b: 40).

Operational Definition: Food expenditures per capita.

Rationale: Food is one of the strict necessities of life. However, it is assumed that as a nation becomes increasingly capable of satisfying more wants, people will expect more and better food and will tend to take food standards for granted, even if these standards are well above absolute needs. Therefore, we take food expenditure as an *index* of (i.e., to be linearly related to) "conventional necessaries," or CSmin. By using per capita measure, we control for population differences.

Data Source: Food-expenditure per capita measures were obtained for 41 nations using the following variables from the Dimensionality of Nations project and the Yale Political Data Program: food expenditure as a percentage of private expenditure (DON); private expenditure as a percentage of GNP (Yale); and GNP per capita (Yale). Appropriate multiplication of these variables yielded our measure. It was assumed that any differences in dates of collection were insignificant.

Maximum Consumption Standards (CSmax)

Conceptual Definition: "The maximum units of consumption which could be allocated by a nation in a given period to consumption standards" (Guetzkow, 1981b: 44).
Operational Definition: Gross national product per capita.
Rationale: CSmax is a simple linear function of the total realized basic capability of a nation and is equivalent to the total basic capability times the generation rate for consumptive goods and services. Since the concept indicates the level of consumption that hypothetically would exist if all of a nation's resources were devoted to that end, GNP per capita seems roughly equivalent to CSmax and allows us to control for population.
Data Source: Yale Political Data program.

Consumption Standards (CS)

Conceptual Definition: "Quantity of goods produced and utilized in the nation for consumption purposes" (Guetzkow, 1980b: 41).
Operational Definition: Private expenditure per capita.
Rationale: Private expenditure per capita provides a measure of consumption controlling for differences in population size.
Data Source: Yale variables: GNP/capita X private expenditure/GNP = private expenditure/capita.

Validator Satisfaction with Respect to Consumption Satisfaction (VScs)

Conceptual Definition: "The satisfactions attained by the nation's validators from the amount and distribution of goods and services" (Guetzkow, 1981b: 42).
Operational Definition: GNP/capita per percentage literate.
Rationale: It is assumed that validator satisfaction is linearly related to GNP/capita per percentage literate. That is, we assume that satisfaction with respect to consumption is directly proportional to GNP/capita, but inversely proportional to the percentage literate.
Data Source: Yale Political Data program.

Office-Holding (pOH)

Conceptual Definition: "The de jure right ... to make the decisions of the nation with respect to both internal and external affairs" (Guetzkow, 1981b: 29).
Operational Definition: (1) Average tenure of last two governments (pOH1); (2) executive stability as indexed by number of chief executives since 1945 over years independent since 1945 (pOH2).

Rationale: Office-holding is assumed to refer to executive or regime stability.
Data Source: DON (pOH1) and Yale (pOH2).

System Stability

Conceptual Definition: The stability of the overall governmental system of a nation.
Operational Definition: Governmental stability as coded by Banks and Textor.
Rationale: Banks and Textor's measures are simply assumed to be adequate measures of the concept.
Data Source: Banks and Textor, *A Cross-Polity Survey* (1963).

Validator Satisfaction (VSm)

Conceptual Definition: "The acceptability of the central decision-maker's program to those with power to authenticate his office-holding" (Guetzkow, 1981b: 29).
Operational Definition: Same as VScs; thus, VSm = VScs.
Rationale: In the INS model, overall validator satisfaction (VSm) is a weighted function of satisfactions with respect to consumption (VScs) and national security (VSns). The latter is determined by the ratio of a nation's force capabilities and potential, plus that of its allies, to the force capabilities and potential of all other nations. For nonaligned nations not engaged in the arms race, this factor is discounted completely, and VSm equals VScs. This conception suggests that in a system characterized by a relatively stable balance of power, VSns will be nearly constant for all nations and thus will contribute little to the variability in VSm. Because this situation seemed to obtain in the referent system, VSm is simply assumed to be dominated by VScs; and no attempt is made to cope with the difficulties involved in giving operational meaning to VSns.
Data Source: Yale Political Data program.

Decision Latitude (DL)

Conceptual Definition: "The degree to which the probability of office-holding of the decision-makers depends on changes in validator satisfaction" (Guetzkow, 1981b: 34).
Operational Definition: (1) Reflected and scaled "freedom of opposition" ratings from DON (DL1); (2) number of political parties reflected and scaled (DL2); (3) DL1 times DL2 scaled to form DL3.
Rationale: (1) DL1 provides an index of the extent to which political opposition is permitted in a nation. We assume that the more restricted political opposition is, the greater the decision latitude. (2) DL2 is used with the assumption that the greater the number of parties, the less the decision latitude of the governmental decision-makers. (3) DL3: Combining the assumptions made with respect to DL1 and DL2, we assumed that the less restricted political opposition is and the greater the number of parties, the less is the decision latitude.
Data Source: DON.

4
The International Processes Simulation

Paul L. Smoker

I. INTRODUCTION

A. COMPARISON OF INS AND IPS

The International Processes Simulation (IPS), like the Inter-Nation Simulation (INS), incorporates theoretical assumptions abstracted from literature relevant to inter- and intranational relations. National characteristics, such as the nature of the political system, are assumed to influence international characteristics, such as alliance structure. Similarly, international characteristics, such as balance of power, are assumed to influence national characteristics, such as national security (Guetzkow et al., 1963: 126; Guetzkow, 1981b: 44). These INS theories have been retained in IPS, either in their original form, as in the case of the programmed assumption concerning probability of a revolution being successful should one occur (Guetzkow et al., 1963: 131; Guetzkow, 1981b: 48), or in a revised form, as in the case of national security. A significant difference between INS and IPS concerns an additional theoretical model that is used to define the

---

Author's Note: Portions of this chapter were originally published under the title "International Processes Simulation: A Description," pp. 315-365 in Jean A. Laponce and Paul L. Smoker (eds.), *Experimentation and Simulation in Political Science,* copyright © 1972 by the University of Toronto Press. A complete computer program for the IPS is reproduced in an appendix to that publication. The author and publisher wish to acknowledge with thanks the permission to reprint of the University of Toronto Press.

central focus of IPS. Major structural features, such as an international cultural and economic system, are included in IPS in such a way that the resulting simulation is consistent with modern theories about global society.

The fact that this metatheory adopts a Parsonian viewpoint is secondary to the general correspondence of the resulting simulation model with modern theoretical positions concerning international relations (Alger, 1968b; Galtung, 1967). These adopt a multilevel systemic, multientity position far removed from traditional balance-of-power theories. They operate through time on many levels, including international, national, and transnational, and incorporate individuals, nations, international corporations, and international governmental and nongovernmental organizations.

B. A PARSONIAN MODEL

The model used (Smoker, 1967c) takes as its starting point an interpretation of national political systems by Karl Deutsch (1964), who used a theoretical framework developed by Talcott Parsons for the analysis of social systems (Parsons, 1951). He argues that a first approximation the four basic requirements of a social system suggested by Parsons—pattern maintenance, adaptation, goal attainment, and integration—can, at the national level, be equated with specific subsystems: individuals and groups who are mainly responsible for pattern maintenance through activities such as practicing cultural values and providing labor; a governmental subsystem mainly responsible for goal attainment of the nation; an economy mainly responsible for adaptation; and a cultural subsystem responsible for social integration.

While Deutsch was not concerned with international relations in his interpretation, it is possible to extend this theoretical position in the following way. A nation-state system is for our purposes defined as a system where interaction between nations is primarily an interaction between goal attainment subsystems; a classical interpretation of this concerns power politics (Schwartzenberger, 1964; Morgenthau, 1960). There is, by definition, no integrative subsystem between nations in such a situation. The situation resembles a zero-sum game where might is right. A nation-state system for a three-nation world is illustrated in Figure 4.1. Interaction between subsystems, represented by squares, is shown by arrows. This system defines nation-state interaction as motivated purely by goal attainment subsystems.

Much of the recent international relations literature speaks of perceived worlds made up primarily of nations.[1] It is possible, however, to construct models of the world containing other behavioral entities (Haas, 1964). In

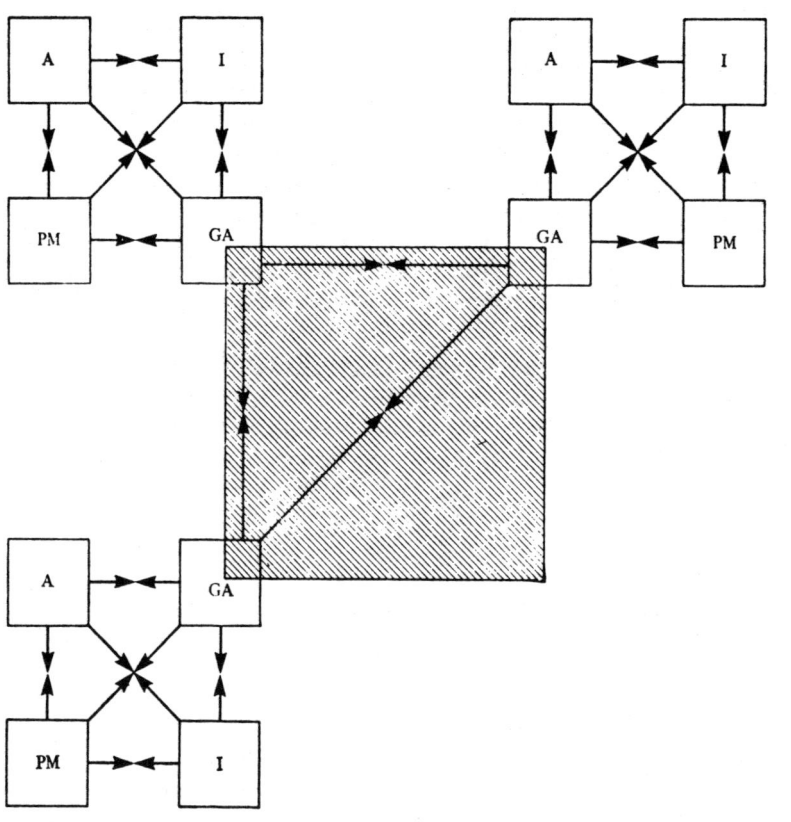

Figure 4.1 A Nation-State System

NOTE: A—adaptive subsystem; I—integration subsystem; PM—pattern maintenance subsystem; GA—goal attainment subsystem; the shaded area represents a nation-state system.

addition to nations, a model might include international governmental organizations, international nongovernmental organizations, international corporations, and various subnational entities. Against this background, it is possible to extend Parson's framework still further to define a model international system:

(1) The pattern maintenance function may be characterized by individuals and families throughout a model international system. The individuals might be referred to as "international" and would represent, at present, a tiny minority in the actual world system. While the number is irrelevant for the theoretical purpose of

constructing an international system's model as defined, international person is increasingly making his presence felt. He may work for international governmental organizations like the United Nations, for any of the more than 2000 nongovernmental organizations,[2] or as an executive for international corporations. He is even to be found in the entertainment and communications business.[3]

(2) The adaptive subsystem might be represented roughly by an international economic system, which includes international corporations. In the world of the future these corporations may play an increasingly important role. General Motors' sales exceeded the gross national product of the Netherlands and 100 other countries in 1965.[4]

(3) The goal attainment subsystem might be represented by an international government. While some organs of the UN are concerned with cultural, educational, or social matters—for example, UNESCO—others, such as the General Assembly and the Security Council, are concerned with world politics and might be seen as performing an international goal attainment function.[5]

(4) The international integrative subsystem may be characterized in world affairs by cultural activities of some nongovernmental organizations (Smoker, 1965b; Brogden, 1966; Angell, 1965) and certain international conferences. The same position is taken in the model international system.

At a general level, the defined nation-state and international systems can be regarded as extreme cases of a world system. This is shown in Figure 4.2. Here, when the international component is insignificant, there exists the extreme case of a nation-state system and, when the nation-state system is insignificant, the extreme case of an international system. Figure 4.2 illustrates a theoretical framework for the overall design of IPS and also provides a basis for constructing important substructures within IPS. The shifting mix of international and nation-state components in this model[6] world system are likely to be critical. The nation-state and international components may be equal in size, but behavior of a model world system in which both are small is likely to differ from that in which both are large.

Two interpretations of Figure 4.2 have been used in experiments conducted with IPS. One interpretation is nearer to nation-state as defined, and is called International Processes Simulation (Nation-State). The other includes a significant international component and is called International Processes Simulation (International). Figure 4.3 illustrates major structural requirements of nation-state and international versions of IPS.

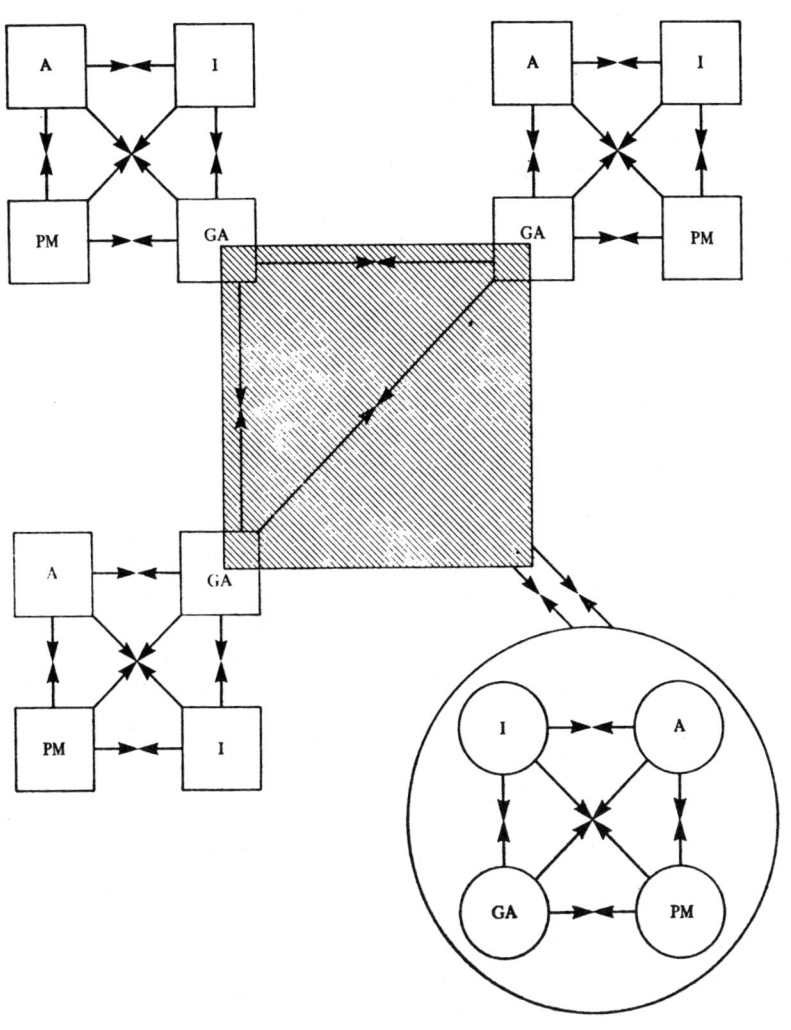

Figure 4.2 A World System

NOTE: A—adaptive subsystem; I—integrative subsystem; PM—pattern maintenance subsystem; GA—goal attainment subsystem.

In fact, many alternative worlds could be constructed by researchers or educators by adjusting parameters in the programmed part of IPS and creating an appropriate data base. Other experiments with IPS could use alternative interpretations of this general model. In order to satisfy these structural requirements some other innovations have been introduced—for

Functional Subsystem	Variable	International Processes Simulation	
		Nation-State	International
Nation-state goal attainment	Nation size (six nations)	Relatively small	Relatively large
Nation-state goal attainment	Military power	Just conventional forces. No nuclear nations.	Four large nuclear nations. One potential nuclear nation.
International and national adaptation	Corporation size and structure (five corporations)	Relatively small. All but one national to begin with (factories all in one nation).	Relatively large. Four international, one national to begin with.
International adaptation	International trade	Relatively little to begin with.	Relatively much to begin with.
International goal attainment	International governmental organization	None at start of simulation.	Full-time international governmental organization at start of simulation.
International integrative	International nongovernmental activity	None scheduled at start of simulation.	Regularly scheduled nongovernmental meetings at start of simulation.

Figure 4.3 Major Structural Differences Between Two Model World Types

example, private citizens, independent corporations, a new economic system, and full-time international organization delegates. These and other structural additions to INS are described below.

II. STRUCTURAL CHANGES IN IPS

A. INTRODUCTION

The structural changes in IPS relative to INS have been determined by the theoretical perspectives described above. INS represents a world system using nations and an international governmental organization (Guetzkow et al., 1963: 107; Guetzkow, 1981b: 26). It consists of components at three levels: individuals (decision-makers), groups (nations), and supra-groups (government alliances and international organizations). IPS incorporates the same three levels, each level undergoing expansion and greater differentiation.

At the international level, a differentiation is introduced between public and private and governmental and nongovernmental. International governmental organizations, international nongovernmental organizations, and international corporations are included in IPS. At the national level, a similar distinction between public and private and a greater role differentiation within national political systems are found. Public and private economic systems exist within IPS, while decision-making roles within each national political structure are: head of state, domestic adviser, foreign affairs diplomat, international organization delegate, citizen, and executive director of a corporation. At the individual level, each role requires at least one person; as a result, a six-nation, five-corporation, single-international organization IPS requires upwards of 40 participants to act as decision-makers.

As in INS, three types of communications exist. Written communication between participants is possible either using message forms or decision forms. Verbal communication is possible through scheduled or unscheduled conferences. In addition, a world press is read by all participants.

In both nation-state and international versions, nations are prototypes and are named Algo, Bingo, Somne, Utro, Yora, and Zena. The three largest nations represent three distinct types of political structures. Algo has a decision latitude (Guetzkow et al., 1963: 115; Guetzkow, 1981b: 33) of 9 on the decision latitude scale, complete government control over all national industry, and relatively little trade with other nations when the simulation starts. Yora also has a high decision latitude, 8, and much control over national industry. Industry in Yora exports significant amounts to groups in other nations. Bingo has a relatively low decision latitude of 4, and a government that does not exercise direct control over industry. Bingo is the largest nation at the start and includes industries with high export potential and consumers with high import potential.

The three smaller nations, Somne, Utro, and Zena, also differ significantly from each other. Somne is allied to Bingo, has industries that sell much to groups in Yora, and even a little to the citizens in Algo. Somne has a decision latitude of 4, exercises no control over industrial enterprises in the country, and is the largest small nation. Utro and Zena are less involved in general political disputes of the tripolar simulation world, and both have a decision latitude of 5. Groups in Zena do most of their trade with groups in Bingo and Somne, while groups in Utro trade mostly with

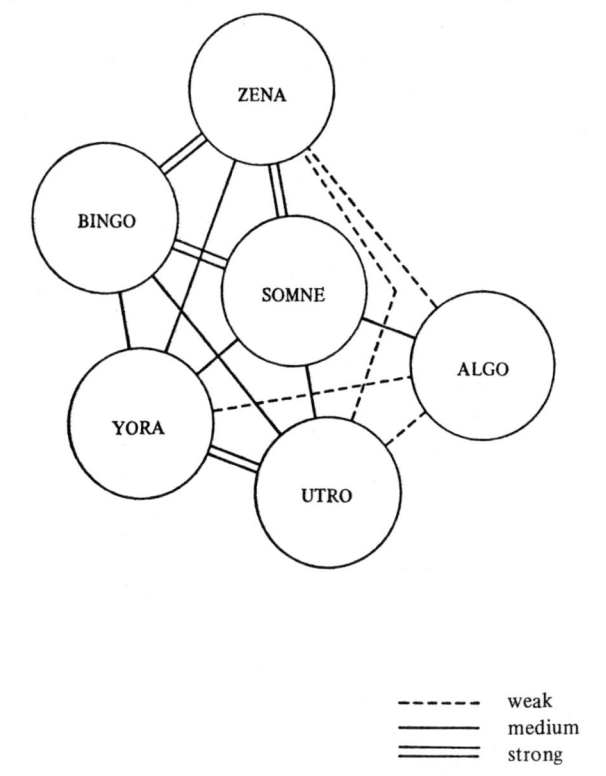

Figure 4.4 Trade Structure

groups in Yora. The trading structure is illustrated in Figure 4.4 using the conventional notion that nations trade with each other. Of course, trade in IPS and international relations is between companies and customers in nonsocialist economies. Most nations do not trade with each other in fact.

B. NATIONAL AND INTERNATIONAL CORPORATIONS: DESCRIPTION

In section I.B, emphasis was placed on national and international adaptive subsystems. National and international corporations in IPS represent these subsystems. In the nation-state interpretation, Algo Manufacturing, Somne Merchandise, Utro Development, and Yora Industrial are completely national at the start of the simulation, with all their factories and plants in one country. The fifth and largest corporation, Bingo

Enterprises, is international. It has 80 percent of its plant in Bingo, the largest nation, and 20 percent in Zena, the smallest. National identity is thus incorporated into nation-state corporations both by integrating the economic structure of each corporation into that of a particular nation and by naming the corporation after that nation.

In the international interpretation, Algo Manufacturing is the only corporation that is entirely nation-based and nation-identified. Globus Products, International Supplies, Magnus Products, and Worldwide Products are the other four corporations, none of which is identified with just one nation. Nonnational identities are deliberately used for these corporations.

In both nation-state and international interpretations, the distribution of each industry within each period is communicated to every participant by using a computer printout from the research and development program described in section III.D. The initial distributions are given in Tables 4.1 and 4.2.

Table 4.1
PERCENTAGE DISTRIBUTION OF EACH INDUSTRY
AT START OF IPS (NATION-STATE)

	Algo	Bingo	Somne	Utro	Yora	Zena
Algo manufacturing	100	0	0	0	0	0
Bingo enterprises	0	90	0	0	0	0
Somne merchandise	0	0	100	0	0	0
Utro development	0	0	0	100	0	10
Yora industrial	0	0	0	0	100	0

Table 4.2
PERCENTAGE DISTRIBUTION OF EACH INDUSTRY
AT START OF IPS (INTERNATIONAL)

	Algo	Bingo	Somne	Utro	Yora	Zena
Algo manufacturing	100	0	0	0	0	0
Globus products	0	40	30	10	0	20
International supplies	0	70	10	0	10	10
Magnus products	0	0	0	10	90	0
Worldwide products	0	40	30	10	0	20

C. NATIONAL AND INTERNATIONAL CORPORATIONS: OPERATION

Each corporation is able to sell three products—basic resources, consumer goods, and force capability—to governments and citizens. To make this possible, a monetary unit, the "ipscript," has been introduced. Trading is carried out using a trade agreement form and a trade termination form.

A trade agreement is concluded when both the seller (a corporation) and the buyer (a government or citizen or international organization) have signed a trade agreement form giving details of the agreement. Simulation control checks that the corporation has sufficient spare productive capacity and the buyer has sufficient funds before the agreement is considered ratified. This is done using the computer program agreement described in section III.H. When ratified, simulation control informs the parties to the agreement via courier.

The trading operations are simplified by two procedures. The first concerns duration of existing trade agreements, which remain in effect until explicitly broken by means of a trade termination form. The second procedure concerns the trade termination form. A trade termination form delivered to simulation control in period n before the trade termination deadline, comes into effect at the next period, $n + 1$. This is implemented by computer program termination described in section III.H.

If the period in IPS is 80 minutes long, the trade termination deadline comes at 30 minutes. The trade agreement deadline then comes after 45 minutes. Trade agreements concluded after this point do not count for the current period and are held over until the following period. Obviously, other experimenters may lengthen an IPS period. Experience suggests that an 80-minute period is the lower time limit for effective operation of IPS.

Because of the distribution given in Tables 4.1 and 4.2 and the relative size of both nations and corporations in IPS (Nation-State) compared to IPS (International), correspondingly different trading structures characterize the starting positions in each case. The starting data are included in program load, which is described in section III.B.

The major decisions of corporations concerning capital investment and research and development are recorded on a corporation plan for the period. During each period, each corporation is given its part of computer printout from the research and development program. This gives its current unit costs on each product to each nation and its production ceilings for the next period. Costs are set to begin with, such that costs in countries where corporations lack plant are higher than for those where plant exists. They include production and distribution costs to each country. Research and development in IPS brings down unit costs so that a company selling heavily to one country can invest research and development funds in that country, using a corporation plan for the period to achieve this goal.

Unit costs are given to each company on the printout of the research and development program. They do not include reductions in costs achieved for mass production. Unit costs decrease by fixed amounts as the size of a particular agreement increases: The bigger the agreement the greater the cut in unit costs. The mass production effect tapers off; above a certain level no extra decrease in costs can be gained by large orders. Company directors are told the size of their mass production effect. They are able to use mass production savings to improve bargaining power in negotiations with prospective customers.

Capital investment by a corporation in a country increases plant and equipment in that country and proportionately increases total production potential of factories in that country. Capital investment, like research and development, can be directed at any nation or combination of nations using corporation plan for the period. In this way a company can change its geographical distribution and influence the international trade structure. Similarly, a government or citizens invest in a corporation using the national investment form. Research and development investment will decrease costs to purchasers in that country. The executive director may or may not pass along these reductions to customers.

D. NATIONAL AND INTERNATIONAL CORPORATIONS: STRUCTURE

Perlmutter (1966) has suggested three structural forms for international corporations: (1) The ethnocentric organization is a nation-based corporation dominated by one set of nationals but having factories abroad. (2) The polycentric organization is made up of autonomous national branches with poor communications. (3) The geocentric organization is worldwide but ethnocentric within its cosmopolitan and international headquarters; communication is good and so is understanding of local conditions. In the international interpretation of IPS, four out of five corporations are international and tend to be polycentric. The fifth is ethnocentric and based in the nation with highest decision latitude. It is possible to represent all three types in IPS.

With ethnocentric corporations, more than half the factories can be placed in one country and all the profit boost goes to one national economy. Cost prices for an ethnocentric corporation can be reduced by research and development. Only the corporation or nation base can provide funds to do this. Any reduction in cost prices for an item would apply to corresponding prices in every country for that corporation. This simulates the spread of innovations found by research.

Cost prices for polycentric corporations can also be decreased by research and development. Government and citizenry can make available research and development funds for subsidiaries in their own nation. But research payoffs in cutting cost prices would apply only to prices for that nation. This simulates bad communications in a polycentric organization and the destructive competition described by Perlmutter. A gradual diffusion of payoff is possible, the speed of diffusion being proportional to the degree to which an organization is moving toward geocentricity. Polycentric organization profits return to the nation base of the subsidiary.

For geocentric corporations, any nation, as well as the corporation itself, can make funds available for research, and research is measured by the sum of all research funds as outlined by Perlmutter. Any payoffs apply to the particular product in all nations, while the profit boost is distributed similarly to a polycentric corporation.

Future experiments with IPS might include national and international banking systems as well as national currencies, which would make possible a number of new economic acts—for example, devaluation of a national monetary unit, credits, and stocks and shares in corporations. This would mean more complexity. The option to start new companies is not included in the simulation at present, but there is no structural reason for this. Streamlining some technical feature, such as computer usage, should make this possible in the future.

Because no banking system exists within the simulation at present, funds allocated for purchasing a particular product (basic resources, say) but not all used for this purpose are converted to that product at the unfavorable rate of 25 ipscripts per unit. This is a weakness in the economic system of IPS.

E. TRADING AND ECONOMIC STRUCTURE

Introducing corporations as distinct entities has made possible a new economic and trading structure. While in INS consumer goods, basic resources, and force capability are produced by governments using generation rates, in IPS citizens can improve their standard of living by buying as many consumer goods as their income allows, and governments can get as much as possible with available income. The trade matrix for IPS is calculated each period by the economic program described in section III.E. Unlike in INS, trade is not under the direct control of governments.

Governments are able to tax citizens and industrial enterprises to raise necessary monies for implementing government policies. Thus, in each period governments are given a computer printout that tells taxable profits on corporations or subsidiaries operating in the country and the total amount of other monies expected in the national economic system. Governments then decide how much tax they require and tax citizens and corporations accordingly. This is done using the budget allocation form.

Funds raised by governments in this way are allocated on a budget allocation form for expenditures on basic resources, capital investment, research and development, and force capability. A citizen's after-tax income is reported on his income form. Similarly, the profits after tax are reported on a profits after tax form. These funds are then used by corporations during the following period. When deciding on taxation levels, governments take into account dividends to shareholders. These payments have no direct programmed consequences in IPS.

Profit and loss accounts for each corporation are calculated each period by the economic program. The computer printout provides a balance sheet for each corporation and gives a complete breakdown of profits by product and nation as well as current inventory. A research and development program uses the total profit figure to calculate profits of each corporation in each nation.

F. OTHER NONGOVERNMENTAL ACTIVITY

In the international interpretation of IPS, international nongovernmental conferences, each lasting five minutes, are scheduled during each period to promote further activity at this level. An invitation is circulated by simulation control, and citizens attend voluntarily. Further nongovernmental activities sometimes evolve from these conferences. The programmed influence of these activities on international opinion is explained later. No such programmed structure is present in the nation-state interpretation.

A new range of political conflicts has become possible in IPS. The role differentiation involved in citizen, foreign affairs diplomat, head of state, and corporation executive has made possible twenty-four types of conflict not previously possible in INS. Citizens now have a demonstration form which may be used any time for antigovernment or antiforeign demonstrations and riots. Details of this form are reported to the world press when it is submitted to simulation control. Governments concerned are also informed. While such acts have no immediate influence on the programmed structure of IPS, under certain conditions they can seriously inconvenience governments by influencing evaluations of others.

While demonstrations and riots enable citizens to make demands on governments in a way stronger than written or verbal communication, strikes provide a method for making strong demands on industry. In IPS a citizen may strike at any time against any corporation with a plant in his country by using a strike form. When a strike takes place citizens lose income for the period of the strike, while corporations lose production in that country. Three strike-breaking methods are available to a government through the internal control form:

(1) The government issues a court order to strikers requesting them to return to work. Citizens are not obligated to accept this order.
(2) The government mans the factory with military forces. Forces used in this way are not available for national defense at the same time. The force required equals loss in citizen's income divided by 25.
(3) The government uses military force to get citizens back to work, but forced labor pushes up production costs by 5 percent.

Citizens can purchase force capability from corporations in IPS. This can be used through the subversion form for two purposes: (1) to undertake assassination attempts against members of their government, and (2) to wage guerrilla warfare. The success of an assassination attempt depends upon the amount of force used for internal control by a government. This is recorded under item 3 of the force utilization form. The outcome of guerrilla warfare is calculated using a war program. If guerrilla warfare is successful, a citizen becomes the new head of state. In both cases the citizens must have previously purchased force and distributed it in the nine national zones using a subversion form.

Force capability purchased by citizens from home industry can represent a purely indigenous subversive uprising. Citizens may be offered arms or subsidized by a foreign power or a foreign corporation. This represents activities of international and revolutionary movements.

A government may protect itself from subversion by inspecting for illegal forces in its nine zones, using the internal control form. Such inspections are considered purges of dissenting elements in which all materials are appropriated and subversives are assumed to be imprisoned. Simulation control is then able to erase any subversive forces operating in the country.

G. GOVERNMENTAL ACTIVITY

Zinnes (1966b), in her comparison of communication in INS and the 1914 crisis, suggests that a lack of indirect governmental channels as alternatives to top-level communication causes severe distortion in INS. Zinnes suggests a decision-making role explicitly responsible for such activities. This has been done in IPS by creating a diplomatic position. Larger nations in IPS may have two diplomats. One of these operates in a dual role as a diplomat and a second international organization delegate. The sole function of an IPS diplomat is to carry out negotiations on behalf of his government.

In the international interpretation of IPS there is a full-time international organization and for each nation an international organization delegate. For ten minutes in each period the international organization recesses and delegates attend a national council meeting in their nations. At all other times they are in the international organization chamber. In keeping with Alger's (1966b) findings, an international organization delegates' lounge is provided, which delegates can use at any time for informal interaction.

Governments can impose a variety of negative sanctions in IPS. They can place tariffs on imports or exports of any or all products. They can place limitations on travel by their citizens to another country (to attend a nongovernmental meeting) or on foreign citizens attending a meeting in their country. All of these acts are implemented using a negative sanction form. Troop movements, mobilization, and war are made possible through the force utilization form. If war is declared, a computer program war calculates outcomes.

On the diplomatic front, three types of conflict behavior are now possible: (1) Diplomatic relations can be broken, established, or reestablished. When broken, direct conferences between diplomats of the two governments are not allowed. (2) An ambassador can be expelled or recalled. (3) A diplomat of less than ambassador status can be expelled or recalled. In diplomatic conflict a continuum of acts from mild to strong is thus available, and a diplomatic form is used for this purpose.

III. PROGRAM CHANGES IN IPS

A. INTRODUCTION

In INS "relations among nations are embodied in the simulation by the postulation of programs of operation with respect to the internal functioning of the several nations consituting the overall inter-nation system. Using these programs, the decision-makers of each nation then freely develop relations between their states as they deem appropriate, given their unfolding circumstances." The simulation is based on "explicit specification of a basic set of variables and programmed relations among them," as well as the variety of additional factors introduced by using human beings as decision-makers within the system (Guetzkow et al., 1963: 104; Guetzkow, 1981b: 23-24). In a similar way, IPS is based on both explicit programmed relationships and unprogrammed activity of human decision-makers. The programmed activities in IPS are incorporated in eight FORTRAN computer programs.

B. PROGRAM LOAD

Program load is used to place starting data in nineteen data files. Starting data are stored with the program in the first instance. The program itself simply places data in the computer's memory.

While all programs are written in GE FORTRAN and use the file conventions of a particular commercial on-line system, it should be possible to modify them to run on other systems without too much difficulty. The bulk of the program is written in relatively simple FORTRAN, which could be modified to suit particular machines.

Since program load is simply a bookkeeping program, definitions and assumptions will not be discussed. All programs involving assumptions about international relations theory are described in detail.

C. PROGRAM FACTS

Program facts can be used at any time during the simulation to provide a comprehensive listing of the state of the simulation environment. It is also of value to run program facts after program load, before the simulation starts. This enables the experimenter to check for any system malfunction that might have occurred while loading the data with program load. In addition, a printout of the state of the world at the start of the simulation is then available for the world press and for simulation records.

Program facts simply reads data currently in store in each of nineteen data files within the computer's memory. When printing information out at the computer terminal, facts adds labels to the information so that the experimenter can check to see that it is correct. As for program load, program facts is a bookkeeping routine and no important assumptions are included.

D. RESEARCH AND DEVELOPMENT PROGRAM

1. Description

The introduction of independent corporations into IPS requires programming of corporations' capital investment and research and development. Both nations and corporations can invest in corporations, the source of investment in part determining geographical distribution of corporations' assets and factories. Capital investment in a nation by a corporation simulates construction of plants in that country and subsequently improves that nation's trading position. Not all investment is used to create new plants. As 5 percent depreciation on existing plants occurs each period, investment is used in part to offset this loss.

Research and development by nations and corporations has the effect of lowering production costs where these include both production and delivery costs. Research and development is directional. A company can invest research and development funds in any particular nation or combination of nations to lower costs, but not necessarily prices, to these countries.

The research and development program converts research and development and capital investment appropriations into research and development payoffs; increases basic capabilities for industries; and creates a continually changing geographical distribution of industrial plants. This, in turn, increases export capability.

2. Definitions

This program represents a completely new set of programmed assumptions. The programmed variables used are defined in the following way:

(1) BCBR: the basic capability of a corporation to produce basic resources
(2) BCCG: the basic capability of a corporation to produce consumer goods
(3) BCFC: the basic capability of a corporation to produce force capability
(4) BCTOT: the total basic capability of a corporation
(5) BCPROD: the total production of a corporation
(6) BRPROD: the total basic resources production of a company
(7) CI: the capital investment in a company in a nation
(8) CITOT: the total capital investment in a company
(9) COSTS: the unit costs of production for each product to each nation
(10) CFPROD: the production of conventional force
(11) CGPROD: the production of consumer goods
(12) IND: the name of the industry

(13) PERC: the percentage of a company in a nation
(14) PROF: the total corporation profits in a nation
(15) PROFBT: the profits before tax of each corporation in each nation
(16) PROFCS: the total profit of a corporation
(17) RANDD: funds invested in research and development
(18) WHO: the nation names

3. Assumptions

The first part of the program implements a research and development routine.

Research and development: Unit costs. The assumption used is that up to a saturation ceiling, the greater the investment in research and development, the greater the payoff in terms of reduction in unit costs. Beyond this maximum an increased investment does not bring any further reduction in unit costs. Thus, for RANDD < RANDDmax,

$$COSTSold - COSTSnew = DELTA \times RANDDlevel,$$

while for RANDD = RANDDmax,

$$A[COSTS(BC)old - COSTS(BC)new] +$$
$$B[COSTS(CG)old - COSTS(CG)new] +$$
$$C[COSTS(FC)old - COSTS(FC)new] =$$
$$DELTA1 \times RANDDlevel, \qquad [4.2]$$

where RANDDmax is the saturation ceiling for investment, DELTA1 is the incremental drop associated with each increase in level of RANDD, and RANDDlevel is the level of RANDD in terms of an interval scale. A, B, and C are constants.

In initial runs with IPS, RANDDmax was made equal to 600 ipscripts. DELTA1 was set at 0.1, the RANDD level was defined on a seven-point scale such that 0 to 99.9 Ipscripts invested became zero RANDDlevel, 100 to 199.9 became one, 200 to 299.9 two, and so on in a linear fashion up to RANDDmax. A, B, and C were all set at 1, thus giving equal research and development payoffs in all three sectors for RANDDmax. By adjusting A, B, and C, the orientation of a corporation might be influenced by giving a bigger research and development payoff in one sector relative to others.

Capital investment: Basic capability. The total basic capability for each corporation is then calculated by assuming that this production potential depends upon how much capital investment there is in the corporation. The nearer to maximum production in the current period, the greater the production potential in the next period. This simulates the fact that if people and machines are not being used to the maximum, then maximum production in the next period is lower because of training and retooling problems. Similarly, the greater the capital investment, the greater the production potential next period because new equipment and personnel are acquired. The same assumptions are taken for each particular product as well as for total production. A company that has been producing to its maximum in consumer goods and not in force capability will find that its basic capability for producing consumer goods will tend to increase relative to its capability for producing force.

Imposed on these two assumptions is a standard depreciation per period. This simulates natural wastage that occurs in both people and machines in every industrial enterprise. The equation representing these three interacting assumptions is

$$\text{BCTOTnew} = [(100 - C)/100] \cdot (\text{BCTOTold} + \text{BCPROD})/(\text{BCTOTold} \times 2) + (\text{CI}/\text{ZETA}), \quad [4.3]$$

where D is the depreciation rate, expressed as a percentage, and ZETA is a multiplier associated with returns on capital investment. The higher ZETA is, the lower are the returns.

Geographical distribution: Profits. The geographical distribution is then estimated by calculating how much of each corporation is in each nation, having taken into account depreciation and new plants introduced by capital investment.

$$\text{PERC}(K,L) = \text{PERC}(K,L) \times \text{BCTOT}(L)/100. \quad [4.4]$$

The percentage of industry L in nation K in absolute figures, depreciation having been taken into account as well as the increase from capital investment, is then used in the equation

$$\text{PERC}(K,L) = \text{PERC}(K,L) + \text{CI}(K,L)/\text{ZETA}. \quad [4.5]$$

This absolute figure is then reconverted to a percentage by dividing by total size of company and multiplying by 100.

This new geographical distribution of factories is then used to determine national distribution of profits for each company. Thus, profits of each corporation L in each nation K are given by the equation

$$\text{PROFBT}(K,L) = \text{PERC}(K,L) \times \text{PROFCS}(L)/100. \quad [4.6]$$

The program then calculates total profits of each corporation and prints out new unit costs, new total and particular basic capabilities, profits by nation and corporation, and new geographical distribution of each corporation.

E. ECONOMIC PROGRAM

1. Description

Because of the changed economic structure, a special program is required to calculate simulated world trade patterns and profit and loss accounts of corporations. Trade between nations in IPS is not directly controlled by government except under special circumstances. Import and export patterns in the simulation depend on the amount of industrial plant in each nation, needs of government and citizenry, and available foreign markets. The economic program calculates an import/export matrix by taking into account geographical distribution of industry and company sales.

The balance sheet of each corporation gives statements of profit and loss on each product (consumer goods, basic resources, force capability) to each nation for each corporation. This is calculated knowing cost price, which changes through research and development, and sale price, which changes through bargaining between corporations and customers. A mass production effect is incorporated into the computer program to simulate effects of decreasing unit costs on increasing quantities of a product. Inventory is also updated by the program.

2. Definitions

Like IPS research and development, this program represents a new set of assumptions in IPS. These assumptions relate to the economic system in operation in IPS, and programmed variables used are defined in the following way:

(1) CORP: the name of the industry
(2) DSTOCK: the change in inventory, or stock, for the corporation
(3) INST: the period number
(4) PERCEN: the percentage of a company in a nation
(5) PRODCT: the production of each corporation of each product
(6) PROFIT: the profit of each corporation on sales of each product to each nation
(7) PROFPN: profit by product and industry

(8) SALES: the sales of each product to each nation by each corporation
(9) STOCK: the stock of each product by corporation
(10) SALEPR: the sales price of each product to each nation for each corporation, expressed as the deviation from the unit cost
(11) TOT: the total trade of a nation
(12) TRADE: the total trade of a nation with each other nation
(13) TOTEXP: the total exports of a nation
(14) TOTIMP: the total imports of a nation
(15) TPROFC: the total profits of a corporation
(16) TPROFN: the total profits of each corporation in each nation
(17) TSALES: the total sales of each corporation in each nation
(18) WHO: the nation names
(19) XMPORT: the imports and exports of each nation to each other nation

3. Assumptions

Mass production: Unit costs. The first part of the program adjusts unit costs to allow for mass production effects. It is assumed that, up to a saturation ceiling, the larger the trade agreement for a particular product to a particular nation, the greater the reduction in unit costs. Thus, for SALES and SALESmax the general expression is

$$\text{SALEPRnew} = \text{SALEPRold} - \text{DELTA2} \times \text{SALESlevel}, \qquad [4.7]$$

and for all other values of SALES,

$$\text{SALEPRnew} = \text{SALEPRold} - \text{DELTA2} \times \text{SALESmax}, \qquad [4.8]$$

where SALESmax is a saturation ceiling for the mass production effect, DELTA2 is the incremental drop associated with each increase in level of SALES, and SALESlevel is the level of SALES in terms of an interval scale. For each corporation, the particular interpretations of these equations for basic resources, BR, say, are

$$\text{SALEPR(BR)new} = \text{SALEPR(BR)old} -$$
$$\text{DELTA2(BR)} \times \text{SALES(BR)level} \qquad [4.9]$$

and

$$\text{SALEPR(BR)new} = \text{SALEPR(BR)old} - \text{DELTA2(BR)} \times \text{SALES(BR)max}. \qquad [4.10]$$

Trade Matrix. The total sales of each corporation to each nation are first calculated using the formula

$$\text{TSALES} = \sum_{J=1}^{J=3} \text{SALES(J)}, \qquad [4.11]$$

where SALES(J) is sales of product J.

The import/export matrix is then calculated using the formula

$$\text{XMPORT} = \text{TSALES} \times \text{PERCEN}/100. \qquad [4.12]$$

This assumes that at production of national subsidiaries relative to total production of a company is a linear function of the percentage of the company within that nation. Having calculated the import/export matrix XMPORT, it is possible to calculate TOTEXP, TOTIMP, TRADE, and TOT by simple additions. The complete trade structure is calculated in this way and subsequently printed out.

The program then calculates a profit and loss account for each corporation. Thus,

$$\text{PROFIT} = \text{SALES} \times \text{SALEPR}; \qquad [4.13]$$

that is,

$$\text{PROFIT} = \text{SALES (unit sale price-unit cost price)},$$

since for each product, SALEPR is the mass production corrected excess of unit sale price minus cost price.

Using this simple formula, the complete profit matrix is calculated and printed out. In addition, the program calculates current stock by using the formula

$$\text{STOCKnew} = \text{STOCKold} + \text{PRODCT} - \text{SALES}. \qquad [4.14]$$

The corporation balance sheet includes STOCKnew and DSTOCK as well as the complete PROFIT matrix for each company.

F. POLITICAL PROGRAM

1. Description

This program has been developed from the programmed relations in INS (Guetzkow et al., 1963: 103-149; Guetzkow, 1981b: passim) and is best understood in terms of INS assumptions. In each period, the program updates current political and economic conditions in each nation. It calculates the probability of holding office, the probability of a revolution, other indicators of office-holding (Guetzkow et al., 1963: 110; Guetzkow, 1981b: 29), and orderly and disorderly transference of power (Guetzkow et al., 1963: 117; Guetzkow, 1981b: 35). It calculates various national attributes and capabilities, such as national security and consumer satisfaction (Guetzkow et al., 1963: 122-127; Guetzkow, 1981b: 39-44), and it estimates national economic variables such as the level of basic resources.

2. Definitions

The programmed political variables used in IPS are:

(1) AF: nuclear force level
(2) AFBEG: nuclear force level at start of period
(3) AFINC: nuclear forces acquired by nation during period
(4) BP: exports minus imports
(5) BR: basic resources of a nation
(6) BRDL: cost in basic resources for forced change in decision latitude
(7) BRINC: increase in basic resources
(8) CF: conventional force level
(9) CS: consumer satisfaction
(10) CS0: starvation level of consumer goods
(11) CFDr: conventional force cost for forced change in decision latitude
(12) CFIC: forces used for internal control
(13) CFBEG: conventional force at start of period
(14) CFDEP: depreciated conventional force
(15) CFINC: increase in conventional force
(16) CSMAX: maximum possible level of consumer goods
(17) CSMIN: the minimum level of consumer goods acceptable to a nation's people

(18) DL: decision latitude
(19) DDL: government-instigated change in decision latitude
(20) DDLV: programmed pressure to change decision latitude
(21) F: sum of nuclear and conventional force
(22) F2: sum of nuclear and conventional forces for two nations
(23) OPI: world opinion index
(24) OVS: political effectiveness
(25) OPIN: opinion of one nation about another
(26) PO: public opinion
(27) PR: probability of a revolution
(28) PHO: probability of holding office in the event of an election
(29) PSR: probability of a successful revolution in the event of a revolution taking place
(30) PSS: probability of system stability
(31) SEC: national security
(32) TOT: total trade of a nation
(33) TRADE: trade of each nation with each other nation
(34) WHO: names of nations

3. Assumptions

Consequences of pressured changes in decision latitude are calculated using the same formula INS uses (Guetzkow et al., 1963: 128-130; Guetzkow, 1981b: 45). Conventional force levels are also updated in a manner similar to INS, by assuming that

$$CFnew = CFDEP + CFINC - CFDL, \qquad [4.15]$$

where

$$CFDEP = CFold \times depc, \qquad [4.16]$$

and depc is the depreciation rate. Similarly, nuclear force is updated using the equation

$$AFnew = AFBEG \times depa + AFINC, \qquad [4.17]$$

where depa is the depreciation rate of nuclear force.

National Security. In INS, validator satisfaction with respect to national security is directly related, within limits, to the ratio of force strength of a nation and its allies to the strongest nation or group of nations not allied with it (Guetzkow et al., 1963: 125-127; Guetzkow, 1981b: 42-44). IPS replaces validator satisfaction with respect to national secirity, with a redefined index called national security. National security is defined using the following considerations.

Richardson (1960), in his study of arms races, developed the concept of directed intentions to extend his model of a two-nation situation to an N-nation situation. Galtung (1964), in another context put forward a sociological model of polarization which appears to apply to various situations ranging from relatively complete polarization (Jenkins and MacRae, 1967) to relatively complex situations in which differential polarization is present (Smoker, 1965b). In the latter type of situation, polarization ceases to be a bipolar concept, and with nations, relations gain an intensive aspect—for example, the degree to which a government is involved with another government. The power political definition of national security used in INS has, therefore, been modified to include degrees of involvement of a nation in behavioral groups. These are defined using Smoker's interpretation of Galtung's polarization model (Smoker, 1965b).

This can be summarized in the following way. Galtung defines a completely polarized situation as one in which all positive relations are within blocks and all negative relations are between blocks. Conversely, in a completely unpolarized situation, it would be impossible to define blocks between which there were a significant difference in distribution of positive and negative relations. Between completely polarized and nonpolarized, the degree of polarization can be defined. Polarization as defined is not necessarily bipolarization. A tri- or N-polarization would also satisfy the criteria of all positive relations within, and all negative relations between, blocs.

If trade is assumed to index a positive relation between nations, then it is possible to define a relative index Fmn, where

$$F\text{mn} = t\text{mn}[(1/T\text{m}) + (1/T\text{n})], \qquad [4.18]$$

to measure the positive bonds between nations. In this definition, $t$mn is the intertrade between the two nations, and Tm and Tn are total trade of the mth and n^{th} nations. This index, which averages relative importance of trade between two nations, has been used in an empirical study of the present arms race (Smoker, 1965b). The adopted model, when applied to seven nations—the United States, USSR, UK, China, Federal Republic of Germany, Poland, and France—for the ten years from 1952 to 1962, gives a strong correlation with actual behavior. If the same model with no allowance for differential polarization is used, the agreement is weaker. On the basis of this study, the national security index in IPS takes differentiated polarization, as defined, into account. For each nation, Fmn is defined as above, and a polarization weighting is calculated according to the deviation of Fmn from the mean value of all Fmn.

The assumption is that the greater the positive deviation of Fmn from the mean, the better the relations between the two nations. The greater the negative deviation from the mean, the more the two nations are opposed to each other. These measures are then used to define behavioral groups and to weight power terms in the national security index.

The program implements this definition of national security by calculating positive deviations RHO of Fmn from the mean F and the negative deviations SIGMA. For each nation it is then possible to define a weighted positive strength,

$$\text{GOOD} = \Sigma F2 \times \text{RHO}, \qquad [4.19]$$

and a weighted negative strength,

$$\text{BAD} = \Sigma F2 \times \text{SIGMA}. \qquad [4.20]$$

National security is then defined in terms of the relative magnitude of GOOD and BAD.

$$\text{SEC} = \text{COEFF} \times \text{GOOD}/\text{BAD}, \qquad [4.21]$$

where COEFF is a weighting parameter.

World Opinion. A Vietnam simulation developed by the Peace Research Centre, UK, and the Canadian Peace Research Institute (MacRae and Smoker, 1967) introduced world opinion as an explicit determinant of the political effectiveness of governments. The underlying assumption was that opinions of foreign political elites, as recorded on the so-called world opinion form, are important to a nation's political decision-makers, the importance of foreign opinion being proportional to the behavioral groupings as defined by Galtung's polarization model. The opinions of political decision-makers of nations which are positively linked carry more weight than those of hostile nations. In fact, the index is constructed so that negative evaluations of foreign political decision-makers of hostile nations cause a positive score on the international opinion scale. In the international interpretation of IPS, the citizen can influence world opinion. If he attends an international nongovernmental conference, the index for his nation is boosted. This means that two complementary effects are incorporated into the index: Relationships between governments are dependent upon current behavioral groupings, while goodwill generated by citizens is not. This is expressed in the program using the equation

$$OPI = OPIN \times (RHO - SIGMA) + GWS, \qquad [4.22]$$

RHO and SIGMA being such that for a particular pair of nations one is always zero, and GWS being the goodwill score generated by citizens. GWS was set at 2 for IPS and was added to OPI by hand.

Consumer satisfaction. The Elder/Pendley studies of consumer satisfaction (1981) suggest that programmed equations for VScs (validator satisfaction for consumption standards; see Guetzkow et al., 1963: 123-126; Guetzkow, 1981b: 41-43) be altered to

$$VScs = constant \times Log_e (CS/CSmin) + constant \qquad [4.23]$$

and

$$CSmin = constant \times Log_e (CSmax/CS_0) + CS,$$

where CS is consumer goods purchased, CSmin is consumer minimum, CSmax is maximum producer goods which could be purchased, and CS_0 is the starvation level.

Basic resources. Basic resources, like force capability, are calculated using the equation

$$BRnew = depbBRold + BRINC - BRDL, \qquad [4.24]$$

but the value of BRnew is then modified to allow for balance of trade. It is assumed that, since balance of payments cannot at the present time be incorporated into IPS without the addition of a banking system, the balance of trade influences a nation's economy. Deviations from the balance boost or hold back growth. Thus, a booster is defined in terms of the difference between exports and imports. This booster, RO, is defined as

$$RO = BP/TOT, \qquad [4.25]$$

and BRnew is then modified by multiplying by (1 + RO). The complete equation for BRnew then becomes

$$BRnew = (depbBRold + BRINC - BRDL)(1 + RO). \quad [4.26]$$

Public opinion. Another innovation from the Vietnam simulation is a public opinion index. It uses current evaluations of political decision-makers concerning performance of national governments. These are recorded on the world opinion form. Only opinions of nationals are used in evaluating performance of their own government. In practice, this means that public opinion is taken as an average of opinions of head of state, domestic adviser, foreign affairs diplomat, international organization delegate, citizen, and business executive. Public opinion is on a one-to-ten scale, as are national security, international opinion, and consumer satisfaction.

Probability of holding office. The INS probability of holding office index (Guetzkow et al., 1963: 111; Guetzkow, 1981b: 30) was reconsidered by Elder and Pendley (1981) in terms of contemporary political theory about stability of regimes and government. They assert that programmed relations in INS tend to express relationships between system stability and its determinants, rather than regime stability. Thus, they argue that the INS equation

$$pOH = a(b - DL)VSm + c(DL - d) \quad [4.27]$$

should be retained, but that it should be interpreted as the probability of system stability, pss. This has been done in IPS.

The new probability of holding office at elections is redefined in terms of public opinion and changes in public opinion. The probability of holding office, pOH, is defined by the equation

$$pOH = 1 - pLO, \text{ where } pLO = M \times DPO + N/PO; \quad [4.28]$$

that is, pLO is the probability of losing office, DPO is the drop in public opinion during the period, PO is current public opinion, and M and N are constants. This equation assumes that the probability of holding office depends both on current levels and current trends in public opinion.

Political effectiveness. INS, overall validator satisfaction (VSm) is defined in terms of two component parts corresponding to national security and consumer satisfaction (Guetzkow et al., 1963: 114; Guetzkow, 1981b: 32). IPS adopts a corresponding strategy, the difference being an increased number of component parts, four against two. Thus, political effectiveness (OVS) is defined as

$$\text{OVS} = e\text{CS} + g\text{NS} + h\text{IO} + i\text{PO} \qquad [4.29]$$

where $e, g, h,$ and i are weighting parameters.

G. WAR PROGRAM

1. Description

The war program calculates outcomes in the event of war. It assumes each nation can deploy forces in four ways: attack, active defense, passive defense, and reserve.

Attack forces are directed against a particular nation or combination of nations. Forces may be transferred to the attack status at any time and are only used when a statement is made to that effect in writing by the head of state. Active defense forces have the capability of destroying oncoming attack forces. They simulate defenses of the antiaircraft gun and antimissile missile type. Passive defense forces cannot destroy incoming attack forces but can protect civilian and/or military installations. They simulate hardened missile sites or fallout shelters. Reserve forces are held to replenish forces of the other three types.

The war program provides governments with a variety of strategies ranging from all-out military conquest (100 percent attack) to completely nonviolent resistance (100 percent passive defense). In addition, attack and defense forces may be deployed against or in protection of any all-civilian, all-military, or civilian-military force to provide another range of strategies.

2. Definitions

The programmed variables used in IPS war are:

(1) ATTACK: force used by one nation to attack another
(2) SHIELD: passive defense forces of a nation
(3) REATAK: active defense forces of a nation
(4) DAMAGE: effectiveness coefficient for ATTACK

(5) PROTEK: effectiveness coefficient for SHIELD
(6) REPULS: effectiveness coefficient for REATAK
(7) DATTAC: losses in ATTACK
(8) DSHIEL: losses in SHIELD
(9) DREATA: losses in REATAK
(10) RATIOS: military/nonmilitary mix of attack and defense forces
(11) RATIO: mean military/nonmilitary mix of all ATTACK forces
(12) BCLOSS: nonmilitary loss from an attack
(13) SUMDAT: sum of DATTAC
(14) WHO: nation names

3. Assumptions

The program calculates loss of attacking forces by assuming attacking forces suffer losses before defending forces, the losses being

$$DATTAC = REATAK \times REPULS. \qquad [4.30]$$

The value of RATIO is then calculated by averaging across all RATIOS, and the total loss in attacking forces, SUMDAT, is calculated by summing all DATTAC for each nation. Passive defense losses are then calculated using the expression

$$DSHIEL = DAMAGE \times ATTACK, \qquad [4.31]$$

where ATTACK has been modified to allow for losses, DATTAC. A correction is then made to allow for protective effectiveness using the equation

$$DSHIELnew = DSHIELold - SHIELD \times PROTEX, \qquad [4.32]$$

and civilian and protective losses are calculated using the equations

$$SHIELDnew = SHIELDold - DSHIEL \times RATIO \qquad [4.33]$$

and

$$BCLOSS = DSHIEL(1 - RATIO). \qquad [4.34]$$

Active defense losses are then calculated by assuming that the greater the other losses are, the greater are these losses. Thus,

$$REATAKnew = REATAKold - CONST(BCLOSS + DSHIEL), \qquad [4.35]$$

where CONST is a constant. The program then reports total attack forces destroyed, passive defense forces left and destroyed, active defense forces left and destroyed, and total civilian losses. The data base is modified by the computer.

H. TRADE AGREEMENT PROGRAM AND TRADE TERMINATION PROGRAM

These two programs operate together on a second computer terminal. They are both bookkeeping programs, and the results of their operations are automatically transmitted to the programs on the other terminals via the data base. In each period the trade agreement program is put into operation each time a trade agreement is sent to simulation control. The program checks whether the agreement is possible, and, if it is, records it in the computer's memory. As a rule, the program is running all the time, up to the trade agreement deadline. After all agreements have been processed, the trade termination program is run. This program implements trade terminations and adjusts the data base for the next period's operation. It also prints out existing agreements for the start of the next period, providing for every participant a hard copy of their own trading situations.

Both these programs are self-instructional and do not permit impossible agreements or terminations. The only time problem the experimenter must observe is to finish using the trade agreement program before implementing the economic program on the other computer terminal. The interlocking nature of the various programs, or modules, is illustrated in Figure 4.5. The war program can be run on either computer terminal.

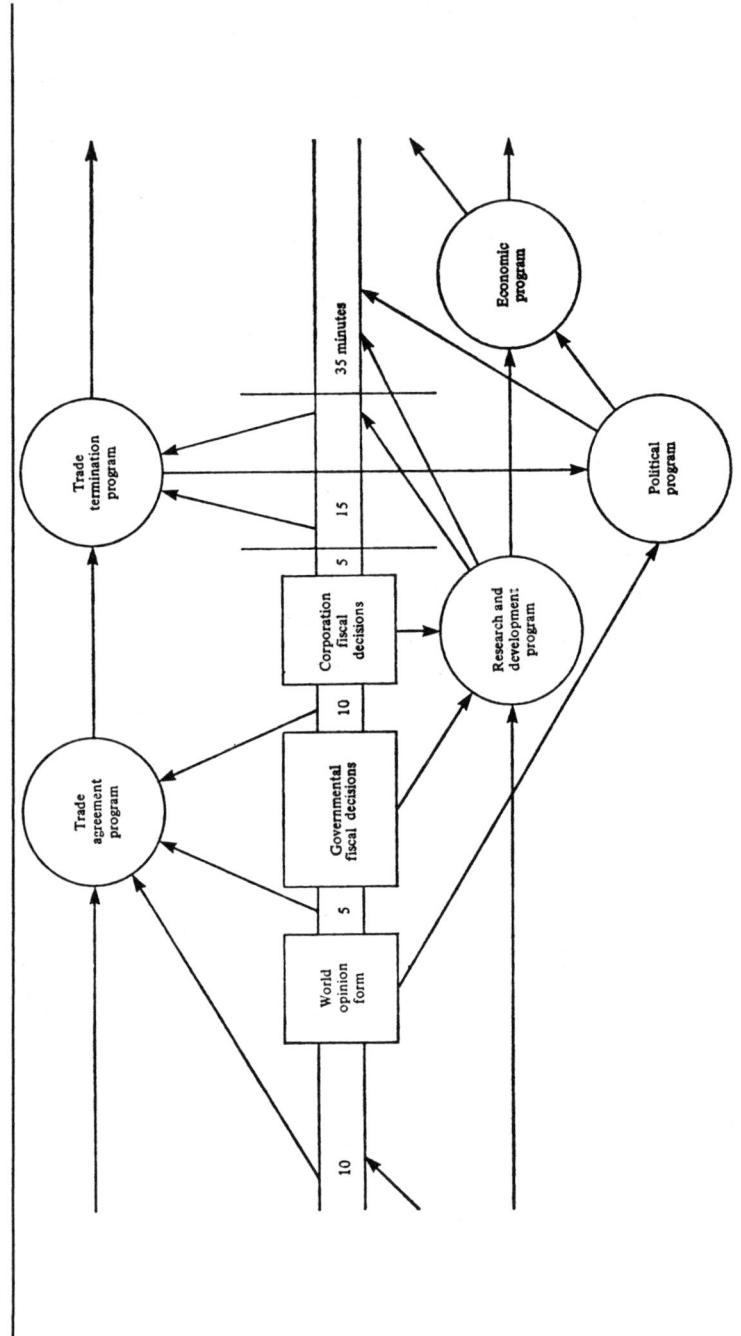

Figure 4.5 Information Flow

NOTES

1. It is easy to confuse models of the world with reality. It can be argued that science will never know what reality is, but will just produce models of reality which are scientists' perceptions. There are many possible perceptions of a reality, all of which can be behaviorally consistent.

2. Details of international governmental and nongovernmental activities are given in *The Yearbook of International Associations* and the monthly publication, *International Associations,* both published by the Union of International Associations, Brussels.

3. Apart from individual globe-trotters, such as international journalists, those on holiday, and students, there have been entertainers with mass international following giving them the status of international man—for example, the Beatles, Bob Dylan, Joan Baez, and Judy Collins.

4. It has been estimated that by the year 1975, through international mergers, overseas investment, and assorted practices, three hundred corporations will control 75 percent of all industrial assets. For details on international businesses, see *Fortune Magazine, World Businesses.* Recently, international business has received increasing attention from international relations theorists.

5. Every international organization has some international aspects, some are goal attainment and others not. International organizations can be placed on a political (goal attainment), nonpolitical (integrative) scale. This has been done elsewhere using empirical data (Smoker, 1965b).

6. The term "model" can be used as a noun meaning representation, as an adjective implying perfection, and as a verb meaning to demonstrate. It is used in the text to imply all of these meanings. It tries to represent states, objects, and events, but is idealized and simplified to include only those propositions considered relevant to perceived reality, and attempts to show what the perceived reality is like.

5

The Simulated International Processer

Stuart A. Bremer

The purpose of this chapter is to describe the computer model for the Simulated International ProcessER (SIPER)[1] as it stands today, and to provide some of the supporting rationale for the way in which it is presently structured. The SIPER model draws upon the INS model for some of its components (see Bremer, 1977, especially Ch. 1), and the description that follows is organized in order to make clear where INS ends and SIPER begins.

The simulation model is composed of two parts. The larger and more complex part of the model specifies how a national decision-making unit attempts to achieve its goals in a changing environment. The smaller and less complex part of the model, borrowed essentially from INS (Guetzkow, 1981b), defines the decision-making environment and specifies the ways in which it changes in response to the behavior of the national decision-making units. It is this second part of the model that we will examine first.

Author's Note: This chapter is an updated version of Chapter 2, "The Simulation Model," pp. 29-80 in Stuart A. Bremer, *Simulated Worlds: A Computer Model of National Decision-Making,* copyright © 1977 by Princeton University Press. The author and publisher wish to acknowledge with thanks the permission to reprint of Princeton University Press. The description of the model was updated by Gary L. Tygesson (Fulcher Research Assistant at Northwestern University) and Michael Don Ward to be consonant with the 3.2 version of Bremer's simulation program, SIPER-Evanston.

THE DECISION-MAKING ENVIRONMENT

The national decision-making unit is embedded in an environment composed of three basic systems: an international system, the national economic system, and the national political system. Each of these presents the decision-making unit with opportunities for achievement as well as obstacles to be overcome.

The International System. The behavior of other nation states in the international system is a major influence on the national decision-making unit. Figure 5.1 presents in diagrammatic form the essential features of a typical simulated international system. The system is small, since it contains only five actors, and tightly bipolar, since the alliance bonds define two mutually exclusive blocs. Furthermore, each bloc is composed of a leader nation that is primarily responsible for coordinating the defense policy of the bloc, and a variable number of member nations that may or may not wish to follow the advice of their bloc leader. The current model does not permit nonalignment, so every member of the system must be affiliated with one of the two blocs.

The size limitation and bipolarity requirements were necessitated by considerations of economy and parsimony. Although the model was originally designed to accommodate ten nations, it became clear that the exponential nature of the cost increase for the larger system capability outweighed the advantages of such a capability at this stage of the research. With a few technical modifications, the computer can accommodate any number of national actors.

The tight bipolarity restriction is a more important and limiting assumption and less easily relaxed within the current model. After much deliberation, it became clear to me that for some purposes I would need to conceptualize an international system as a two-bloc system.[2] In the future, it is my intention to provide for the inclusion of nonaligned nations, but the modifications required are theoretical, not technical.

As Figure 5.1 indicates, there are three kinds of interactions that link the national actors. Trade is an important way for nations to acquire economic and military goods, while aid serves as an instrument for bloc leaders to reward and bolster the economies of bloc members. Hostile interactions are represented in the model as well. A good number of the decision-making rules to be discussed later in this chapter govern the amount and direction of these flows, and further discussion will be postponed until that time. It should be noted here that, unless exogeneously changed, the alliance structure remains constant for the duration of a simulated international system.

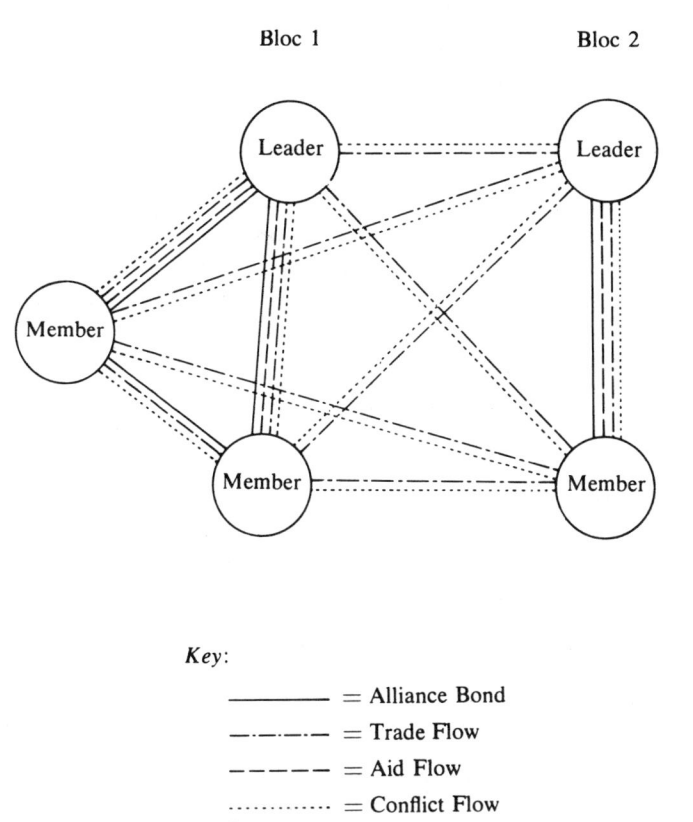

Figure 5.1 The International System

The National Economic System. The national economic system is composed of three sectors of economic activity: consumption, investment, and government. Consumption refers to that sector of economic activity concerned with the production of "final goods" with which "the population replenishes or increases its energies and ministers to its wants and needs" (Heilbroner, 1966: 13) The value produced by this sector will be referred to as consumption satisfaction (CS).

Investment refers to that sector of economic activity concerned with the production of value that has the characteristic of being able to produce more value (Heilbroner, 1966: 14).

For our purposes, the government sector will be equated with that aspect of economic activity concerned with the maintenance of the internal and external security of the system.[3] Other governmental economic activities are considered to be either consumption (such as government transfer payments) or investment (such as subsidies to industries). The value produced by activity in this sector has the characteristic of being capable of destroying other value. This will be called force capability (FC).

Value production occurs when resources are allocated to an economic sector. These resources, the factors of production, are represented in the model by a unidimensional measure of resource capability, total basic capability (TBC). Allocation to the investment sector increases the resource capability of the national system in the future; hence, total basic capability may be thought of as the accumulated past basic capability (BC) production.

The value produced by an allocation of TBC to an economic sector depends upon the size of that allocation and the efficiency of the economic sector. Each sector has associated with it a generation rate that states the output of the sector given a unit input of TBC. For example, the CS sector may have a generation rate of 1.4 for a particular nation, in which case an allocation of 100 TBC units will produce 140 units of CS value. Each nation has a set of three generation (GR) rates (CSGR, BCGR, FCGR) that may be considered analogous to what the economists call opportunity costs, and these rates will differ from nation to nation in response to their level of development and degree of specialization.

There is a second kind of value accumulation that occurs in the economic system. FC value accumulates in such a way that at least part of the value produced in the present time period will be available for use in a future time period. Accumulated force capability is called total force capability (TFC), and the level of this variable determines the amount of force capability that can be used in defense of the nation at any time.

These two value reservoirs, TBC and TFC, are assumed to depreciate, and, to maintain constant levels, allocations to the investment and defense sectors are necessary. The rate of depreciation for TBC (DBC) is either 2 percent, 5 percent, or 10 percent, depending upon a stochastic determination in which each rate is given an equal probability of being used. The rate of depreciation for TFC (DFC) is also 2 percent, 5 percent, or 10 percent, depending upon a stochastic determination as discussed above.

We can now establish some basic relationships in equation form.[4] The amount of CS value produced in a particular time period is

$$CS = CSP \times TBC \times CSGR,$$

where CSP is the proportion of national resources allocated to consumption. Similarly, the BC value produced in one time period is

$$BC = BCP \times TBC \times BCGR$$

and the FC value produced is

$$FC = FCP \times TBC \times FCGR.$$

CS value is completely consumed in a period of time, but BC and FC value accumulate in the following ways:

$$TBC_{t+1} = TBC_t + BC_t - (DBC_t \times TBC_t)$$
$$TFC_{t+1} = TFC_t + FC_t - (DFC_t \times TFC_t)$$

DBC and DFC are the selected depreciation rates discussed earlier. That is, the levels of basic capability and force capability at the next time point are simply the present level plus the current production, minus depreciation.

The allocation of resources to consumption, investment, and defense and the setting of values for CSP, BCP, and FCP, constitute major decisions which have far-ranging political consequences for the simulated national systems, and it is to the nature of these consequences that we now turn our attention.

The National Political System. In the previous section, we discussed a set of decisions concerned with the allocation of resources to the production of value. This set of decisions involves the authoritative allocation of value, which, according to Easton (1965a), is the domain of the political system. The making of decisions necessarily entails the existence of a set of decision-makers, and in this context the term "decision-makers" may be thought of as parallel to the concept of elite. Whether we consider them the "influential," as Lasswell does (1965: 4-6), or the "active population," as Rashevsky does (1947: 146-149), "by an 'elite' we mean a very small (usually less than .5 percent) minority of people who have very much more of at least one of the basic values than have the rest of the population" (Deutsch, 1968: 63). In an Eastonian sense, our "decision-makers" are the authoritative allocators of the system.

In the previous section, we specified that economic activity in the consumption sector produced value that was consumed by the "population." These consumers, which, in conformity with the INS model, we shall call validators, may be thought of as the masses or nonelite. We need not be concerned at this level of abstraction with the question of who *is* and who *is not* a member of the elite and, therefore, a part of the decision-making unit. We need only postulate that the population of a nation can be divided up for analytical purposes into those who have more, and those who have less, control over the behavior of the nation.

We begin our discussion of the programmed relationships between the decision-makers and validators with a consideration of the demands the validators make upon the decision-makers. The demands fall into two areas: (1) The validators expect a certain flow of CS value into their hands. (2) The validators expect a certain level of national security. The specification of these demand functions follows the formulations used in the INS (Guetzkow, 1981b).

With regard to the first demand, let us assume the existence of a minimum level of CS value flow below which the nation cannot fall without ceasing to exist. This may be thought of as the subsistence level or simply the maximum deprivation that the validators will endure. We will call this variable CSmin, and it is a function of the CS value production potential of the nation (CSmax). CSmax is, in turn, a function of the value productive resources of the nation, TBC, and the productivity of the consumption sector, CSGR (Guetzkow, 1981b):

$$CSmax = TBC \times CSGR$$

Thus, CSmax is the amount of consumption goods that would be produced if all of a nation's resources were allocated to that purpose.

The minimum CS value flow (CSmin) is defined as[5]

$$CSmin = a_1 \times CSmax.$$

Since a_1 is assigned a proportion ranging from .6 to .9 based on a nation's size, the effect of this equation is to stipulate that when the maximum possible consumption production is rather small, the minimum fraction of national resources which must be allocated to consumption will be large. Thus, larger and more developed nations must devote proportionately less to meeting the minimum demands of their population than smaller and less developed nations. CSmax and CSmin represent the maximum and minimum demands of the validators with respect to CS value flow.

The validators give support to the decision-makers in response to the level of CS value flow at any point in time as related to this minimum and maximum. This support is manifested in the variable of validator satisfaction with respect to consumption satisfaction (VScs). VScs is dependent on two factors: (1) For consumption near minimum consumption standards, validator satisfaction depends on the relation of consumption satisfaction to minimum consumption levels. (2) Once minimum consumption standards have been met, larger increases in consumption are necessary to produce corresponding changes in validator satisfaction [Guetzkow, 1981b].

The mathematical formulation of these two factors is as follows:[6]

$$VScs = a_2 \times \log_e \left[\frac{CS}{CSmin} + 1 \right] + a_3$$

The constant a_3 assures that BScs will be 1 when the production of CS value is at the minimum level. As the ratio of CS production to CSmin increases, CSmin increases. The constant a_2 rescales VScs to range from 0 to 10, and the natural logarithm produces a "saturation" curve of decreasing marginal gain per additional CS expenditure. Nations reach the upper boundary for CScs (10) when CS production is four times the minimum level of consumption satisfaction. In an aggregate sense, then, the support the validators give to the decision-makers is partially a function of the level of the CS value flow, the value productive resources of the nation, and the efficiency of the mechanisms that produce the CS value.

The second area of validator demands is national security. Here we postulate that the validators expect a distribution of world FC favorable to their national security, as well as a favorable distribution of potential force capability. The support the validators give to the decision-makers in response to the satisfaction of this demand is called validator satisfaction with respect to national security (VSns). However, in determining the distribution of world force capability, the validators do not perceive internal coercive forces as factors in their decision. Since TFC includes forces for the control of external and internal systemic threat, we want to remove the force capability devoted to internal control (FCic) from the support equation. That equation is:[7]

$$VSns = a_5 \left[\frac{\sum_{\text{self + allies}} (TFC - FCic + a_6 TBC)}{\sum_{\text{non allies}} (TFC - FCic + a_6 TBC)} \right] + a_7$$

The minimum value of VSns is 1.0, and the maximum is 10.0. A VSns of less than 1.0 indicates that the nation should be considered "disengaged from the armaments race" (Guetzkow, 1981b), and a favorable balance of forces ceases to be a demand for the validators. In this case, support is solely dependent on consumption flow.

The aggregate support for the decision-makers, called VSm, is a weighted average of the two support factors discussed above (Guetzkow, 1981b):

$$VSm = a_8 \, VScs + a_9 \, VSns$$

It is clear that political systems differ in the degree to which decision-makers are dependent upon validator support for their continuation as decision-makers. The power to disregard the wishes of the validators is called decision latitude (DL; see Guetzkow, 1981b). Political systems with low decision latitude may be considered open (Rosenau, 1966: 27-92), flexible (Wright, 1955: 543-553), nondirective (Kaplan, 1957: 55-56), or accessible (Gregg and Banks, 1965: 602-614). In any event, this may be considered a structural variable that mediates the relationship between the decision-makers and validators.

DL is not necessarily constant. It is assumed that the validators will periodically seek to change the political system by making it more responsive to their wishes or demanding more leadership from the decision-makers. In the model, a unit increment in DL, a unit decrement in DL, and no change in DL are equally likely outcomes of a stochastic decision process in any given period of time. The variable DDL introduces random shocks into the relationship between the decision-makers and validators, to which the nation must adapt.[8]

Returning now to the question of the relationship between the degree to which the validators are satisfied and the stability of the political system, we assume, as INS does, that (Guetzkow, 1981b)

$$pOH = a_{10} + a_{11} \, VSm - a_{12} \, VSmDL + a_{13} \, DL;$$

pOH, as it is used here, is a measure of the stability of the system as suggested by Elder and Pendley (1981b).

We see, then, that as validator support goes up, stability also increases, and as decision latitude rises, stability increases. The middle term, however, specifies that when the political system is more democratic (low DL), each unit increase in VSm brings a greater increase in stability than when the system is more authoritarian (high DL). The rationale is that an authoritarian nation whose stability rests primarily on oppression, gains relatively little additional stability from increased validator satisfaction, while the opposite is true for more democratic nations.

It will be recalled that in the VSns formulation there was a term, FCic, or force capability, devoted to internal control. The role of coercive forces in relation to the control of internal threats to the political system is well established (Gurr, 1970), and it is assumed that the decision-makers will allot some proportion of their total force capability to the performance of this function. The importance of this force will become clear when we consider another way in which the validators may manifest their support, or lack of support, for the decision-makers.

Revolutions may occur in the simulated nations, and their occurrence is dependent on four factors. If the overall validator satisfaction (VSm) is above a revolution threshold, a_{14}, revolution is not considered possible. If this threshold value is not reached, then the probability of revolution is dependent upon the nature of the political system and the level of coercive forces, in the following manner (Guetzkow, 1981b):

$$PR = a_{15}DL - a_{16}\left[\frac{FCic}{TFC}\right] + a_{17}$$

According to this equation, the more authoritarian the regime, the greater the probability of a revolution, *unless* this tendency is offset by the maintenance of a relatively large internal security force.

The final decision as to whether or not a revolution occurs depends upon a stochastic decision process. Should a revolution occur, however, there are substantial costs to the national system. All FC devoted to internal Control (FCic) is considered lost in defense of the system. Furthermore, there are substantial losses in the productive capacity of the system: 20 percent of the nation's TBC is assumed lost in the event of a revolution. On the other hand, there are benefits to be gained from a revolution in the form of momentary increases in the overall validator satisfaction. In the period following the revolution, a two-unit increase in VSm is credited and a one-unit bonus is given in the period after that (Guetzkow, 1981b).

It should be clear by now that we have described a set of conceptual variables, which we may use to define the predecisional and postdecisional states of a simulated nation, and a set of relationships that determine the transformation of the system given the outcome of the decisional stage. It is to this stage that we now turn our attention.

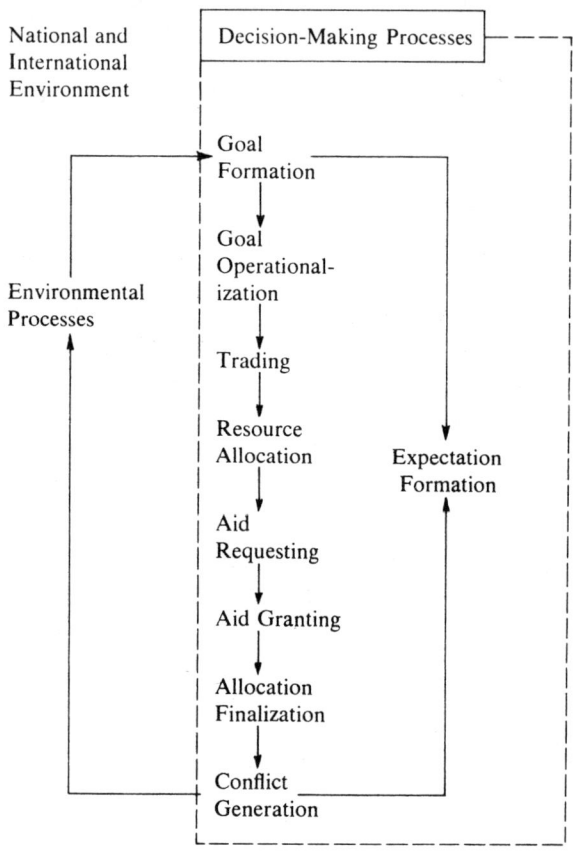

Figure 5.2 Decision-Making Sequence

THE DECISION-MAKING PROCESSES

Having specified the national and international environment of the decision-making units, we can attend to the decision-making and information-processing rules that govern the behavior of the national actor. These rules can be viewed as a substitute for the human participants found in the INS model, and they consist of nine basic processes, which are diagrammatically presented in Figure 5.2. Tracing through this diagram, we can see the sequence of operations that a simulated decision-making unit undertakes in the course of one unit of time. After assessing the environment, the decision-making unit first sets its general goals for the current period (goal formation), and then proceeds to identify the specific things that should be done if these goals are to be attained (goal operationalization). The next four processes (trading, resource allocation, aid-requesting, and aid-granting) are used in an attempt to meet these specific needs by utilizing international and national resources. After all these alternatives have been explored, a final set of decisions concerning resource allocation is made (allocation finalization) and expressions of hostility are transmitted to other members of the international system (conflict generation). The set of decisions made in such a way modifies the decision environment according to the formulations discussed in the previous section. The remaining process (expectation formation) is used for making predictions about the future behavior of other states. These predictions are used in the goal formation and conflict generation processes. In the remaining part of this chapter, we will examine each of these nine processes in detail.

Goal Formation. Nations are open, complex, adaptive systems and, as such, their behavior is purposive. Their behavior is intended to reduce the perceived discrepancy between the present state of the nation and some desired future state of the nation. We are concerned here with the national definition of that desirable future state.

Defining completely the state of a complex system, be it present or future, would require an extraordinarily large number of dimensions. Theory and prudence tell us, however, that it is essential for us to carefully select a subset of these dimensions for scrutiny.

The first goal area to be so isolated is political stability. Decision-making elites have, as a major goal of their behavior, the retention of their decision making positions. The elites will endeavor to use the resources of the political and economic systems at their command to make their positions of command secure. This can, of course, have far-ranging consequences. As North (1962: 198) pointed out, "during the summer of 1914 ... the Austro-Hungarian leadership, feeling threatened by the spectre of Pan-Slavism, put forward the preservation of the dual Monarchy at all costs as their major policy goal."

The second goal area that will guide the behavior of the decision-making elite of a nation is economic growth. The expansion of national productive capability has been, particularly in this century, a major objective. Organski (1958: 57) has stated, "Wealth is [a] goal that is sought to some extent by every nation."

The third end toward which national behavior is directed is national security. By this, we mean that nations act to further the continuation of their existence in the face of real or imagined external threats: "Each political unit aspires to survive. Leaders and led are integrated in and eager to maintain the collectivity they constitute together by virtue of history, race or fortune" (Aron, 1967: 72) Political stability, economic growth, and national security by no means constitute an exclusive set of national objectives; they are, however, universal among nations and clearly prominent in the literature of international relations.

Our task of specifying the goals that guide nations is far from complete, however, for as Singer (1961: 86) has stated, "goals and motivations are both dependent and independent variables, and if we intend to explain a nation's foreign policy, we cannot settle for the mere postulation of these goals. We are compelled to go back a step and inquire into their genesis and the process by which they become the crucial variables that they seem to be in the behavior of nations." In specifying the process by which goals are set and reset, we have relied heavily on the work of Cyert and March (1963: 26-43). Their formulation of goal determination in a business firm suggests a pattern for such behavior in all complex organizations, including nation-states.

Organizations set levels of aspiration in areas of meaningful achievement, and in the short run seek to attain these levels. In the long run, however, these aspiration levels themselves are subject to change. The result of this process is a dynamic homeostatic equilibrium of aspiration and achievement. In what follows, we will show how this formulation is applied in the political stability and economic growth goal areas.

The Goal of Political Stability. We have posited that decision-makers act to make their positions secure. The degree of security they seek at any given time, we will call the nation's aspiration level of political stability (ALPOH). The current value of the aspiration level for political stability is dependent upon three factors: (1) the past aspiration level for political stability; (2) the degree to which the past aspiration was achieved; (3) the achievement of a significant other nation with regard to political stability relative to one's own achievement. The way in which these three factors enter into the setting of the aspiration level for political stability (ALPOH) is outlined in Figure 5.3. Initially, the aspiration level for this period is set equal to a predetermined proportion, b_1, of last period's level. If b_1 is greater than 1.0, then the present aspiration level will be higher than the past aspiration level unless subsequently altered; if b_1 is less than 1.0, the opposite holds true. The value of b_1 represents the teleological inertia of the system with respect to the goal of political stability. Since goals change slowly and incrementally, this coefficient indicates the influence of past goals upon present goals.

The second step in this decision process represents an adaptive or learning component. It is a simple feedback loop with b_2 and b_3 being the rates of adaptation. Both coefficients are positive; hence overachievement leads to a higher aspiration level and underachievement leads to a lower

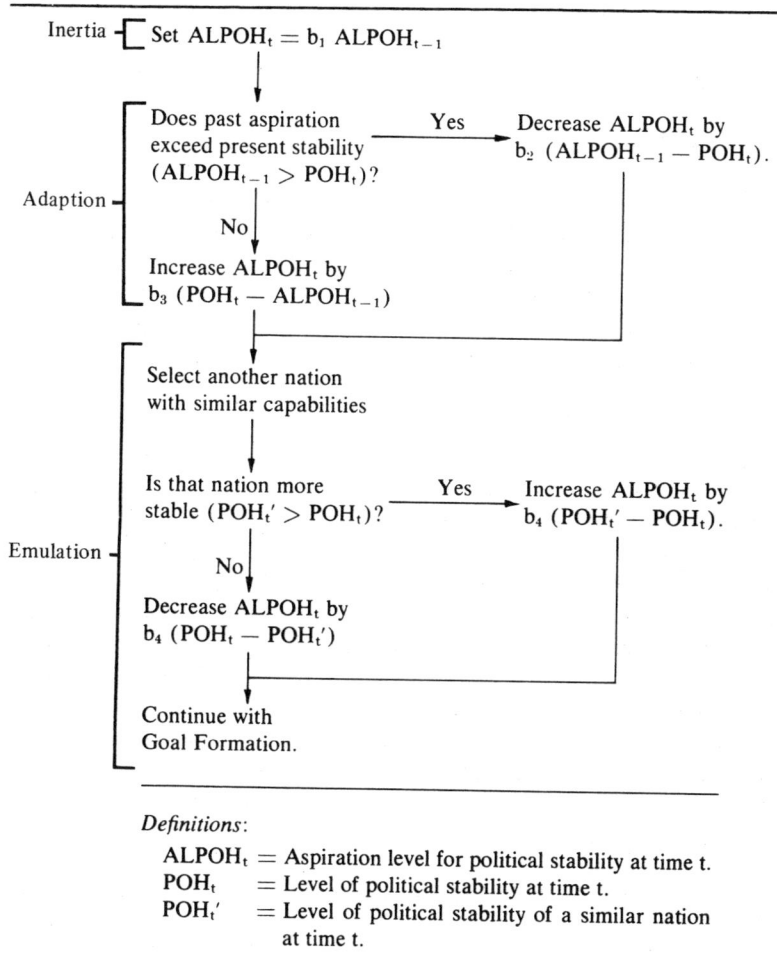

Figure 5.3 Goal Formation (political stability)

one. The relationship between over- and underachievement is not symmetrical, however.

We will assume that nations (given encouragement) will more readily raise their aspiration levels and more reluctantly lower them when failure is encountered. Hence, b_2, the amount that the aspiration level for political stability will be decreased (given failure to achieve the aspiration level set in the previous period), is less than b_3.

The third consideration in setting this aspiration level centers on the relative achievement of other nations in this goal area. That is, it is assumed that the achievement of significant other nations with regard to political stability in relation to one's own achievement will condition the aspiration level. The coefficient b_4 may be considered the propensity to emulate. Since its value is assumed to be greater than zero, the aspiration level of a nation will be increased by the attainment of a higher level of political stability by another nation that is deemed to be significant.

The significant other nation is chosen on the basis of similarity of resource capability and level of development. The nation most similar to the self nation on these factors will be selected for comparison.

The Goal of Economic Growth. The aspiration level for economic growth (ALGRO) is assumed to operate in the same manner as the aspiration level for political stability. The steps involved in setting this aspiration level are outlined in Figure 5.4. The coefficients b_5 through b_8 correspond to the coefficients b_1 through b_4. The first, b_5, specifies the propensity to raise or lower the aspiration level for economic growth, regardless of what has happened internally or externally in the immediate past. The next two parameters, b_6 and b_7, govern the degree to which success or failure in fulfilling previous aspirations modifies present aspirations. Once again, we assume that b_6 is less than b_7; hence, success fosters a greater amount of increase in the aspiration level than failure engenders in the opposite direction. The last parameter, b_8, determines the degree to which the achievement of other nations in the area of economic growth causes a nation to increase or decrease its own aspirations in this area.

The Goal of National Security. As we indicated earlier, nations are assumed to be grouped into alliances, and the model, as it presently stands, does not allow for the position of nonalignment. Furthermore, the international system is bipolar in nature, with a major power functioning as the leader or dominant member in each bloc. The perspectives of bloc leaders and bloc members are sufficiently different that their behavior in regard to national security questions deserves separate treatment.

However, there are some common elements in their decision processes. National security is identified with the ability to successfully counter the use of coercion by other nations. Hence, when we speak of the aspiration level for national security (for both bloc leaders and bloc members), we will be referring to the level of defense that is considered adequate for countering external threat.

Since national goal-setting behavior is anticipatory in nature, we have modified Singer's (1958: 90-105) threat equation (threat = intent × capability). That is, the national desire is for an ability to counter not simply *present* threat, but also *future* threat. Accordingly, our formulation equates expected threat to the product of expected intent and expected capability. In a later section, we will discuss specifically how these expec-

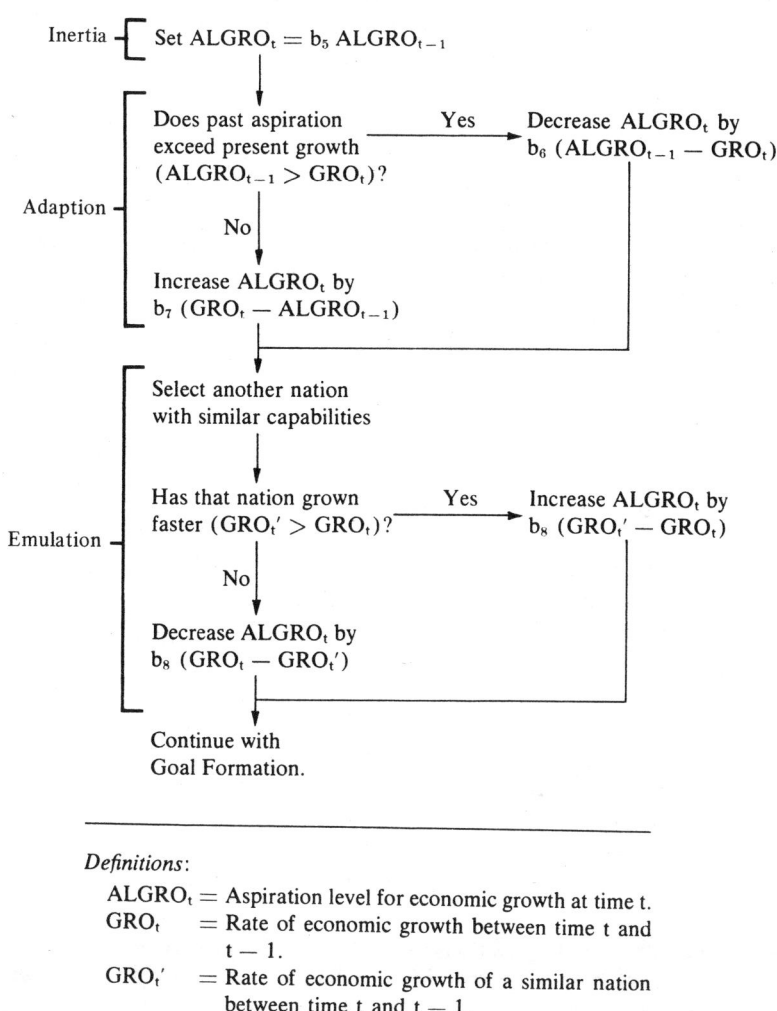

Figure 5.4 Goal Formation (economic growth)

tations are arrived at in the model, when we examine the expectation formation process.

When a nation scans its environment for possible threats to its security, the search pattern must be selective. The limitations of time and resources prevent the nation from treating all nations as potentially equally threatening. In the present model, a simulated nation assumes that those nations in the international system with which it has not entered into mutual security agreements are potentially threatening. The alliance structure serves as a guide in simplifying the search for enemies.

The Bloc Leader. When the leader of an alliance bloc ponders the question of national security, the nation perceives the question in terms of bloc security. As the leader of a bloc, the nation takes upon itself the duty of evaluating the security position of its alliance vis-à-vis an opposing alliance. Leadership confers larger responsibilities than does membership, and the security interests of the leader become intertwined with those of the group. Accordingly, the goal of national security merges with the goal of bloc security.

The gap that the alliance leader watches closely, then, is the difference between the amount of threat expected from the opposing bloc and the amount of threat-countering ability that its own bloc will have in the future.[9] If the bloc's counter-threat capability is adequate, then the alliance leader will be content with current defense commitments and those of its allies. If, on the other hand, the counter-threat capability is not judged adequate, then a revision of alliance security policy will be sought.

Figure 5.5 outlines the decision processes that the bloc leader executes in setting its own aspiration level for national security and deciding what defense allocation its allies should make. As mentioned above, nations are sensitive to expected threat, and expected threat is equal to the product of expected intent and expected capability. One of the differences between bloc leaders and bloc members is their estimate of expected intentions. Intent in the threat calculation is considered to be the probability that a given nation's force capability will be used against one's own nation. Hence, the upper bound of intent is 1.0, and the lower bound is 0.0.

The first step in the decision process incorporates the assumption that, in the case of alliance leaders, expected intent is always at the maximum value of 1.0. There are several reasons for this. It is assumed that the special responsibilities of leadership make a nation more cautious in its security calculations, and therefore the nation will, in all likelihood, wish to be able to counter the worst of all possible situations. It can do so, in part, because of its larger resource base and the associated consequence of being able to work with such a pessimistic view without being overwhelmed. And, of course, there is some realism contained in the special paranoia of bloc leaders as their prominence and centrality in the international system make them primary targets for other nations.

The next two steps in Figure 5.5 involve computing the amount of threat that the opposing alliance is likely to present in the next time

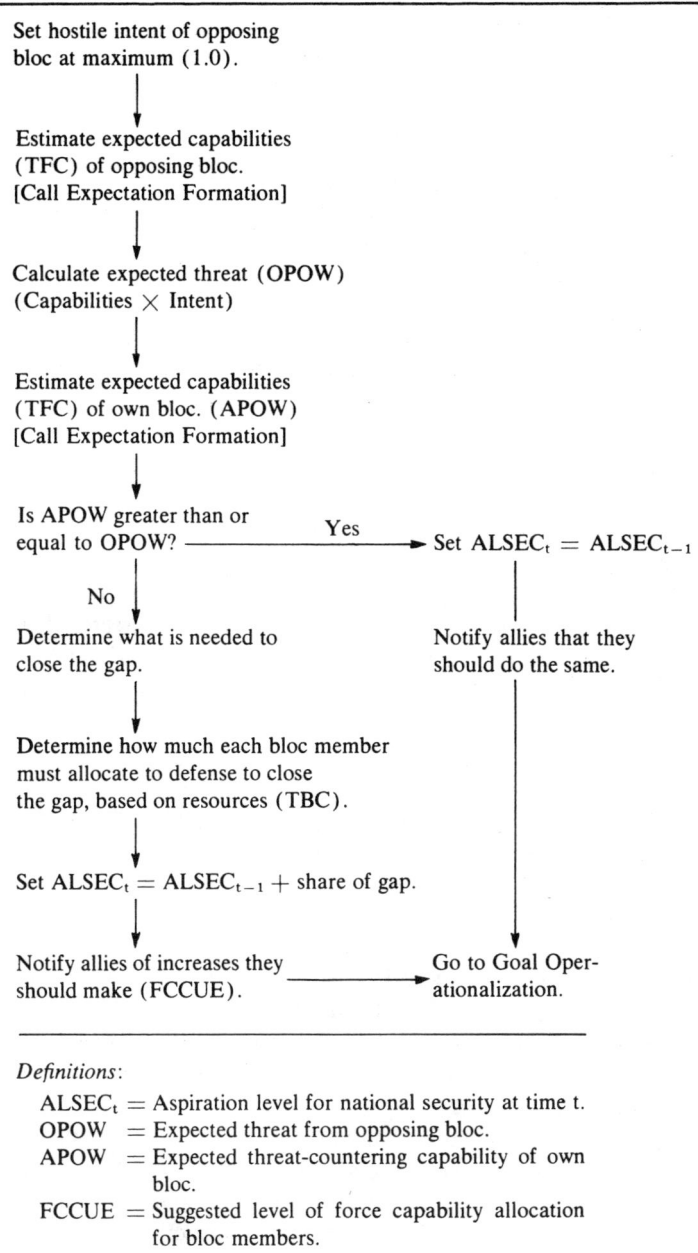

Figure 5.5 Goal Formation (national security, bloc leader)

period (OPOW). Since intent has been set at 1.0, the calculation reduces to this:

$$\text{OPOW} = \sum_{}^{\substack{\text{non} \\ \text{allies}}} \text{TFC}_{t+1}$$

The expected value of TFC_{t+1} is given by the application of one of the information-processing rules to data concerning a nation's past behavior with regard to total force capability levels, and is described in a later section.

The next step is simply to estimate the amount of counter-threat capability (APOW) of the leader's own alliance; this is calculated according to the following formula:

$$\text{APOW} = \sum_{}^{\substack{\text{self}+ \\ \text{allies}}} \text{TFC}_{t+1}$$

With these estimates of the future threat capabilities of both blocs in hand, the bloc leader is ready to decide whether a change in its aspiration level for national security is necessary If APOW is greater than OPOW, then the leader's aspiration level for national security (ALSEC) will remain unchanged. If This relationship does not hold, then a series of steps is undertaken to formulate a defense policy for the alliance that will close the gap.

The leader first considers the amount by which the alliance, as a whole, must increase its military strength to counter the expected threat. The leader then computes the share of the increase that each ally should contribute, based on its respective resource capability. The leader then modifies the aspiration level for national security in accordance with what is considered to be its fair share of the additional defense burden. In addition, the leader transmits cues (FCCUE) to its allies, suggesting to them an appropriate level of defense allocation. This completes the determination of the aspiration level for national security for a bloc leader.

The Bloc Member. Turning to Figure 5.6, we see that the bloc member (like the bloc leader) reacts to the expectation of threat. For the most part, however, the member cannot afford to assume the worst, and is not so much concerned about the security of the bloc as its own security. These and other factors compel the alliance member to be more discriminating in an assessment of threat. To do so, the alliance member examines the verbal conflict behavior, hostile communication (HOST), of each nonallied nation in order to make estimates concerning the future inten-

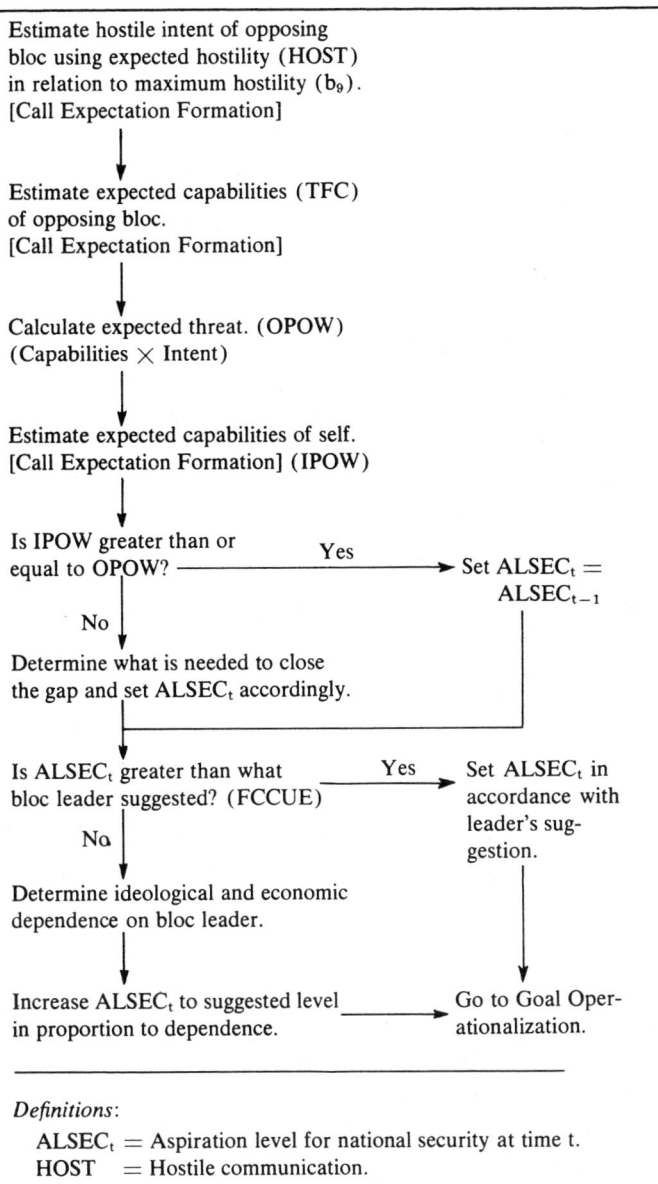

Figure 5.6 Goal Formation (national security, bloc member)

tions of these nations. The following formula summarizes the first three steps in Figure 5.6:

$$\text{OPOW} = \sum_{}^{\text{non allies}} b_9 \times \text{HOST}_{jt+1} \times \text{TFC}_{jt+1},$$

where TFC has the same meaning as above, and HOST_{jt+1} is the amount of verbal hostility the nation expects to receive from nation j in the next time period. The coefficient b_9 is a parameter that indicates the propensity to discount verbal statements when estimating intentions.

The fourth step in the decision process entails the use of the expectation formation process to predict the level of armaments the bloc member can expect to have available in the next period (IPOW). After this determination, the member nation compares expected threat (OPOW) to its own expected threat-countering capability (IPOW). If the comparison is favorable for the bloc member, then the aspiration level for national security is tentatively assigned the same value it had in the previous period. If, on the other hand, IPOW is less than OPOW, the aspiration level is raised by an amount sufficient to close the expected gap.

The bloc member now has a tentative aspiration level for national security, but it also has received a cue (FCCUE) from its bloc leader suggesting a certain level of armaments that would be appropriate according to the leader's assessment of the world situation. The last steps in Figure 5.6 deal with reconciling these views and setting a final ALSEC. If the leader's estimate (FCCUE) is less than or equal to the member's own estimate (ALSEC), then the member acquiesces and accepts the leader's policy. If, on the other hand, the bloc leader's estimate is more pessimistic than the member's, and the leader's estimate is greater than the member's, a negotiation process is begun, and the outcome is determined in the following way.

The outcome of the negotiation process is dependent upon the amount of power the leader exercises over the member at the time of the negotiation. Etzioni (1965) identified three basic types of power in his discussion of political integration. These are utilitarian or economic power, identive or ideological power, and coercive or military power. Working with this power typology, Denis Forcese (1968) found that only the first two of these were effective in coordinating the behavior of alliance leaders and members. Forcese's findings were based largely on data generated by the INS model. We have made the outcome of the bargaining process dependent upon the amount of utilitarian and identive power that the leader exercises over the member.

Utilitarian power is likely to be most effective when the bloc member is highly economically dependent upon the leader (EDEP) by virtue of past trade and aid flows. This latter condition varies from 0 to 1.0 and is computed in the following way:

$$EDEP = \frac{\sum_{\text{past mt periods}} (TRADE_1 + AID_1)}{\sum_{\text{past mt periods}} \sum_{\text{all nations}} (TRADE + AID)}$$

The numerator in this equation indicates how much trade and aid the bloc member has received from its bloc leader (nation 1) in the past, and the denominator is the total amount of trade and aid it has received from all nations during the same period. Thus, economic dependency reflects the degree to which the bloc member's economic transactions with the outside world have been dominated by its bloc leader.

Identive power reflects a kind of moral suasion that an alliance leader can exert by the manipulation of symbolic rewards. We postulate first that the greater the ideological difference between leader and member, the less identive power the leader will be able to exercise over the member. Since we are again looking at the situation from the bloc member's point of view, we are interested in measuring ideological dependency (IDEP). The preliminary formulation states:

$$IDEP = 1 - \frac{|DL_i - DL_1|}{DL_i + DL_1}$$

where IDEP varies from 0 to 1.0, and 1 is member i's bloc leader. The numerator of the term on the righthand side of the equation measures the absolute difference in decision latitudes of the member and leader. The denominator normalizes this difference so that the value will be between 0 and 1.0. The result is that IDEP will be at its maximum when the member's DL is the same as its leader's, and it is at its minimum when they are on opposite ends of the decision latitude continuum. Thus, the further apart the member and leader are ideologically, the less dependency.

Identive power will be maximally effective and identive dependency will be higher when the world is ideologically heterogeneous and less effective when ideological differences are slight. Consequently, IDEP is modified by a term that takes into account the between-nation variance in decision latitude. This variance is greatest when one-half of the nations are on each end of the DL continuum, and smallest when they all have the same DL. Hence, the standard deviation of the distribution of DL values among the nations in the international system is normalized by the maximum value it may attain with a given system size.

The complete equation for IDEP is

$$\text{IDEP} = \left[1 - \frac{DL_i - DL_1}{DL_i + DL_1}\right] \times \frac{\sigma_{dl}}{\text{Max } \sigma_{dl}}$$

In general, then, when the leader and member are quite *similar* ideologically, as reflected in their DL values in a world that is characterized by high ideological diversity, the bloc leader will be able to greatly influence the member's behavior by the manipulation of symbols. If they are considerably *different* ideologically and the world is relatively homogeneous, then this type of influence is not likely to be as effective.

The compromise forged between the bloc leader and member, if only tacitly, is based upon the average of EDEP and IDEP in the following manner:

$$\text{ALSEC} = \text{ALSEC} + (\text{FCCUE} - \text{ALSEC}) \times \left(\frac{\text{EDEP} + \text{IDEP}}{2}\right)$$

Consequently, if a bloc leader has absolute power over a member (EDEP and IDEP equal to 1.0), that member would raise its own estimate of security needs, ALSEC, to the level, FCCUE, suggested by its leader. Proportionately less power means proportionately less increase, and if the bloc leader has no power over the member (EDEP and IDEP equal to 0), then the bloc member would totally disregard the leader's wishes.

At this point we have completed the setting of aspiration levels for the simulated nations. We now turn to the consideration of how these aspiration levels are to be attained.

Goal Operationalization. At this stage, each nation has a set of aspiration levels it wishes to attain. The next thing the simulated nation does is to operationalize these goals in terms of laying out a tentative resource allocation budget, and the steps in this procedure are outlined in Figure 5.7. The first steps involve making preliminary estimates as to what

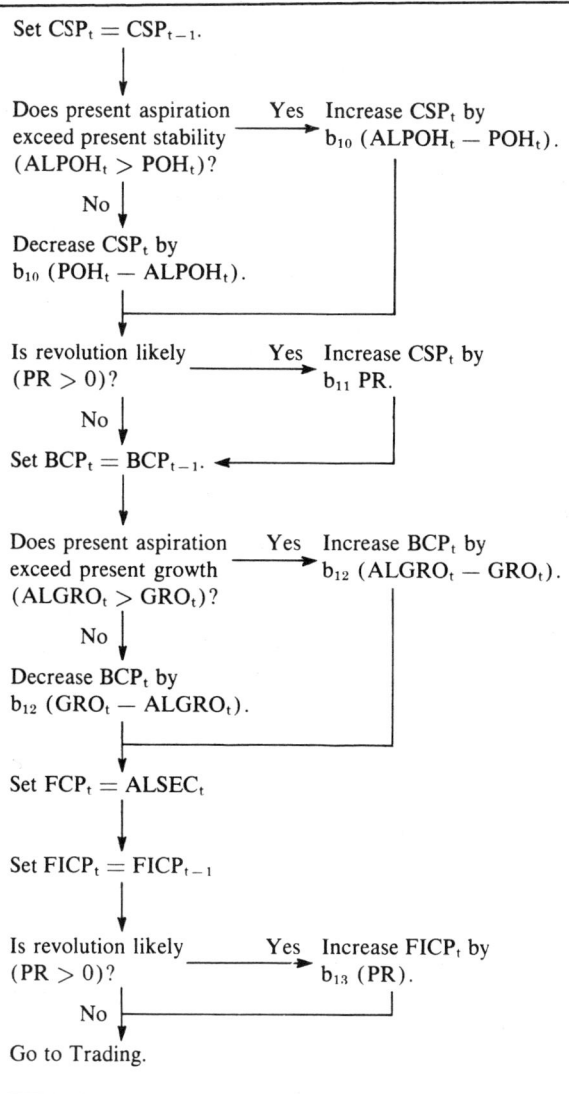

Figure 5.7 Goal Operationalization

Definitions:
CSP_t, BCP_t, FCP_t = Proportion of resources allocated to consumption, investment, and defense sectors, respectively.
$FICP_t$ = Proportion of force capability devoted to internal security.

proportion of its resources will have to go to consumer goods (CSP) to achieve its aspiration level for political stability (ALPOH). In equation form, the procedure looks like this:

$$CSP_t = CSP_{t-1} + b_{10} (ALPOH_t - POH_t) \times CSP_{t-1} + b_{11} PR_t$$

The first term embodies the idea that such decisions are incremental in nature, and the second states that the amount of revision is related to the degree that goal achievement has failed in the past. The third term causes the system to react when political stability is threatened by crisis. Parameter b_{10} is the goal operationalization rate, and b_{11} represents the propensity of the regime to react to crisis of support by acceding to the validator's wishes with an emergency CS allocation.

The proportion of resources needed to achieve the growth aspiration level (ALGRO) is the next concern of the simulated nation. The proportion (BCP) is determined in the following way:

$$BCP_t = BCP_{t-1} + b_{12} (ALGRO_t - GRO_t) BCP_{t-1}$$

GRO_t is the proportionate change in total basic capability from time $t-1$ to the present time t. As in the case of the consumption allocation decision, the past allocation for capital goods is adjusted, based on how successful the nation has been in attaining its growth goal. A higher than desired rate of growth will produce a drop in capital investment, while the opposite condition will cause the proportion of resources devoted to capital goods to increase.

The proportion of resources devoted to national security concerns (FCP) is set equal to the ALSEC level previously established.

$$FCP_t = ALSEC_t$$

The remaining allocation decision involves the establishment of the proportion of current total force capability (TFC) that will be used for internal control (FICP).

$$FICP_t = FICP_{t-1} + b_{13} PR_t$$

The maximum value of FICP is .30, as it is in the INS model. The form of this equation is such that if the probability of a revolution (PR) is zero, then the proportion of forces allocated to internal control does not change. As revolution becomes more likely, then, the internal security forces are increased proportionately. Hence, a threat of revolution prompts the decision-making unit to attempt raising both consumption levels and internal security force levels.

This set of decisions completes the goal operationalization process of a simulated nation. It now has a set of concrete objectives, which, although not necessarily consistent with one another, can serve as a basis for evaluating and selecting specific alternatives.

One major profitable alternative open to the nation is the exchanging of goods with other nations, and it is this process that we will consider next.

Trading. International trade entails certain noneconomic costs, which we will call sovereignty costs. The kinds of costs referred to here have been alluded to by John Maynard Keynes: "Let goods be home-spun wherever it is reasonably and conveniently possible.... We do not wish... to be at the mercy of world forces.... We wish to be our own masters, and to be as free as we can make ourselves from the interferences of the outside world" (Pen, 1966: 93).

Pen concluded, "Nationalism leads to protection, the deliberate choking-off of imports with the intention of reserving the home market for home producers" (1966: 94). Nations accomplish this through import duties, quotas, excise taxes, manipulation of public health and administrative rules, government purchase restrictions, import permits, and, of course, the state trading monopoly.

The process that governs this activity is outlined in Figure 5.8. The simulated nations set import limits for each of the three kinds of goods. These import limits (IMLIM) are a function of the size of the national economy and the particular priority that a specific type of goods has in the tentative allocation mix. The import limit on all imports (TOTIM) is

$$\text{TOTIM} = b_{14}\text{TBC},$$

where b_{14} is the international trade autarchy factor, or propensity to import. This total figure is apportioned among the three types of goods according to the relative magnitude of the sector values produced by the goal operationalization process. Thus, the import limit for a specific good, such as BCs would be

$$\text{IMLIM}_{bc} = \frac{\text{BCP}}{\text{CSP} - \text{CSMF} + \text{BCP} + \text{FCP}} \times \text{TOTIM},$$

where CSMF is the proportion of national resources that must be allocated to the consumption sector to satisfy the CSmin requirement. Hence, if CSP, BCP, and FCP were .86, .10, and .04 respectively, and the fraction of

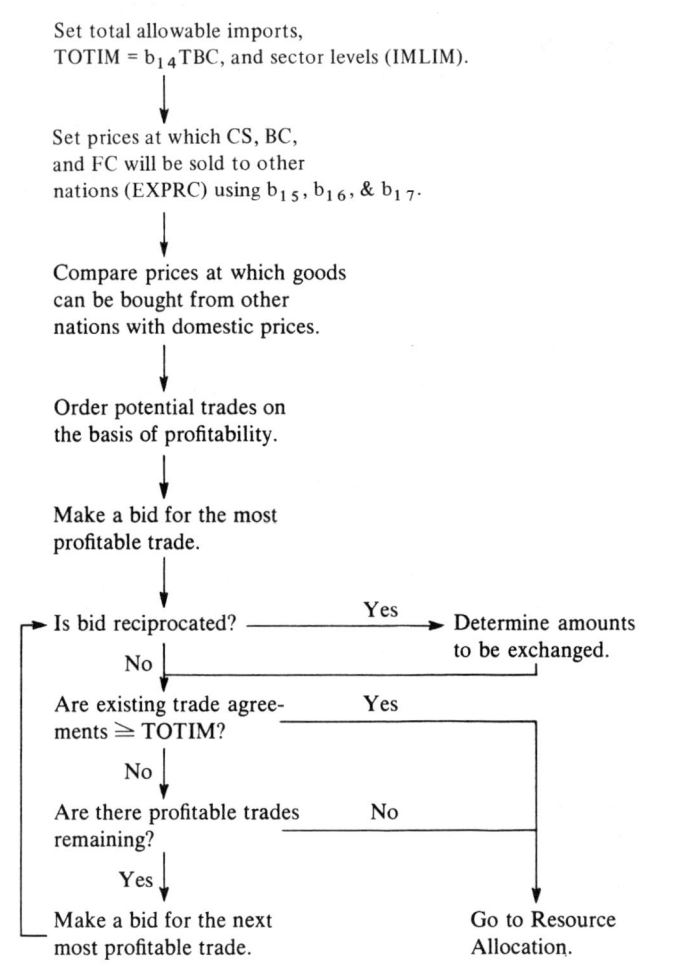

Figure 5.8 Trading

resources that must go to consumption, CSMF, is .8, then the CS, BC, and FC shares of the total imports would be 30 percent, 50 percent, and 20 percent respectively.

In addition to deciding in the preliminary trading stage how many foreign goods will be allowed to enter the nation, the nation must also decide the prices at which it is willing to sell its goods to other nations. The national set of export prices (EXPRC) is a function of a series of factors.

The basic unbiased price, or what might be considered the equal profit price, is given by the following rather formidable formula:

$$EXPRC_{ijkl} = \frac{GR_{jl} \times GR_{il} \times (GR_{ik} + GR_{jk})}{GR_{ik} \times GR_{jk} \times (GR_{il} + GR_{jl})}$$

This formula states the amount of good l that nation i would want from nation j in exchange for one unit of good k. GRi1, GRi2, and GRi3 are nation i's generation rates for CS, BC, and FC goods respectively. The terms of trade given by this formula are such that nations i and j would derive an equal amount of profit by concluding a trade on these terms.

The profit split appears to be a powerful norm in human interaction. Simmel (1950), Durkheim (1957), Homans (1961), and Schelling (1963: 47) are just a few of the authors who have noted its prominence. In referring to the INS trade negotiations, Sherman (1963: 47) commented, "These findings demonstrate the pervasiveness and importance of the 50-50 profit splitting norm for the prediction of the negotiation outcome."

On the other hand, we have reason to suspect that there are factors which produce a departure from the equal profit price. The first one we shall consider is the preference among allies for trading with one another.

If we may define alliances as formal agreements among nations to be responsive to one another, then we may postulate that this general state of responsiveness will lead allies to reduce their export prices to one another. Furthermore, it is reasonable to suggest that allies frequently interact and negotiate on a wide range of matters, and consequently the costs of trading are reduced (Pruitt, 1962: 5-18). By the same reasoning, the cost of trading with nations that are not frequently interacted with, and to which one is not responsive, are higher. Consequently, EXPRC is modified:[10]

$$EXPRC_{ijkl} = EXPRC_{ijkl} - b_{15} (2 \times ALLY_{ij} - 1) \times EXPRC_{ijkl},$$

where $ALLY_{ij}$ equals 1 if i and j are allies, and 0 otherwise. The parameter b_{15} is the alliance preference pricing factor, or, alternately, the price increase (expressed as a proportion) that a nonally receives.

The relative economic strengths of the two nations involved is yet another factor that may affect export prices. There are, of course, two ways this can be manifested. One line of argument states that the terms of trade are such that, in effect, richer nations charge poorer nations more than they charge other richer nations and in this way are able to exploit poorer countries. On the other hand, Sherman (1963: 32) observed in INS trading patterns a "paternalistic attitude toward the smaller under-developed countries" on the part of larger countries. The consequence of this would be that richer nations charge poorer nations less than they charge other richer nations. Both of these factors are embodied in the following modification of EXPRC:

$$\text{EXPRC}_{ijkl} = \text{EXPRC}_{ijkl} + b_{16} \left[\frac{\text{TBC}_j}{\text{TBC}_j + \text{TBC}_i} - \tfrac{1}{2} \right] \times \text{EXPRC}_{ijkl}$$

If b_{16}, the economic strength pricing factor, is greater than zero, then export prices are adjusted according to the ability to pay, and are thus of benefit to poorer nations. If, on the other hand, b_{16} is less than zero, trade prices are biased in favor of the wealthier nations. The fractional term following this parameter assesses the relative size of the national resource bases, as they differ from equality. For example, if a potential trading partner has twice the total basic capability of the price-setting nation, then the price for each good would be increased (or decreased, depending upon the sign of b_{16}) proportionately by one-sixth of the value of b_{16}.

The final factor that enters into pricing decisions is risk, and in international trade, two kinds of risk are involved. The first is the possibility that one nation will fulfill its part of the bargain, while another nation will not. Also, since trade is not a simultaneous exchange, the risk involved requires compensation. The second, more indirect form of risk is that associated with whether or not the goods sold to a nation will enable it to act contrary to the selling nation's interests at some future time. Trading-with-the-enemy legislation is one means by which nations attempt to minimize this latter type of risk. Accordingly, the following formula stipulates an increase in the profit derived from trading with a hostile or distrusted nation to compensate for the increased risk:[11]

$$\text{EXPRC}_{ijkl} = \text{EXPRC}_{ijkl} + b_{17} \frac{\text{HOST}_{ij}}{\sum\limits_{\text{all nations}} \text{HOST}_i} \times \text{EXPRC}_{ijkl}$$

HOST_{ij} represents the hostile feelings that nation i feels for nation j at the present time. If the price-setting nation, i, feels no hostility toward the potential trading partner, j, then no price increase is made. If, on the other hand, all of i's hostility (represented by the denominator in the equation above) is directed at nation j, then the full degree of increase stipulated by b_{17} is made.

This completes the setting of export prices for the simulated nations, and we can return to Figure 5.8 in order to understand the rest of the trading process. The trading process itself begins with each nation computing the foreign and domestic prices for each commodity and preparing a list of profitable trades, rank ordered by profitability. A trade round consists of each nation making a bid to trade a given commodity to a specific nation for another specific commodity. After each nation has bid its most profitable trade, a check is made to see if any trade offers have been reciprocated. If this is not the case, then a new trade round is begun and the nations bid for their next most profitable trade. This is again followed by a reciprocity check, but this check includes bids made in both the first and second rounds. Trade rounds continue until all nations except one have either reached their import limit and/or have no profitable trades yet to bid. When this state is reached, trade ceases.

The reciprocation of bids entails agreement on the terms of trade, and it is only the actual quantities that remain to be determined. These quantities are based on the smaller of the two import limits of the two nations involved, and the trading continues.

Resource Allocation. At this stage in the decision processes, a simulated nation begins to evaluate its overall position with reference to all goal areas. Prior to this point, activity in each goal area was carried on independently from activity in the other goal areas. The problem of goal conflict is considered at this point, and a resolution of any such conflict is sought; Figure 5.9 outlines the steps in this process.

Before this evaluation can take place, however, the nation must adjust its allocation decisions in accordance with any trade commitments that may have been made. This process involves the shifting of resources into sectors where export commitments have been made and away from sectors where import commitments have been received. Consequently, the values for CSP, BCP, and FCP (the tentative proportional allocation decisions) may require some adjustment.

The nation, at this point, considers the possibility that it may have overextended itself. If the sum of CSP, BCP, and FCP is greater than 1, the nation is faced with a deficit and a budget crisis. In the event of this situation, the following processes are activated to resolve the crisis.

First, a new emergency budget is drafted, based on two factors: (1) the size of the commitment that has been made in each sector, as indicated by the tentative proportional allocation decisions; and (2) the national pri-

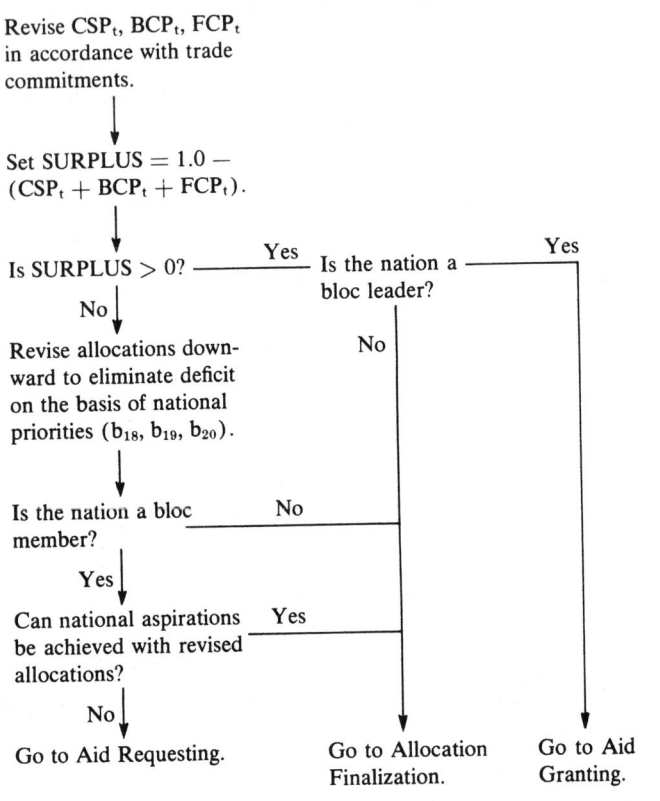

Figure 5.9 Resource Allocation

ority for each sector. This latter set of values, which may be considered budget-crisis-resolution weights, indicates in a critical situation the degree of importance ascribed to each sector. Accordingly, the revised CS allocation would be

$$CSP = \frac{b_{18} CSP}{b_{18} CSP + b_{19} BCP + b_{20} FCP} \times (1 - EXCEPT - CSMF),$$

where b_{18} is the parameter denoting relative priority assigned to the area of political stability. The new values for BCP and FCP are calculated in a way analogous to that for the parameters b_{19} and b_{20}, indicating the relative priorities of economic growth and national security. The multi-

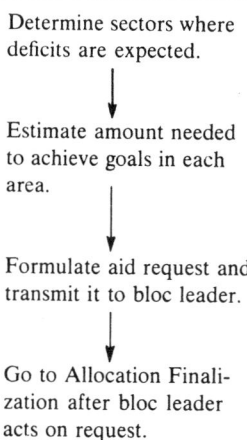

Figure 5.10 Aid-Requesting

plicative term in the equation, subtracting the sectors exempted from reallocation (EXCEPT) and the CS maintenance factor (CSMF), represents the resource base available for budget reallocation. The nation now has a budget that is acceptable, but not necessarily desirable, in terms of its consequences.

Aid-Requesting. The nation may find, for example, that the resulting level of consumption (after adding CS to be imported and subtracting CS to be exported) is far short of its perceived need, if its aspiration level for political stability is to be achieved. It may, under these circumstances, make a request for a grant of CS value from another nation in the international system. The steps in this process are outlined in Figure 5.10.

However, there are some basic rules constraining nations in making aid requests. In the future we may want to relax some of these constraints, but for the moment they are considered necessary simplifications.

The first of these constraints specifies that alliance leaders may not make aid requests, since such requests would compromise their position of authority and undermine their prominence in their alliance. Alliance members, on the other hand, when aid is required, direct requests only to the leader of their alliance. This is a constraint that we reluctantly impose and resolve to relax in the future.

Within these constraints, a nation requests aid of specific commodities to the degree that its prior considerations revealed a discrepancy between the value level needed to achieve a goal and the value level that is expected as a consequence of fulfilling budget decisions.

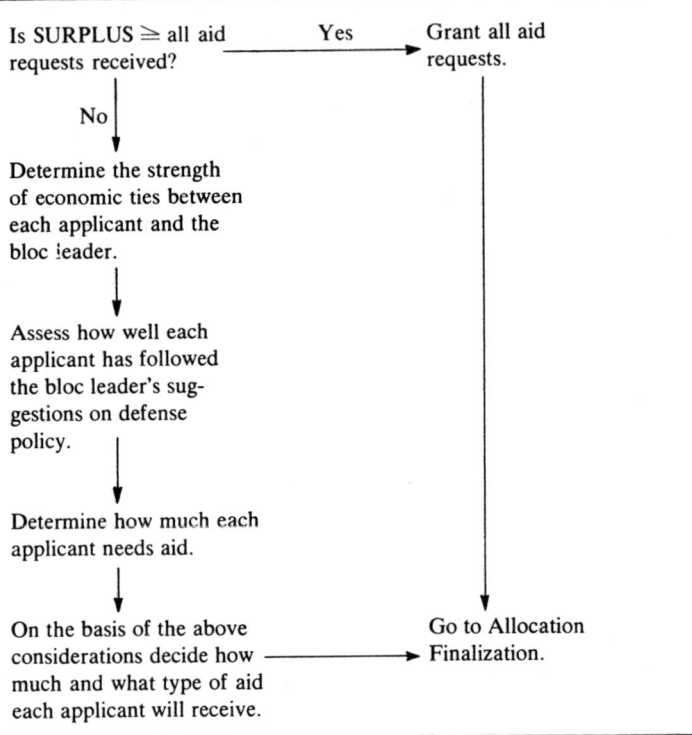

Figure 5.11 Aid-Granting

Aid-Granting. A bloc leader, then, may be confronted with a large number of aid requests, and the rendering of decisions concerning these requests proceeds in the manner outlined in Figure 5.11. There are four factors that exert control over the granting-of-aid decisions. First consideration is given to the leader's economic ability to fulfill the aid requests it has received. If the leader has found that it can meet its aspiration levels and have uncommitted resources remaining, it will consider aid requests; if not, any aid requests it has received will be ignored. On the other hand, if the leader's surplus permits all aid requests to be granted without sacrificing the attainment of its own goals, it will grant all requests.

In the event of a situation in which the leader has a surplus, but this surplus is not adequate to satisfy all the aid requests, the leader must decide how much and to whom aid will be given. There are three criteria that a bloc leader uses to make such decisions.

The bloc leader's first consideration is the degree to which the requesting nation's economy and its own are interdependent. The greater the economic linkages between the two nations, the greater the share of available aid resources the requesting nation will receive. The economic linkage with nation j, $ETIE_j$, is

$$ETIE_j = \frac{\sum_{\text{past mt periods}} TRADE_j}{\sum_{\text{all nations}} \sum_{\text{past mt periods}} TRADE_{jl}}$$

The numerator of this equation indicates the amount of exports that the aid-requesting nation, j, has directed to the bloc leader considering the request, over the past mt periods of time. The denominator yields the aid-requesting nation's total exports to all nations over the same period of time. Thus, $ETIE_j$, which varies from 0 to 1, indicates the degree to which nation j, the aid-requesting nation, has concentrated its trade with its bloc leader.

The bloc leader's second consideration is the degree (reflected in the value of $DTIE_j$) to which the aid-requesting ally has followed previous suggestions concerning defense policy. This value is produced by an algorithm, which has as its essential component, a Pearson product-moment correlation coefficient. The alliance leader's suggested allocation (FCCUE) and the aid requester's final allocation to the defense sector (FCP) are correlated over time, and the resulting coefficient is rescaled in such a way that an r of -1.0 yields a $DTIE_j$ value of 0, and an r of $+1.0$ corresponds to a $DTIE_j$ value of $+1.0$.

Finally, consideration is given to the need of the aid-requesting nation as embodied in its request relative to other nation's requests. Relative need is assessed according to the following formula by relating each nation's request of aid to the total requests that have been received.

$$NEED_j = \frac{AIDREQ_j}{\sum_{\text{allies}} AIDREQ},$$

where AIDREQ is defined as the value of an aid request measured in the number of units of TBC that the leader would need to allocate to meet the request. The total value of aid that the requesting nation, j, receives from its bloc leaders, l, designated $TAID_{lj}$, is as follows:

$$TAID_{lj} = \frac{(NEED_j + ETIE_j + DTIE_j)}{3} \times SURPLUS_l$$

We then can see that need, economic ties, and defense ties are weighted equally in the determination of the share of the bloc leader's available resources (SURPLUS) that each aid-requesting nation receives. The total for each receiving nation is then divided among the various commodities, in relation to the degree that each commodity was originally requested by the nation.

Allocation Finalization. The final steps in the resource allocation process are outlined in Figure 5.12. If aid has been given, then the value production schedule must be adjusted to produce the CS, BC, and FC units that have been promised. If aid has been received, then the production mix may need to be altered to take into account the type and amount of aid received. It is possible that the nation may still have uncommitted resources (SURPLUS greater than zero), and in the event this is true, the remaining resources are allocated to the value sectors, proportionate to the relative size of the existing sector commitments.

Conflict Generation. Nations may express hostility toward one another during each time period, and the process that generates these conflict flows is outlined in Figure 5.13. The first step in the determination of hostility levels involves a reaction factor. The action-reaction phenomenon has frequently been discussed, and the work of Zinnes (1966b: 474-502) is particularly relevant here. Zinnes examined both historical and simulated data and found a positive relationship between "x's expression of hostility to y and y's perception of unfriendliness," and that "there is a positive relationship between the perception of unfriendliness and the expression of hostility" (1966: 477). However, we will add to this basic formulation the proposal that nations react to expected hostility by anticipating how hostile another nation will be in the future, with the aim of deterring that behavior. Accordingly, the expectation formation process, to be discussed shortly, is used to yield a value for $HOST_{jit+1}$, and the equation is

$$HOST_{ijt+1} = b_{12}\ HOST_{jit+1},$$

where $HOST_{jit+1}$ is the amount of hostility nation i expects from nation j in the next period, and $HOST_{ijt+1}$ is the amount of hostility that nation i is considering sending to nation j in that same next period.

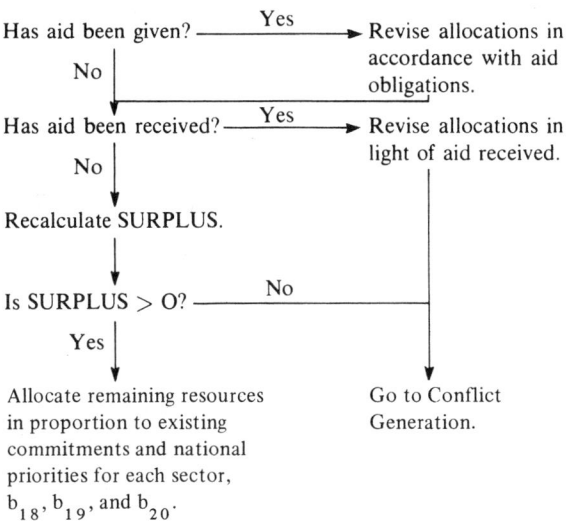

Figure 5.12 Allocation Finalization

There are factors that work to repress the expression of hostility, and three kinds of factors that modify the expression of hostile feeling have been included. The first of these factors comes into play when there are great power differences between actor and target. Rummel (1965: 143) reports a significant positive association between the discrepancy in military power between a pair of nations, and the level of threats, accusations, and protests that pass between the nations. Brody and Milstein (1967) found that if a weaker simulated nation perceived hostility emanating from a stronger one, it was less likely to respond with verbal hostility than if the hostility were emanating from a weaker nation. This finding has been partially supported in analyses using real-world data, as well. Erich Weede (1969: 1) reports, "Powerful states are more likely to engage in verbal conflict activities than relatively powerless states."

Hence, the next steps outlined in Figure 5.13 involve computing the expected force differential, again calling upon the expectation formation process. If the force differential is positive, then HOST is increased by the following amount:

$$b_{22} \frac{TFC_{it+1} - TFC_{jt+1}}{TFC_{it+1} + TFC_{jt+1}}$$

170 SIMULATED INTERNATIONAL PROCESSES

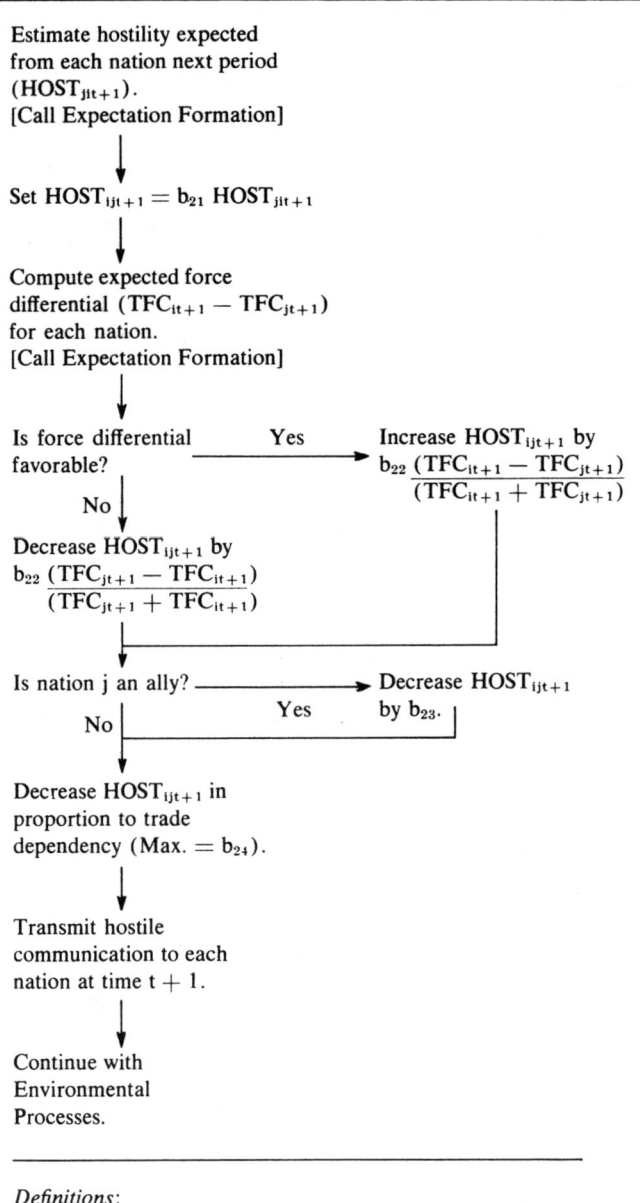

Figure 5.13 Conflict Generation

Estimate hostility expected from each nation next period ($HOST_{jt+1}$).
[Call Expectation Formation]

↓

Set $HOST_{ijt+1} = b_{21} HOST_{jt+1}$

↓

Compute expected force differential ($TFC_{it+1} - TFC_{jt+1}$) for each nation.
[Call Expectation Formation]

↓

Is force differential favorable? —Yes→ Increase $HOST_{ijt+1}$ by $b_{22} \dfrac{(TFC_{it+1} - TFC_{jt+1})}{(TFC_{it+1} + TFC_{jt+1})}$

No ↓

Decrease $HOST_{ijt+1}$ by $b_{22} \dfrac{(TFC_{jt+1} - TFC_{it+1})}{(TFC_{jt+1} + TFC_{it+1})}$

↓

Is nation j an ally? —Yes→ Decrease $HOST_{ijt+1}$ by b_{23}.

No ↓

Decrease $HOST_{ijt+1}$ in proportion to trade dependency (Max. = b_{24}).

↓

Transmit hostile communication to each nation at time $t + 1$.

↓

Continue with Environmental Processes.

Definitions:
   $HOST_{ijt}$ = hostile communication sent by nation i to nation j at time t.

The division term normalizes the force differential value so that it varies from -1.0 to 1.0, and this modified value determines the fraction of b_{22} that will be added to the value of HOST. Thus, if the expected levels of force capability are two-to-one in favor of the acting nation i, then one-third of the value of b_{22} would be added to the hostility level.

If, on the other hand, the expected force differential is negative, then the level of hostility will be lowered by a certain fraction of b_{22}. This fraction is also determined by the above equation. Thus, if the expected levels of force capability are two-to-one in favor of the target nation, then the acting nation will lower its hostility level by one-third the value of b_{22}. The second factor operating in the conflict generation process takes into account the effects of alliances on the expression of hostility between nations. Zinnes (1966b: 484-486) found that there is a tendency for a nation to perceive less hostility from an ally than a nonally, and to express less hostility to an ally than a nonally. Consequently, it is postulated that a nation will be willing to overlook a certain amount of hostility from an ally in the interests of preserving the alliance. Hence, the next set of steps in Figure 5.13 involves determining whether or not the target nation is an ally, and if so, the level of hostility is decreased by the amount b_{22}.

The third and final set of steps in Figure 5.13 takes into accont the effect of close economic ties on the expression of hostility. The reasons for including this term are similar to those given above for the alliance factor. The stronger the economic dependence, the more effort will be made to repress the expression of hostility, up to a maximum value, for the sake of maintaining economic ties. The relevant formulation is:

$$b_{24} \frac{TRADE_{ji}}{\sum_{\text{all nations}} TRADE_i}$$

The numerator in this equation indicates the amount of exports the target nation, j, sent to the acting nation, i, in the last trading round, while the denominator indicates the total amount of exports the acting nation received in that trading round. In the context of the total equation, the reduction in the level of hostility will be proportional to the target nation's share of the acting nation's total import. The greater the import dependency of the latter on the former, the more the hostility level will be decreased, up to the maximum, b_{24}.

Putting all these component parts together yields the following equation:

$$HOST_{ijt+1} = b_{21} HOST_{jit+1}$$

$$+ b_{22} \frac{TFC_{it+1} - TFC_{jt+1}}{TFC_{it+1} + TFC_{jt+1}}$$

$$- b_{23} ALLY_{ij}$$

$$- b_{24} \frac{TRADE_{ji}}{\sum_{\text{all nations}} TRADE_i}$$

Expectation Formation. In the previous sections, reference has been made to the development of expectations by one nation vis-à-vis the future behavior of another nation. In this section, I will discuss how these estimates of future behavior are formulated.

The central thesis here is that nations use information-processing rules to forecast the behavior of other nations. Since much national behavior is, in part, anticipatory in nature, it is a matter of no small importance how this future behavior is estimated. An underlying assumption of all the information-processing rules to be discussed here is that the best estimate of future behavior is to be found in the analysis of past and present behavior.

The particular type of forecasting rule used seems to be dependent on two considerations: (1) the perceived accuracy of the information at hand, and (2) the underlying pattern that is thought to characterize the behavior of the nation being considered. Each of these two dimensions has been divided into two categories. The information at hand may be considered accurate or approximate, and the behavior pattern may be either stable or changeable. Thus, there are four combinations:

(1) approximate information, changeable behavior
(2) approximate information, stable behavior
(3) accurate information, changeable behavior
(4) accurate information, stable behavior

As we shall see, there is an information-processing rule corresponding to each pair of assumptions.

Before considering each of these in turn, it may be useful to gain an overall view of the entire expectation formation process. The steps in the process are laid out in Figure 5.14, and, as is apparent, a single parameter, b_{25}, governs the whole process. Looking at the first step on the left, we see that the assumptions about information and behavior need not be made by the decision-making unit. (We will return later to this alternative and explain in more detail what happens when b_{25} is set equal to zero, and for the moment take the yes branch of the assumptions question.)

The next two steps are branching operations that determine which of the four pairs of assumptions is held by the decision-making unit. Moving from right to left in Figure 5.14, we will examine accurate information, stable behavior.

Accurate Information, Stable Behavior. Setting b_{25} equal to four invokes rule 4 as the forecasting rule to be used, and rule 4 specifies that

$$X_{jt+1} = X_{jt} .$$

That is, the level of behavior by nation j in the next time period is assumed to be equal to that emitted in the present time period. This rule stipulates that under the conditions of accurate information and stable behavior, the best estimate of what is likely to happen in the future is what is happening presently. For obvious reasons, this has been labeled the No Change rule.

Accurate Information, Changeable Behavior. When the appropriate value has been assigned to the controlling parameter, the decision-making unit is forced to use rule 3, which is:

$$X_{jt+1} = X_{jt} + (X_{jt} - X_{jt+1}).$$

Thus, the level of behavior by nation j in the next time period is taken as the present level plus the last change. Since changes in behavior are seen as disjoint and incrementalistic in nature, this rule is labeled the Disjoint Change rule.

Approximate Information, Stable Behavior. Under these circumstances, rule 2 is invoked for forecasting purposes. It states that

$$X_{jt+1} = \frac{\sum^{\text{past mt periods}} X_j}{mt}$$

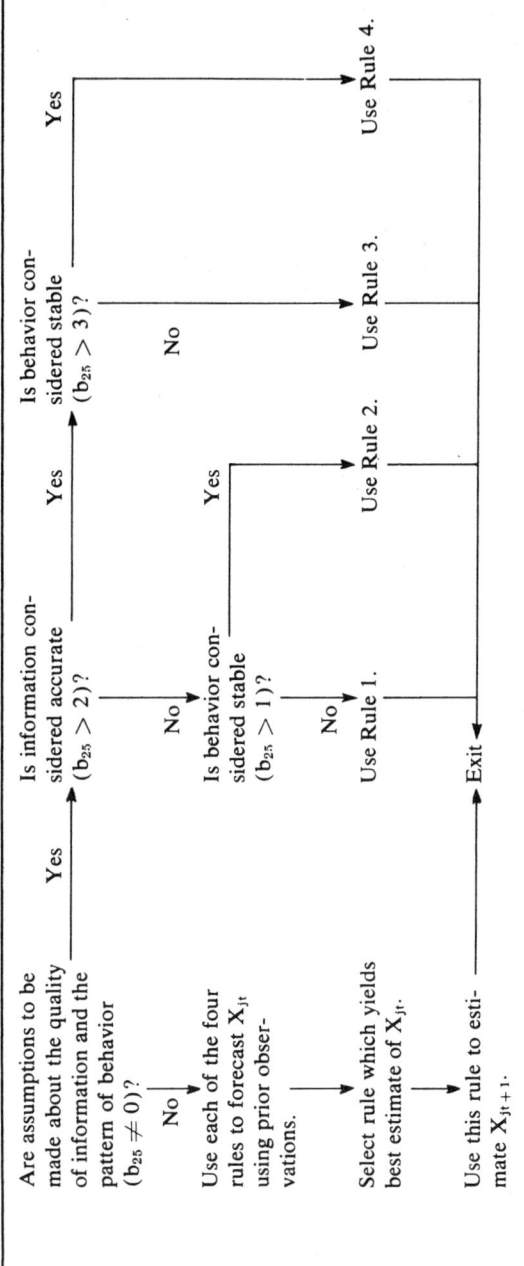

Figure 5.14 Expectation Formation

The level of behavior to be emitted in the next time period is estimated as the average level of behavior over the last mt time points. Since the error in the information is assumed to be normally distributed, the mean value is thought to be the best estimate, given that no fundamental change in the behavior pattern is expected. This rule is labeled the Central Tendency rule.

Approximate Information, Changeable Behavior. The last in this set of four rules, rule 1, specifies that

$$X_{jt+1} = a + \beta(t+1),$$

where a and β are the constant and slope of the regression line relating the behavior X to time over the last mt time points. Error is assumed to be normally distributed, but the expectation is that there is a linear trend in the pattern of behavior. This rule is identified as the Trend rule.

Thus, by setting b_{25} equal to one of the four values discussed, we can force the decision-making unit to consistently use one of the four information-processing rules. As we suggested earlier, there is still another option that remains to be discussed. This is the Best Fit rule.

Setting b_{25} equal to zero specifies that only empirical considerations will be used to develop forecasts, and no a priori assumptions will be made about the accuracy of information and stability of behavior. Simply stated, rule zero stipulates the use of that rule (from among the four previously discussed) that hindsight suggests would have yielded the most accurate prediction had it been used in the previous period. As we can see in Figure 5.14, this is done by using all four rules to estimate the present level of behavior, X_{jt}, and then using the rule that produces the best estimate to predict the future value, X_{jt+1}. Hence the designation, Best Fit rule. With this rule, a nation may not constantly use the same rule if, by experience, it learns that another rule is more accurate, and some elementary learning and adaption are possible with respect to the expectation formation process.

This set of five rules by no means exhausts the variety of rules that could be formulated, but the rules do represent some interesting and different prediction processes. Since there are 5 nations, each of which may be assigned a different rule, and 5 rules, there are 25 possible combinations.

Let me trace the few remaining steps in the model's execution sequence. At this point, each of the simulated nations has made decisions about resource allocation, trade, aid, and conflict in light of its knowledge and expectations about the environment, and these decisions become inputs into the processes (described in the first part of this chapter) that specify how the environment is altered. Following these alterations, the cycle begins again as the simulated nations endeavor to cope with their redefined environment.

NOTES

1. SIPER is a next-generation simulation model developed in the project on Simulated International Processes (SIP) at Northwestern University.

2. This is not an uncommon response to this type of problem. Newton resolved his n-body problem by reducing it to a 2-body problem (the sun and each planet individually), and one solution to the problem of the n-person game involves transforming it into a 2-person game by merging two of the players into one coalition.

3. This assumption does not seem unreasonable, since governments are typically defined as social institutions having a legal monopoly on the use of force.

4. In many of the equations which follow, subscripts will be used to denote variables. The following will hold, unless otherwise noted.

Subscript	*Referent*
i	the decision-making nation
j	a nation other than the decision-making nation
l	a bloc member's bloc leader
t	the present time period
t + 1	the next time period
t - 1	the preceeding time period

When the variables used in an equation pertain to the decision-making nation, i, and/or are measured at the present time period, t, the subscripts are omitted. Thus, a fuller notation of the equation $CS = CSP \times TBC \times CSGR$ would be: $CS_{it} = CSP_{it} \times TBC_{it} \times CSGR_i$.

5. The INS equation produced decreasing values for CS_{min} when the value of CS_{max} was greater than one-half the constant k (380,000) and negative values for CS_{min} when CS_{max} exceeded k, as observed by Charles D. Elder and Robert E. Pendley (1981: 67). The new equation, consonant with the verbal theory of INS and SIPER, was borrowed from Pendley (1966).

6. The INS equation for VS_{cs} was replaced by the Elder and Pendley (1981: 72) formulation. The new equation, with parameters estimated by Gary L. Tygesson and Michael D. Ward, is consonant with the verbal theory of INS and SIPER.

7. Guetzkow (1981b). In order to simplify the equations which follow, we will denote summation operations in the following way.

Notation	*Meaning*
$\sum_{\text{all nations}}$	sum of the indicated variable(s) for all nations in the system

$\sum\limits_{\text{allies}}$ sum of the indicated variable(s) for those nations allied to the decision-making nation

$\sum\limits_{\substack{\text{non-}\\\text{allies}}}$ sum of the indicated variable(s) for those nations not allied to the decision-making nation

$\sum\limits_{\substack{\text{past mt}\\\text{periods}}}$ sum of the indicated variable(s) over the past mt time points, including the present

$\sum\limits_{\substack{\text{self+}\\\text{allies}}}$ sum of the indicated variable(s) for the decision-making nation and its allies

8. In the original INS model, provision was made for the decision-makers to initiate increases in decision latitude. It was not included in this extension because an inspection of INS data indicated the option was seldom used by participants, and it was thought desirable to simplify the model somewhat by its exclusion.

9. This formulation is similar to the Lagerstrom-North (1969) anticipated-gap model.

10. The notation scheme used in some of the equations that follow is a mixture of mathematical and computer convention. For example, in strictly mathematical terms, the equation $a = a \times b$ makes sense only if b is equal to one, since $a \times b = a$ must also be true. In computer languages, however, the equals sign indicates that the value to its left is to be assigned that value which results after the operations on the right of the sign have been performed. Thus, $a = a \times b$ is sensible, but $a \times b = a$ is not. This is the explanation of why, in some of the following equations, the same variable will be found on both sides of the equals sign.

11. For a discussion of the effects of hostility on trade, see Gift (1969).

Simulated International
Processes: Interpretations

6
Generational Development in Modeling

Joseph J. Valadez and Gary L. Tygesson

Work toward the development of a simulation of international processes was begun in 1956-1957 by Harold Guetzkow while at the Center for Advanced Study in the Behavioral Sciences. At that time a single all-computer simulation and a few manual games for examining crisis situations were in existence. Guetzkow's goal was "to develop a creative, balanced simulation of the overall international scene, using a vehicle that would facilitate explicitness and cumulative work" (1981a: 13). He conceived of a simulation as "an operating representation in reduced and/or simplified form of relations among social units [i.e., entities] by means of symbolic and/or replicate component parts" (Guetzkow, 1959: 184).

The Simulated International Processes (SIP) project developed three simulation constructions during its tenure (1957-1972) at Northwestern University (see Guetzkow, 1981a, for SIP's history). The Inter-Nation Simulation (INS), the "first-generation" model, is a person-computer formulation. The participants are divided into nation teams (about five), with each person representing a head of state, a defense minister, or a foreign minister. In these roles the participants interact with members of their own nation-team and other nation-teams with the purpose of making a variety of national and international political, economic, and military decisions. These decisions are then fed into a computer program to assess and delineate the state of each simulation nation for the next round of decision-making. The length of a simulation is determined by the number of such decision-making periods the experimenter chooses to run. The INS has been used for studying a host of hypotheses, including those associated with nuclear proliferation (Brody, 1963a), the role of collective goods for effecting alliance cohesion (Burgess and Robinson, 1969), and the influence of psychological characteristics of heads of state on decision-making (Driver, 1977).

The International Processes Simulation (IPS), developed by Paul Smoker at Lancaster and Northwestern Universities, is a second SIP person-computer simulation. This new model introduced an international system composed of international governmental and nongovernmental organizations, multinational and national corporations, and a larger set of participating nations (about ten; Smoker, 1981). It is interesting that Smoker anticipated the criticisms of the INS as formulated by Modelski (1970) when he developed his simulation. The IPS represents a quantum change from the INS by incorporating these many elements as well as establishing a program structure that is considerably more complex than the INS (Guetzkow, 1981a: 14).

Throughout the period in which Smoker was developing his IPS, there was a growing interest in all-computer formats. Through the initiative of Stuart A. Bremer, the Simulated International ProcessER (SIPER) was formulated and the third SIP model established. SIPER (Bremer, 1977, 1981) is "an all-computer specification of a revised and updated version of the Inter-Nation Simulation" (Guetzkow, 1981a: 14). An all-computer version of the simulation is particularly expeditious as a research tool in situations when it is considered "desirable to replace all human decision-makers by computer routines so that many options can be considered relatively quickly" (Smoker, 1970b: 2).

As detailed discussions of these three models are presented elsewhere (Guetzkow, 1981b; Smoker, 1981, 1972, 1968; Bremer, 1981), we should like to focus this essay on a comparison of their formated structures as products of Guetzkow's diversification strategy for developing SIP models.

COMPARISONS OF SIP GENERATIONS

The following discussion inspects three schematics depicting the salient processes of each SIP simulation, comparing and contrasting their diverging characteristics.

Personnel in the INS (Figure 6.1) include the simulation control team and decision-makers for the simulated nations. The former group is composed of researchers and technicians whose responsibility is to (a) establish the political, military, and economic parameters for each nation at the start of each period,[1] (b) process through the computer the decisions made by the nation heads, (c) feed back the results of these decisions to the

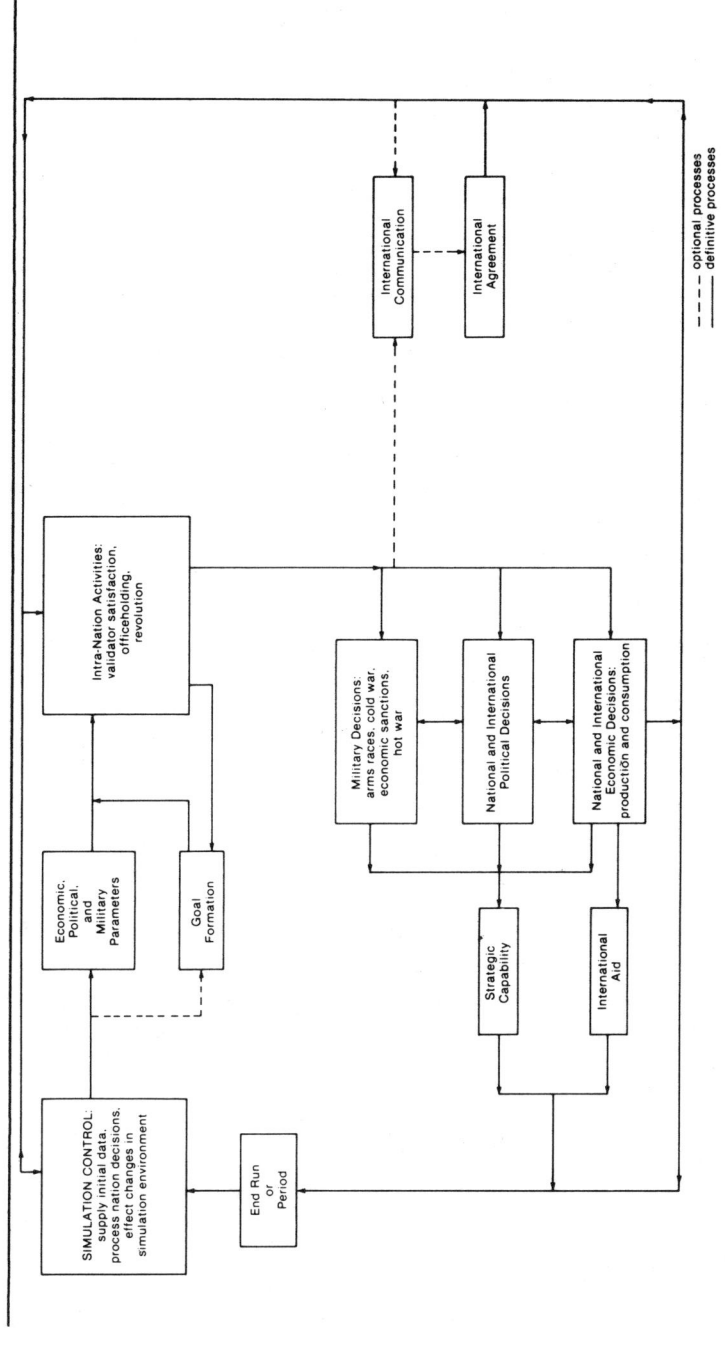

Figure 6.1 INS Schematic (Guetzkow and associates)

nation players, and (d) stipulate changes in nations that result from war or revolution. Simulation control may also be thought of as an information center through which ground rules and programmed relationships can be clarified for decision-makers. Receiving copies of all internal communications (hostile and peaceful), the control team has a comprehensive overview of simulation activities.

National decision-makers have the responsibility of achieving the "goals" of their own nation. Nation goals are either established by the control team or the nation itself. Using these as a rubric, nations acting independently and/or through coalitions formulate national and international economic, political, and military policy for each simulation period.

National and international decisions are interrelated in that events taking place on one level are of consequence to the other. This is evident in office-holding, asserted to be a "mainspring of the inter-nation simulation" (Guetzkow, 1981b: 29). The probability of a government regime retaining such is dependent upon the level of validator satisfaction in its own nation. Validators are conceptually represented nation actors "who occupy positions of influence outside the formal governmental structure" (Guetzkow, 1981b: 29). If they are satisfied, they will support the central decision-maker's tenure in office. If they are not satisfied, they will support the efforts of an aspiring decision-maker to acquire office. Two routes for maintaining validator satisfaction are to keep consumption standards and national security high. Events in the simulation can inhibit these. For example, an international arms race could challenge a governmental leader to invest his country's basic resources into weapons capability. Though he may be able to maintain his power position relative to other countries with this decision, he may do so at the price of reducing consumption standards in his own. Though national security would be high, consumer satisfaction would be low. Thus, the probability of his government retaining office could be reduced. (See Guetzkow, 1981b: 30-32 for a presentation of the equation calculating office-holding.)

Decisions regarding economic, political, and military activity in the simulation are forwarded to simulation control at the conclusion of each period (± 60 minutes). Inserting these outputs into the programmed relationships of the INS, the control team then generates the economic, political, and military parameters for each nation for the next period. Also calculated are validator satisfaction, probability of office-holding, the probability of a revolution occurring, the outcomes of war, and whether new governments have come to power in the simulation.

There are a great many similarities between the Inter-Nation Simulation (INS) and the International Processes Simulation (IPS) (Figure 6.2). Both consist "of components at three levels, that is, individuals (decision-

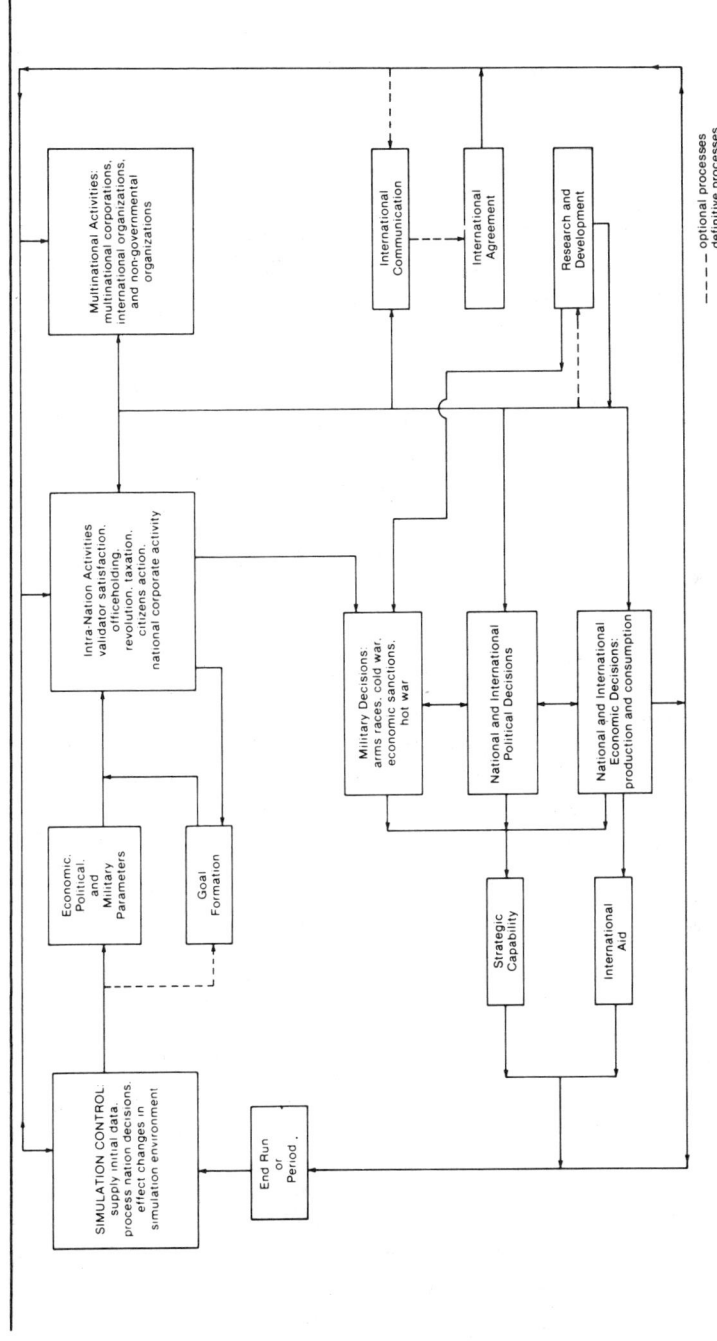

Figure 6.2 IPS Schematic (Smoker)

makers), groups (nations), and supragroups (governmental alliances and international organizations)" (Smoker, 1981: 107), though in the IPS each level is expanded and differentiated. The principal difference between them is that in the IPS, "major structural features, such as an international cultural and economic system, are included" (Smoker, 1981: 102). For example, citizens and international non-governmental organizations are represented by simulation participants in the IPS rather than solely in a conceptual manner (as validators) as they were in INS. Since these groups now have the potential for trade, lobbying, and resisting governmental dicta, they enrich and complicate decision-making considerations in the model.

Probably the most salient feature of the IPS is its multinational corporate structure. Smoker observed (1981: 108) that nations in the INS are often discussed as though they traded goods when in fact this role is subsumed principally by corporations, be they private- or state-controlled. In IPS, multinationals trade with each other, with national corporations, with citizens, and with nongovernmental organizations. Each of these transactions is contractually negotiated in writing. In addition to basic resources, the corporations can also supply weapons technology to either nations or citizens. The purchasing power of these entities is dependent on their pool of operating capital.

One method through which nations in the IPS obtain operating capital is taxation of citizens and corporations. This function constitutes a set of checks and balances between governments and the other groups. For example, citizens dissatisfied by oppressive taxation could revolt; yet if they are not taxed at all, then government services which support their quality of life cannot be provided. A similar relationship exists between nations and corporations. High taxation could force retaliatory price hikes; low taxation could exclude a nation from the marketplace due to an insubstantial cash flow.

The remaining component of the IPS in Figure 6.2 refers to the capacity of nations and corporations for technological advancement through investment in "research and development."[2] Though directing resources away from immediate use, support of research and development can have long-term payoffs, which increases power, status, and the quality of life for those so affected.

Stuart Bremer (1977) developed an all-computer simulation, the Simulated International ProcessER (SIPER; see Figure 6.3), the third SIP model, programming a set of empirically grounded decision-making and information-processing rules to replace the human participants of INS and IPS. Broadly speaking, this five-nation, bipolar model consists of three

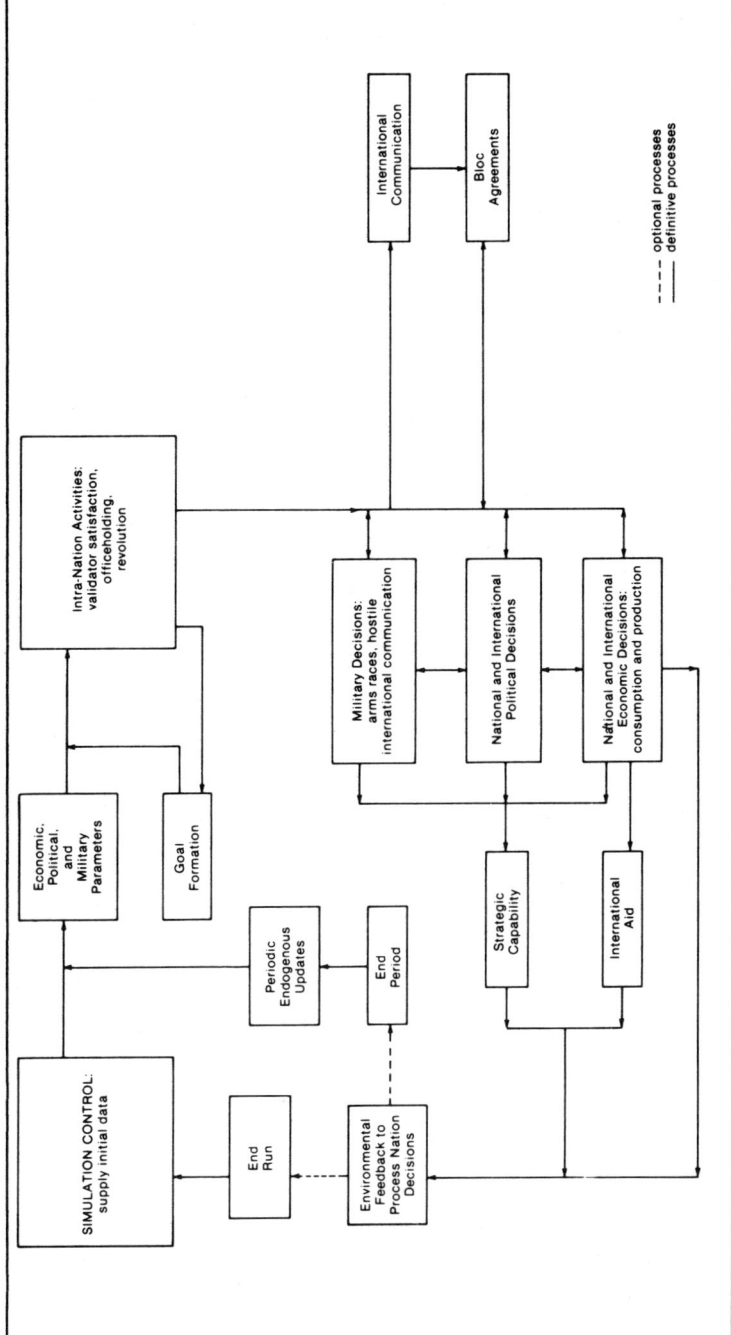

Figure 6.3 SIPER Schematic (Bremer)

components: input data, decision-making processes, and environmental feedback processes.

Since both the decision-making and environmental feedback processes are programmed, the sole human participant in SIPER is the simulation operator. As in INS and IPS, the operator supplies the initialization data and the decision-making parameters[3] for each of the five nations. After establishing and inputting these conditions, the simulation runs independently without further human intervention. Outputs are generated by a computer program for as many periods[4] as the operator specifies. By altering the input data and/or parameters, the simulation operator can experiment in a prototypic fashion with national attributes, similar to the way INS and IPS do through preselection of participants (cf. Hermann and Hermann, 1967) and referent nations. In this manner, SIPER can generate a wide range of varying decision-making profiles without human participants.

As in INS and IPS, goal formation and execution of strategies for goal achievement represent the core of the all-computer decision-making process.[5] In SIPER, however, these are the product of Bremer's set of mathematical algorithms (herein personified as the "programmed decision-maker"). The programmed decision-maker (a) sets national goals for stability, growth, and defense at the beginning of each period, and (b) then attempts to realize these by drawing upon national and international resources. The latter processes are linked to a computer program making decisions for resource allocation, trade, aid-granting, aid-receiving, and budget revision. After a systematic inspection of the numerous alternatives they generate, the programmed decision-maker sets final resource allocations for each national production sector so as to realize earlier goals set for the simulation period. In capsule form, this outlines a single period of SIPER. At the end of each period, the programmed decision-maker also has a political option available: to send expressions of hostility to other nations in the international system. This option is discussed later in this chapter.

The impact of these decisions on the economic, political, and military sectors of the national economy is ascertained and recorded by SIPER's environmental feedback processes. These results then automatically generate new outputs in terms of which national goals are formulated by the programmed decision-maker for the subsequent simulation period. This differs from the INS and IPS in which the effects of decisions and programmed processes are relayed to nation players by the control team.

Thus, "artificial intelligences" have been created as substitutes for the humans involved in both control and game activities.

SIPER's programmed environment is closely related to that of the INS. Having borrowed the programmed relationships from this person-computer model, Bremer adapted them to a Keynesian three-sector economy. The level of activity in each sector is based upon the amount of resources allocated by the programmed decision-maker, the production capability of the nation, and the growth and depreciation rates of each economic sector. This economic process is then linked to a national political system. The latter requires that the programmed decision-maker maintains (a) the consumption satisfaction of validators, and (b) a high level of national security. The consequence of not achieving these is an increased likelihood of revolution. Revolution, though increasing validator satisfaction, vitiates national economic and political processes due to a breakdown of internal control.

In sum, the programmed environment (i.e., the economic, political, and military systems) determines the events and changes the system given by the formulations of the programmed decision-maker (i.e., goal formation and resource allocation). These activities may be on national or international levels. In the subsequent time period, the programmed decision-maker then attempts to "cope" with these changes. The programmed decision-maker formulates new national goals based on outputs from the preceding period.

SIPER reduces dramatically the plurality of actors involved in INS and IPS. Physically, all human participants, except the simulator, are replaced by programs. Conceptually, a single programmed decision-maker reduces the number of participants in the decision-making process by operating as "head of state" for each nation (varying the decision flow slightly for bloc members as distinguished from alliance leaders). At the international political level, variety is further restricted by the inability of nations to be nonaligned. Each must be a member of a bloc (as determined prior to the first period by the human operator). As it is, the alliance structure also constrains expressions of international cooperation since diplomatic exchanges are impossible. There are no independent actors at the international level. The nongovernmental organization and conference forums of INS and IPS and the multinational corporations of IPS are nonexistent. At the national level, SIPER does not include the innovative private sector introduced by Smoker (1981: 106-114) in IPS (represented by activities such as strikes and civil violence). The programmed decision-maker functions without the apportioned authority, responsibility, and the variety of the INS and IPS "cabinet" structure. This degree of abstraction may become problematic, such as in the event of a revolution, when it is not clear where the new decision-maker "comes from" or whether the "new regime" represents qualitative policy alternatives.

SIPER also represents a reduction in the behavioral options available to the decision-maker at both national and international levels. While the goals of political stability, economic growth, and national security are quite broad, the cost of programming the decision-making process is the exclusion of human ingenuity and psychological factors in initiating behavior to meet those goals. Bremer (1977: 30) found such limitations necessary because of the need for parsimony in such an elaborate model. "Defining completely the state of a complex system . . . would require an extraordinarily large number of dimensions. Theory and prudence tell us, however, that it is essential for us to carefully select a subset of these dimensions for scrutiny" (1977: 40-41). This does not restrict activity in the economic sector, where nations can either produce or trade for desired goods, so much as in other national and international sectors. For example, if production after trade falls short of national goals, bloc members may request aid to the extent that the leader has a surplus. Political and military behavior is far more constrained. Conflict in the national system has only one dimension in SIPER, i.e., revolution, as contrasted with a wide range of dissident domestic behavior in INS and IPS. While conflict may be transmitted internationally in the form of hostile communication, there are no degrees of conflict, such as war (as in INS and IPS) or direct economic sanctions (as in IPS). Generally speaking, the only conflictive behavior that nations may display is that which might be implicit in trade and aid, and through hostile communication. As already discussed, aid potentials are constrained by the alliance structure. Alliance formation and dissolution, while possible in SIPER, occurs only as the simulation operator mandates such exogenously. Even then, a posture of nonalignment is not permitted in SIPER's international system.

RESEARCH DIVERSIFICATION THROUGH GENERATIONAL DEVELOPMENT

Proceeding from this comparative overview of salient processes in each generation of SIP's global models, questions remain concerning the evolution of the simulations. Do the three SIP models offer different methodological leverage? INS, with its emphasis on governmental decision-making, provides a quasi-experimental laboratory (see Raser, Campbell, and Chadwick, 1970) for exploring social psychological processes influencing the behavior of heads of state (see Druckman, 1968; Hermann and Hermann, 1967). IPS, an expanded system including a variety of nation and internation actors and a multiplicity of behavioral options, is a similar but more elaborate device than INS for inspecting national and transnational economies, conflicts, and the social psychologies of decision-makers. Smoker (1981), by improving structurally the person-computer format through embellishing the economic and political components, makes the generational leap allowing more holisitic, interdisciplinary examination of global processes than is available with the INS. Bremer (1976: 316) concluded: "In my opinion, the IPS is the best man-machine simulation to be found in the social sciences today." Thus far, the potential for social psychological investigation with the IPS has been explored less than it has with the INS. By contrast, the only social psychological component in SIPER is that which is exhibited in the artificial intelligence of the programmed decision-making rules. The all-computer model's salient advances have been on other fronts. These have been achieved principally through the integration of economic, political, and military processes within the goal formation, budgetary decisions in a simulated three-sector economy. Though the all-computer simulation is specialized and thus does not have the versatile quasi-experimental laboratory environment of its predecessors, it does provide a new and innovative method for exploring macro theories of international affairs through inspection of empirically grounded nation and inter-nation decision-making models. SIPER can be characterized as the culmination of technological and methodological advances of earlier SIP research.

As displayed in Figures 6.1-6.3, IPS and SIPER reveal their descendance from INS. Though enhancing the programmed environment, Smoker maintained the basic INS morphology in his formulation of IPS. His deviations from it consisted mainly of including a multinational corporate structure, more complex governmental and nongovernmental relations, and research and development components; also, "inter-nation communication" was developed as a definitive rather than an optional process, as it had been in the parent model.

SIPER's developments derive from the move from a person-machine to an all-computer format, in the replacement of human decision-making participants by artificial intelligences, as embodied in algorithmic decision rules. Characteristic of the shift to formalized decision procedures is the case of bloc alliances. Bloc agreements are a part of the "structured program" rather than a function of "free activity" (see Guetzkow, 1981b), as they are in INS and IPS, yielding rigid, narrow alliance processes. In its current SIPER format, bloc alignment is mandatory; there is not a "no-bloc" option. Guetzkow's strategy of allowing the inter-nation activities to evolve, given the specification of intranational decisions (Guetzkow, 1981b) has now been programmed, eliminating opportunity for freewheeling, creative processes by humans in the evolution of "solutions" at the international level. Although there is a reformulation of allocations as more information is fed back by allies to leader (see Bremer, 1981: Figure 5.2), the algorithms specifying the goals themselves do not change throughout the sequence of runs, as is possible in INS and IPS, when goals are modified by the human participants as need arises. Thus, by removing the human participants, SIPER is able to exhibit explicitly the full complement of its decision processes, even though they be narrowed and constrained because of the strategy of using an all-computer format. When compared with the initial all-machine simulation a decade earlier by Benson (1961), SIPER is a much enriched formulation, even as it seems constrained and abbreviated when matched with INS, especially when compared with IPS.

Development of the three SIP models should be attributed, at least in part, to Guetzkow's "predilection . . . to work in teams. . . . These include a 'super-team' in the form of the International Relations Program . . . at Northwestern, 'sub-teams' through which [he] executed the Inter-Nation Simulation, and 'side-teams' which served to stimulate and challenge [his] efforts as others went in alternative directions" (Guetzkow, 1970: 34-36). By cultivating variety in his intellectual environment, he encouraged diversification of research interests and diverging simulation developments based on his seminal Inter-Nation Simulation. The INS can be considered the first-generation SIP simulation, a prototype from which incremental improvements were advanced.

Diversification of research efforts through a strategy of generational improvement for SIP models has nurtured three distinct models, each a methodologically propitious research instrument for diverging scholarly audiences. Though the SIP trident has made substantive analytic thrusts (Guetzkow and Valadez, 1981a), comparatively speaking, SIPER must be considered to be in an early, formative stage. Though its equations have been refined recently by Tygesson and Ward (Bremer, 1981: Author's Note), there are still serious limitations, as Bremer and his associates (1979: 2) summarized for the Moscow IPSA Congress:

> A five-nation international system is too small and the assumption of bipolarity too restrictive for us to be able to approach the com-

plexity of the real world. The simulated nations must be more directly connected to real-world counterparts and not remain the largely hypothetical constructs that they are now. The national economic and political systems must be reformulated in order to bring them more in line with and take advantage of recent theoretical and empirical work. And, perhaps most of all, we see that the model must be empirically grounded.

The lineage of the three SIP models has often been described in terms of three generations—i.e., INS, IPS, and SIPER. (Guetzkow, 1981a, 1970). Actually, however, SIPER and IPS are both progeny of INS. Thus, it is only chronologically and in degree of mechanization, not in substance, that IPS can be understood as a second-generation model and SIPER as a third-generation model.

Since their initial construction, INS, IPS, and SIPER have each undergone considerable refinement and elaboration. INS has been subjected to numerous validity tests for inspecting the congruence of INS's outputs with data from a referent system (Chadwick, 1966d; Guetzkow and Valadez, 1981b). A substantive refinement of INS was contributed by Elder and Pendley (1981), who after detailed inspection of the simulation's programmed assumptions (see Guetzkow, 1981b) reformulated the equation calculating the probability of officeholding and reconstructed the economic submodel.

Smoker, in addition to inspecting IPS's validity (Smoker, 1969d), has also elaborated its programmed format in recent years. Inspired by the work of Jay Forrester (1971) and others (Cole et al., 1973; Mesarovic and Pestel, 1972), Smoker integrated a "limits to growth" component into the IPS so as to investigate the impact of the "world problematique" (Meadows et al., 1972), on global political and economic processes. Smoker rechristened this expanded version of the IPS, which includes a complement of ten nations (including a citizenry) and the limits to growth component, the Global Systems Simulation (GSS). This formulation has a capability for simulating exponential growth, resource depletion and scarcity, and an energy crisis in a model of national and international processes.[6]

Since the early version of SIPER (Bremer), all-computer simulation research has taken a new direction for increasing the validity of global modeling. Following completion of the project on Simulated International Processes (SIP), Guetzkow and his group at Northwestern initiated a follow-on project: Computer Simulations for Decision-Making in International Affairs (CS-DM-IA). The CS-DM-IA group (Guetzkow, Hollist, and Ward, 1977) theorized that through construction of modular simulations the components of international processes can be individually elaborated and refined. Ward and Guetzkow (1979: 12) identified areas for which competing modules are currently being constructed: cooperation and conflict, alliance behavior, distribution of wealth, arms processes, and political-economic interaction in trade and aid. "Once analyzed, these 'mini-models' are specified as computer simulation modules operable both independently and within the context of a more comprehensive simulation framework," namely, SIPER-Evanston (Guetzkow et al., 1977: 6). Because each mini-module is based on specific theoretical constructs, through experimentation each may be developed to increase the validity of the entire simulation.

Bremer and his associates, since relocating to the International Institute for Comparative Social Research at the *Wissenschaftszentrum* in Berlin, are also taking a "New Look at SIPER" through "Cumulative Efforts in Sociopolitical Global Modeling" (Bremer et al., 1979). Currently, they are reformulating important components of the model (1979: 2; but see Hoole, 1979; Lebanon, 1979; Wallace, 1978). Cusack is developing a national resource allocation process distinguishing clearly between economic and political processes (Bremer et al., 1979: 19-21). Pollins, following Bremer's (1977) conclusion that SIPER "constantly underpredicted . . . trade volume" (Bremer et al., 1979: 4), is focusing on international trade. In a third study, Widmaier is identifying deficiencies and proposing revised equations in the political submodel determining political stability and revolutions (Bremer et al., 1979: 13-18). Bremer himself is devoting attention to international conflict-generation processes (Bremer et al., 1979: 7-13). He is able now to move from the specification of his model in terms of earlier WINSAFE out comes (see Raser and Crow, 1964) to reference system data for twenty-five countries over the nine-and-a-half-year period from January 1966 to June 1975.

SUMMARY OVERVIEW

The construction of three distinct simulations of international processes has been nurtured by Guetzkow within the context of team research. This strategy fostered formulation of a prototype (INS) and two follow-on models (IPS and SIPER). The former was developed through concentrated effort for designing the basic structure of the programmed environment and defining salient variables. As Guetzkow's "sub-team" carried out several INS runs investigating fundamental questions in international affairs, "side-teams" pursued diverging paths for ameliorating the overall simulation environment. With IPS, Smoker expanded the prototype, adding a complex multinational economic system and citizenry. Bremer, in SIPER, formalized both micro and macro processes in international affairs, precluding the variability deriving from the use of human decision-makers. Both of these latter simulations represent generational improvements upon the INS in terms of technological complexity and theoretical sophistication.

A second benefit of research diversification in SIP has been that each SIP model focuses on a different level of analytic specificity. The spin-off effect has been to provide three research instruments suited to diverging scholarly audiences: INS for social psychological research of decision-making; IPS for examining effects of multinational corporate and private citizen activity in global society; SIPER for complete formalization of institutional processes through mathematical equations.

For Guetzkow (1970: 48), "years of life with the Inter-Nation Simulation have been most demanding. . . . [T] he pangs involved in confronting the problems of peace and war through the use of a simulation which is perhaps 'too big' and 'too soon' " have been penetrating. It seems reasonable to suggest that his diversification strategy is part of the reason for the tone of this retrospect. Guetzkow's side-teams, by offering alternative models, increased *demand* for his attention, which was already abundantly occupied; by encouraging two second-generation models (IPS and SIPER), he invited more torments. Was SIP now much too big and a second-generation model much too soon? The substantive contributions of Simulated International Processes to international relations theory are comprehensively documented; the correspondences between simulations and "realities" in international affairs are clearly delineated (Guetzkow and Valadez, 1981a, 1981b). Diversification of research for simulating international processes has not only produced a wealth of scholarly work, but has already laid the foundation for a third generation of simulations (GSS and CS-DM-IA) and a third generation of simulation scholars.

NOTES

1. Parameters include: decision latitude (DL), basic capability (BC), force capability (FC), nuclear FC, probability of revolution (pR), validator satisfaction (VS), and the probability of office-holding (pOH; see Guetzkow, 1981b).

2. Some INS experiments, such as Brody's (1963a) series, also included a capacity for research and development. The amount of this activity in the INS, as with other budgetary decisions, was determined by heads of state.

3. Parameters include aspiration levels, national priorities, reaction buffers, and alliance structure. The set of input parameters is much larger than that required for the INS or IPS.

4. A version currently in use (SIPER-Evanston) has simulated up to forty periods. As in INS and IPS, the period is an abstract time frame which may be used to represent, for example, a year or a decade.

5. "Nations are open, complex, adaptive systems and, as such, their behavior is purposive. Their behavior is intended to reduce the perceived discrepancy between the present state of the nation and some desired future state of the nation. We are concerned here with the national definition of that desirable future state" (Bremer, 1977: 40).

6. Personal communication with Paul L. Smoker, Richardson Institute for Peace and Conflict Research, Lancaster University, England, 1971-1974.

7
International Relations Theory: Contributions of Simulated International Processes

Harold Guetzkow and Joseph J. Valadez

Cumulative research is a world concern in the building of social science. Alker and Bock (1972) created a milestone in collating some seventy-five articles in international relations, taken principally from the *International Encyclopedia of the Social Sciences (IESS)*. Their synthesis of the literature included studies representing various interdisciplinary thrusts and differing methodological orientations. The verbal theories and empirical analyses which the authors condensed from these works were grouped under four central categories: "participants and perspectives," "behaviors and processes," "international systems," and "resources, arenas, environments." Their syntheses are used in this essay as comparative material to display, the substantive contributions from work in global simulations as carried out from 1957 to 1972 by persons remotely and closely associated with the project on Simulated International Processes (SIP).

The central substantive research of the project has been conducted through three simulation models: the Inter-Nation Simulation (INS), the International Processes Simulation (IPS), and the Simulated International ProcessER (SIPER). These simulations represent steps in the cumulation

Author's Note: A precis of this chapter was presented by Guetzkow at the Tenth World Congress of the International Political Science Association, Edinburgh, August 1976. Great thanks are given to Hayward R. Alker, Jr., Peter G. Bock, Charles D. Elder, and Charles and Margaret Hermann for detailed comments on the manuscript as a whole. The scrutiny of Richard A. Brody, Wayman J. Crow, Daniel Druckman, and Dennis P. Forcese on our use of their work is particularly appreciated. Preparation of this chapter was supported by the Fulcher Chair of Decision-Making at Northwestern University, Evanston, Illinois.

of knowledge, the latter two being built upon the former (Valadez and Tygesson, 1981).

The Inter-Nation Simulation (INS; see Guetzkow, 1959, 1981a, 1981b; Alker, 1968), developed in a person-machine format, emphasizes foreign policy processes. Surrogate decision-makers occupy political leadership positions within an international system consisting of as many as ten nations. Critical relationships necessary to the maintenance of the inter- and intranational system are programmed into the computer environment of the simulation. These programmed relationships circumscribe the behavior of the human participants. Studies using the INS have included such topics as the impact of psychological characteristics, ideological perspectives, economic processes, and systemic properties of decision-making, with an emphasis on social psychological variables. Considerable attention has been given to the functioning of these factors in crisis situations. Overall, the simulation may be considered as nation-state-centered (Modelski, 1970).

The International Process Simulation (IPS; see Smoker, 1970, 1972, 1981) encompasses the international system as a whole, emphasizing transnational processes more than does the INS. Its participants explicitly represent multinational corporations and international governmental organizations. It is a greatly enriched person-computer simulation when compared with the state-centric INS. It includes a large variety of socioeconomic and technological components, allowing multilevel decision-making.

The Simulated International ProcessER (SIPER; see Bremer, 1970, 1977, 1981) was developed at about the same time that Smoker was completing the analysis of his IPS runs. Although SIPER is an all-computer simulation, a major achievement, given its comprehensiveness, it tends to focus more upon transnational economic processes than its precursor, the INS. Its trade and aid programs are more detailed than those included in the INS. By having "artificial intelligence" routines rather than humans make policy decisions (as was done in both INS and IPS), SIPER uses programmed algorithms with different modes of decision-making. The all-computer format required an explicit formalization of each component beyond that of the INS or IPS.

Philosophical and methodological aspects of the Simulated International Processes (SIP) project will be neglected for the nonce, since they have been treated elsewhere (Guetzkow, 1959; Chadwick, 1967; Guetzkow, 1969c; Christensen and Butterworth, 1976; and Thorson, 1976). It is important, however, to remind the reader that simulation is but a "heuristic device for theory development in international relations research" (Guetzkow, 1959: 183). The major metatheoretical contribution of SIP consisted in the realization that the "Inter-Nation Simulation was...

[but] a theoretical construction" (Guetzkow, 1970: 42-43). Despite phenotypic resemblances, INS and IPS are neither sociopsychological laboratory experiments in small-group behavior nor in organizational processes, as has been elaborated elsewhere (Guetzkow, 1976: 250).

Given the foregoing overview of the simulations, we will examine substantive developments in Simulated International Processes (SIP). In our essay on "correspondences" (Guetzkow and Valadez, 1981b), an attempt was made to assess the validity of the outputs of the simulations in a punctiform manner. This essay tries to assess the outputs of the simulations in a macroscopic manner, using Alker and Bock's "Propositions about International Relations" (1972) as a template for exhibiting the varied theoretical contributions of scholars working in SIP. Although this essay is written to stand alone, readers are encouraged to reread the Alker-Bock inventory, inasmuch as their work provides definitions and a substantive context for our exposition.

It would have been possible to utilize the treatises of Arbatov (1973), Aron (1967), or Deutsch (1978) as patterns in terms of which to view SIP products. But in order to be more encompassing, the thoughtful eclectic work of Alker and Bock (1972) was chosen as a framework. It is one of the very few available "propositional inventories" in international relations (LaBarr and Singer, 1976: 78-79). The "survey of scientific findings" in McGowan and Shapiro's *The Comparative Study of Foreign Policy* (1973) did not give enough coverage in its chapter on "systemic variables" to include the materials designated by Alker and Bock as "international systems" and "resources, arenas, environments." Alker and Bock's "major interest in empirical research leads [them] to emphasize ... the most general and significant empirically based explanatory propositions" (Alker and Bock, 1972: 388). As all but 6 percent of the 113 contributors in international relations to the *International Encyclopedia of the Social Sciences* were Americans, the *IESS* is more representative of scholarship in the United States than in other parts of the world. The "inventory distills the major empirical assertions about international relations in the IESS.... In almost every case, the original source makes an empirical argument which on occasion is supported by operational, replicable statistical data; this fact justifies, to some extent, our calling the main assertions ... propositions rather than mere hypotheses" (Alker and Bock, 1972: 488-489).

As predicted earlier, "tighter bodies of verbal theory are being developed" (Guetzkow, 1959: 189). In Alker and Bock's codification of contributions in international relations from the *IESS*, each component of theory is listed as a proposition or a definition and is numbered accordingly. In our references to their synthesis, we have noted this number rather than pagination. For instance, Proposition 3.1 refers to the first segment of the third section ("behaviors and processes") in Alker and Bock's inventory. Using this numerical coding scheme, they are able to relate theories which are similar in content. For example, Proposition 3.11 means that the proposition is the first subcomponent following Proposition 3.1 and is closely related to it. (The introductory section of Alker and Bock's paper, "An Analytic Framework for Characterizing International Relations," was also numerically coded and includes the 1.00 series of propositions.) The propositions of the 2.00 through 5.00 series refer to the four major sections of international relations theory of their work, as listed at the opening of this chapter. Paragraphs labeled as "definitions" distinguish key concepts used in the propositions which follow them; these are also numerically ordered. Thus, Definition 4.1 refers to the first definition in the section pertaining to "international systems."

Lexical considerations affect the terminology of this presentation in our attempt to juxtapose the products of the simulations within the framework of the Alker and Bock inventory. Inasmuch as simulations are "simply another form of theory" (Guetzkow and Hollist, 1976: 336), we do not use the customary social science vocabulary in reporting the findings. For example, we do not state or imply that analyses either *support* or *disconfirm* theories and verbal speculations. In referring to the materials developed in simulation, we label such as "outputs" rather than "data," since the former term does not suggest that the simulated products are empirical, generated from the "real" world, as is usually connoted by the term "data." Because our concern is to display the gains and spin-offs from simulations, we focus on the SIP studies as heuristics for *clarification, refinement,* and *elucidation* of existing theories. We have also devised a vocabulary to distinguish Alker and Bock from the INS researchers. The former we call "integrators," "synthesizers," and "summarizers"; the latter we label "researchers," "simulators," and "investigators."

We are now able to proceed in presenting the findings of the work in SIP, first for INS and then from the work in Smoker's IPS and organization of the materials; to the extent feasible, we proceeded from concern with the behavior of individuals through analyses centering on international systems.

I. OUTCOMES FROM STUDIES IN THE INTER-NATION SIMULATION (INS)

Most of the work to date in the simulation of international relations has used the Inter-Nation Simulation (INS), modified in a myriad of ways depending on the purposes of the user. Many of its inadequacies (Guetzkow and Valadez, 1981b; Modelski, 1970; Bremer, 1976), especially its narrow focus on the nation-state system, are dramatized in the step-changes made by both Smoker and Bremer in their successor formulations.

Information relating to the format of the ten Inter-Nation Simulations, such as the number of participants and nations involved, and the length of time scheduled for each period, are included in Table 7.1. Of the several investigations analyzing these INS simulations, some were not considered principally because they focused on specific historical cases (see Guetzkow et al., 1964; Hermann and Hermann, 1967; Rosenband, 1968). The twenty-one INS studies discussed here involve three conceptual domains: (a) Variables believed to affect "participants and perspectives in foreign policy decision-making" are explored by Driver (1977); Crow and Noel (1977); Hermann (1969, 1972); Robinson, Hermann, and Hermann (1969); and Shapiro (1966b) in ordinary and crisis situations. (b) "Transnational phenomena, as related to integrative perspectives and coalitional behaviors" were researched by several simulators. Forcese (1968, 1976) and Nardin (1965b) examined alliance cohesion as affected by political influence (in its coercive and noncoercive forms) and voting behaviors within blocs. Burgess and Robinson (1969) explored a theory of collective action based on an economic theory of bloc cohesion in the INS. Brody (1963a), Wright (1963), and Zinnes (1966b) investigated international military relationships, dynamics of intra-bloc and inter-nation threat and hostility, and nuclear weapons proliferation as affecting inter- and intra-nation cohesion. Druckman (1968), Druckman and Ludwig (1970), Cappello (1972), and Ruge (1969, 1972) studied ethnocentrism, national stereotyping, and cultural backgrounds of decision-makers in international affairs. (c) "Inter-nation violence in international relations" was examined by Raser and Crow (1969)[1] in the context of a strategy allowing capacity to delay response; by Hermann et al. (1974) in the case of surprise attack from an unidentified source; and by Caspary (1963), who analyzed communication patterns between nations during hostile times.

There are many detailed descriptions of the programmed environments and scenarios of the Inter-Nation Simulation (INS) (Guetzkow, 1962; Guetzkow, et al., 1963; Guetzkow and Valadez, 1981b). The INS operates in a series of periods. Each lasts about sixty minutes and is equivalent to one or two or five years in the simulation. Though the number of periods varies from one simulation to another, there are usually about eight or nine periods. The participants in the INS are divided into nation teams, with each person representing a principal decision-maker—a head of state, a defense minister, or a foreign minister, for example. In these roles the participants engage as decision-makers in a variety of political and economic activities. For instance, in every period each decision-maker allocates national resources in an effort to achieve the goals he has developed for his own nation. In order to remain in office, a decision-maker must successfully pursue at least one goal—to satisfy the political elites which validate office-holding in their own countries. If this is not accomplished, "support" is withdrawn from the government and a new government assumes office. The decisions national leaders make are used to reckon the probabilities of war, of revolution, and of office-holding. Typical calculations for each nation are their GNPs, consumption standards, conventional and nuclear force capabilities, and investment potentials.

A. PARTICIPANTS AND PERSPECTIVES IN FOREIGN POLICY DECISION-MAKING

The following section considers foreign policy processes as affected by personal cognitive styles and beliefs of decision-makers. Such are examined both in crisis and noncrisis situations, and in group versus nongroup decision-making contexts. Substantive INS findings are displayed in terms of Alker and Bock's section on "participants and perspectives" of their *IESS* synthesis.

DRIVER: CONCEPTUAL COMPLEXITY AND TRUST

In discussing "participants and perspectives," Alker and Bock (1972: 398-421) exhibit "possible sources of irrationality in various phases of the foreign policy process" (Propositions 2.25-2.27, as summarized in their Figure 3, p. 444). Driver's investigation in this area included varied personal tendencies of decision-makers in the Inter-Nation Simulation (INS) as determinants of aggression among powerful nations (Driver, 1977). In her appraisal, Margaret Hermann (1977: 337) noted how "person-machine simulation ... allows the researcher some [experimental] control over the situations that the political leader experiences, which is not generally available to the researcher in the field." Driver's employment of decision-making teams with differing personal characteristics puts the INS to such a use by examining their effects on decision-making. Driver collaborated with Brody (1963) in the operation of the INS runs, assembling surrogate decision-makers within each "nation" in terms of their conceptual styles. Intending to isolate psychological variables related to conflicts precipitated between the large nations in these runs, Driver (1977: 338-339) selected for his analyses variables focusing on personal differences. Two of them were: (a) the characteristic level of complexity of conceptual or cognitive structure, and (b) the level of trust of the decision-makers. Teams high in

Table 7.1
CHRONOLOGY OF INS FORMATS AND STUDIES

Location and Date	Number of Runs	Number and Length of Periods per Run over Number of Days	Number of Nations: Total Number of Participants	Types of Participants
Chicago, IL 1960	17	12:50–70 min:4 days	7:357	North Shore and northern Chicago high school students [on the basis of cognitive complexity scores]
Studies: Brody (1963)		Nuclear proliferation		
Driver (1977)[a,b]		Cognitive complexity, trust, and aggressiveness		
Caspary (1963)		Bellicose leaders and inter-nation conflict		
Zinnes (1966)		Inter-bloc threat and hostility		
Shapiro (1966)[a]		Cognitive complexity and moral rigidity		
Wright (1963)[a]		Block organization		
Great Lakes, IL 1963	11	6:1 hr:1 day	6:325	Naval petty officers
Studies: Hermann (1969)		Crises and action in foreign policy organizations		
Robinson, Hermann, and Hermann (1969)		Search behaviors during crisis		
Hermann (1972)		Threat, time, and surprise in crises		
Hermann, Hermann, and Cantor (1974)		Response in surprise strategic attack		
Chicago, IL 1964	4	8:90 min:2 days	9:36	High school and college students
Study: Nardin (1965)		Alliance cohesion		
San Diego, CA 1964	24	1:4 hr:1day	6:384	Naval recruits
Study: Crow and Noel (1977)		Risk-taking and nationalism vis-à-vis military response as individuals and groups		
San Diego, CA 1964	11	12:70 min:2.5 days	5:240	Naval recruits
Studies: Raser and Crow (1969)		Deterrence through a "capacity to delay response"		
Druckman (1968)[c]		Ethnocentrism and decision-making roles		
Druckman and Ludwig (1970)		Cultural stereotyping by decision-makers		
Robinson, Hermann, and Hermann (1969)		Search behaviors during crisis		
Ohio State University 1966	10	6:65 min:1 day	7:220	Army, Navy, and Air Force ROTC cadets at Ohio State University, mostly junior and senior university students
Study: Burgess and Robinson (1969)		Bloc cohesion through collective versus private reward		
St. Louis, MO 1966	13	7:65 min:1 day	10:208	University and high school students
Studies: Forcese (1968, 1976)		Alliance cohesion through identive, utilitarian, and coercive power		
Oslo, Norway 1967	2	9:na[d]:na	8:48	Political science majors (mellogaf), 20-24 years old
and University of Oregon 1967	2	9:na:na	8:48	Political science majors, juniors and seniors
Studies: Ruge (1971, 1972)		Political images in decision-making		
Mexico City c. 1964	2	9:na[d]:na	7:65	First-year psychology students
Study: Cappello (1972)		Inter-nation threat and hositility		

a. These researchers analyzed outputs of 336 participants from seven INS nations (Driver, 1977: 338; Shapiro, 1966: 6-7; Wright, 1963: 39).
b. Driver (1977: 337) examined outputs from 16 of the 17 INS runs.
c. Druckman (1968: 49) analyzed outputs from 176 participants from 5 nations.
d. Not ascertained.

cognitive complexity consisted of persons whose thinking tended to be abstract and elaborate, involving rich linkages among many concepts underlying information-processing for decision-making purposes. In contrast, other large nations were composed of participants whose thinking tended to be more concrete and less complex.[2] For the second variable, decision-makers rated high in their propensity to trust were those tending to perceive credible threats less frequently than their distrustful counterparts. A chi-square test indicated a significant inverse relationship between complexity and distrust, the latter being appraised by the California F-scale (χ^2 [1] = 8.17, p = .005; see Driver, 1977: 341).

These sets of personal characteristics generated quite different outcomes in the events of the simulation. Participants with concrete conceptualizations who were distrustful of other nations created more conflictful situations using more direct, violence-oriented actions than those decision-making teams with the abstract styles. In total, the behaviors of the 32 large powers were examined in sixteen runs. In 10 cases there was no measured aggression; 9 of the 10 cases involved decision-makers possessing high, abstract cognitive complexity (binomial test, p = .02). In 22 cases there was aggression of some kind, ranging from provoked arms increases to unprovoked arms increases to the making of war plans and conduct of war itself; 15 of the 22 cases involved decision-makers possessing concrete, less cognitive complexity (binomial test, p = .067). When attitudinal components are added, such as the distrust represented in the F-scale, there is enhancement in the tendencies toward aggression (Driver, 1977: 344). As Driver (1977: 350) summarizes his findings, "nonaggression is largely a product of high complexity . . . whereas serious aggression seems due . . . to the incidence of low complexity" with high distrust.

Shapiro's (1966) complementary analysis of Driver's INS work provides additional insight into the relationship between cognitive structure and decision-making. His specific interest concerned complexity as it influenced national leaders' perceptions of conflict as either a moral issue or one politically instrumental (1966b: 1). He hypothesized that concrete thinkers perceive conflicts influenced by inflexible moral standards (1966b: 4). Correlating moral perception scores of simulation participants (obtained through content analysis messages sent by decision-makers; see Holsti, 1963[4]) with F-scores (authoritarian personality test) and the Situational Interpretation Test (SIT; Holsti, 1963: 7), he concluded that "cognitively rigid individuals tend to perceive conflicts at a moral level" (F-scale: r = .51, p < .01; SIT: r = .69, p < .01; Holsti, 1963: 10-11).

Alker and Bock note the influence of "*idiosyncracies* of decision-makers (their differing resources and perspectives)" as operating at the "participants and perspectives" level of analysis (Definition 3.12). The results from the Driver work, as supplemented by Shapiro's analyses, explicate facets of the "psychological significances" noted by Alker and Bock in Proposition 3.25. The simulators operationalized "perceived complexity of situation," handled "fear" versus trust, and made an assessment of the "ideological devaluation of rationality" by relating this to moral standards (as exhibited in the integrators' Figure 3; 444). Further, the INS results specify the inverse relation between trust and cognitive rigidity, including its moral component, and their joint association with the level of aggression deriving from foreign policy decisions. Thus, by increasing the level of specificity, the Driver-Shapiro conclusions extend Alker and Bock's Proposition 3.26 in its assertion that "decision-makers are more likely to be irrational . . . when they experience affect-laden involvement."

But Driver is not reductionistic in his emphasis on the importance of psychological characteristics. Though complex decision-makers tended to avoid serious aggression, he found (1977: 350) that the nature of the situation was also important. "The only 'war condition' which is necessary for serious aggression in general among high complexity [decision-makers] . . . is military superiority; without it, no high complexity group in this series of INS runs ever committed an act of serious aggression ($p = .06$, binomial test."

Note how the Driver-Shapiro analyses posit a reversal of the direction of causality stated in Alker and Bock's Proposition 3.27a. In codifying works from the *IESS*, the synthesizers assert that "foreign policy processes tend to be more rational when . . . richer and more varied available information decreases personality-based selectivities." They also mention in the footnote to their schematic representation of "possible sources of irrationality in various phases of the foreign policy process" the inclusion of "personality factors" (even though such are not explicitly represented in the figure itself; see Alker and Bock, 1972: Figure 3; 444). In a converse fashion, the experimenters in the INS were able to increase "rationality" by employing these very "personality-based selectivities" as represented in complex cognitive processes to secure more adequate problem-solving.

CROW AND NOEL: INDIVIDUAL AND GROUP DECISION-MAKING AFFECTING LEVELS OF MILITARY RESPONSE

In their standardization of the *IESS* and other materials, Alker and Bock noted that "perspectives of elites" are "the determining factor in reactions to a perceived international crisis" (Proposition 2.28). This concern with the effect of psychological factors of decision-makers on international affairs was delineated by Crow and Noel (1977: 392) in their study of a simulated international crisis, using as participants 384 of 1124 Naval recruits chosen on the basis of three attitudinal variables, i.e., risk-taking, nationalism, and militarism. The simulation consisted of an attempt to reenact the Mexican Government's military response at the time Texas declared its independence in 1836.

Quite similar to the focus of Driver, Crow and Noel were concerned with the impact of underlying decisional style, in this instance exploring the propensity of their decision-makers to take risks. The national leaders prone toward high risk-taking in the simulation responded to crisis with higher levels of military force than those rated as low risk-takers ($F[1,24] = 9.27$, $p < .01$; Crow and Noel, 1977: 400). This outcome parallels the decision-makers in Driver's study who were concrete in their thinking. Just as the latter employed more violence, so those preferring risky rather than conservative choices in the Crow and Noel situation opted for "heavy counter-rebel action *plus* destruction of infiltration and supply lines," on *both* sides of the border.

However, when these same risk-preferring decision-makers in Crow and Noel's exercises were constituted as groups required to reach consensus, they pulled back to military action confined within their own borders, a response isomorphic to the Mexican government's response at the Alamo ($F[1,24] = 15.89$, $p < .01$; Crow and Noel, 1977: 400). The finding indicates that "group foreign policy-making," as designated by Alker and Bock (Proposition 3.251), is *not* "diluted by group sharing [of responsibility] so as to cause a 'risky shift' toward more reckless policy choices" (Proposition 3.27). Alker and Bock also note that "foreign policy decision processes tend to be significantly more psychologically rational (and sometimes organizationally as well) when the decision situation . . . includes group pressures for consensus that dispel the more deviant and unrealistic private situational definitions" (Proposition 3.28c). It is regrettable that the same probe of individual versus group decision-making was not part of Driver's experimental situations, so that operation of abstract, complex cognitive processes of the individual functioning alone as solitary chief of state might also have been examined.

In researching cognitive complexity, Driver explored a concomitant, conditioning psychological process, namely, the interacting effect of mistrust. In a like manner, Crow and Noel checked out dispositions of decision-makers tied substantively to events in the simulation by analyzing the impact of militarism and nationalism upon levels of response made in the crisis of the Texan insurrection.

Using scales developed by Shure and Meeker (1965), Crow and Noel selected as decision-makers persons who exhibited "aggressive militarism versus nonbelligerence," and those whose postures were designated as "authoritarian nationalism versus equalitarian internationalism." Decision-makers whose perspectives were rated as aggressively militaristic produced significantly higher levels of military response than did their nonbelligerent counterparts ($F[1,40] = 5.38$, $p < .05$; Crow and Noel, 1977: 400). As Alker and Bock note, "Ceteris paribus, heightened crisis increases the political power of specialists in violence, *participants* whose *perspectives* tend to further increase crisis intensities" (Proposition 2.29a). The militarism reflected in simulation response level was neither diminished nor enhanced when the individual decision-makers came to their decisions in committee.

In contrasting decision-makers with national versus international postures, as assessed in terms of the Shure and Meeker factor scores on "authoritarian nationalism versus equalitarian internationalism," Crow and Noel's nationalistic participants reacted to the crisis with high levels of military response ($F[1,20] = 11.08$, $p < .01$; Crow and Noel, 1977: 401). This result parallels Alker and Bock's assessment of nationalism's "association with violent 'excesses'" (Proposition 2.44a, using Definition 2.122).

When the simulation leaders perceive the intentions of their neighboring power, the United States, as expansionistic, there is also a heightened military response ($F[1,20] = 11.08$, $p < .01$; Crow and Noel, 1977: 401); this contrasts with decision-makers who conceive of their opponent's "territorial ambitions [as] minimized" (1977: 399). This response is exacerbated when the former decision-makers operate as a committee ($F[1,20] = 5.56$, $p < .05$; 1977: 401). In the group configuration, the level of military response is the highest obtained in Crow and Noel's experiments: These decision-makers in committee opted for "counter-rebel action *plus* destruction of infiltration and supply lines" on both sides of the border" *plus* commando raids into [U.S.] territory . . . *plus* destruction of principal supply lines in [U.S.] mountains and naval blockage . . . *plus* preventive action against [U.S.] Regular Forces" (1977: 391).

In discussing "reactions to a perceived international crisis," Alker and Bock stress the importance of the "perspectives of elites," as was noted above, including therein "their appreciation of the nature of the situation and the net gains and net losses probably associated with alternate courses of action" (Proposition 2.28). Yet, in contrasting participants from the Crow and Noel runs who were advised that their chances were from 25 to 35 percent in favor of losing (versus 75 to 65 percent in favor of winning), there was no effect of such probabilities, either when the decision-makers were acting alone or when they acted in committee.

In using an experimental design in which characteristics of the person and the context may interact with each other, as such effects are captured in statistical analyses of variance, Crow and Noel illumine the intricacies involved in understanding leadership in international affairs. For example, Alker and Bock note that "national decision-making elites tend to be less xenophobic, less isolationist," and that "these attitudes correlate negatively with aggressiveness" (Propositions 2.40, 2.41). Although this state of affairs is confirmed in the experiment, Crow and Noel's work allows its refinement, in that there is a heightening of the level of military response even when the decision-makers operating in committee are (a) international in orientation and (b) perceive their opponents' intentions as expansionistic ($F[1,20] = 5.56$, $p < .05$; 1977: 401). Another example of the complication in the relationships involved in decision-making, above and beyond direct effects, is demonstrated in Crow and Noel's finding of a greater reduction in the level of military response for decision-makers (*when* in committee) whose chances of winning were higher than for those whose chances of winning were low ($F[1,24] = 4.29$, $p < .05$; 1977: 400).

It is encouraging that more research is being done on leadership in political situations, as has been categorized by Paige (1977: Chs. 5, 6) and focused by Hermann in her "Statement of Issues" (Hermann with Milburn, 1977: 1-24). Although both Driver and Crow and Noel have isolated important underlying determinants of decision-making behavior in their work with cognitive complexity and risk preferences, the influence of these fundamental styles is powerfully affected by the context within which the leaders perform. Whether the leaders operate alone as heads of state or in committee-like councils makes a difference (Crow and Noel, 1977). Their styles of thinking interact with the contents of their attitudes, such as mistrustfulness (Driver, 1977) and militarism and nationalism (Crow and Noel, 1977). Further, the very substance of their perspectives, such as their perceptions of their opponents' intentions and the assessment of their chances for winning and losing, prove to be intermeshed. In these ways the simulation findings go beyond the formulations of Alker and Bock, as the latter delineated the *IESS* findings about participants and perspective with respect to foreign policy decision-making.

ROBINSON, HERMANN, AND HERMANN: CRISIS AND FOREIGN POLICY DECISION PROCESSES

Kelman (1968: 223) judged the Inter-Nation Simulation (INS) as "perhaps the most promising source of alternative experimental approaches," due to its capacity for eliciting from participants "motivations that have a real-life character." This aspect of the INS explains its capacity for probing topical areas that elude conventional empirical approaches. In international relations this problem is particularly severe (see Hermann with Milburn, 1977: 19-24). Studies, for example, of social psychological factors affecting decision-making during critical policy formation are difficult because of the inaccessibility of political leaders. The Hermanns and Robinson utilized the INS in their study of crisis. The research consisted of analyses of INS outputs from a series of 11 runs conducted at the Great Lakes Naval Training Center (Hermann, 1969: Ch. 3). Three[4] completed studies (Hermann, 1969: Chs. 4-7; Robinson et al., 1969; Hermann, 1972) examined some differences in "behavior processes" in crisis (Definitions 2.08 and 2.081) as encompassed by Alker and Bock (1972: 421-462).

Conceiving of "action-inaction as policy alternatives," Hermann concluded that "actions taken in crisis are more likely to be hostile [χ^2 = 3.63, p = .03] ... and less likely to be cooperative [χ^2 = 8.83, p = .002] than actions in noncrisis" (Hermann, 1969: 73, 88). But Hermann does not oversimplify in his analyses. He explored influences of participants' definitions of the situation, finding that "crisis is more likely to result in action than a non-crisis if the decision makers perceive that (1) the agent was not friendly [U = 49.0, p = .004] [or] (2) the agent was hostile [U = 4.0, p < .001]" (1969: 122). As alker and Bock remark, "a major part of the variance in general patterns of meaning assigned by foreign policy elites can be described in terms of a finite-dimensional 'frame of reference' ... labeled in ... 'hostile-friendly' terms" (Proposition 2.25). The Hermann work indicates that such designation may be used not only for description, but also for prediction of proclivities for action in crisis as contrasted with noncrisis situations in the simulations.

These analyses flesh out components in Alker and Bock's Proposition 2.28 explaining wherein the "perspectives of elites" are "the determining factor in reactions to a perceived international crisis." Hermann concludes that "crisis is more likely to result in action than a non-crisis if the decision makers perceive that ... the agent acted deliberately" rather than accidentally (U = 15.5, p = .004; 1969: 122). As earlier reported, Crow and Noel found that those intentions of the agent perceived as "expansionistic" increased action; within the context of "crisis and foreign policy processes," Hermann observed that in INS crises the goal of national survival is a prime consideration. When national decision-makers perceive national goals as threatened, they are more prone to take action than if such were not (χ^2 = 14.40, p < .001; 1969: 117). Further, if the goal imperiled was thought to be of high priority before the crisis, action is more likely to occur (U = 36.5, p = .01; 1969: 121). Also, "in crisis as compared to noncrisis, the frequency of consensus among decision-makers as to the national goals affected by the situation is increased" ($\chi^{,2}$ = 7.17, p = .004; 1969: 159).

Hermann probed further to discover to which aspects of the crisis the simulation participants seem to be reacting, in terms of the three elements also included in Alker and Bock's definition (2.08) of such—namely, "(a) surprise; (b) a short time period available for an appropriate response; and (c) the likelihood of highly valued or disvalued consequences of such responses." The INS participants' perception of high threat in conjunction with a short decision-making time *and* with the situation of surprise were related to whether action was taken "when national survival was endangered" ($\chi^2 = 3.94$, p = .04; $\chi^2 = 7.25$, p = .008, respectively; 1969: 117).

Hermann's analysis complements Driver's work on the association of cognitive complexity with hostile action, as reported above. Contrary to Hermann's a priori expectation that "in crisis as compared to noncrisis, the more the decision makers perceive a situation to be ambiguous, the less likely is action to occur" (1969: 108), such was found *not* to be the case. He suggests then, a posteriori, an alternative explanation, "an inability to tolerate ambiguity in crisis as compared to noncrisis." As mentioned above, Driver noted that persons with concrete conceptualizations, who also were distrustful (this is congruent with Hermann's findings concerning perception of agents as hostile), created more conflictful situations involving more direct, violence-oriented actions. Is this a root explanation of Hermann's interpretation that "if crises do make an ambiguous situation harder to withstand, then taking a definite position, through an action response, may provide a method of reducing the ambiguity" (1969: 112)? Alker and Bock view the matter broadly, positing that "foreign policy decision processes tend to be significantly more psychologically rational . . . when the decision situation as defined by the policy makers . . . involves less ambiguous cognitive and more compelling evaluative aspects" (Proposition 3.28).

Colleagues from the Western Behavioral Sciences Institute (Raser and Crow, 1969) replicated the Great Lakes experiment in part at the San Diego Naval Training Center. Outcomes in both simulations with respect to search processes under crisis were congruent. "Under crisis, both the search for alternative courses of action [$\chi^2 = 4.22$, $p < .05$; $\chi^2 = 13.6$, $p < .01$] and the actual number of such alternatives considered by the political decision makers are reduced [$\chi^2 = 5.62$, $p < .01$; $\chi^2 = 9.77$, $p < .01$]"[5]. Further, "although the absolute amount of information search does not expand in crisis, relatively more information search than alternative search occurs [$\chi^2 = 6.24$, $p < .01$; $\chi^2 = 23.55$ $p < .01$]" (Robinson et al., 1969: 91). These results were further probed by Hermann working alone; he discovered that the reduction in alternative solutions identified by the national decision-makers was related to the magnitude of the threat involved in the crisis ($F = 37.37$, $p < .01$) and the shortness of the time available for response ($F = 13.58$, $p < .01$) rather than to the element of surprise ($F = .48$, n.s.; Hermann, 1972: 199). It seems that in times of crisis decision-makers tend to behave in the Inter-Nation Simulation as concrete, low-complexity thinkers (as identified by Driver above), irrespective of their normal cognitive proclivities.

In addition to the consequence of more hostile action, as both Driver and Hermann indicate, "in crisis as compared with noncrisis, the decision-makers' confidence in the ability of their decisions to protect the affected [national] goal[s] is decreased [$\chi_2 = 15.01$, $p < .01$; $\chi^2 = 39.02$, $p < .01$]" (Robinson et al., 1969: 89). As the latter authors early speculated, "lack of confidence ... may have the positive effect of motivating a [decision-making] unit to search for support" (1969: 93). Later analysis found such to be the case ($U[24,24] = 3.65$, $p < .001$; Hermann, 1969: 186). As Hermann (1969: 177) states, "in crisis as compared to noncrisis, the amount of search by the decision makers for support of their decision is incresed." This permits one then to understand the concomitant tendency of the decision-makers to increase the frequency of communication within their nations during crisis ($U[24,24] = 2.52$, $p = .006$; 1969: 187). As Alker and Bock indicate, "members of policy-making committees" have "needs to conform" (Proposition 2.27d), as might well be the case when they are liable to misperceptions in crisis, having less than full confidence in their own decisions.

Weaving the findings of international relations research a la Alker and Bock with the three analyses made of the Robinson et al. INS simulation, a sketch of "behaviors and processes" in crisis may be formulated, as presented in Figure 7.1a. An integration can be made as follows: Others are perceived by the decision-makers as unfriendly, especially when they are conceived as acting deliberately. National goals, especially survival goals, are thought to be endangered. There is a reduction in search for alternative solutions, with fewer alternatives considered. The situation is ambiguous. The decision-makers have low confidence in their own decisions. Support from other policy-makers is sought; there is greater consensus on the priority of the imperiled goals. There is communication among decision-makers. There is preference for cautious but hostile solutions, as the often surprising threats develop into a crisis, with time constraints on decision-making.

COMMENTS

The outputs from the three analyses made by Hermann and his collaborators constitute core behavioral processes in crisis which are affected

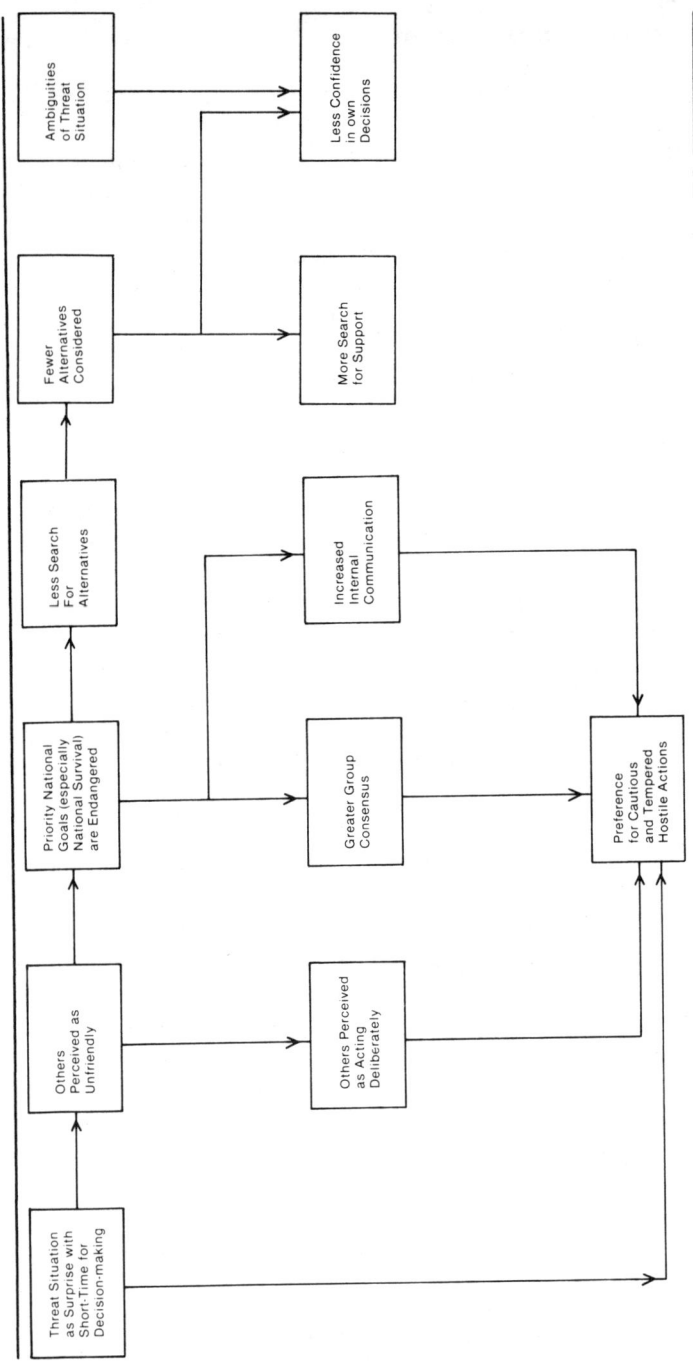

Figure 7.1a Integrative Flowchart Depicting Crisis Processes
NOTE: This chart attempts to schematize findings summarized by Alker and Bock (1972) and produced in the IWS simulation analysis of Robinson et al. (1969) and Hermann (1969, 1972).

by both personal style and long-term orientations, as demonstrated in INS by Driver and by Crow and Noel. The work interrelates psychological, social psychological, organizational, and political components. Note how one may overlay the core processes in crisis with previously existing quasi-exogenous elements, as has been done in Figure 7.1b. Driver's investigation suggested that cognitive complexity and the level of trust of national leaders was significantly related to their propensity for inter-nation aggressive action in the INS. As Alker and Bock argue, these psychological traits may underlie and exacerbate behavior, yielding "crisis expectations." In Crow and Noel's simulations, social psychological factors such as nationalism and militarism were associated with increased levels of hostile inter-nation action.

In all, the INS work has refined "behaviors and processes," as Alker and Bock (1972: 422) sought, "in terms of participants, their identifications or loyalties, their particular objectives, their belief systems or other predispositional characteristics, the kinds of physical and symbolic behavior involved, the situational contents of their acts, [and] the related outcomes and effects."

In analyzing of the effects of crisis on decision processes in the Great Lakes runs, Hermann (1972: 195-206) was able to compare experimenter with participant ratings, finding great differences in outcome; only some five of the dozen relationships found by the observers were also produced in the ratings of the actors (1972: Table 6; 208). This great difference between the images of the participants and the "realities" was noted by Ruge (1972) in her probes of the extent to which hostile and friendly evaluations of other nations are affected by (a) the decision-maker's own psychology, and (b) environment information. The fundamental question she posed (1972: 300) concerned whether "the image which an actor has of any particular environment consists of internal or external components. By internal components is meant the collection of personality factors, internalized cultural and social norms, and experience.... By external image components is meant those elements from the environment which are perceived and included in the image." Of the 96 INS participants interviewed, a significant number tended to use themselves rather than external factors as a referent when asked to evaluate other nations ($z = -3.3$, $p < .0005$; 1972: 302). This tendency was not related to learning occurring within the simulation itself; "participants in the simulation [were no more likely] to make realistic estimates of each other at the close of the experiment than at the beginning [$z = -.04$, n.s.]" (1972: 304). Established self-images of participants persisted as "yardsticks" for assessing inter-nation affairs at the beginning and at the end of the INS experiment ($z = -.04$, n.s.; 1972: 304-305).

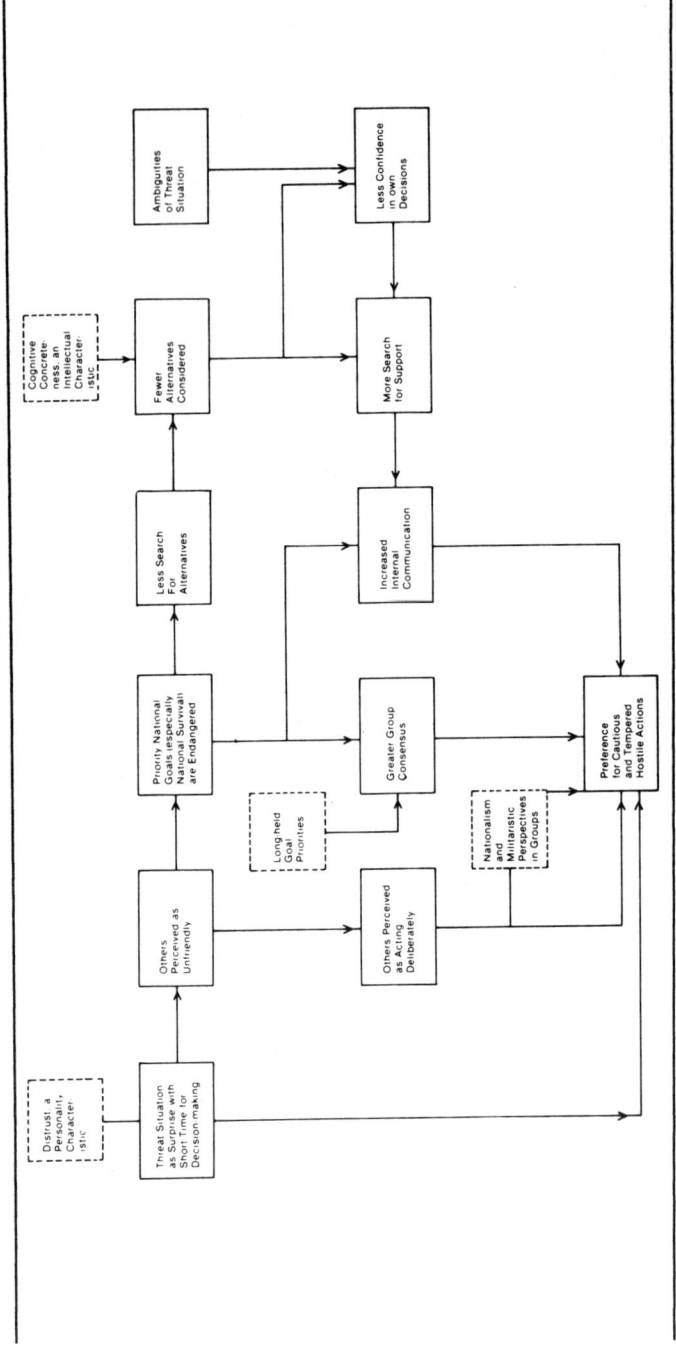

Figure 7.1b Amended Integrative Flowchart Depicting Crisis Processes, with the Addition of Quasi-Exogenous, Long-Term Components

NOTE: The dozen original variables in solid-lined boxes are from Figure 7.1a; the four added variables in broken-lined boxes are from Driver (1977); the notion of using an overlay of Figures 7.1a in Figure 7.1b is from Alker and Bock (1972).

B. TRANSNATIONAL PHENOMENA, AS RELATED TO INTEGRATIVE PERSPECTIVES AND COALITIONAL BEHAVIORS

The previous studies focused on foreign policy processes in decision-making, especially in crisis, as they reflect personal styles and belief systems, the "participants and [their] perspectives" (Alker and Bock 1972: 398-421). The following analyses focus on transnational phenomena; as such they are exhibited in the context of alliances and other international behaviors (Alker and Bock, 1972: 447-479). Once again, the studies are arranged across various levels of analysis, from the individual through relations among nations, following the overall format employed by Alker and Bock in their presentation of "propositions about international relations."

DRUCKMAN: INTER-NATION COHESION AS AFFECTED BY ETHNOCENTRISM

Druckman (1968) investigated ethnocentrism in the INS, as it operates in the context of relations among nations. He was concerned about the tendency for ethnocentric individuals to "be more favorable to members of one's own nation than to out group members" (1968: 46-53). Drawing from a wide variety of field and laboratory studies dealing with social psychological conceptualizations of the nature of roles, Druckman explored INS outputs to see how decision-makers occupying various positions in the eleven Raser-Crow person-computer simulations (1964) expressed their ethnocentrisms. As a first step to check his contention that "ethnocentric bias should be present in a simulation setting judged to be homomorphic to the 'real world' " Druckman (1968: 47) tested for the presence in the simulations of an attitude central to the concept of ethnocentrism, namely, preferences for in-group members.

Four composite attitudes (evaluation, liking, respect, personality strength)[6] were assessed for (a) fellow participants in the individual's own simulated nation, (b) individuals constituting his allies, and (c) those constituting his enemies. As reported in Table 7.2, the hypothesis of in-group preference and out-group enmity was not contradicted. For all variables, the individual's own nation was strongly preferred, as contrasted to the nations of either his allies or his enemies. These results are in agreement with the central tenet of ethnocentrism, i.e., preference for ones own nation. This output is congruent with Alker and Bock's proposition that contemporary loyalties to one's own nation are strong (Proposition 2.13). Further, the INS outputs indicated gradations in ethnocentrism. As recorded in Table 7.2, participants showed greater liking for

Table 7.2[a]

MEAN HALO EFFECTS[b] OF OWN NATION, ALLIES, AND ENEMIES, AND SIGNIFICANT MAIN EFFECTS FROM DRUCKMAN'S ANALYSIS OF VARIANCE ARRANGED BY ATTITUDE

Attitudes	Mean Halo Effects		
	own nation	allies	enemies
Evaluation	.44	-.01	-.22
Liking	.50	.02	-.28
Respect	.32	-.04	-.13
Strong personality[c]	.21	.01	-.10

	F Ratios		
	main effect own vs. ally	main effect own vs. enemy	main effect ally vs. enemy
Evaluation	91.63***	186.21***	14.75**
Liking	71.47***	152.30***	12.35**
Respect	60.72***	87.00***	3.24
Strong personality	19.47***	35.70***	5.01*

a. This table is adapted from Tables 1 and 2 of Druckman (1968: 54-56). These scores were taken from the "final structure" row of those tables which includes outputs from 10 runs. All "halos" have been multiplied by (-1).
b. With "mean halo effects," the higher the mean in a positive direction, the more favorable the attitude.
c. "Strong personality" refers to the perceived potency of the personalities of individuals in a nation.
* $p < .05$; ** $p < .01$; *** $p < .001$; df = 9 (Druckman, 1968: 52, n 7).

their own nation than for their allies. Individuals show significantly less preference for their enemies than their allies in three of the four attitudinal groupings obtained in the Raser-Crow simulations.

But Druckman was not satisfied with mere description of gradations of ethnocentrism with respect to allies and enemies. There are a variety of competing theories regarding ethnocentrism and the status of an individual in society. "Some theoretical orientations and findings suggest that high status roles are most ethnocentric while others suggest that the ethnocentrism of lower status roles is strongest" (1968: 60). Druckman's analysis of these contradicting predictions explored three roles of varying status among the simulation decision-makers: the central decision-makers (CDM) versus the aspiring central decision-makers, or office seekers (CDMa) and the external decision-makers (EDM)—the participants involved in foreign affairs.

In their examination of the contents of the stereotyping by the decision-makers, Druckman and Ludwig (1970: 230) found the "most commonly used traits in characterizing in groups were 'cooperative,' 'friendly,' and 'peaceable,'" while the description of allies and enemies "included both positive and negative traits," such as "cooperative" and "aggressive."

Druckman (1968: 60) summarized his theoretical interests thus:

> Learning theory and reinforcement theory predicts [sic], on the basis of the contiguity of reward and group membership, that high status roles should be more ethnocentric than low status roles. . . . [Researchers] noted the mechanism of "status giving" used by lower status members for making the most needed members most dependent on the group for rewards they could not get elsewhere. The use of this power mechanism might serve to make the most important members (e.g., CDM) most loyal to the group. An alternative hypothesis, offered by several investigators, is that lower status members (e.g., CDMa) should be most ethnocentric. This hypothesis is based on concern for status mobility or on compensatory satisfaction derived from vociferous ethnocentrism. Concern for status mobility was a structural characteristic of the role of aspiring Central Decision-Maker in the simulation. Thus, on the basis of both low status and concern for status mobility, the CDMa is predicted to be the most ethnocentric role. However, from a learning theory perspective, the concomitance of frustration and group membership forms the basis for the prediction that lower status members, who are presumed to be most dissatisfied, should be least ethnocentric.

Mean halo effects[7] of the attitudinal ratings for the three simulation decision-makers are recorded in Figure 7.2. Druckman's (1968: 62) application of the Duncan multiple range test suggested that their responses followed the scenario hypothesized in status mobility theories. The higher-status central decision-maker (CDM) indicated significantly less in-group adulation and out-group derogation than did the lower-status aspiring central decision-maker (CDMa).

In seeking understanding of the foreign minister's (EDM) deviation from the other decision-makers, Druckman examined theories describing characteristics of roles exhibiting low ethnocentrism. The "equal-status contact" hypothesis supports the notion that roles with the most international contact are the least ethnocentric (1968: 60). In the

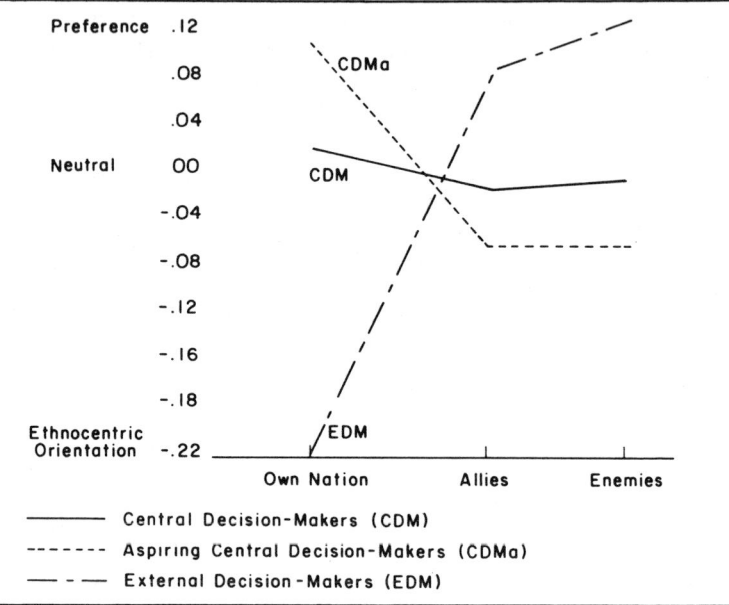

Figure 7.2

NOTE: Adapted from Druckman (1968: Figure 2; 60); halos multiplied by (—1). Each variety of line represents a decision-maker's preference for his own nation, allied nations, or enemies (see key).

simulation, this role was that of the foreign minister (EDM). Druckman (1968: 61) further theorized that the foreign minister may see his role as one that favorably interprets the needs of other nations to his own decision-makers so as to gain the concessions required for improved relations.

The operation of ethnocentrism in terms of the decision-making roles occupied by the participants in the Raser-Crow simulation, as analyzed by Druckman, permitted study of transnational attitudes with respect to other nations in terms of the alliance structures. In another simulation,[8] Ruge (1972) developed a complementary analysis tapping the relation of images about intentions to membership in alliances, going beyond statements of ethnocentric preference. Inspecting the levels of friendly intentions that the INS nations held for each other, Ruge (1972: 299) found that 83 percent of the nation ratings for own bloc members were "friendly," whereas only 35 percent of the ratings[9] for inter-bloc nations were such. A significant chi-square test of these outputs (χ^2 [1] = 14.07, $p < .001$)[10] indicated that nation actors were more friendly to nations within their own blocs than to those in opposing blocs. A second set of analyses concerned own-bloc nations vis-à-vis neutrals. Of these, 66 percent of the ratings were friendly. Comparing these bloc-/neutral-nation ratings with intra-bloc ratings of 83 percent, chi-square failed to reach significance ($\chi^2[1] = 2.35$, n.s.), suggesting that nations were as friendly to neutral nations as to members of their own bloc. These same own-bloc/ neutral ratings versus inter-bloc ratings, however, did exhibit a significant chi-square ($\chi^2[1] = 8.78$, $p < .01$). In an interesting bypath in her analyses, Ruge found that a nation with friendly intention was one that was pessimistic about the intentions of other nations toward itself ($\gamma = .59$; gamma calculated using 141 observations recorded in Ruge, 1972: Table 4; 307).

The three role divergences (i.e., CDM, CDMa, EDM) found by Druckman in terms of ethnocentrism failed to appear when Ruge analyzed levels of friendly and hostile intentions. Yet both studies indicate that position within the transnational matrix, as defined by in-groups and out-groups, are associated with both preferences and perceptions of intentions of friendliness. Even more, Druckman was able to delineate the way in which particular decision-making roles were linked with variations in ethnocentrism. These simulators enable us to enrich the conclusion reached above in the examination of foreign policy-making per se, in which stress was placed on "foreign policy decision-makers' *external* frame of reference as a multidimensional factor space within which meaning is assigned to the behavior of other international participants" (Alker and Bock, 1972: 408; change in italics is ours). Druckman and Ruge were able to examine the way an "internal" organizational structure, within which the decision-makers are embedded through roles and alliance membership, is also associated with the perceptions of preferences and intentions.

FORCESE: THREE TYPES OF POWER AFFECTING ALLIANCE COHESION

It is also possible to move from the perspective of the participant to the level of the nation-state, as it operates transnationally in the context of alliances. In their discussion of alliance cohesion, Alker and Bock referred to several critical variables that may be involved in maintaining such organizations. With respect to Proposition 3.18, these include mutual economic benefits, commonly shared interests and perspectives, and military power. Using a variation of the Inter-Nation Simulation (INS) with university and high school students, Forcese (1968; 1976) investigated the relative influence of these three variables. He employed Etzioni's (1975) conceptual framework for analysis of organizational functioning of alliances distinguishing three forms of power: "utilitarian (economic) power, identive (ideological or symbolic) power, and coercive power [threatened or actual use of physical force]."

Forcese (1976: 180) hypothesized that "alliance organization cohesion would vary with the intensity" of these forms of power. Employing thirteen runs of the INS, the researcher was able to elucidate relationships among these variables. He focused upon each form of power; four simulations were oriented to probe each type. "During one additional run [the thirteenth] the three independent variables were allowed to vary simultaneously" (1968: 48). Each simulation had two military blocs, each consisting of four nations; two other nations remained neutral. The experimenter considered it essential to maintain tension between the blocs. He did this in two ways. Differences were established between the blocs from the outset by providing each side with world histories presenting diverging orientations, so that each bloc might view the other as an opponent (1968: 47). The second method of inducing tension was by having the simulation director cause sporadic guerrilla attacks upon each bloc. These assaults were performed so that "the participants attributed them to their antagonists in the opposing alliance organization" (1968: 51).

The simulation findings are quite clear: "Both utilitarian power and identive power significantly affected the degree of alliance organization cohesion ... while the coercive variable was ineffective" (Forcese, 1976: 181). This conclusion was based on results derived from two forms of analysis. In the first, the level of alliance cohesion was measured in each set of four simulations wherein only one of the three forms of power varied in strength. Each type of power was individually correlated with the level of alliance cohesion. These results are contained in Table 7.3. Analysis of the outputs obtained from the thirteenth simulation, in which the three variables operated simultaneously, produced results that refined these earlier findings. Multiple regression analysis "indicated virtually no correlation [$r = .01$] between coercive power and alliance cohesion, but did indicate correlations of .92 and .95 for the utilitarian and identive variables respectively" (Forcese, 1968: 95-100).

These simulation outputs order the relative effects of the central variables which Alker and Bock list in Proposition 3.18, referenced above. Though the cumulators did not comment therein about the relative strength of the three variables, they were more explicit elsewhere. Discussing cooperative processes, they suggested that common interests among members and mutual utilization of each other's talents are "more persuasive than coercive influence ... [for] increasing joint capabilities" (Proposition 3.371). The authors think it probable that an ideology would develop which justifies alignment to their common interests and norms

Table 7.3
FORCESE'S SIMULATION OUTPUTS FOR THREE POWER VARIABLES[a]

Power Variable	Mean Cohesion	Correlations of Power and Cohesion			
		run 1	run 2	run 3	run 4
Utilitarian power[b]	12.67	.90*	.96*	.91*	.99*
Identive power[c]	11.18	.88*	.93*	.96*	.80**
Coercive power[d]	9.67	.81**	.78**	.82**	.83**

a. Decimals have been rounded to two places.
b. Taken from Tables I-IV, N = 6 (Forcese, 1968: 86-89).
c. Taken from Tables V-VIII, N = 6 in Tables V-VII and N = 7 in Table VIII (Forcese, 1968: 91-94).
d. Taken from Tables IX-XII, N = 7 (Forcese, 1968: 96-99).
* $p < .01$; ** $p < .05$.

(Proposition 2.36). Focusing on the utilitarian character of alliances Alker and Bock, cited historical materials to illustrate this aspect of transnational behavior. Principal benefits derived from membership include supplementing military capabilities, "the right to move forces across a nation's territories, to deploy forces in a territory, to gain influence or to gain prestige" (Proposition 3.12).

Alker and Bock's encyclopedic material regarding political integration of nations is consistent with Forcese's INS outputs. Both sets of findings tend to isolate utilitarian and identive power rather than coercive power as central in maintaining the organization (Proposition 4.121).

BURGESS AND ROBINSON: THE EFFECTS OF COLLECTIVE AND PRIVATE BENEFITS ON INTER-NATION ALLIANCE COHESION

Burgess and Robinson's (1969) analysis of coalitions and coalition behavior through the Ohio State University version of the Inter-Nation Simulation (OSU-INS) explicates processes involved in alliances. Their research explores collective action in terms of the economic theory of "public goods" (1969: 194-195). An impetus for this research was to apply the theory of collective action, as developed by Mancur Olson (1965) to the study of cohesion and effectiveness of voluntary associations, such as inter-nation coalitions and alliances.

As classified by Olson, the "benefits produced by an association may be *collective or private*" (1965: 195) and are related to its performance. According to the theory of collective action, voluntary associations may achieve effectiveness and cohesion by providing their members scarce private benefits in addition to the collective advantages which constitute the group's raison d'être (1965: 199).

The cohesion and effectiveness of a five-nation experimental coalition threatened by a hostile nation were studied within the OSU-INS setting.[11] Behavioral and attitudinal information was obtained from the output of ten person-computer simulation exercises. Five of these were designed to produce only *collective* benefits; the other five supplemented collective benefits with *private* benefits. Collective benefits primarily centered on military support. Private benefits were created through the coalition supplying individual nations with funds "to enhance internal political stability and ... promote economic growth of each nation. These benefits were created from resource allocations to the coalition organization by each member of the coalition and ... [then] redistributed according to collective decision" (1965: 203-204).

Burgess and Robinson's principal purpose in their research was to ascertain whether "coalitions facing common and constant threat are more cohesive and more effective if they supplement collective benefits with private benefits than if they produce collective benefits exclusively" (1969: 205). As Alker and Bock indicate in Proposition 3.202, it is an accepted norm among Western powers to nurture potential and continuing allies with private benefits.

Burgess and Robinson (1969: 206) used five indicators of cohesion "measured on an eight point Likert-type scale. These included participants' perception of the (1) Friendliness, (2) Trustworthiness, (3) Helpfulness, (4) Cooperativeness of each of the other nations ... [and] (5) the Likelihood of war ... between his nation and every other nation in the simulation." Four measures of effectiveness were also employed using the Likert-type scale: "each participant's assessment of (1) the effectiveness of the coalition, (2) the likelihood that the coalition would succeed in maintaining peace, (3) the contribution of the coalition to maintaining national security, and (4) the effectiveness of the coalition in attaining domestic goals" (1969: 206-207). All 150 participants from the five coalition nations were asked to indicate their perceptions on these nine scales. Analyses of variance performed on these simulation outputs yielded eight significant effects: "The evidence obtained from the perceptual data indicates the presence of private benefits increases cohesion among the members of coalition and results in higher ratings of coalition effectiveness by its members" (1969: 213).

Other outputs from the ten simulations relevant to Burgess and Robinson's hypothesis were also analyzed. These consisted of assessments of the coalition by external decision-makers (EDM) and the central decision-maker (CDM) at the end of each meeting of the coalition. Coalitions "that produce only collective benefits evidence greater desire for moderate or radical change in policies than coalitions that produce both collective and private benefits [$\chi^2 = 29.34$, p $<$ .001]" (1969: 215). Other evidence consisted in the "EDM's appraisal and recommendation to his CDM ... with respect to the 'correctness' of the coalition's policies. Once again, the coalition that supplemented collective benefits with private benefits was viewed more favorably [$\chi^2 = 20.2$, p $<$ .001]" (1969: 215).

Burgess and Robinson concluded that a coalition which included private as well as collective benefits for its member nations was perceived by its members to be more cohesive and effective than those which provided only collective benefits. The former type of coalition also was given greater approval by its members than those of the latter type.

The OSU-INS study complements the outputs obtained from INS runs conducted in St. Louis by Forcese, as reported above. Forcese says that "the economic interests of member nations are of pressing salience in affecting alliance or organization cohesion. Indications were that if nations perceived the possibility of economic benefits by virtue of alliance affiliation, then their association with the alliance was more pronounced" (Forcese, 1976: 181). Burgess and Robinson found that alliance cohesion and effectiveness increased when member nations obtained private benefits in addition to mutual, shared rewards.

Nardin's (1965b) investigation of bloc cohesion in a special series of four INS runs also developed conclusions reinforcing some of those of Forcese. Identive components within blocs were tapped by Nardin (1965b: 36) as he studied levels of association between alliance membership and (a) mutual ratings of friendship (r = .63, p $<$ .01); (b) frequency of bilateral agreements (r = .36, p $<$ .01); and (c) common actions as agreed upon through inter-bloc voting in the simulation's international organization (r = .31, p $<$ .01). In his exploration of such integrated behaviors in alliances, Nardin also examined intra-bloc conflict. He found that there was a lower expectation of war between bloc members, in contrast to higher expectations of war between those nations in opposing blocs (r = $-$.50, p $<$ .01).

Ruge (1969), along with Cappello (1972), is one of the few experimenters who has analyzed the influence in simulations of cultural backgrounds on transnational activities. In her work, already described above, she conducted two runs of a simulation with Norwegian (N = 48) college students, which she then was able to compare with an analogous pair of runs conducted by Raser in the United States (N = 48). Since "multilateral activity clearly represents a much larger part [of foreign policy] for Norway than it does for the USA ... , Norwegian participants in the simulate [were expected] to pay more attention to and to make more use of the multilateral institutions available to them than their American colleagues" (Ruge, 1969: 205). This tendency was exhibited in Norwegian alliance behavior, too, in intra-bloc trade. Nearly half (45 percent) of their "shipments took place between alliance partners," whereas in the U.S. runs this amounted to only about a quarter (27 percent; 1969: 208). This transnational affiliative tendency was also noted in the international agreements made and acted upon. The Norwegians gave the International Organizations (I.O.) on average 3,070 units of basic resources (BR) and 16,345 units of military force (MF); the I.O. was also a point of trade with an average of 22 shipments per simulation run. The American participants had less interaction with the I.O., with no BRs, an average of some 157 MFs, and traded but one and one-half shipments to the I.O. per simulation run. The Norwegian and U.S. decision-makers were significantly different (χ^2 [2] = 38.38, p < .001). In a presimulation "social opinion survey," the Norwegian students were found to agree significantly more often (on a seven-point Likert scale) than the U.S. students that "nuclear weapons [should be] controlled by a supranational organization rather than by individual nations [difference of means = .92, p < .05]" (Ruge, 1969: 205).

BRODY: EFFECT OF NUCLEAR PROLIFERATION ON ALLIANCE COHESION

In their section pertaining to "international systems," Alker and Bock (1972: 463-479) consolidated speculation about future inter-nation relations. They suggested that the international configuration will become a multipolar arrangement with structural and functional features of a "reconciliation system." Bureaucratic and group mechanisms would integrate nations; individuals would identify with the international system and give their loyalties to it; governments would have more information available and thus be less dependent on coercive practices (Proposition 4.17). Brody (1963a) was also concerned about the future of the international system, specifically with respect to the potential effects of the proliferation of nuclear weapons technology on smaller countries. He explored these effects, focusing on the "cold war" system of alliances modeled in a series of seventeen Inter-Nation Simulation (INS) runs.

To study this "n^{th}-country," problem Brody divided his INS runs into two time segments. The first phase (consisting of about six hours of play) simulated the thermonuclear pair as leaders of two bloc alliances; only the bloc leaders possessed nuclear weapons. At the beginning of the second phase (again consisting of about six hours of play) Brody intervened, purposefully giving nuclear weapons capabilities at the beginning of the seventh period to all nations, thus generating an nth-country world (1963a:

712). Brody's investigation included analysis of the behavior and structure of each bloc both prior and subsequent to the spread of nuclear weapons. Alker and Bock suggest that "nations will prefer self-reliant to collaborative problem-solving means" but only "to the degree... perceptions of advantage... argue for... such alternatives" (Proposition 2.21c). These "alternatives" include entering into alliances. In the event of inter-nation conflict, nations try to develop a network of collaborative international relationships, which castigates common enemies (Proposition 2.36) and creates security for bloc members.

Brody's analysis of insecurity in the INS pre-spread bloc structure indicated that both blocs perceived external threat and hostility ($z = 5.40$, $p < .00003$; $z = 5.20$, $p < .00003$; 1963a: 716-719). The tendency for mutual bloc members to perceive threat and hostility simultaneously from the external bloc was strong ($r [40] = .88$, $p < .0005$; 1963a: 719-720). Hostility generated in the simulation was most frequently transmitted externally rather than internally in the bloc ($z = 3.84$, $p < .00007$; 1963a: 717). Blocs were cohesive units recognizing external enemies to whom members were mutually hostile. Another indicator of bloc cohesiveness was the tendency for interaction to occur internal to the bloc with significantly greater frequency than external to it ($z = 4.17$, $p < .00003$; 1963a: 725). In this regard, communication most often occurred with the bloc's superpower (U [5, 5] =0, $p < .004$; 1963a: 731). Alker and Bock assert that bloc cohesiveness arises from reliance of members on nuclear deterrence. They propose that the nuclear deterrence benefit obtained from bloc alliances "symbolizes for its members their own interdependence" (Proposition 4.162).

Other reported outputs produced by Brody's analysis are in agreement with Alker and Bock's proposition concerning catalysts for alliance formation. Both the simulator and the synthesizers suggest that the imminence of international violence and the perception of threats and hostility from external enemies ferment bloc cohesiveness (Definition 2.08, Proposition 4.1611).

Zinnes (1966b) also analyzed INS outputs obtained from Brody's series of simulations, focusing on the relationship between inter-bloc perceptions of threat and acts of hostility. Her conclusions complemented Brody's report that mutual perceptions of threat and hostility existed between the blocs. Exploring the existence of an interactive, circular relationship between threat and hostility, she found that one country's hostility is associated with (1) a second country's perception of threat and unfriendliness (Leary score: .43, $n = 42$, $p < .01$; Leary score: .49, $n = 42$, $p < .01$; 1966b: 487), and (2) the expression of hostility by a country as threatening and unfriendly (Leary score: .34, $n = 42$, $p < .01$; Leary score: .49, n = 42, p < .01; 1966b: 487). The interactive relationship between perceptions of threat and unfriendliness underscore Zinnes's prediction that hostility is a reciprocal phenomena. This was borne out by statistical analysis (r = .51, n = 30, p < .01; 1966b: 485). In selective analysis concerned with uncovering variables affecting a conflict syndrome, Zinnes found that threat perceived by blocs is related to the frequency of interaction between them. "[T]he greater the perceived threat [and perceived unfriendliness], the less the interaction [r = -.36, n = .42, p < .05; r = -.56, n = 42, p < .001]" (1966b: 491).

Cappello (1972), inspecting outputs from an INS with Mexican participants, reached similar conclusions to those of Zinnes, but in an inverse sequence. His experimental group with restricted inter-nation communication "felt they did not have enough information" when compared with a control group without such restriction (t = 2.5, p < .02, df = 17). Those with restricted communication also tended to perceive that other nations were more hostile toward their own nation (t = 1.76, p < .05, df = 17) and that they themselves had more hostile intentions toward others (t = 1.80, p < .05, df = 17), as compared with the control group. These perceptions were not contradicted by behavioral outputs; "the proportion of hostile messages is much larger in the experimental than the control group [χ^2 = 169.95, p < .001]" (1972: 42-43).

Zinnes's analysis, in addition to extending Brody's investigation of inter-bloc behavior, also raises questions with respect to the direction of causal linkages in inter-bloc hostility. The synthesizers propose that imminent hostility and perceived threat prepare a social environment conducive to the maintenance of alliances (Proposition 3.013 per Definition 3.05, Propositions 3.12, 3.13; Definition 2.08). The INS outputs indicate that "a decision-maker's perception of a hostile environment is a function of two ... factors: international alliance structure and the extent to which the decision-maker has received hostile communication" (1966b: 494). A principal characteristic of the alliance structure influencing the mutual hostility between blocs in the INS was their limited interaction (r = -.71, n = 42, p < .001). The communication limitations which are related to the alliance system (z = 4.17, p < .001; 1966b: 491) are also related to the mutual threat perceived between blocs.

In further structural analyses of the blocs, Brody (1963a: 729) found that they were hierarchically ordered into two levels, with nuclear powers holding dominant roles (U [8, 10] = 0, p < .001). This hierarchical arrangement was indicative of the nonnuclear leaders' dependency on nuclear members (U [5, 13] = 13, p < .05; 1963a: 722-723). Though Brody was able to delineate this relationship, he stated that there was no substantive evidence that this dependency was due either to the threat perceived by the bloc members or to the desire to maintain cohesiveness in the bloc (1963a: 726-727).

Wright (1963) pursued this line of inquiry further, inspecting various attitudinal variables as they relate to maintaining the central position of nuclear nations in blocs. He concluded (1963: 13) that nations which received the most communication (the nuclear powers) were also the most respected nations ($\chi^2 = 70.4$, $p < .01$). Further analysis suggested that rates of communication were also related to (a) the expressed attraction one nation had for another (range of $r = .59$ to $.65$, $n = 672$, $p < .01$; 1963: 70), and (b) one nation's perception of another nation's attraction to it (range of $r = .21$ to $.35$, $n = 672$, $p < .01$; 1963: 75).

Subsequent to the spread of nuclear weapons in Brody's INS runs, there were drastic alterations in the tight bipolar international system. The perception of external threat was reduced ($z = 4.66$, $p < .0003$; Brody, 1963a: 732), while the perception of threat from within the bloc increased (U [18, 18] = 108.5, $p < .05$; 1963a: 735). Cohesiveness of the bloc was reduced; blocs tended to communicate outside of their bloc as frequently as they did within it ($z = .79$, $p < .05$; 1963a: 736). Former nonnuclear powers were as likely to communicate with external bloc leaders as with their own bloc leader (U [5, 5] = 12, $p < .05$; 1963a: 744). The tight bipolarity of the prespread international system fragmented in the nth-country future.

Though there is apparent breakdown of the tight bipolar system in the nth-country future, Brody notes that there is no concomitant breakdown of the hierarchical structure within each bloc. Nations with nuclear weapons capabilities prior to the spread maintain their position of leadership (U [8, 10] = 0, $p < .001$; 1963a: 742). Brody (1963a: 744; italics omitted) concluded that "the hierarchies [within blocs in the pre-spread and post-spread world] appear to be based on the economic differential."

Brody's delineation of the transition to the post-spread international system and his conclusion that hierarchies were maintained within blocs are both in agreement with Alker and Bock's Proposition 4.17. Brody's findings indicate that although hierarchical structures are maintained in alliances due to the economic strength of the superpowers, communication with nations outside of the bloc also develops. Within Zinnes's framework, this may mean reductions in the perception of threat and hostility between nations of different blocs. Given that Wright correlates frequency of communication and respect, the reduction of communication within blocs in an nth-country future may also mean that nations have less respect for their allies. Thus, Brody's INS analyses are not entirely congruent with Alker and Bock's speculation (Proposition 4.17) that in the near future the world scene will evolve into a "reconciliation system," given the proliferation of nuclear capability.

COMMENTS

The studies by Druckman, Forcese, Burgess and Robinson, and Brody, as complemented by the works of Nardin, Ruge, Zinnes, and Wright, indicate how processes at the decision-making and transnational levels of analysis are related to integrative perspectives and cohesive behaviors in coalitions and alliances. The articulation of the simulation studies with the concerns of Alker and Bock (1972) in terms of their syntheses about loyalties (pp. 404-407), alliances (pp. 429-430), and future systems (pp. 478-479), is not possible on a proposition-to-finding basis. However, there are many congruences, as have been mentioned in the detailed presentations made above. Their "propositions about international relations" encompass the sweep of transnational phenomena exhibited in the simulations using the INS or variations thereof.

Druckman's findings concerning ethnocentrism with respect to in-groups versus out-groups emphasize the importance of endogenous processes, as represented in roles, in terms of both status mobility and contact theories. As Ruge's analyses suggest, it would be important to understand more adequately how ethnocentrisms become transformed into perceptions of various bloc members' intentions, as such are structured in the INS. The attitudinal components in transnational activities, as reflected in indentive modes of behavior in friendships and agreements, in bilateral as well as in coalitional voting behaviors, were clearly exhibited in the studies by both Forcese, and Burgess and Robinson.

Forcese's finding of the relative unimportance of coercive mechanisms in building cohesion *within* blocs was counterbalanced by the emphasis given to the identive and economic components in his simulations, as then explicated by Burgess and Robinson in terms of the theory of public and private goods. The benefit obtained politically, low expectation of war, was explored by Nardin as he (like Forcese) sought to understand integrative mechanisms of alliances.

In the end, these transnational processes seem not only to be self-reinforcing, building further cohesion within integrating groups, but also augmented by exogenous components, as was dramatized in the comparative studies done by Ruge with Raser, as they involved participants of contrasting nationalities, Norwegian and American. There was a background propensity of the Norwegians for multilateral and collaborative behaviors in international arenas that was lacking in the Americans; these a priori tendencies with respect to transnational activities were exhibited in their simulations.

Brody's investigation of alliance cohesion in an nth-country future concluded that member nations of a bloc in the post-spread world perceived much less threat and hostility from the external bloc, but tended to perceive much more of these from within their own. These findings add perspective to Alker and Bock's Proposition 3.013 (per Propositions 3.12 and 3.13), that expectations of international violence and perceptions of threat from nations are cohesive for alliances. In the Brody simulation these perceptions were reduced and thus also lessened the integrity of the blocs.

Though the cohesion of the two blocs was shaken in the nth-country future, the blocs' hierarchical structures persisted. Brody suggested that this was due to the economic superiority of the superpowers relative to the smaller nations. Forcese's finding was congruent with Brody's—that utilitarian power was a major influence maintaining alliances. This interpretation is in agreement with Alker and Bock's Proposition 2.21c, that nations prefer to act independently of alliances unless they are not strong enough to hold their own. In Brody's analyses the economic benefits derived from association with the superpowers in alliances seemed to sustain the blocs, even after nuclear proliferation.

In overview, INS research on "transnational processes" has contributed to understanding two components of social, political, and economic internation relations—namely, "social processes of conflict and cooperation," in ordinary contexts as well as in crises (Alker and Bock, 1972: 447). For conflict, simulators exhibited variables leading to or exacerbating such behavior both within and among blocs; for cooperation, they developed theory delineating processes that maintained bloc cohesion and nonbellicose inter-nation relations.

C. INTER-NATION VIOLENCE IN INTERNATIONAL RELATIONS

Alliances sometimes lead to war and sometimes to peace. But as Alker and Bock indicated, "the crystallization of limited alliances into more enduring multifunctional and antagonistic blocs does tend to intensify and expand international conflict, at least when an arms race is involved" (Proposition 3.132). In the Brody-Driver runs of the Inter-Nation Simulation as detailed above, war occurred between the two superpowers, once in each of three of the sixteen simulations during the six periods before the proliferation of nuclear capability.[12] Caspary's (1962) analysis of the communication between the superpowers in each of the systems indicated there was less communication among those six superpowers that went to war than among those that did not ($n = 6,26$; $t = -3.58$, $p < .01$); content analysis of those communications indicated that hostility was greater among those superpowers that went to war (n = 6,26; t = 2.85, p < .02). Hostility was also reflected in the participants' ratings of their trust of each: That trust was significantly lower in those systems that went to war than in those developing without war (n = 6,26; t = -5.17, p < .01). This latter result is complementary to that noted in a separate analysis of the same sixteen simulations reported above by Driver (1977: 344), who found that there is enhancement of tendencies toward aggression of all kinds (including the conduct of war) when a decision-maker is distrustful.

RASER AND CROW: FEEDBACK FROM THE CAPACITY TO DELAY NUCLEAR STRATEGIC RESPONSES

In another experiment, conducted by Raser and Crow (1969) and involving 325 Naval recruits in the top 25 percent of their class in a dozen runs of the Inter-Nation Simulation, wars occurred in seven of the twelve runs, with "major powers acting for 'deterrent' or 'responsive' purposes" (Proposition 3.041). The simulation environments were arranged so that the behavior of the nations could be checked before and after obtaining capacity for making a delayed military response (CDR)—i.e., by possession of both weapons and command-and-control invulnerability. Despite expectation that the ability to respond at a time considered propitious would increase the "stability of the deterrence situation" (1969): 138), it was found that a nation's willingness to engage in military action to achieve national goals significantly increased (p < .05): "Strategic war was much more probable when [a nation] had CDR, primarily because [it] was more belligerent and aggressive and more ready to make war" (1969: 149).

The decision-makers in the other INS nations perceived the change in the superpowers as they gained invulnerability. The CDR nations were thought of as less cautious (p < .03) and more likely to precipitate war (p < .02; 1969: 145). The CDR nations were reckoned as stronger (p < .0001) than prior to their known possession of invulnerability. Loss of CDR capacity caused a shift in views. The CDR nations were then thought to be weakened (p < .0005; 1969: 144). As Alker and Bock summarized the debate over effectiveness of deterrence, the "amount of threat experienced depends on threat perceptions related to other parties' ... capabilities" (Proposition 3.31).

These findings on the perceptions the INS nations held of each other were obtained as verbal responses to questionnaires. These views were also enacted by the decision-makers in the simulation runs, as they conducted their foreign affairs. Instead of stabilizing the nuclear situation by securing invulnerability, as had been hypothesized, Raser and Crow's nations with a capacity for delayed response actually increased their first-strike strategic aggressions some three fold. In retaliation for these first strikes, the opponents countered with more than a doubling of missile launchings, thoroughly destabilizing the simulated worlds. Further, "there was a strong correlation between... possession of CDR and *increased* magnitude of wars" (1969: 148).

International relations theory à la Alker and Bock posits that "a major incentive for increasing military power and technology (armaments) is the perceived utility of first, the threat, and second, the use of physical violence as a major means of influence" (Proposition 5.02). Among the Raser and Crow nations, there was a strong trend for the superpower's opponents to be deterred when it possessed the capacity for delayed response (p = .08; p = .07 on verbal responses to two scenarios); after losing CDR, nations were less able to deter opponents (p = .09; p = .02; 1969: 147).

The use of first strikes and retaliatory strikes was rampant. But was the large difference in the amount of violence exhibited in the Raser and Crow nations (as compared with those involved in Brody and Driver's work) due to the former's use of military personnel as participants (as contrasted with the latter's use of suburban high school students as surrogates for the decision-makers)? Through the cooperation of Dr. Rogelio Diaz-Guerrero of the National University of Mexico, two replication runs were made of the dozen simulations reported above by Raser and Crow. The 40 male students in their second year of studies (comparable to U.S. junior or senior college students) "were similar, for the most part, in their reactions" to the U.S. participants (Crow and Raser, 1964: 10). No wars occurred in the two Mexican runs. "Systematic differences in response to the questionnaire items... seemed to be related to a culturally based predisposition for the Mexican participants to respond to stress and frustration with a passive rather than an active response" (1964: 11). In later analyses of the Mexican runs, Cappello (1972: 45) reached converse conclusions saying that "what Crow and Raser attributed to passivity and the avoidance of threatening situations can be explained more simply by the level of communications and the number of messages exchanged."

In discussing the dynamics of international crisis, Alker and Bock saw the expectation of imminent violence as a principal variable (Definition 2.08). When delineating contexts ripe for outbreaks of violence, they suggested "military preparations" and "exchanges of threats" (among other behaviors) as antecedents to warlike behavior (Definition 3.013). In Raser and Crow's analysis, the acquisition of CDR by nations in their INS constituted an escalation in military preparedness; the nations also exchanged threats. In sum, Raser and Crow have isolated important, albeit neglected, "effect[s] of invulnerability and the consequent capacity-to-delay response on the nation's sense of its own strength, on its aggressiveness, and on its willingness to engage in war to achieve national goals" (1969: 149; italics omitted).

HERMANN, HERMANN, AND CANTOR: SURPRISE ATTACKS FROM UNIDENTIFIED SOURCES

Raser and Crow (1969) had included a questionnaire probe of reactions of the nations in their INS experiment to "accidental, pre-emptive, and catalytic war." They found that a significant number of their decision-makers in the superpower nations shifted from recommendation of a retaliatory strike to recommendation of a nonmilitary response when possessing the capacity for a delayed response (CDR; $p < .05$). There was an opposite reaction when the nation lost CDR ($p < .01$; 1969: 146). Hermann, Hermann, and Cantor (1974) had a similar focus in their study of response of INS nations to an imminent strategic attack from an unidentified source. In such circumstances, will the nation counterattack or delay the response? Rather than use a questionnaire, these investigators coded the responses of their surrogate decision-makers. They found (1974: 95) that "with none or only some of their nuclear weapons defended, the nations tended to counterattack (71% counterattacked and 29% delayed a response), whereas nations with all their nuclear weapons defended tended to delay a response (71% delayed a response and 29% counterattacked)" ($n = 14,7$; $tau = .33$)[13]. Note that these reactions are the inverse of those reported above when the sources of provocation are identified.

The Hermann et al. study also investigated "factors other than the invulnerability of weapons systems ... involved in maintaining the stability of deterrence in an extreme crisis" (1974: 75). This included research into the problem of surprise attack from an unidentified source in ten replications of the INS. At the end of the simulation runs, decision-makers in each of the six INS nations were told that momentarily "their nation was to be attacked by a large military force from an unidentified force" (1974: 80). Two decisions were possible: either immediately retaliate or absorb the strike and then assess the situation before reacting, given uncertainty about the identity of an aggressor. The identification "problem becomes far more acute if the number of nuclear powers expands. For example, a third nation might seek to precipitate a catalytic war between two hostile states to further its own objectives" (1974: 79). Their research examined the responses of decision-makers and variables which influenced such decision-making.[14]

Regression analyses indicated that independent variables such as perceived ambiguity of the situation, self-esteem, degree of group interaction, degree of perceived tension in the world, extent of nuclear capability, and economic strength were significant components influencing whether a nation would launch weapons in retaliation.[15] Each of these relations was studied in some detail, as follows.

The outputs from the ten simulations indicated that the more uncertain decision-makers were of the attacker's identity, the less likely they were to retaliate (β [6,32] = -.37; t = 2.72; p < .01).[16] On the other hand, simulation nations that thought themselves certain who their attacker was, counterattacked. But whether the situation was perceived as accidental or not made no difference concerning whether or not the reaction was counterattack or delay.

Self-esteem of decision-makers was negatively correlated with the decision to counterattack (β [6,32] = -.35; t = 2.56; p < .05). Persons with high self-esteem tried to ignore the presence of danger by using avoidance behavior to deal with stress, while those low in self-esteem tended to overinterpret potential threats (1974: 86). Alker and Bock's cumulative research from the *IESS* provides related material indicating that when "the sense of national security is ... precarious ... [decision-makers are] more aggressive" (Proposition 3.063). In the simulation, low self-esteem of a head of state was strongly associated with his decision to launch weapons in response to an attack by an unidentified party (p < .05). Yet another personal characteristic, cognitive complexity, found by Driver and others to be negatively associated with aggression (as reported above), was unrelated to the decision outcomes in this simulation.

Analysis of the Hermann et al. simulation outputs indicated that counterattacks tended to occur in nations with governmental decision styles that involved little group interaction (β [6,32] = -.32; t = 2.61; p < .05). Alker and Bock suggest that "group sharing" may "cause a 'risky shift' toward more reckless policy choices" (Proposition 3.27d). In the INS, decision-makers working in groups tended not to retaliate against unknown attackers. This output is parallel to Crow and Noel's (1977) report that decisions made by groups of militaristic, risk-taking individuals were less aggressive than those made by individuals acting alone. Further, these decision-makers, even though working in groups, did not "more actively examine policy alternatives" (as is predicted by Alker and Bock in Proposition 3.27d) than did those decision-makers working without consultation with their colleagues. These outputs are incongruent with Alker and Bock's summaries.

The degree of existing tension in the world constituted an important influence. Decision-makers who perceived a high degree of tension were more likely to counterattack than those who perceived less tension (β [6,32] = .32; t = 2.51; p < .05). Alker and Bock propose that "if threats go beyond a certain magnitude, the tension level becomes so high that decision-makers are likely tempted to go to war regardless of whatever realistic calculations of probable military consequence are available" (Proposition 3.32).

Crow and Noel's (1977) study of crisis in the INS complements both of these analyses in suggesting that increased levels of international tension reduce the input of information into decision-making and cause leaders to rely on prearranged coercive strategies rather than searching for viable alternatives.

In contrast to the social psychological factors (ambiguity, self-esteem, and tension), two national attributes were found to be of importance. The decision to counterattack was related to the strength of a nation's force capability. The INS outputs indicated that nations with smaller force capabilities were more likely to launch their weapons than were powerful nations (β [6,32] = -.32; t = 2.50; p < .01). Hermann et al. argued that a likely reason for this response is that the greater a nation's weapons capability is, the more confident it is that some useful proportion of its force will survive a surprise attack. Further, the larger a nation's economic capabilities are, the more likely it is to launch a counterattack (β [6,32] = .37; t = 3.45; p < .01).

The Hermann et al. study of crisis decision-making processes in the situation of surprise attack from an unknown source provided important elaboration for and disagreement with aspects of the international relations theory sketched by Alker and Bock, that in times of precarious national security nations tend to behave aggressively. If they perceive threats to exceed some arbitrary point, there is likelihood that the nations will go to war. Hermann et al. (1974: 99) summarize their findings succinctly: "Counterattacks on warning tended to be launched by nations with substantial economic capability but little force capability whose decision makers were low in self-esteem, perceived the situation as relatively unambiguous, interacted very little in making decisions, and perceived a high degree of tension already existent in the world."

COMMENTS

The amount of violence taking the form of wars in the various Inter-Nation Simulations varied widely from one experimental situation to another. Could these differences perhaps be related to the latent levels of assertiveness and passivity of the participants?

Although there are many causes of war, as Alker and Bock (1972: 425-435) document so well, each group of INS experimenters, given resource and time constraints, was able only to probe the outputs of its simulations with respect to a very few variables. The findings focus largely on whether immediate or delayed response is made to strategic attack, regardless of its source, as such might be represented in "first strikes." The analyses of long-term social psychological, military, and economic background characteristics reveal that only some of such variables are related to immediate violent responsiveness.

Given the efficacy of intra- and inter-bloc information flow processes obtained from the capacity to delay response (CDR), it would seem that CDR might be related to alliance cohesion. However, when this hypothesis was explored intensively by Raser and Crow, no clear effects of CDR upon alliance cohesion were found (1969: 148), whether cohesion was measured in terms of relative frequencies of inter-bloc versus intra-bloc communication, in terms of a questionnaire probing friendliness, or through a content analysis of the messages themselves judged in terms of an "index of solidarity."

It is fascinating to note how relationships reported in the two earlier sections of this chapter vary as the context shifts from "crisis" (section I.A) and "transnational" (section I.B) behaviors to those elicited in the context of inter-nation violence (section I.C). For example, cognitive complexity is closely related to aggressiveness when enemy actors are identified; when the source is unidentified the relationship seemingly disappears! Yet other relationships persist, as in the tendency of mistrust as a component of international tension to be associated with aggressive behavior in crisis, regardless of whether the adversaries are identified or not.

Perhaps the most serendipitous finding, unmentioned by Alker and Bock, was the discovery by Raser and Crow of a powerful short-term feedback. Once the decision-makers in a nation secured the capacity for delaying their response to provocation by the acquisition of greater invulnerability, they themselves tended to become more provocative, destabilizing the international deterrent system.

II. OUTCOMES FROM STUDIES IN SMOKER'S ENRICHED IPS: A PAST WORLD COMPARED WITH AN ALTERNATIVE FUTURE

Alger's (1978: 233) conclusion that "proposals for change in the present international order ... require creative thought about ... future global order" can be explored within the malleable context of inter-nation simulations. By structuring independent, experimental variables while holding others as controls, it is possible to examine in a quasi-experimental way global impacts of diverging political, economic, social, and/or military models. Using this approach, Smoker (1969a) analyzed fourteen variables dealing with conflict acts—six domestic (n = 342) and eight foreign (n = 145)—that developed in a series of sixteen two-day runs of the International Processes Simulation (IPS).[17] Decision-making teams operated in two modifications of the enriched environment. The simulated "past world" was composed of small nations, conventionally armed with nation-based industries conducting little international trade and developing virtually no structures of processes at the international level. An "alternative future" consisted of "four massive nuclear superpowers, large international corporations, much trade, and a large international political and social system" (Smoker, 1969a: 8).

Comparative examination of Smoker's frequency distributions of conflict acts in both modifications of the IPS suggests important differences. For both domestic and foreign variables, the past world (of conventionally armed nations with nation-based industries) was about 50 percent more violent than the alternative future (of four nuclear superpowers and pervasive multinational corporations). In the past world, 95 domestic acts of conflict were precipitated, while 50 were exhibited in the alternative future. On an international level, 240 foreign acts of conflict occurred in the past as opposed to only 102 in the alternative future. The significance of these differences between the past world and the alternative future was assessed by examining the respective frequencies of both the foreign and domestic conflict acts on a binomial distribution ($p < .0001$ and $p < .0001$, respectively).

Though there is a clear reduction in the absolute frequency of conflict acts in the IPS alternative future, do these simulations represent the reconciliation system proposed (Proposition 4.17) by Alker and Bock (Haas, 1964)? In the simulation of an alternative future, the threat of holocaust may effect a reduction in the frequency of foreign conflict acts rather than mutual reconciliation of differences. Smoker noted 10 wars in the future system (1969a: Table 6). Though this is a reduction from the 21 that developed in the past world, there is no indication of internation reconciliation. A prominent consequence of nuclear weapons capability and a transnational corporate economy in Smoker's alternative future is the relative stability found at both domestic and foreign levels of analysis. Thus, the IPS outputs are more suggestive of a trend toward negative peace as defined by Alker and Bock (Definition 3.07a), where there is decreasing war rather than the positive peace embodied in a system of reconciliation.

In addition to examining these simulation outputs, Smoker developed other substantive findings by comparing factor analyses of conflict acts from the past-world and alternative-future modifications of the IPS. As listed in Table 7.4 (Smoker, 1969a), the past foreign conflict factor (3) exhibits

Table 7.4
ORTHOGONAL FACTOR ANALYSES ABOUT CONFLICT IN A PAST WORLD AND AN ALTERNATIVE FUTURE FROM SMOKER'S INTERNATIONAL PROCESSES SIMULATION[a]

Variables	A Past World Factor 3 N = 36	Alternative Future Factor 1 N = 36	A Past World Factor 2 N = 36	Alternative Future Factor 2 N = 36
1. Assassinations	24	-07	03	-02
2. General strikes	12	09	(82)	(92)
3. Guerrilla war	27	(82)	02	-12
4. Purges	49	08	(50)	01
5. Riots	-13	23	(84)	06
6. Antigovernment demonstrations	-09	-13	(73)	(76)
7. Antiforeign demonstrations	23	02	33	11
8. Negative sanctions	(81)	21	05	-05
9. Severance of diplomatic relations	-09	(60)	-10	(57)
10. Expulsion/recall of ambassador	03	(64)	16	17
11. Expulsion/recall of lesser official	01	01	00	-04
12. Wars	(85)	(93)	10	14
13. Troop movements	(88)	(74)	01	-06
14. Mobilizations	(68)	43	-23	09

a. Decimal points are eliminated; thus, 24 = .24. Loadings greater than 50 are in parentheses. The factors exhibited here were taken from Smoker (1969a: Table 6). The matchings of Factors 3 and 1 and Factors 2 and 2 for past and future, respectively, were developed by Smoker (1969a).

four appreciable loadings: negative sanctions, wars, troop movements, and mobilizations—all foreign conflict variables. The more complex alternative future, though having significant loadings (Factor 1) for classic foreign conflict indicators (wars and troop movements), now also includes variables representing internal instability (guerrilla war) and diplomatic conflict (severing of diplomatic reactions and expelling or recalling of an ambassador). In contrast to the past world, negative sanctions failed to materialize in the factor representing conflict in an alternative future.

The domestic conflict factors also displayed diverging patterns for the past and future systems. In the former, general strikes, purges, riots, and antigovernment demonstrations were significantly loaded, while the latter included two internally directed acts (general strikes and antigovernment demonstrations) and one externally directed (severing of diplomatic relations).

A salient characteristic of the alternative future modeled in the IPS is the interrelationship between foreign and domestic conflict acts; for the past world the interrelationship is dichotomous with respect to these two categories of conflict. The variables which Smoker initially structured to define each system and thus produce these diverging effects are among those which Alker and Bock mentioned (1972: Proposition 3.24 and as displayed in Figure 2: 440) as having impact on foreign policy. But as Smoker's IPS outputs indicate, Alker and Bock's proposition could be enriched to include the relationship between these variables and both foreign and domestic conflict acts. Alker and Bock's material needs to suggest that within complex world systems (as exemplified by the IPS alternative future) *inter*national aggression is related to *intra*national instability.

Diplomatic "violence" (severing of diplomatic relations and expelling or recalling of an ambassador) is exhibited in the future world system but not in the past. Though such events are consistent with Alker and Bock's Proposition 3.40, that "the development of more rapid and reliable ... communication, together with the growth of the ... multi-functional industrial state, have transformed the conduct of diplomacy," their theory may now be refined. Though the synthesizers enumerate eight characteristics of this conduct (Propositions 3.401-3.408), they do not discuss diplomacy as conflict such as occurred as appreciable loadings (Smoker, 1969a: Table 4) in both Factors 1 and 2 of the future world. Smoker's IPS outputs suggest that as the world system increases in complexity, diplomatic relations may become an important channel for inter-nation conflict.

Research on alternative futures with simulation may assist our refinement of theories in international affairs. Though Smoker's past world displays greater incidence of conflict acts relative to the future alternative, conflict in the latter (be it foreign or domestic) may have greater repercussions throughout the system, intra- and internationally. Smoker elucidates diplomacy as a dynamically defined political activity, demonstrating how in a world of nuclear superpowers and international corporations, diplomacy moves beyond its traditional role as "a special case of international communication" (Definition 3.18) to one which also includes its use as an act of foreign conflict.

III. BREMER'S SIPER: HISTORICAL CONTEXTS, TRADE AND FOREIGN POLICY EXPECTATIONS

Throughout their synthesis of the *IESS* materials, Alker and Bock were sensitive to contextualizing their propositions about international relations within historical frames of reference. Embracing a similar orientation, Bremer (1977) examined four variables (productive resources, political stability, military capability, and international hostility) operationalized in twenty-four runs of the Simulated International ProcessER (SIPER).[18] Each of the thirty simulated nations presented different historical backgrounds. Bremer created distinct national histories by setting at varied levels the initial parameters of each nation governing their economic, political, and military characteristics. The initial parameters were (a) economic: resource allocations for consumption, investment and defense, and international security; (b) political: nations sending conflict and nations receiving conflict; and (c) military: total basic capability, total force capability, validator satisfaction, probability of office-holding, decision latitude, and probability of revolution (1977: 112-118).

A second substantive focus of Bremer's research concerned the influence of trade and policy expectations on four variables (productive resources, political stability, military capability, and international hostility). The two forms of trade policy operationalized in SIPER included a "free-trade" model in all nations for twelve of the twenty-four SIPER runs, and a "constrained-trade" policy (operating in the other twelve runs) in which allies were charged 20 percent less for exported goods, while nonallies were charged 20 percent more. A second experimental variation, involving "the rule to be used [by decision-makers] for developing expectations as to the future behavior of other nations," contrasted "status-quo" versus "future-oriented" policies. In the former, modeled in twelve of the twenty-four runs, decision-making was based on information derived from "the current situation rather than on some expected future state of affairs" (1977: 104). In the latter, nations were permitted "to adapt to—and learn from—prior experience in their forecasting behavior" (1977: 105).[19]

Bremer's principal finding was that the initial nation-state system configurations used in each of the twenty-four SIPER runs tended to explain at least 83 percent of the total variance for each of the four variables: productive resources (98.2 percent of the total variance explained), military capability (97.3 percent), political stability (91.3 percent), and international conflict (83.2 percent; 1977: 114-120). Of the some 7.5 percent variance remaining (on average), status-quo and future-oriented policy alternatives accounted for 22.2 percent, while trade policy explained only .5 percent. The combined effect of the two policy areas explained on average 22.7 percent of the variance; the remaining 77.9 percent was attributed to residual factors generated by stochastic processes in SIPER (1977: 112, 128-132).

While these findings reaffirm the desideratum that we analyze internation processes from a comparative perspective, they further suggest that research of international affairs inspect with greater depth historical patterns of nation characteristics analogous to those Bremer manipulated to set initial nation parameters in the twenty-four SIPER runs. These results, though they do not elucidate *how* history influences the SIPER parameters, augment the salience of historical nation differences for explaining variance among SIPER runs for each of the four dependent variables (productive resources, political stability, military capability, and international hostility), and exhibit the negligible impact of policy variables. In so doing, these outputs raise questions concerning the use of ceteris paribus clauses as theoretical qualifiers sans investigation of historical characteristics of nations under research. Though Alker and Bock tend to contextualize their synthesis historically and are sensitive to the pitfalls of ahistorical research, the integrators could constrain their proposition (Proposition 3.28abc) on efficacies of information-gathering and expectation formation phases of foreign policy-making by discussing the differences among nations due to their diverging histories.

In summary, two principal findings emerged from Bremer's analysis of SIPER outputs: (a) Historical differences among nations tended to explain much of the variance for each of the four dependent variables (productive resources, political stability, military capability, and international hostility), averaging 92.5 percent, while (b) "expectation rules" (status-quo versus future-oriented) and trade policy alternatives (free-trade versus constrained-trade) explained but small amounts of the remaining 7.5 percent variance. Implications of these results reaffirm tenets of comparative historical analysis of nations. Salient variables to be inspected should include those which Bremer utilized in establishing initial parameters for the thirty SIPER nations studied.

CONCLUSIONS

Rather than repeat the summaries made in the course of presenting the findings, these conclusions will attempt to integrate schematically analyses of the outputs from the ten simulations and their associated studies encompassed in the project on Simulated International Processes (SIP). In his article in Hoole and Zinnes's volume on quantitative international politics, Bremer (1976) discusses several SIP studies individually but does not view them in unison. It is possible, however, to display fifty-three variables reported in our chapter with the schematic in Figure 7.3.[20] The number of multiple mentions of simulators in the following discussion indicates, in our judgment, the amount of overlap among the SIP studies.

It is intriguing to note the extent to which the rubrics used by Alker and Bock (1972), in synthesizing articles from the *IESS* and complementary sources, have been embodied in the work of the SIP simulators. Propositions were developed in all four categories. In Table 7.5 are enumerated the propositions and definitions from Alker and Bock used in displaying findings from the analyses of the simulations. Overall, about one-quarter of the items developed by Alker and Bock have been encompassed by the simulators in their analyses. Thus, our use of the inventory vindicates Alker and Bock's (1972: 387) hope that their report might "be of value in different ways to its different readers."

One may use Singer's (1961) notion concerning "levels of analyses" in categorizing the work of our SIP collaborators. Although refinements are possible, it seems judicious to conceive of the variables schematized in Figure 7.3 as those related to decision-making as contrasted with those involving macro-political, social, and military processes. As indicated in the coding in Figure 7.3, some 40 percent of the boxes involved variables at the individual and person-to-person decision-making level; 60 percent may be characterized as describing national, foreign policy, and international processes. Let us now attempt to discuss the findings in summary fashion at these two levels of analysis, even though they have been presented in detail in this essay in five separate sections.

MACRO-INTERNATIONAL PROCESSES

Perhaps the most revealing outcome of the work in Simulated International Processes (SIP) is found in Bremer's (1977: Ch. 3) discovery that the "historical differences," as he labels them, accounted for some 83 to 98 percent of the variance in the levels of performance of his simulated nations with respect to productive resources (TBC), military capability (TFC), and political stability (POH). The historical differences in his

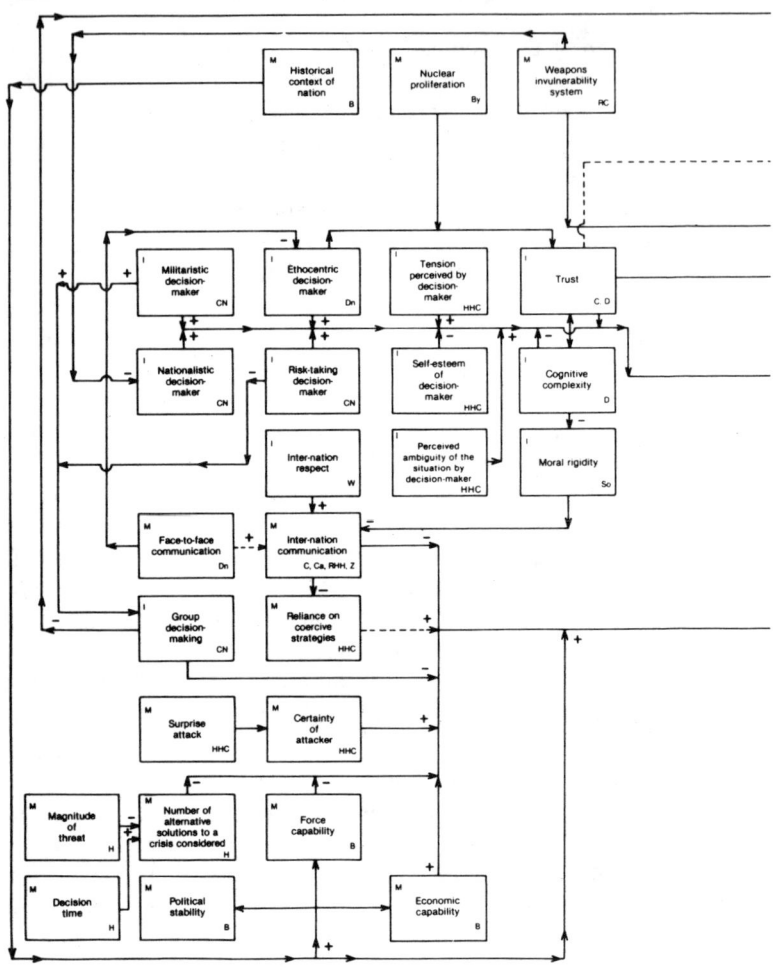

Figure 7.3 Substantive Outcomes

NOTES: Solid line = obtained linkages; broken line = implied linkages; + = positive relationship; — = negative relationship.

Arrows are included as heuristic devices to indicate association of a variable with related variables; they are not intended to assert causality. When two or more arrows join to form a single one, this does not indicate an interaction effect, but that each variable was reported to have a separate relationship with the same variable.

Boxes are coded in the upper-lefthand corner with I or M to signify individual/small-group activity and macro/system process, respectively.

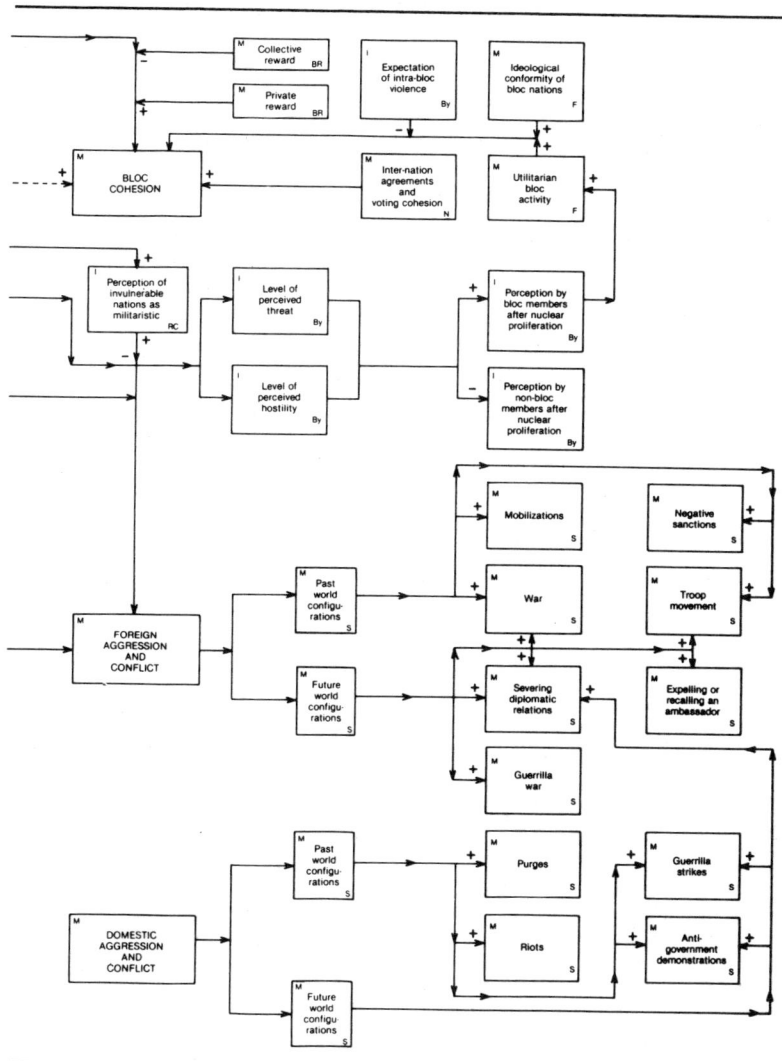

Boxes are coded in the lower-righthand corner with letters indicating their reference:

B	= Bremer (1977)	H	= C. F. Hermann (1969, 1972)
By	= Brody (1963a)	HHC	= Hermann, Hermann, and Cantor (1974)
BR	= Burgess and Robinson (1969)	N	= Nardin (1965b)
C	= Caspary (1963)	RC	= Raser and Crow (1969)
Ca	= Cappello (1972)	RHH	= Robinson, Hermann, and Hermann (1969)
CN	= Crow and Noel (1977)	S	= Smoker (1969a)
D	= Driver (1977)	So	= Shapiro (1966b)
Dn	= Druckman (1968)	W	= Wright (1963)
F	= Forcese (1968, 1976)	Z	= Zinnes (1966b)

This schematic was designed by Joseph J. Valadez.

Table 7.5
LIST OF PROPOSITIONS AND DEFINITIONS FROM ALKER AND BOCK, CITED WHEN DISPLAYING SUBSTANTIVE OUTCOMES OF SIP[a]

Four Section Headings of Alker and Bock			
Participants and Perspectives	Behaviors and Processes	International Systems	Resources, Arenas, Environments
$N^b = 44$	$N=50$	$N = 17$	$N = 14$
2.13	3.01	4.12	5.02
2.08*	3.04	4.16	
2.12*	3.05*	4.17	
2.21	3.06		
2.25	3.07*		
2.26	3.12		
2.27	3.12*		
2.28	3.13		
2.29	3.18		
2.36	3.18*		
2.40	3.20		
2.41	3.24		
2.44	3.25		
	3.26		
	3.27		
	3.28		
	3.31		
	3.32		
	3.37		
	3.40		

a. Proposition and definition numbers are carried to two decimal places only.
b. N consists of the total number of propositions (excluding definitions) posited by Alker and Bock (1972).
* Denotes a Definition rather than a proposition.

twenty-four systems were the result of his having established "six different initial system configurations . . . under four different sets of parameter values" (1977: 81). As Bremer's findings dramatize, the "historical" context of natural processes is critical in determining the outcome effects.

The SIP findings summarized below exhibit historical variations due primarily to differences in interventions and to different initial conditions and parameter settings. It is imperative to remember that the SIP simulations were designed to diverging specifications because of the theoretical concerns of the simulators.

Smoker's findings supported historical relativity in intra-nation as well as inter-nation relations in his research on foreign and domestic conflict in past-world and alternative-future formulations of the International Processes Simulation (IPS). Factor analyses of domestic and foreign conflict revealed different loadings for past and future worlds. The past-world domestic factor included exclusively general strikes, purges, riots, and antigovernment demonstrations; the future-world domestic factor included but two of these—general strikes and antigovernment demonstrations—but also a foreign conflict dimension, severing of diplomatic relations. In a similar fashion, the loading of items in the factor analyses of foreign conflict varied as one moved from past to future. Severing diplomatic relations, expelling or recalling an ambassador, troop movements, and war were all found as loading on foreign conflict in the past. One of the "domestic" variables (guerrilla war) which had *not* loaded on the domestic factor for either past or future now loaded on the future factor representing foreign conflict.

Such historical effects—whether they are due to nation and system configuration as established by initial conditions and parameter settings, as in the Bremer simulation, or whether they are due to the interaction of variables within the simulation as it represents different time segments, as in the Smoker simulation—constitute an important part of the raison d'être for the use of simulations for theory construction. It seems impossible to represent the contextual impacts of past and present conditioning variables in ordinary language.

Coalitions and Blocs

When Brody reviewed the literature on the behavior of the international system in terms of the proliferation of nuclear capability, he found much disagreement about its potential effects (Brody, 1963a: Ch. 2). Some argued the spreading of nuclears would enhance alliances; others contended that ties among members of a given bloc would be loosened where members of the alliance were in possession of an autonomous nuclear force. In Brody's n^{th}-country study, the distrust of and hostility toward nonallied nations prior to the spread of nuclear weapons changed after their spread to smaller nations. As Brody (1963a: 745) summarized the change in the post-spread system, "(1) threat external to the bloc is reduced; (2) threat internal to the bloc is increased."

The simulators also viewed ways in which blocs were made more cohesive. Burgess and Robinson (1969) investigated economic factors affecting blocs. They found that coalitions which rendered private benefits to individual nations in addition to collective advantages were more stable than when collective rewards had been the sole source of benefit. Forcese

(1968) also concluded that utilitarian features of bloc membership were significant in maintaining internal cohesion. His investigation indicated that ideological similarities among allied nations were equally as important as utilitarian functions. Nardin's (1965b) and Brody's (1963a) investigations report concurring findings. The former researcher observed that alliance membership was associated with benefit yielding international agreements. The latter found that cohesion increased among nations when they mutually perceived threat and hostility from enemies.

Thus, the simulators investigated both facets of alliance processes, their strengthening and their weakening. Note how the conceptualizations by the various researchers tended to form a common language when the verbal theory was formulated for simulation purposes, whether the original language was that of strategic theory (as in the case of political scientist Brody) or in terms of Etzioni's theory of action (as in the case of sociologist Forcese).

DECISION-MAKING PROCESSES AT THE INDIVIDUAL AND GROUP LEVEL

Various determinants and consequences of conflict constituted the central core of the simulators' investigations of decision-making, whether such behavior occurred at the individual level per se or among individuals as they formed teams and councils for decision-making purposes. It is useful to conceive of the processes taking place at the individual level as explicating the action at the macro level. It is for this reason that the long-touted imperative to keep the levels of analysis quite distinct and separate seems to have been neglected by the researchers using simulation.

In Driver's (1977) analysis of cognitive style, political decision-makers evidencing low cognitive complexity and distrust of other nations tended to engage in serious aggression. For Brody's (1963a) investigation, distrust of other nations' heads of state also surfaced as a factor associated with inter-nation conflict. Distrust tended to be related to the perceived amount of threat and hostility from other nations. Other investigators extended the list of variables, concluding that low self-esteem, perceived situational ambiguity, and tensions (Hermann et al., 1974), as well as proclivity for risk-taking and militaristic and nationalistic attitudes (Crow and Noel, 1977), are positively associated with increases in international conflict.

The tight interlocking of macro and micro mechanisms in the outputs of the simulations was also found to hold with respect to the studies involving the capacity to delay response. In Raser and Crow's study of the destabilizing international effects of a weapons invulnerability system developed by simulated superpowers, nations with such were perceived by others as militaristic and likely to precipitate war, a finding again confirmed by Crow and Noel's conclusion that the most militaristic leaders were also the most bellicose. In the former study, the shift in perceptual orientation in the international community suggests that acquisition of weapons invulnerability may be related to less powerful nations' perceived threat and hostility, as discussed by Brody (1963a: 745).

This focus on psychological components associated with inter-nation aggression and perceived hostility and threat tied intimately into the existence of social processes in the small. Shapiro's (1966b) analysis of Driver's outputs focuses on systemic factors related to precipitation of conflict. He suggested that distrust associated with rigid, unelaborated cognitive styles leads to reduced communication between nations. Zinnes's (1966b), Cappello's (1972), Caspary's (1963), and Robinson et al.'s (1969) analyses concentrating on this variable concluded that the reduction in flow of information between nations was strongly related to the emergence of inter-nation hostilities. In theorizing about causal linkages, these researchers suggested that in crisis situations, restricted information input tended to induce decision-makers to rely on prearranged coercive strategies. Druckman's and Zinnes's INS outputs indicated that communication flow between nations was vital for sustaining inter-nation tranquility. Druckman (1968) demonstrated that decision-makers in the INS who have continuous contact with individuals of equal status from other nations exhibit virtually no ethnocentrism. Zinnes's research led to a related relationship, namely, that nations in the INS which most respected each other also tended to communicate most frequently. Maintenance of information flow among nations is a recurrent theme in many of the person-computer simulations included in the work on Simulated International Processes.

When communication among decision-makers takes place in groupings, one finds that the dynamics of such committees and councils influence the foreign policy outputs of the simulated nations. Crow and Noel (1977) and Hermann et al. (1974) concluded that decisions formed through group interaction tended to be less aggressive than those made by individuals. But there are interactive effects, too. Nationalistically oriented groups tend to become more rather than less belligerent. To come full circle, macro variables such as the nation's economic and force capabilities increase the hostility of the group's response to crises, such as a threat of surprise attack (Hermann, et al., 1974).

Couched in extant theory on ethnocentrism, Druckman's (1968) INS study exhibited another feature of group structure. His analysis demonstrated that there are differing degrees of ethnocentrism, depending upon a person's hierarchical position. Decision-makers aspiring to a high status displayed the greatest dislike for other nations, allies and enemies alike. But as always, external situational factors influence outcomes, too. When there is surprise with a high threat, accompanied by short decision time, there is a reduction in the number of alternative solutions to the crisis considered and an increased likelihood of hostile responses by groups (Hermann, 1969, 1972).

The work from eighteen researchers involved in the ten simulations we have examined can be summarized in terms of the three different tacks utilized in their studies.

Many developed their simulation runs to contrast initial conditions, as, for example, in Driver's and Shapiro's comparison of complex and less complex participants, and in Forcese's examination of nations with utilitarian versus ideological versus coercive mechanisms for the development of bloc cohesion. Druckman also embraced this approach for his comparative analysis of ethnocentrism among heads of state, aspiring elites, and foreign diplomats; as did Crow and Noel in their study of militaristic, risk-taking, and nationalistic politicos in group and individual decision-making contexts; and Robinson et. al. for study of decision-making in crisis versus noncrisis; and Smoker for examining past-world and alternative-future systems in the IPS. Bremer's comparison of SIPER historical systems represents this approach in an all-computer environment.

A few simulators were able to introduce experimental interventions per se, as when Brody interpolated into his runs the spread of nuclears to the small nations, and when Raser and Crow, and Hermann et al. gave notice of a surprise attack.

Many utilized the outputs of the simulations in post hoc ways either when analyzing their own runs or those of others, as in Caspary's analysis of bellicose leaders in crises and in Shapiro's inspection of interaction effects between morals and cognitive complexity in decision-making. Zinnes used this approach when examining perceived threat and hostility as affected by inter-nation communication; so did Wright in his study of the relationship between inter-nation respect and communication, and Ruge when examining cultural differences between Norwegian and U.S. participants in the INS environment. Following through on Forcese's research, Nardin analyzed intra-bloc conflict and ideological components of bloc cohesion through post hoc analysis of simulation outputs.

Of all the experimenters involved in SIP, the Hermanns utilized their own simulation runs more than others, even piggybacking on work of the Western Behavioral Sciences Institute to secure replication of their findings.

The more than fifty variables as interrelated in several hundred hypotheses, all within the context of initial conditions and parameter estimations of SIP simulations, have yielded a rich analysis. Components of this study have included investigations of (a) international relations as influenced by heads of state and their perspectives in foreign policy decision-making; (b) transnational phenomena, including economic and political collective action, military relationships, and cultural dispositions as these relate to integrative perspectives and coalitional behavior; and (c) effects of domestic and foreign conflict on international affairs in contexts with planned strategies, as well as in the case of surprise attack. These findings constitute the substantive corpus of the project on Simulated International Processes.

Figure 7.3 integrates fifty-three variables schematically. Variables not depicted, though researched by SIP and previously discussed in the body of the text (such as Ruge's [1969, 1972]) are typically those requiring interstitial theories linking them substantively to the holistic display in Figure 7.3.

By exhibiting these outputs in terms of current theories in international affairs, have we vindicated Guetzkow's (1959: 188) early belief, stated prior to formulation of any of the SIP models, that "inter-nation simulation will be of heuristic value in clarifying our theories of international relations"? As we concur with Alker and Bock's (1972: 489) impression that "much of the [qualitative and] quantitative, empirical literature suffers from a lack of theoretical power," it may be that another application, in addition to clarification, would be to elaborate, integrate, refine, and contradict existing theories about international affairs, which we have at various times attempted in this chapter. Through displaying two decades of SIP research, we hope, as did Alker and Bock (1972: 488), also to have "help[ed] significantly to increase the understanding and control of international relations." Though the nascent state of our models augurs ill for "control," increases in "understanding" may be a pragmatic way that outputs from Simulated International Processes contribute to theory-building in international relations.

NOTES

1. Crow and Noel's series of exercises used an all-person version of the INS.
2. The amount of psychological research concerned with cognitive complexity has increased over the last ten years. During this time there have been several studies (Richardson and Soucar, 1971; Bavelas et al., 1976) suggesting there is need for refinement of the methods used for measuring cognitive complexity. Louise (1974), examining the intercorrelation of three tests measuring cognitive complexity, found that two widely used measures, the Bieri Role Construct Repertory Test and Schroder's Paragraph Completion Test, were not significantly related. In his study,

Driver employed the Situational Interpretation Test (SIT), which was not considered in these critical reviews.

3. Communications sent by decision-makers were either directed to other heads of state or released to the World Times, the simulation news bureau (Shapiro, 1966: 7).

4. The Hermann et al. (1974) study was completed, thus making four works, but it is not discussed until section C of this chapter.

5. For chi-square tests in this paragraph, the first score is derived from the Great Lakes runs of eleven simulations, while the second is from the dozen Western Behavioral Sciences Institute runs. The MIT games were also analyzed by Robinson et al., but they are eliminated here, since we are limiting our exposition to outcomes obtained in the INS.

6. Data for Druckman's analysis were acquired from the participants in eleven Raser-Crow simulations (1964) using a personality trait booklet. These ratings were consolidated into four principal attitudes judged to be indicators of ethnocentrism (Druckman, 1968: 50-53).

7. As indicated in note b to Table 7.2, mean halo effects are judged along a positive-negative continuum. For effects recorded in Figure 7.2, the higher the score in a positive direction, the greater is the preference; negative scores indicate ethnocentric bias.

8. Simulation participants consisted of political science student volunteers in both Norway (N = 48) and the U.S. (N - 48). They were randomly assigned to nations and roles. The runs in the United States were conducted by John R. Raser at the University of Oregon, under the auspices of the Western Behavioral Sciences Institute.

9. Ruge (1972: 299) reported mean scores recorded at the various points of the Likert scale.

10. We calculated this chi-square using a 2 × 2 table. The seven points of the Likert scale were collapsed to form two cells: friendly scores (points 5.1-7) and nonfriendly/hostile scores (1-5).

11. The hostile nation was "manned by participant-observers. This threat to the coalition was created for control purposes: it insured a minimally viable coalition because of the threat-cohesion principle ... and it permitted the establishment of experimental control over threat perception so that observed variance could be attributed to the treatment effect" (Burgess and Robinson, 1969: 203).

12. War also occurred in another system after proliferation, but only once.

13. "This statistic indicates that information about the availability of a weapons survivability system reduces the probability of errors in predicting the type of decision by 33% on the average" (Hermann et al., 1974: 95).

14. Of the 60 nations involved in the simulation, 39 made responses classified as either a decision to counterattack or a decision to delay retaliation. These 39 were used in subsequent analysis.

15. Of the 11 independent variables hypothesized as influencing the decision to retaliate, only the 6 reported were statistically significant. The nonsignificant variables were: nuclear force capabilities for defense, cognitive complexity, situation considered accidental, number of alternatives available, and the extent of isolation of the simulated nation in the international system (Hermann et al., 1974: Table 3).

Self-esteem was measured using Cohen's (1953) 13-item self-ideal discrepancy measure. Ambiguity was rated on a four-point scale by participants shortly after notification of the attack (Hermann et al., 1974: 88). Degree of group interaction was measured through content analysis of inter-nation messages and conferences (1974: 90). Participants recorded their perceptions of world tension using a ten-point scale at the beginning of each decision period (1974: 26). Nuclear capability and economic strength were obtained through computer output of the INS programmed relations.

16. Beta-weights are standardized (Hermann et al., 1974: Table 3).

17. The International Processes Simulation (IPS) was developed in the Northwestern University project on Simulated International Processes (SIP; Smoker, 1981). See Valadez and Tygesson (1981) for a discussion of the differences between INS and IPS, both involving person-computer formats. See Guetzkow and Valadez (1981b) for analysis of IPS validity. The first four runs of the set of sixteen were used for debugging; the analyses were done on twelve runs. Two types of decision-makers operated the simulation. The first were adult professionals from industry, the military, commerce, and politics. In the second, sixteen- and seventeen-year-old high school students were the participants.

18. See Valadez and Tygesson (1981) for a discussion of SIPER's all-computer environment as contrasted with the person-computer formats of the INS and IPS.

19. There was overlap of these four policy variations as represented by the following table:

		TRADE POLICY	
		Free-trade	*Constrained-trade*
EXPECTATIONS	Future-oriented	runs 1-6	runs 13-18
	Status-Quo	runs 7-12	runs 14-24

20. These forty-three variables include most of those discussed above. Variables which would have made the schematic discursive are not represented.

8

Simulation and "Reality":
Validity Research

Harold Guetzkow and Joseph J. Valadez

To the student of politics who is a poet, simulations of international relations must be works of art, constructions that fulfill aesthetic needs. To the student of politics who is a social scientist, simulations are theories that, like other claims to knowledge, need verification. When scholars are policy-influencers, they seek to apply simulations to the affairs of actual states and international organizations, in order to guide them in the direction of their own values. The aesthetician may work without the constraints of reality; both social scientists and policy-influencers, in their attempts to understand and to shape the processes and outcomes of

Authors' Note: This chapter is an updated and revised version by the authors of Harold Guetzkow's "Some Correspondences between Simulations and 'Realities' in International Relations," pp. 202-269 in Morton A. Kaplan (ed.) *New Approaches to International Relations* (New York: St. Martin's Press, 1968). Preparation of this chapter was supported by the Gordon Scott Fulcher Chair of Decision-Making, held by Harold Guetzkow in the Political Science Department at Northwestern University. An overview of an earlier version was presented to the Norman Wait Harris Conference in celebration of the Seventy-Fifth Anniversary of the University of Chicago in June 1966. This work has benefited greatly from research supported by the JWGA/ARPA/NU project on Simulated International Processes (Advanced Research Projects Agency, SD 260), conducted within the International Relations Program at Northwestern University, 1959-1972. Special thanks are due the Carnegie Corporation of New York for providing the opportunity for work during 1966-1967.

international politics, accept the challenge that their simulations must be anchored empirically, yet not be bound by such "realities." To gain confidence in their simulations, the social scientists may check them against scholarly work in general. Further, they should compare their constructions with "realities"—empirical descriptions of the world of nation-states and international organizations. Comparisons of simulation theory with extant verbal theory have been made elsewhere (Guetzkow and Valadez, 1981a). This will compare some aspects of simulations of international processes with corresponding empirical materials obtained from political, economic, and military studies of international affairs.

USE OF SIMULATIONS FOR THEORY-BUILDING IN INTERNATIONAL RELATIONS

Although simulations are expensive, given the primitive technologies of today, some limited exploration of their potential values in the study of international relations is under way, which Sidney Verba (1964) and Shubik (1975: 279-294) have reviewed. Here are three possible values of their use by the social scientist:

(1) Simulations *enable scholars to build syntheses beyond the capability of the individual,* as is now being realized in the Project LINK global economic model (Hickman and Klein, 1979).

(2) Simulations *demand an explication and then an articulation of theory usually not required by the vernacular,* as Herrera and members of the project team for the Latin American World Model (1976) illustrate vividly in their critique and reconstruction of the computerized model of the club of Rome (Meadows et al., 1972).

(3) Simulations, once created, *are vehicles for experimental work, providing devices for both replication and variation,* as Bonham and his associates (1976) have dramatized in their exciting analyses of the cognitive maps of the Yom Kippur war.

However, a simulated construction is but theory. It provides no shortcut or magical route to the "proof" of the validity of the verbal and mathematical components it contains. Thus, there is a need for a systematic examination of the extent of the congruences between empirical analyses of world processes and simulations of international relations. This essay attempts such an examination.

It is still convenient to employ the definition[1] of simulation of behavioral processes written some years ago: "an operating representation, in reduced and/or simplified form, of relations among social units (or entities) by means of symbolic and/or replicate component parts" (Guetzkow, 1959: 184).

Within the perspective that simulation is operating theory, let us proceed with our central task: To what extent are simulations of international processes being verified? Probing reveals that the problems involved in verifying simulation theory are not basically different from those involved in establishing validity for symbolic theory in the languages of the historian or the mathematician (Hochberg, 1965; Kress, 1974). The Association for the Advancement of Science on "The Validation of Scientific Theories" seem still to hold true (Frank, 1954: esp. 3-36). Charles F. Hermann (1967b) has investigated the sweep of validation problems in games and simulations. The present essay however, addresses itself to only a segment of the gamut. Omitted herein, for example, is an examination of the validities involved when simulations are used for such purposes as prediction and exploration of policy alternatives and alternative counterfactual universes, as well as a discussion of the use of simulation in education (Alger, 1963; Guetzkow and Cherryholmes, 1966; Cherryholmes, 1966b; Coleman et al., 1966a, 1966b; Robinson et al., 1966; Suransky, 1980). However, as Hermann (1967b: 220) pointed out, "for the most part the various purposes for conducting games and simulations do not negate the need for criteria we can use to estimate the degree of fidelity with which one system (the operating model) reproduces aspects of another (the reference system)." Bremer (1976: 312-315) recently focused the validation problems by contrasting the use of simulations as "quasi-laboratory settings" for exploring hypotheses versus their use in "macrovalidity" studies contrasting simulation outputs with empirical findings.

VALIDITY AS HOMOMORPHISM OF THEORY AND EMPIRICAL ANALYSES

When policy-influencers and scholars handle the contents of international politics, seldom is there explicit reference to the evidential base from which assertions are constructed, whether these statements are based on fragments of cocktail conversation or on the propositions of formalized verbal theory. "Facts on file" as reported in news media are but interpreted reports of journalists (Gamson and Modigliani, 1965: 47-78). Nor are the "inside dopester's" anecdotes to be taken at face value, for often such a participant observer of a decision group is only an intimate member with vested interests. As William D. Coplin (1966: 562) pointed out in his comparison of verbal theories with simulation theory, "the lack of congruence between the assumptions of the simulation and the assumptions of the verbal theories does not necessarily indicate that the simulation model lacks validity, since the verbal theorist has no monopoly on valid hypotheses." Thus, in seeking to establish simulation theory, it is imperative to make checks not only against another set of theories, but also against empirical observations.

It would seem impossible at the outset to achieve a strict and complete isomorphism between the "realities" of world processes (the reference system) and simulation materials, in compliance with May Brodbeck's (1959: 374) stipulation that "there must be a one-to-one correspondence between the elements of the thing of which it is the model." In the early stages in the construction of simulations there is at best a homomorphism, in which many entities in one system may be represented by fewer entities in the other system, with but some correspondence in the relationships among the coalesced entities (Beer, 1965: 223-231). The homomorphic many-to-one relationships may eventually be differentiated to the extent of forming isomorphic one-to-one relationships, in which the materials "resemble one another as systems . . . in ways which do not depend on the particular elements of which each consists" (Kaplan, 1964: 263). But to have a complete isomorphism the model might be as complex and intractable as the reality. It is ironic that sometimes simulations are so large that they defy intuitive understanding. Yet is this not exactly one reason why simulations hold promise? Someday they may permit us to reach beyond the limitations of verbal and mathematical formulations.

Some homomorphy may exist among outputs as well as between the very processes which result in such outputs. As we analyze the correspondences between simulations and "realities" sometimes an internal process, like the representation of the decision-making within foreign offices, helps produce an outcome of some validity, such as the constellation of internation alliances. At other times, less often because of lack of appropriate research, an internal process will be judged to be of some validity because the very process itself has some congruence with corresponding processes in the reference data.

In verifying theory, the simulations' constructions are compared with reference materials of the "real world" (Kaplan, 1964: Chs. 23, 36). This testing of hypotheses may be done with different degrees of accuracy, ranging from rough-and-ready appraisals of the behavior of the individuals and groups involved in world politics to rigorous, systematic comparisons with content analyses of diplomatic documents (North et al., 1963) and with careful coding of interactions among international representatives (Alger, 1966b, 1968a). The lack of correspondences between the simulations and the empirical materials indicates the extent of nonverification.

Reference materials used in assessing correspondences may be abstract and prototypic in nature, embodying processes that are supposed to hold more generally, since they have been derived from a gamut of studies made in the field and laboratory (as Herbert C. Kelman (1965) and his associates have developed in their *International Behavior*). Or, reference data may be used which are more concrete and systematically gathered from operations within the international system, such as those Wright presented in *A Study of War* (1965). The extent to which processes within the international system differ from those found in noninternational materials is largely unknown today. To what extent does the simplification achieved in the conventional laboratory experiment of the psychologist make the findings a valid reference for the outputs generated in the simulation exercise (Barber, 1966: 8-13)? May the phenomena found in the field of noninternational affairs be used as a legitimate probe of the validity of a global simulation?

In posing the verification problem in the study of international relations, our distinctions are overdrawn. More than that, our colleagues in the enterprise believe the emphasis on validation distorts the fertile and specific roles games and simulations might have "in constructing international relations theory" (Raser et al., 1970: esp. 183-185). As is widely recognized in the methodology of science, work is not done analytically with empirical materials without constructing at least implicit theories about the *denotata*, as events are selected from the entire population of such items and then a few reported events characterized. Sense impressions are "validated" by perceiving and then reinterpreting them in terms of individual theories of history, as Richard Snyder and Glenn Paige believe happened in Truman's conceptualization of the cables from Korea on June 24, 1950 (Snyder and Paige, 1958: 359). Practitioner and scholar alike work with materials at varying levels of abstraction (Guetzkow, 1966a: 264-267), sometimes "correcting" data in terms of theories and at other times "editing" such theories because of the data. "Our longing is for data that prove and certify theory, but such is not to be our lot," according to contemporary methodologists (Webb et al., 1966: 10). However, by using some systematic rigor in making comparisons between simulations and realities, by taking reference data largely from extant international systems rather than from laboratory and field research about noninternational phenomena, and by finding in simulations internal processes and outputs which correspond to reference processes as well as reference outcomes, a convergence of evidence is gained which increases the credibility of the theoretical constructions of simulations.

ASSESSMENTS OF CORRESPONDENCES: SIMULATIONS AND EMPIRICAL FINDINGS

Let us now examine assessments of the congruence that simulations of international relations have with analyses made of empirical materials derived from world processes. Inasmuch as but one work (Bonham, 1967) on the validation of either the RAND/MIT political exercises or TEMPER has been recorded so far, the studies to be surveyed in this chapter center largely on the Inter-Nation Simulation (INS) and its variations: the International Processes Simulation (IPS) and the Simulated International ProcessER (SIPER).[2] This limitation is great; therefore, our findings may *not* be extrapolated broadly. In a later section of this chapter we also refer to a series of comparative validity studies carried out by Bremer (1977: Chs. 5, 6) of the INS and SIPER. Each of these three simulations (INS, IPS, and SIPER) was developed in association with the Simulated International Processes (SIP) project at Northwestern University. An overview of SIP's development from 1957 through 1972 is presented elsewhere in this volume (Guetzkow, 1981a).

No attempt is made to rehearse materials presented elsewhere. *Simulation in Social Science: Readings* (Guetzkow, 1962c) and its sequel, *Simulation in Social and Administrative Science: Overviews and Case-Examples* (Guetzkow et al., 1972), providing general background. The book Guetzkow and his colleagues assembled, *Simulation in International Relations: Developments for Research and Teaching* (Guetzkow et al., 1963), describes the Inter-Nation Simulation (INS) in considerable detail. A summary presentation is given in an earlier essay, "A Use of Simulation in the Study of Inter-Nation Relations" (Guetzkow, 1959), which is reprinted as Chapter 2 of the Guetzkow et al. (1963) *Developments* volume; this essay was updated for IBM's 1964 Scientific Computing Symposium on Simulation Models and Gaming (Guetzkow, 1966a). The newcomer may find Verba's (1964) or Geutzkow and Hollist's (1976) review of this work useful in providing further orientation to simulation in international relations.

Findings on the correspondences between simulations and realities will be discussed from a substantive point of view. The studies summarized will cover first the "Decision-Makers and Their Nations" and then "Relations Among Nations." The assessment of correspondences between each unit of simulation and reference materials is reported on a five-point scale after the relevant research is discussed, as a *correspondence rating*. A summary of these assessments of congruence is contained at the end of each of the substantive sections of this chapter, in Tables 8.3, 8.5, 8.11, 8.14, 8.15, and 8.20, with a final summation in Table 8.22. A correspondence rating is given in parentheses following the discussion of each of the 136 comparisons between simulations and realities in international relations. The rating of correspondence is either "much" (M), "some" (S), "little" (L), "none" (N), or "incongruent" (I). "Much" and "some" were used to describe the correspondences where the findings obtained in simulation and reference materials were judged not to be different from each other at levels of significance of 5 percent or less, or between 5 and 10 percent, respectively. A rating of "little" was assigned when the sets of materials indicated relationships between variables to be in the same direction but clearly of different magnitudes. If significant relationships were in opposite directions, a rating of "incongruent" was given. When the findings from reference materials were not significant in the simulation materials, or vice versa, the designation "none" was made. In some cases statistical tests were not available; we then made intuitive ratings. Though in most instances we conformed to this coding scheme, on occassion we did deviate. Whenever referent materials consisted of anecdotal information rather than statistical analyses, we never judged a correspondence greater than "some," in order to reflect the speculative nature of this information. When Bremer's (1977) analysis of the Inter-Nation Simulation (INS) and the Simulated International ProcessER (SIPER) validity are presented (see pp. 312-325) it will be feasible to be rigorous in the application of our coding rules.

While viewing the substantive findings, it is important to realize not only that the correspondences are based on very limited analyses of realities, the reference data, but that severe methodological difficulties are encountered in studying the comparisons, as has been found in making comparisons among nations (Eckstein and Apter, 1963: Part II; 39-94) or between societies (Naroll and Cohen, 1968). The coarseness of our measuring instruments themselves (Guetzkow, 1965c: 25-31) implies further limitations. These problems are codified in Przeworski and Teune (1970: Part II; 91-131). Two difficulties of special prominence indicate that the entire effort of this attempt to survey the correspondences at this time should be viewed with much circumspection: (1) In all instances the matching of variables in the reference and simulation materials has been an intuitive process, usually based upon phenotypic judgments of the authors. (2) In most instances, in neither the reference nor the simulation materials has attention been given to the problem of the reliability of the data and outputs. Yet, unless both sets of materials can be replicated, a lack of correspondence may be due to variations coming from unreliability rather than to invalidities of the simulation per se.

Immediately after the original correspondence ratings had been completed (Guetzkow, 1969d), George Modelski carried out a reliability analysis which he reports as follows:

> Out of these 24 studies Guetzkow elicited 55 instances for each of which he made a judgment of correspondence between simulations and international realities or, in other words, an assessment of the fidelity with which the simulation represented the real world. In each such instance he gave an explicit rating of "Much," "Some," "Little," "None," or "Incongruent" correspondence. Guetzkow

found that 38 out of 55 comparisons carried out by him merited a rating of "Much" or "Some" correspondence in 13 cases "Little" or no correspondence was found, and 4 cases were clearly incongruent [Guetzkow, 1969d: 253].

The extent of agreement between the Modelski and Guetzkow ratings was examined by J. Krend (1969). The overall correlation statistic for these two sets of observations (Pearson's $r = .96$) is statistically significant at the 0.01 level or better. Overall, again, Guttman's coefficient of predictability (lambda) showed a value of .047, which is small and means that the differences between the observers making the judgments were small if not insignificant (Modelski, 1970: 112-113).

Valadez examined the same works, and, without knowledge of Guetzkow's own ratings, also assigned correspondence ratings to these same 55 cases. In general and with some exceptions, his judgments correspond quite well with Guetzkow's. Taking as his baseline the cited literature, this coauthor found 30 of 55 cases to merit ratings of "much" or "some" correspondence. In 4 instances only did these two scores diverge by as much as two degrees.

We then can readily agree with C. F. Hermann's (1967b: 225) position that "multiple validity criteria are needed because of the error in measurement and because of the recognition that criteria can be only assertions about 'reality.'" It is hoped that the reader will not find the demands on attention involved in pursuit of the 136 comparisons which follow too great to bear. When patience yields, skip to the six summary tables (8.3, 8.5, 8.11, 8.14, and 8.23) and then proceed to the conclusions and the epilog.

INTER-NATION SIMULATION

"DECISION-MAKERS AND THEIR NATIONS"

In considering "Decision-Makers and Their Nations," it is convenient first to discuss individuals serving in the INS as surrogates for the descision-makers of the world. Atention will be given next to these humans assembled in groups, along with the political, economic, and military programs which function together as representations of the nation-state.

Humans as Surrogates

Because of the difficulties involved in programming the decision-making within a nation, given the present development of work in "artificial intelligence" (Feigenbaum and Feldman, 1963; Schank and Colby, 1973), humans are used in the Inter-Nation Simulation to handle these activities. These simulations are *not* being used as a "synthetic environment" in which to explore the psychological characteristics of individuals as subjects in an experiment (Kennedy, 1962: 27-29). Given the perspective of simulation as theory, the participants may be considered as surrogates, focusing upon their outputs as inputs into other components of the simulation as a whole. It was realized early that humans "bring both their own personal characteristics into the model and their own implicit theories of the way in which nations should behave" (Guetzkow, 1959: 188). It was noted also that "eventually it will be necessary to appraise these personal styles of decision-making and organizational presuppositions, so that their influence on the evolving inter-nation interaction may be studied" (Guetzkow, 1959: 188). There is now evidence on the ways in which the decision-making occurs within simulation, and these findings may be compared with results obtained from analyses of empirical materials. The following discussion will consider three aspects of the behavior of the surrogates as derived (1) from their personal characteristics, (2) from their education, and (3) from their ethnicity.

Personal Characteristics. Perhaps the most focused evidence available on the impact of personal style on outputs from the humans who constitute the decision-making units within the Inter-Nation Simulation is presented by Michael J. Driver (1965, 1977) in his essays, "A Structure Analysis of Aggression, Stress, and Personality in an Inter-Nation Simulation" and "Individual Differences as Determinants of Aggression in the Inter-Nation Simulation." Richard A. Brody (1963a) and Driver selected 336 participants for their sixteen runs of the simulation on the basis of each individual's cognitive simplicity/complexity. Driver found that outputs of the high seniors and graduates who served as his decision-makers conformed to the findings obtained in many other situations (Harvey et al., 1961; Schroder et al., 1967). Driver (1977: Table 13.1; 342) noted how those surrogates with simpler conceptual structures, as determined on a pretest, tended to involve their nations in more aggressive behavior than did those with more complex, abstract conceptual structures ($\chi^2 = 7.1**3$ $p <.005$; correspondence rating: much).

This same characteristic was investigated by Hermann et al. (1974) in a study of decision-making in response to an unidentified attack. The simulators hypothesized that cognitive complexity of the participating 325 U.S. Naval petty officers would be inversely related to the decision to counterattack a suspected foe. This prediction was found to be consistent with Driver's conclusion that individuals with less complex cognitive structures tend to exhibit more aggressive behavior than the more complex thinkers. The correlation, though in the predicted direction ($\beta = -.13$,

$b = -.12$, $s = .15$, $t = .84$, $df = 11/27$)[4] was weak (correspondence rating: little).

The success of Suedfeld and his associates in adapting the complexity concepts and techniques to historical, archival materials (Suedfeld and Tetlock, 1977; Suedfeld and Rank, 1976) gives one further confidence in the homomorphy of the simulation and the reference materials offered by Driver and the Hermanns. "Complexity of the messages produced by governmental leaders was significantly lower in crises that ended in war" (Suedfeld and Tetlock, 1977: 169).

The operation of personal characteristics of surrogates within simulations may be pinpointed, too, both in terms of a particular set of personality traits, namely "self-esteem" and "defensiveness," and in terms of a particular situation, namely "crisis." Personal characteristics are related intimately to the way in which individuals handle crises (Basowitz et al., 1955; Funkenstein et al., 1957; Janis, 1958; Lazarus, 1964; and Selye, 1956). Margaret G. Hermann (1965) has replicated aspects of these phenomena (Lazarus and Baker, 1956) concerned with self-esteem and defensiveness in her observations of 163 U.S. Naval petty officers (average age, 32.5 years) who conducted decision-making in eleven replications of a crisis-permeated simulation of policy-making (C. F. Hermann, 1969: Ch. 3). Along with many other outcomes she found that as the simulated crisis produced more negative affect, the decision-makers high in self-esteem and high in defensiveness ("avoiders") decreased their attempts to seek aid from other nations and they decreased their search for information about the threat. Conversely, those low in self-esteem but high in defensiveness ("affiliators") increased their attempts to affiliate and increased their search for information (M. G. Hermann, 1965: 73). The affiliation attempts by these two types of participants (along with four other types, reflecting the intricacies involved in personality analyses) are presented in Figure 8.1. The results are statistically significant ($F = 4.37^{**}$; correspondence rating: much).

Self-esteem, independent of defensiveness, has been found to be associated with avoidance behavior (Hermann and Hermann, 1967; Block and Thomas, 1955; Cohen, 1959; Leventhal and Perloe, 1962; Silverman, 1964). Hermann et al. (1974) examined this personality characteristic in U.S. Naval petty officers as it related to the decision to launch nuclear weapons in response to a simulated unidentified attack. Predicting self-esteem to be inversely related to this decision, the simulators monitored some ten INS runs conducted at the Great Lakes Naval Training Center. Statistical results strongly supported this hypothesis ($\beta = -.35$, $b = -.33$, $s = .13$, $t = 2.56$, $df = 6/32$, $p < .05$; correspondence rating: much; Hermann et al., 1974: 88).

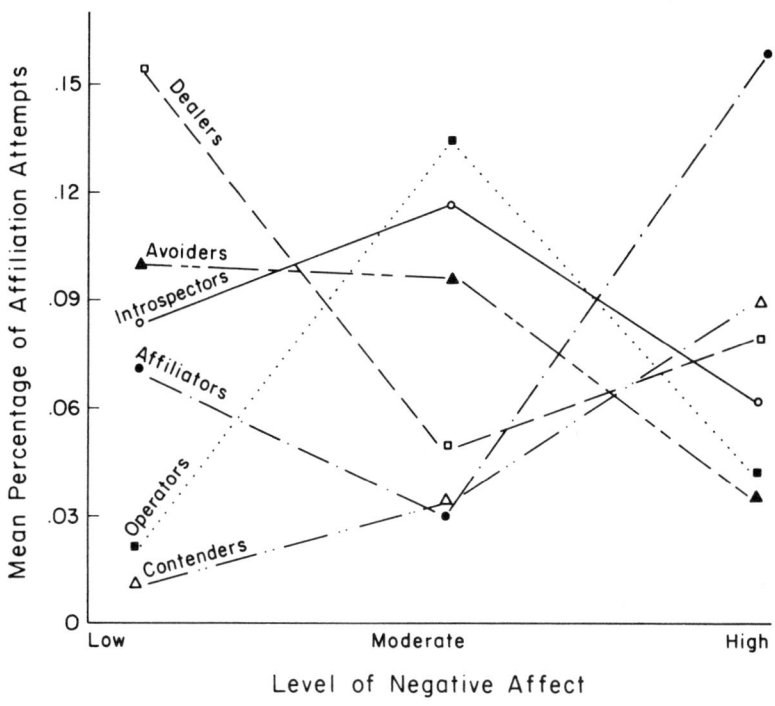

Figure 8.1 Margaret G. Hermann's Study of the Relation of Rated Negative Affect to Affiliation Attempts in an Inter-Nation Simulation

SOURCE: Adapted from M. G. Hermann (1965: Figure 1; 56).
NOTE: The levels of negative affect were obtained from ratings of three phrases (e.g., "injurious to my nation") made in response to each of seven threatening international events, by 163 U.S. Naval petty officers serving as decision-makers for the six nations operated in eleven simulations.

Hermann-like findings corresponding to field and laboratory work reported by Harold M. Schroder et al. (1967) have been obtained in a "tactical game situation" less rich than the Inter-Nation Simulation, in which crisis was created by increasing information loads. Using three measures of information-handling (delegated information searches; self-initiated information searches, as presented in Figure 7.2; and integrated utilization of sought-for information in subsequent decision-making), Streufert et al. (1965) obtained statistically significant impact of levels of information load upon information-handling by 185 college students, assembled into fourteen teams serving as decision-makers. And using the same personality measures employed by Driver in his operation with Brody of the Inter-Nation Simulation, the researchers obtained dramatic as

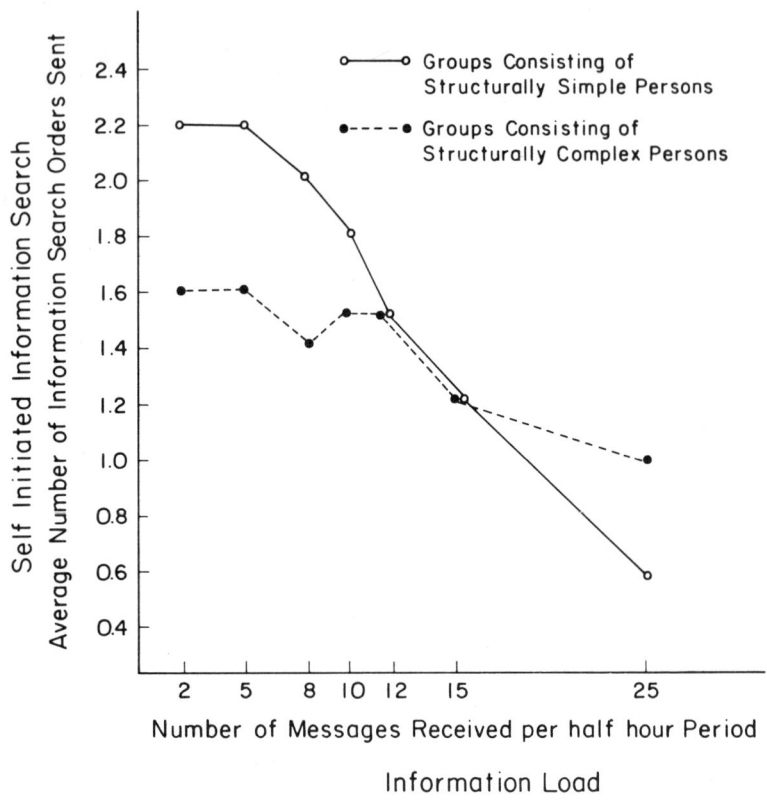

Figure 8.2 Findings from "A Tactical Game" on the Relation of Levels of Information Load on Information-Handling by "Complex" and "Simple" Individuals Under "Crisis" and "Noncrisis" Conditions

SOURCE: Struefert et al. (1965: Figure 2; 739).
NOTE: Decision-makers in this game were 185 college students, assembled into fourteen teams.

well as statistically significant differences in the effects of crisis upon information-handling for those surrogates with structurally complex styles, as contrasted with those with structurally simple styles (broken versus solid lines in Figure 7.2; correspondence rating: much).

Thus, both in ordinary and in crisis situations within two simulations, the surrogate decision-makers behaved in ways similar to ways other individuals act in field and laboratory studies. In the end, however, it may be expeditious to use surrogates who match particular international actors for work within the Inter-Nation Simulation. An attempt to encompass the entire personality of the participants was made by M. G. Hermann (Hermann and Hermann, 1967) in her use of a semantic differential instrument and the California Psychological Inventory (CPI), which yielded a profile of some thirteen traits in a disguised simulation of the activities within and among the countries that became involved in World War I during the summer of 1914. Working as a clinical psychologist, Hermann prepared personality profiles for each of ten actors who played significant roles in the 1914 crisis, on the basis of personal letters, autobiographical materials, and biographies. Then she matched these profiles to those of potential participants, choosing ten from an available population of 101 high school graduates for use as surrogates. The findings from this pilot study are suggestive: One realization with matched participants (M-Run) came closer to producing an output similar to the unfolding of historical events, as they are described by the historian Luigi Albertini (1953), than did a second realization (A-Run), in which another ten surrogates were less well matched than in the M-Run (correspondence rating: some). More definitive validation study covering key personal characteristics of relevance to policy-makers acting in the international scene awaits the production of comparable research in reference materials.

Inspection of Raser's matrix of comparisons among Western and non-Western political decision-makers, who were subgrouped into bureaucratic, military, and nonmilitary categories, suggests that there is a tendency for such leaders to be located at the high end of each continuum describing personal characteristics of ordinary populations. For example, in characterizing political decision-makers of the twentieth century, Raser said, "They are typically dominant, articulate, flexible, opportunistic, able to think *abstractly* as well as concretely, occasionally low in *self-esteem* but more often very self-confident, able to tolerate ambiguity, and willing to take at least moderate risks" (1966: 164; italics ours). If this is the case, surrogates who have too wide a range of variation in their personal characteristics should not be selected (correspondence rating: little). Driver (1966), however, argues that such is not the case, inasmuch as extreme differences occur on occasion, as in leaders as different as Stalin and Khruschev, with many in the middle ranges, as in men as similar as Adenaur and Erhard. Driver fears contrarily that "our surrogates may not be widely distributed enough. What high school boy can match de Gaulle's rigid grandiosity?" (Driver, 1966).

To this point our review of the operation of personal characteristics in the Inter-Nation Simulation has focused on their impact upon the outputs of the surrogates. It is also of interest to know to what extent the very processes producing the consequences are themselves homomorphic to those which create outcomes in the reference system. Are the "right" outputs being produced for the "wrong" reasons? There are three

Table 8.1
C. F. HERMANN'S QUESTIONNAIRE FINDINGS ON PERCEPTIONS OF ALTERNATIVE SOLUTIONS IDENTIFIED IN NONCRISIS AND CRISIS SITUATIONS IN AN INTER-NATION SIMULATION[a]

Alternative Solutions:	Participants' Perception of Alternative Solutions[b]	
	in Noncrisis Situations	in Crisis Situations
number of participants who perceived few alternatives	87	103
number of participants who perceived many alternatives	34	18

a. Adapted from Hermann (1969: Table 24; 171).
b. A total of 121 U.S. Naval petty officers served as decision-makers for six nations operated by them in eleven simulations. *Fewer alternative solutions* were perceived in crisis than in noncrisis. A chi-square test was statistically significant ($\chi^2 = 5.62; p < .009$).

researches of relevance which examine how processes of perception mediate the impact of personal characteristics upon outcomes in the simulation.

(1) Studies of President Woodrow Wilson and Secretary of State John Foster Dulles made by other researchers suggested to Michael J. Shapiro that their personal styles exemplified the frequently verified relations between cognitive rigidity and a tendency to perceive conflicts in moral rather than instrumental terms, and also to be relatively unreceptive to change. Using Driver's measures of cognitive style, as derived from the Adorno/California F-Scale and the Schroder/Streufert Situational Interpretation Test (SIT), (1966b: Table 1; 10). Shapiro checked whether the same processes held within these Brody-Driver simulations. He found that cognitive rigidity correlated significantly ($r = .51**$ for the F-Scale; $r = .69**$ for SIT) with the extent to which 336 high school students, serving as participants, evaluated environmental stimuli in moral catagories, as revealed in coding the messages generated in the course of the simulation. But he found that neither rigidity measure was correlated with fixity of beliefs and attitudes about decision-makers in other nations (the r's being -.01 and .12, respectively; correspondence rating: some; 1966b: Table 2; 12).

(2) Using a model developed by Ledyard Tucker and Samuel L. Messick (1963), Driver (1977) was able to measure changes in the dimensionality of the perceptions of the nations' decision-makers as they moved from ordinary to tense to dangerous situations within the 112 simulated nations

in his research with Brody (1963a). Corresponding to the findings in laboratory and field situations, including those analyzed in studies of natural disasters (such as panics during fires and floods), Driver noted that the dimensionality of the perceptions of the 336 high school students used as surrogates changed curvilinearly, from simple to more complex to less complex, as the inter-nation situation moved from run-of-the-day interaction through conflict and into war (Schroder et al., 1967: 66-81; Driver, 1977: 353). Driver found that even the content of the framework, in terms of which of the other nations were perceived as similar or different from one another, varied as the distinctions among the nations were made in terms of two to three, and then three to five, and then reduced to two or three dimensions again. For example, Driver (1962: 243) noted that "economic power dimensions are first transformed into military power and finally replaced altogether by alliance concerns as the clouds of war gather" (correspondence rating: much).

(3) In quite a different way, C. F. Hermann obtained findings which converge with those of Driver, and noted that in crisis as compared with noncrisis there was a tendency—slight, but statistically significant—for his petty officers to perceive "events as involving a number of different alternatives or only one or two alternatives" (as displayed in Table 8.1), even though content coding revealed no such differences in frequency in alternatives found in messages and conference statements exchanged in the course of the simulation (Hermann, 1969: 171). In his illustrations from the literature on international crisis behavior of political decision-makers, Hermann listed observations (1969: 161-165) that also are congruent with Driver's findings (correspondence rating: some).

In all three of these sets of findings there is somewhat convergent evidence as to how processes of perception operate within the surrogate decision-makers in realizations of the Inter-Nation Simulation. Two processes are displayed: the correlation of cognitive rigidity with the extent to which participants evaluate environmental stimuli in moral categories, and the tendency toward reduction in the perceived richness of the situation in crisis. The reference data used in making the comparisons with the simulations consisted of case materials, along with anecdotal observations. The evidence samples but limited aspects of perceptual phenomena, even though both ordinary and political decision-makers were compared with the surrogates. A codification of perceptions and misperception in international politics was completed by Jervis (1977) after the studies reviewed immediately above were undertaken. Its use of both laboratory experiments and international cases summarizes rich evidence of the common ways in which the "processes of perception" operate in the human, whether the individual is in the (simulation) laboratory or the foreign office. Within these confines, it seems the outputs deriving from the personal characteristics are being produced for at least some of the "right" reasons.

Impact of Training/Professionalism/Background. Just as the Joint War Games Agency of the government of the United States from time to time has involved very high civilian and military officials in its political-military exercises, as part of each year's opening activities at the United Nations the central decision-makers of the countries of the world may want to explore their problems through simulation. Thus far, achievements in securing surrogates who actually participate in international affairs have been modest. Dorothy L. Meier (1965) has completed two runs of the Inter-Nation Simulation involving some forty-one members of the diplomatic corps at the consular and secretarial levels, drawn from twenty-six foreign embassies in Washington, D.C., and from the U.S. Department of State. These runs, set to play the contemporary situation for a year or two forward from 1964, have been replicated using both high school and college students—seventy-two of each (Nardin and Cutler, 1969). Impressionistic observation suggests there were not important differences in at least many of the ways in which the simulations were operated by the three types of surrogates (Meier and Stickgold, 1965; correspondence rating: some). This observation is congruent with one of the "tentative" findings of Lincoln P. Bloomfield and Barton Whaley which "shows an amazing uniformity of 'U.S.' responses to dangerous situations" in replication of the "same games using different levels and types of personnel" (Bloomfield and Whaley, 1965: 869; correspondence rating: some).

In pilot work in a set of exercises within a socioeconomic model of American society enabling "simulated interest groups ... to make decisions on given public policy issues during specific future time periods," Boguslaw et al. (1966) found that their seven "professional and administrative staff" participants secured the adoption of more policies than did seven graduate students in political science and business administration. "Conference transcripts show that more experienced subjects focused their attention on fewer issues which they regarded as critical." The authors also remarked that "it is, of course, possible that some variable other than experience, e.g., personality, may account for these observed differences" (Boguslaw, et al., 1966: 54; correspondence rating: incongruent). More adequate analyses of the impact of professionalism on the behavior of surrogates is imperative, so that continued reliance upon impressionistic reports will be unnecessary. Certainly the ideology and orientation of the decision-makers toward international affairs would seem to be an important component in the background of international decision-makers. Yet, Philip F. Beach and Guetzkow found no relationship between the content of policy decision exhibited within the simulations and the participants' orientation toward international affairs as assessed before their participation in the simulations (Guetzkow et al., 1962; correspondence rating: none). However, this finding may be merely an indication of the inadequacy of our measuring instruments, inasmuch as Shapiro demonstrated a statistically significant tendency in the simulations for participants with rigid cognitive structures to attach moral rather than instrumental values to the actions used in executing foreign policy, paralleling the tendency of Wilson and Dulles, both men of intense religious orientation, to bring a moral outlook to affairs of state. In addition, Wayman J. Crow and Robert C. Noel (1977) were able to show that at least one component of the surrogates' world view, militarism, was related to their escalation responses.

This latter work is now considered in more detail. In a complex environment specially designed to mirror features of the TEMPER model, Crow and Noel secured written responses on a pretest from 384 U.S. Naval enlisted personnel (in training), which ranged from "disengagement with insurgents" (Level 1) through "declaration of war, occupation of winding river basin, establishment of military control there, and establishment of defensive and/or offensive positions in mountatins separating the basin from southeastern Utro" (Level 11; Crow and Noel, 1977: 390-391). Using Gerald H. Shure's questionnaire (Shure et al., 1965) on "aggressive militarism versus nonbelligerence," Crow and Noel found that those surrogates who indicated on the pretest they would rely on the "use of force, threats, and power in international diplomacy . . . [versus avoidance of] belligerent means" (1977: 393) when confronted with the necessity for military response, tended to levels invoking larger and more offensively oriented forces in making their verbal responses about escalation during the simulations ($F = 5.38*$, $df = 1/40$; Crow and Noel, 1977: 400; correspondence rating: much).

Impact of Cultures/Nationalism. A simulation of international affairs is different from simulations of intra-national social and economic processes, in that it needs to represent the multicultural, multinational characteristics of the reference system. On the face of it, this factor seems to be of obvious importance. Yet, the anecdotal report of a day's run in 1959 with eighteen foreign college students (Noel, 1963b: 89-94) indicated no radical "difference of kind" obtained in using surrogates from different cultures, even though the representation from nation to nation consisted of Africans, Asians, Europeans, Latin Americans, and North Americans (correspondence rating: some).

Usually simulations are operated with participants who have similar cultural backgrounds and are all of the same nationality. Raser and Crow (1964: 10) have realized two runs of the Inter-Nation Simulation with

Mexican college students at the National University of Mexico: "Looking at the over-all pattern of the results, it can be concluded in general that the observed regularities... obtained with U.S. participants... held under the changed condition of the cultural background" (correspondence rating: some). There were differences between the U.S. and Mexican participants "that seemed to be related to culturally based predisposition for the Mexican participants to respond to stress and frustration with passive rather than an active response" (1964: 11). Consider the nature of the differences: The Mexicans exchanged more messages and they placed more emphasis on the formalities and phrasing of their communications, and in the course of the simulation they focused more on international issues and less on matters of international economic growth. Could these differences also have been the result of differences in literary achievement (the Mexican participants had about two more years' education than the participants from the United States) and policy orientation (the forty-six Mexican participants were students in liberal arts, while the 240 U.S. participants were Navy recruits)?

In fact, it may be possible to produce many of the differences between the cross-cultural populations through preselection of surrogates, as M. G. Hermann did with respect to personal characteristics. Crow and Noel, too, demonstrated this capability later in their East Algonian Exercise with respect to aggressive militarism. Based on such evidence as that assembled by H.C.J. Duijker and N. H. Frijda (1960, Ch. 5), Otto Klineberg (1964: 142) concluded that "we may find differences in 'mode' or average or central tendency, but there will always be overlapping." Thus, it would seem possible to represent at least some important cross-cultural differences through the judicious selection of participants from within a single culture.

Suppose such capability in the representation of cross-cultural differences were realized as part of the initial conditions of a simulation designed to incorporate multinational properties. Would it lack a representation of the nationalism which plays such a dominant role in contemporary international affairs? In terms of the work of Crow and Noel, it seems not, as they have shown that nationalistic predispositions, measured through presimulation attitudes on authoritarian versus equalitarian internationalism, carry over into the operation of the simulation itself. In the East Algonian Exercise, the more nationalistic participants tended to give responses involving more escalation ($F = 4.50^*$, $df = 1/29$; correspondence rating: much; 1977: 401).

More dramatic, perhaps, is the congruence which Daniel Druckman (1968) obtained with findings from the empirical literature about ethnocentrism, when he obtained special data from Raser and Crow's (1964)

Table 8.2

BONHAM'S FINDINGS ON THE ATTITUDES OF
FRIENDLINESS AND UNFRIENDLINESS BETWEEN
NATIONS IN A SIMULATION OF
DISARMAMENT NEGOTIATIONS[a]

	Attitudinal Relationships Between the Nations[b]		
For All Runs: Attitudes of:		*Nations Being Rated (mean ratings)*	
	"United States" ("USA")	*"Soviet Union" ("USSR")*	*"United Kingdom" ("UK")*
"USA" toward	—	-2.5	+3.3
"USSR" toward	-2.8	—	-1.3
"UK" toward	+3.3	-1.3	—

a. Adapted from Bonham (1971: Table 5, 309).
b. A total of 66 college students, half undergraduate and half graduate, served in 11 simulation runs. The two participants on each team were asked to rate their attitudes toward the other two nations in the negotiations on a scale of +5 (FRIENDLINESS) to -5 (UNFRIENDLINESS). No statistical tests of significance were reported.

exploration of the effects of capacity to delay response in nuclear war in their WINSAFE II research. In the trial-by-trial development of the eleven Raser and Crow simulations, Druckman found an enhancement of the in-group bias for their own nations of the 176 U.S. Naval recruits serving as participants (correspondence rating: much). Thus, just as the perceptual processes were shown to have important impact upon the personal outputs of the surrogates, so it would seem that the surrogates' identifications with their own nations in these simulations produced evidence of predispositions which operated in a fashion homomorphic to the ethnocentrism of cultures and nationalities.

Using an all-person simulation technique, Bonham (1967, 1971) has made checks of the congruences involved in his eleven efforts to replicate the East-West disarmament negotiations of the mid-1950s. In the style of the political-military exercise, his work employed a conventional role-playing of the concrete historical situation through a somewhat abstract representation, as was done for World War I by the Hermanns (1967). Although Bonham (1971: 307-308) felt the "cultural variations between the American and Soviet negotiators were not duplicated in the simulation.... There is some evidence, however, that the *attitudinal relationships* between the parties to the subcommittee negotiations were duplicated in the simulation," as exhibited in Table 8.2 (correspondence rating:

some). These findings seem similar to those obtained by Druckman (1968), in the sense that there is friendliness among in-groups and unfriendliness toward out-groups.

Thus, it would seem that some approximation of the functioning of cultural and national characteristics can be realized within the person-machine simulation of international affairs. In his examination of the relevancies of "national character" to international relations, Bernard C. Hennessy (1962: 46) concluded that foreign "policies are made largely by cosmopolitan elite groups who appear to be on the whole little affected by national character or modal personality traits." Even though the importance of personal characteristics in decision-making is well accepted—be they linked to leadership or grounded in nationality and culture—could it be that the current degree of congruence between simulations and "realities" in international relations suffice, for the moment?

On the other hand, when an all-person or a person-computer format is used for a simulation, why not take advantage of the ethnic characteristics and nationality of the surrogates by employing participants from many cultures? Instead of operating simulations with participants of a single cultural background, it seems useful to operate multinational simulations in which the nations are each composed of surrogates with different nationalities, although the participants within each of the nations might have the same nationality. "Face validity," as C. F. Hermann (1967b: 221-222) put the matter, will then be gained, and the correspondences of the surrogates in the simulations to the decision-makers of the world may become a bit less problematic.

Summary. A compilation of the authors' judgments rating the correspondences between simulations of international processes with "general materials from field and laboratory" and "materials from international relations" is given in Table 8.3 following. It is not surprising that the surrogates in simulations behave remarkably like humans, although the subtotals in Table 8.3 suggest that they resemble decision-makers of the internation scene (much = 2, some = 6) less than they do more ordinary mortals observed in field situations and within the laboratory (much = 6, some = 2). In general, the homomorphies hold for crisis and noncrisis situations. Correspondences are found for the outputs, as in terms of the inter-entity production of violence (Driver, 1977) and alliance (Bonham, 1971); correspondences are found, also, for the intervening processes, as for perception (Driver, 1962, 1977) and nationalism (Druckman, 1968; Crow and Noel, 1977). However, only a few of the multitude of components comprising the varying personalities diverse backgrounds and multi-nationalities have been assessed. Through the use of preselection of the participants, it may be possible to represent in the human surrogates in

Table 8.3
ASSESSMENTS OF CORRESPONDENCES BETWEEN SIMULATIONS AND "REALITIES" IN INTERNATIONAL RELATIONS REGARDING *DECISION-MAKERS AND THEIR NATIONS*: HUMANS AS SURROGATES

Decision-Makers		Correspondence with General Materials from Field and Laboratory		Correspondence with Materials from International Relations	Ratings
Personal Characteristics	(M)	Complexity (Driver, 1977)	(S)	Matched characteristics (Hermann & Hermann, 1977)	(M) 5
	(L)	Complexity and response to unidentified attack (Hermann, Hermann, & Cantor, 1974)	(L)	Skewness of characteristics[a] (Raser, 1965)	(S) 3
	(M)	Self-esteem, and response to unidentified attack (Hermann, Hermann, & Cantor, 1974)	(S)	Rigidity and moral orientation[a] (Shapiro, 1966b)	(L) 2
	(M)	Self-esteem, defensiveness, affect, and information search in crisis (M. G. Hermann, 1965)	(S)	Decision Alternatives in Crisis[a] (Hermann, 1969)	(N) 0
	(M)	Complexity and information handling (Streufert, Suedfeld, & Driver, 1965)			(I) 0
	(M)	Dimensionality of perceptions in crisis (Driver, 1962)			# = 10

(Table 8.3 continued p. 274)

Table 8.3 (Continued)

Decision-Makers	Correspondence with General Materials from Field and Laboratory		Correspondence with Materials from International Relations		Ratings
Impact of Training Professionalism Background	(I) Professionals vs. students (Boguslaw, Davis, & Glick, 1966) (N) IR beliefs (Guetzkow, Brody, Driver, & Beach, 1960)		(S) Diplomats vs. students[a] (Meier & Stickgold, 1965) (S) U.S. officials vs. students (Bloomfield & Whalye, 1965) (M) Militarism (Crow & Noel, 1977)		(M) 1 (S) 2 (L) 0 (N) 1 (I) 1 ## = 5
Impact of Culture/Nationalism	(S) Multicultures (African, Asian, European, Latin American, North American) (Noel, 1963b) (S) Cross-cultures (Mexican/U.S.) (Raser & Crow, 1964) (M) Ethnocentrism (Druckman, 1968, 1965)		(M) Nationalism (Crow & Noel, 1977) (S) Ally/adversary (Bonham, 1971)		(M) 2 (S) 3 (L) 0 (N) 0 (I) 0 ## = 5
Correspondence Ratings	(M) "Much" (S) "Some" (L) "Little" (N) "None" (I) "Incongruent"	6 2 1 1 1 ## = 11	(M) "Much" (S) "Some" (L) "Little" (N) "None" (I) "Incongruent"	2 6 1 0 0 ## = 9	(M) 8 (S) 8 (L) 2 (N) 1 (I) 1 ## = 20

a. Materials involving anecdotes and case illustrations.

simulations an important sample of the attributes of decision-makers of the world, be they decision-makers for nations, for companies overseas, or for governmental and nongovernmental international organizations.

Surrogate Groups and Programs as "Nations"

In making an assessment of "decision-makers and their nations," it is useful not only to consider the decision-makers per se, but also to explore how the surrogates function when assembled as decision-making groups, as well as how the consequences of their decisions are programmed as the outputs of their nations. "Individual and group components of the Inter-Nation Simulation are meshed into an operating model through both structured and free, self-developing interactive processes. In general, programmed assumptions are used for setting the foundations of the simulation, serving to provide operating rules for the decision-makers whereby they may handle the political, economic, and military aspects of their nations" (Guetzkow, 1981b: 64). Let us now examine aspects of the validity of the processes within these "nations" in the simulation. In addition to giving attention to the extent of the congruences occurring between simulations and "realities" with respect to the roles, group structures, and internal communication patterns within the decision-making organization involved, we will give an evaluation of the national programs.

Organizational Characteristics: Decision-Making Groups and Roles Therein. In their East Algonian Exercise, Crow and Noel (1977: 400-401) demonstrated the effects of an organizational context upon their decision-makers, at least in one experiment with respect to one output—the level of military response used to control a simulated military insurrection. Those with high-risk preferences tended to respond throughout at a higher level than those with low-risk preferences ($F = 9.27**$, $df = 1/24$). But in both instances, as the individual moved from private decision-making to a situation in which there was a high probability of winning the war and in which he needed to come to consensus with three other "top-level leaders of Algo, all equal in authority and resonsibility" (1977: 387), there was a reduction in the level of response ($F = 4.29*$, $df = 1/24$). Some writers about politics (e.g., Acheson, 1960; Neustadt, 1960) believe that a committee system tends "to inhibit innovation, boldness, and creativity with the result that any decision is a consensus or compromise based on the lowest common denominator of agreement" (Crow and Noel, 1977: 396). As Henry Kissinger (1962: 356) speculates, "the system stresses avoidance of risk rather than boldness of conception."

In two of Crow and Noel's other experiments in the East Algonian Exercise, in which military response levels made in the course of rendering individual "pregroup" judgments were compared with the outcomes of group consensus, there were no clear effects of organizational context shown, despite the similarity of these experiments to the one mentioned earlier. In one, there was an interaction effect between the simulated situation and the organizational context, but in a contrary direction. When the opponent was presented as highly aggressive the decision-makers shifted to a significantly ($F = 11.1*$, $df = 1/20$) higher level of military response as a result of group decision—in this experiment, from a level of 7.4 to 9.2 (1977: Table 15.4; 401)—a result contrary to current verbal speculation among students of politics. Yet, such findings are in keeping with results from social psychological experiments by M. A. Wallach and N. Kogan (1965), in which group discussions permit shifts to accept greater risks because "each individual can feel less than proportionally to blame for the possible failure of a risky decision" (Crow and Noel, 1977: 396; correspondence rating: incongruent). Both results may be valued, although there is dissatisfaction with the limitations of both criteria: the unsystematic nature of field observation and the lack of "richness" of the laboratory.

More in line with the results from these social psychological experiments were simulation outputs reported by Hermann et al. (1974: 89). In accordance with Kogan and Wallach's (1967) findings, the simulators expected that group decision-makers were less likely to respond aggressively to an unidentified attack and accept the risk of delay. Statistical analysis of simulation outputs did not contradict this hypothesis that groups mitigate aggressive decision-making ($\beta = -.32$, $b = -.31$, $s = .12$, $t = 2.61$, $p < .05$; correspondence rating: much; see note 4).

In his simulation study of crises in foreign policy-making, C. F. Hermann (1965) probed the development of consensus within sixty-six decision-making groups comprising eleven runs of an Inter-Nation Simulation with U.S. Naval petty officers as participants (see pp. 261-266). In an "event and decision form," Hermann (1969: 206-207) queried his participants a number of times as to whether a crisis they "recently or are now experiencing" had made the nation's goals "easier/harder to attain," covering such goals as "office-holding," "alliance development," and an ability to "preserve nation as separate unit." Although this experimenter demanded no actual group decision after focused discussion on the matter, as was the case in the East Algonian Exercise conducted by Crow and Noel (1977), crisis induced considerably more consensus, as measured by the agreement among three or four office-holders within each nation that "one or more goals had been made more difficult to attain" (1969: 159). In a set of forty-eight paired samples of crisis versus noncrisis events, consensus existed for two-thirds of the noncrisis situations; the consensus increased significantly ($\chi^2 = 7.2$, p. = .004) to 100 percent in the crisis situations (1969: Table 18; 159). In discussing his hypothesis that "In crisis as compared to non-crisis, the frequency of consensus among decision-makers as to the national goals affected by the situation is increased," Hermann (1969: 155-157) indicated that such a tendency toward increased consensus is documented by the general literature on conflict (Mack and Snyder, 1957: 234) and on disaster (Thompson and Hawkes, 1962: 278), and by the specific case studies of U.S. decision-making within the Korean (Snyder and Paige, 1958: 375) and the Cuban (Larson, 1963: 225) crises (correspondence rating: some).

This relationship between crisis conditions and intra-group communication processes was further investigated in the Robinson et al. (1969) study of intervening variables influencing group consensus in two sets of INS simulations—at the Great Lakes Naval Training Station and the Western Behavioral Sciences Institute—and the all-person MIT political game. The acts of searching for information and alternatives are typically characteristic of decision-making (Lasswell, 1956); the simulators expected that the time pressures of crisis situations may inhibit these, thus accelerating group decision. It was suggested that this decision-making may thus be based on a deficient intelligence system. Previous research has reported that one reason the search for alternative courses of action becomes limited in crisis is that decision-makers tend to be satisfied earlier than during times of stability (Simon, 1957; March, 1962). Though the MIT game produced nonsignificant results ($\chi^2 = .10$, n.s.), both INS studies produced findings corresponding to empirical research suggesting that there is less search for alternative courses of action in crisis (Great Lakes: $\chi^2 = 4.22$, p. < .05; WBSI: $\chi^2 = 13.60$, p < .01; correspondence rating: much). The number of alternatives open to national leaders is perceived by them to be significantly less in crisis (Snyder and Paige, 1958; Holsti, 1965). This same reduction occurred in the simulation studies (Great Lakes: $\chi^2 = 5.62$, p < .01; WBSI: $\chi^2 = 9.77$, p < .01). As before, the MIT game exhibited nonsignificant findings ($\chi^2 = .10$, n.s.; correspondence rating: much).

As part of the starting conditions within the Inter-Nation Simulation, roles are designated within each group responsible for the nation's decision-making—a procedure which contrasts with the usual RAND/MIT practice of having each "team" work without assigned activities for any participant in their political-military exercises. In this way, an attempt is made within INS to induce a "division of labor" among the participants so that each position gains its perspective, as commonly occurs in roles found in bureaucracies (Katz and Kahn, 1966: Ch. 7, 171-198). Thus, the group as a surrogate tends to function less as a small, "face-to-face" group, instead taking on some characteristics of an organization (Guetzkow and Bowes, 1957).

Druckman's (1965, 1968) study of ethnocentrism indicated that tendencies toward "bias" as found in laboratory and field studies (Rosenblatt, 1964) occur among the roles within the simulation. For example, those in low-status roles within the simulated executive decision-making groups in WINSAFE II (Raser and Crow, 1964), especially the marginal decision-maker who was aspiring to office, were found to be "most favorably disposed toward the in-group and least favorably disposed toward all out-groups, allies and enemies" (Druckman, 1968: 62). Likewise, following observations made by Gordon Allport, Leonard Berkowitz, Robert Hamblin, and George Homans, Druckman (1968: 61) theorized that "the role with the most international contacts with opposite members of equal status ... should be least ethnocentric." Druckman found that "the foreign minister or external decision-maker was the least ethnocentric role" (1965: 124-125; cf. Druckman, 1968: 62). The external decision-maker rated his own group least favorably and the out-group's allies and enemies most favorably (correspondence rating: much). Thus, role differentiations in the Inter-Nation Simulation may be homomorphic to those which occur in government offices handling decision-making for countries within the international system, although there is no direct evidence on this matter from a study (Argyris, 1967) made within the U.S. Department of State.

Organizational Characteristics: Organization Structure and Internal Communication Processes. In seeking to represent a structured government rather than a decision-by-committee process, the Hermanns used five people within each of their "nations" in the simulations. In this way these experimenters were able not only to specify roles for their surrogates, but also to develop "special-task subgroups" (by establishing "two policy groups in each government"), to provide indirect "mediated communication," and to introduce an "authority hierarchy" with "formalized rules" and "defined subordination" (C. F. Hermann, 1969: 45-54; see also above, pp. 262-265, 266-267, 275-276). These elements were chosen so as to conform to the prescriptions developed by Morris Zelditch and Terrence Hopkins (1961: 472-473) for establishing an organization in a laboratory setting.

An analysis of the communications within the "nations" (C. F. Hermann, 1969: 48-51), as shown in Table 8.4, indicates that the Hermanns succeeded in inducing the development of organizational structures (correspondence rating: some). Further, the communication patterns responded to the impingement of crisis, as was shown to have been the case in the international system during the summer of 1914 (Holsti, 1965), as well as during October and November 1962, during the Cuban crisis (Runge, 1963). Hermann (1969: 177-185) discovered that "in crisis as

Table 8.4

C. F. HERMANN'S TABULATION OF TWO-WAY COMMUNICATION CHANNELS BASED ON NUMBER OF MESSAGES WRITTEN BY DECISION-MAKERS IN AN INTER-NATION SIMULATION[a]

Communication Analysis[b] Messages Written via Two-Way Channels:[c]	Within Government						Between Government Members and Aspiring Decision-Makers			
	CDM & IDM	CDM & FDM	CDM & EDM	EDM & IDM	EDM & FDM	IDM & FDM	ADM & CDM	ADM & FDM	ADM & IDM	ADM & EDM
Number of Two-Way Channels	43	44	45	38	19	2	34	7	4	14
Total Messages in Two-Way Channels	524	461	411	300	86	9	209	33	16	46
Average Number of Messages in Two-Way Channels	12.2	10.5	9.1	7.9	4.5	4.5	6.2	4.7	4.0	3.3

a. Adapted from Hermann (1969: Table 1; 49).
b. CDM = central decision-maker; IDM = internal decision-maker; FDM = force decision-maker; EDM = external decision-maker; ADM = aspiring decision-maker.
c. The messages were generated by 325 U.S. Naval petty officers serving as decision-makers for the 6 nations operated in 11 simulations. Between each combination of roles, the highest possible number of two-way communication channels was 66. No statistical test of differences are given.

compared to non-crisis, the volume of communication among decision-makers within the foreign policy structure of a nation is increased," with a probability of this result occurring by chance less than .01 (one-tailed test; correspondence rating: some).

The correspondences between the literature of organizational behavior and the operation of the simulated nations are not as clear with respect to Hermann's hypothesis on the contraction of authority during crisis. He asserts (1969: 161) that in "crisis as compared to non-crisis, the number of decision-makers exercising authority in the decision process is decreased; that is, a contraction of authority occurs." Although Hermann determined the number of individuals in a simulated nation who actively participated in deciding how the government should respond to a situation (1969: 164), he found no significant differences between crisis and noncrisis behaviors. However, the participants frequently tended to perceive fewer decision-makers as active in crisis decisions (1969: Table 26; 171-173).

It is interesting to note that in Dean Pruitt's systematic research on twenty-eight case studies within the "Office of XYZ Affairs" of the U.S. Department of State, no significant relationship was found between crisis and either the number of officers or agencies involved in a decision, although a number of his seventeen respondents volunteered the information that "fewer people are consulted as time pressures go up" (Pruitt, 1964-1965: 25). The evidence Hermann (1969: 161-163) presented from his reference materials in supporting his authority-contraction hypothesis, however, is largely illustrative, citing the perceptions of men who have occupied the position of Assistant Secretary of State, such as Roger Hilsman (1959: 372) and Harlan Cleveland (1963: 638) describe. Hermann's simulation seems to be homomorphic to both these sets of reference data, which showed no contraction at the behavior level, although participants from both the simulation and the reference systems stated they perceived such contraction of authority (correspondence rating: some).

Evaluation of Variables Comprising National Programs.[5] To this point, our comparisons of outcomes in simulations to those in the reference systems have centered upon the functioning of the participants, as individuals or in groups. It also is possible, however, to examine aspects of the validity of the programmed segments separately from their person-machine outputs. This research is analogous to the findings presented earlier (pp. 266-268) on the extent to which personal outputs are mediated by intervening perceptual mechanisms which have some correspondence to those occurring in the reference materials—are the "right" results being produced for the "right" reasons? The following discussion is devoted to results from studies undertaken at Northwestern University. To date, validities of some twelve of the twenty-nine "Programmed Assumptions" of the Inter-Nation Simulation (INS) have been assessed by the work of Chadwick (1966a, 1966b, 1966c, 1966d, 1967). He operationalized seventeen variables (1967: Table 1; 179) from INS theory in data derived from Rudolph Rummel's (1966a) Dimensionality of Nations (DON) project — comparing correlations among indices of INS variables (1966d: Table 3; 15) represented in an Inter-Nation Simulation conducted by Brody (1963a) and Driver (1977) with those among empirical indices of these variables in a reference system of some sixty-four nations in the mid-1950s (Chadwick, 1967: Table 2; 180). Charles Elder and Robert Pendley (1966: 10-11; 1981), using another approach, in which relations hypothesized in INS theory were developed as differential equations, have contributed assessments of aspects of the political and of the economic programs. The use of core variables in INS theory is analogous to the use of human beings as surrogates, in that "whole sets of variables in the complex of national and international life are represented by simplified, generic factors supposedly the prototypes of more elaborate realities." Hence, one hopes that a programmed relation among such prototypic variables "provides a condensed version of a gamut of real-life activities, similar to the way in which probability distributions are used by simulators to represent elaborate, underlying mechanisms that are too complicated to detail" (Guetzkow, 1981b: 24).

National Programs Involving Political Variables. Elder and Pendley (1981) have developed an assessment of Programmed Assumption 1 (Guetzkow, 1981b: equation 2.1). This hypothesis asserts a relationship between the probability of the decision-makers' holding of office (pOH) and the way their chances for remaining in office depend upon how satisfied their validators (be they masses and/or elites) are with their performance (VSm). This programmed assumption indicates that the closeness of the realtionship of pOH and VSm depends upon the decision latitude (DL) which their political structures allow; governments with wider latitude find their office-holding (pOH) is less directly dependent upon the extent to which they please those who validate their office-holding (VSm). Elder and Pendley challenged the definition of office-holding given in INS theory, querying whether it did not pertain to the stability of the government rather than to the regime, according to the formulations of David Easton (1965b: 219). By using measures for some sixty-two- nations in the mid-1950s, as derived from various data sources, Elder and Pendley discovered that the equation underlying Programmed Assumption 1 accounted for only 5 percent of the variance in a pOH-type measure of regime stability, but accounted for some 25 percent of the corresponding measure of system stability (Elder and Pendley, 1981; correspondence rating: some).

In contrast to Elder and Pendley's approach, Chadwick (1966a), for purposes of analysis, simplified INS theory into a series of two-variable, monotonic functions.[6] Components of Programmed Assumption 1 were analyzed one by one, with similar results. In a reference system of some sixty-four nations in the mid-1950s, Chadwick (1967: 181-184) found that the relation between pOH, indexed as regime (rather than as system) stability, and VSm was not statistically significant ($r = .06$); there was a statistically significant relationship ($r = .30*$) between pOH and DL. However, when the simulation was operated, both of these relationships were realized: The relation of pOH to VSm was $.99**$, an artifact due to a regrettable error by the calculators in omitting the mediating effects of DL; the relation of pOH to DL was $.56**$ (Chadwick, 1966d: 15; correspondence rating: some).

Programmed Asumption 2 relates validator satisfaction (VSm) to its two components: satisfaction with consumption standards (VScs) and satisfaction with national security (VSns; Guetzkow, 1981b: 31). In Chadwick's (1967: 184-186) research, VScs correlated somewhat significantly with VSm ($r = .19*$) in the reference system of the mid-1950s; it correlated significantly ($r = .51**$) within the simulation (correspondence rating: some). National security satisfaction (VSns) did not correlate with Vsm in this same reference system ($r = -.15$); it correlated significantly but weakly ($r = .23*$) in the simulation (Chadwick, 1966d: 14-15; correspondence rating: none).

The behaviors of the variables included in Programmed Asumptions 8 and 21, concerned with revolution (Guetzkow, 1981b: 37, 47) were not found by Chadwick to be congruent, with one exception: The relationship specified between the probability of a revolution occurring (pR) and validator satisfaction (VSm) proved to be significantly negative ($r = -.41**$) in the reference materials (Chadwick, 1967: 186-188), although of lesser magnitude; it also was significantly negative in the simulation ($r = -.29**$; Chadwick, 1966d: 15; correspondence rating: much). Chadwick's research also indicated that although Programmed Asumptions 17 through 29, concerned with "consequences of pressure changes in decision latitude" (Guetzkow, 1981b: 44-58) were all realized in the simulation, the relationships postulated between DL and VSm in Programmed Assumption 17, between DL and basic capability (BC) in Programmed Assumption 18, between force capabilities (FC) in Programmed Assumption 19, and the feedbacks from these three in Programmed Asumption 20 did not prove out in the reference materials (Chadwick, 1966d: 14-15; correspondence rating: none).

A tabulation of the findings involving the political variables is included in Table 8.5. Overall, there was but a modicum of congruence between the reference materials from international relations and the outputs generated in the simulation.

National Programs Involving Economic Variables. In keeping with the challenge issued by Noel (1963a) in his theoretical work on economics within the Inter-Nation Simulation, Elder and Pendley (1981) examined portions of the INS model in terms of both economic theory and data. Focusing on Programmed Assumptions 11, 12, and 13 (Guetzkow, 1981b: 41-42), the interrelations among a nation's basic capability (BC), consumption standards (CS), and validator satisfaction (VSm) were probed in considerable detail. In validating the relations posited in equations 2.4 and 2.7 (Guetzkow, 1981b: 41-42) between the minimum consumption standards (CSmin) and the maximum possible (CSmax), given the nation's capability, Elder and Pendley (1981: Figure 3.4) found reference data for some thirty-eight nations in the mid-1950s related curvilinearly rather than linearly. An alternative equation was constructed which represents the programmed relationship between CSmin and CSmax as curvilinear (Elder and Pendley, 1981). In this improved form, the economic submodel of the INS explains some 92 percent of the variance (correspondence rating: much). In checking the validity of CS, the relation of ongoing consumption (as a ratio of CSmin), to an index of validator satisfaction with consumption (VScs), they found a correlation of .75**, calculated over forty-one nations (Elder and Pendley, 1981; correspondence rating: much).

Chadwick's component-by-component analysis revealed in some cases less congruent results. The correlation between basic capability (BC) and consumption standards (CS) in some sixty-four nations in the mid-1950s was .87** in the reference system (Chadwick, 1967: 186). An extremely high relationship of .95** occurred in the simulation (Chadwick, 1966d: 15; correspondence rating: much). Vis-à-vis equation 2.7 (Guetzkow, 1981b: 42) the correlation between VScs and CS was .60** in the same reference system. However, the programmed relation failed to be realized ($r = .15$) in the simulation (Chadwick, 1966d: 14-15; correspondence rating: little). These discordant results between reference system and simulation, with the simulation producing either too strong a relation or too weak a relation between the variables, indicate that adjustments are needed in the model in order to increase its value.

National Programs Involving Military Variables. In developing the INS model which distinguishes nuclear from conventional force capabilities, Brody (1963a: 698) secured counsel in 1959-1960 from military experts in the specification of both his parameters and his equations. Further work in the style of Elder and Pendley, however, has not yet been done in evaluating his programs. Chadwick's findings on military variables are few and negative. In researching the components of Programmed Assumption 16 (Guetzkow, 1981b: equation 2.8), Chadwick (1967: 188-190) found that neither the reference data on sixty-four nations in the mid-1950's nor the simulation materials produced any clear relationship between validator satisfaction with respect to national security (VSns) and the nation's present force capability or its war potential (as represented in its BC; Chadwick, 1966d: 14-15; correspondence rating: none). Chadwick challenged INS theory, too, developing a somewhat different index of national security. He then found a general relationship between this (reformulated) VSns index and (as a set) force capability, threats, accusations, and protests (Chadwick, 1967: 189).

Summary: Surrogate Groups and Programs as "Nations." Table 8.5 is the record of our assesments of correspondences between simulations of international relations and "realities" with respect to the operation of the surrogate groups and the programs which are meshed into "nations." Only three of the twenty-one assessments compared simulation materials with more "general materials from field and laboratory"; thus, almost all the comparisons were made with materials referring to the international system. Some of these were quite rigorous in conception, particularly the work on the operation of the programmed political, economic, and military variables, taken as prototypes. It is interesting to note that as the comparisons become more rigorous, the congruence seems to become less. It is recognized that only a third of the programmed assumptions of the INS model have been assessed; the number of free variables examined is small, contrasted with the number within the simulation which might have been examined. It is disturbing to have one incongruency occurring simultaneously with the fifteen homomorphies, even though the latter vary widely in their levels of correspondence.

"RELATIONS AMONG NATIONS"

In our examination of "decision-makers and their nations," surrogates and programs were composed so as to constitute nation actors within the inter-nation complex. Let us now examine the validities obtained within the simulations when the relations among these "nations" are contrasted with "realities" on international relations—the referent system.

In generating "relations among nations," INS exhibits characteristics of a "self-organizing system" (Guetzkow, 1962c: 89-90). How can these apsects be included in an assessment of the correspondence between the simulations and the reference systems? Terry Nardin utilized notions of

Table 8.5

ASSESSMENTS OF CORRESPONDENCES BETWEEN SIMULATIONS AND "REALITIES" IN INTERNATIONAL RELATIONS REGARDING *DECISION-MAKERS AND THEIR NATIONS*: SURROGATE GROUPS AND PROGRAMS AS "NATIONS"

"Nations"			Correspondence with Materials from International Relations			Ratings	
Organizational Characteristics	(I)	Risk-taking in groups (Crow & Noel, 1977)	(N)	Greater effort to obtain information in crisis (Robinson, Hermann, & Hermann, 1969)		(M)	4[b]
	(M)	Risk of delay during unidentified attack (Hermann, Hermann, & Cantor, 1974)				(S)	4[b]
	(S)	Consensus in groups in crisis[b] (Hermann, 1969)	(S)	Internal communication volume increases in crisis (Hermann, 1969)		(L)	0
	(M)	Fewer alternatives perceived in crisis (Robinson, Hermann, & Hermann, 1969)	(S)	Contraction of authority[a] (Hermann, 1969)		(N)	1
	(M)	Less search for alternatives in crisis (Robinson, Hermann, & Hermann, 1969)				(I)	1
						# =	10[b]

(Table 8.5 continued p. 286)

Table 8.5 (Continued)

"Nations"	Correspondence with Materials from International Relations			Ratings
		in Politics		
	(S) Office-holding as system stability (Elder & Pendley, 1980)	(N)	Validator satisfaction (Chadwick, 1966d, 1967)	
National Programs	(S) Office-holding as regime continuance (Chadwick, 1966d, 1967)	(M)	Revolution (Chadwick, 1966d, 1967)	
	(S) Basic capability and consumption standards (Chadwick, 1967)	(N)	Decision-latitude (Chadwick, 1966d)	
		in Economics		(M) 4
	(M) Consumption standards (Elder & Pendley, 1980)	(M)	Basic capability and consumption standards (Chadwick, 1966d)	(S) 3 (L) 1 (N) 3
	(M) Consumption satisfaction (Elder & Pendley, 1980)	(L)	Consumption satisfaction (Chadwick, 1966d)	(I) 0 # = 11
		in Security		
		(N)	Security satisfactions (Chadwick, 1966d)	
Correspondence Ratings		(M) "Much"	7	(M) 8[b]
		(S) "Some"	6	(S) 7[b]
		(L) "Little"	1	(L) 1
		(N) "None"	4	(N) 4
		(I) "Incongruent"	1	(I) 1
			# = 19	# = 21[b]

a. Materials involving anecdotes and case illustrations.
b. Includes correspondence ratings of the following general materials from field and laboratory: (M) Bias in the internal/external roles of decision-makers (Druckman, 1968, 1965). (S) Organizational structure (Hermann, 1969).

Brody (1963a: 714) and Rummel (1963: 22) in creating variables which characterized the relations among the nations, taken two at a time. He measured "distance" with respect to economic prowess between the U.S.S.R. and India in the reference system, for example, and measured the difference between Yora and Zena in the Inter-Nation Simulation, using the differences for the gross national product and (for the third through sixth periods of 1962-1963) for basic capability (BC), respectively. With fifteen countries in the reference system, data may be compiled for 105 pairs; with nine nations in the simulation, for each run 36 pairs may be constituted. Nardin, with the help of Neal E. Cutler, utilized materials produced in two simulations, an original simulation (INS-16) consisting of six runs (Meier, 1965a; Meier and Stickgold, 1965), and its replication (INS-19), consisting of four runs. A population of 360 pairs was available from the ten simulations (Nardin and Cutler, 1969). In addition to characterizing each pair of nations in terms of its dissimilarity in national wealth and development, Nardin and Cutler composed differences among the nations with respect to type of regime, as indicated by decision latitude (DL). The alliance memberships of each pair were characterized, also, according to how they differed in perceptions of the likelihood of war occurring between them. Further, Nardin and Cutler used measures of interaction among the pairs, including their communications, their exports, and the number of treaties they signed with each other. The twenty-one possible relations among these measures were checked for their reliability by comparing the Nardin replication (INS-19) with the Meier-Stickgold simulation (INS-16), with the finding that only two relations were importantly discrepant (Nardin and Cutler, 1969).

Nardin and his associates, including Harry Targ (Targ and Nardin, 1966), devoted themselves exclusively to the use of variables constituted from pairs of nations. Others have probed "relations among nations" using variables which characterized the external behaviors of the nation, even though the variable itself was an attribute of the nation, in the style of the fifty-seven "raw characteristics" of Arthur S. Banks and Robert B. Textor (1963: 18-20). For example, Chadwick included for each nation its exports and imports, as well as the number of agreements into which it entered which were of a military and/or an economic/cultural nature—all variables which reflect its relations with other members of the international system. In these contrasting ways, researchers have captured some of the "variations in the unprogrammed activities, which emerge as the nations relate to each other within the developing overall system" (Guetzkow, 1981b: 24).

Communication structures and processes used for handling the "relations among nations" will be examined first. Then, characteristics of alliances and their involvement in the use of force will be surveyed briefly. Finally, aspects of the "interaction patterns," including those concerned with cooperation and conflict, will be assessed. It should be noted that in the Inter-Nation Simulation, "with the exception of the rules for the conduct of war, there are no programs prescribing the relations among nations. The basic strategy used in the construction of the simulation has been to allow free development of the inter-nation relations" (Guetzkow, 1981b: 64). Inasmuch as no research on the homomorphies between simulations of international relations and "realities" has as yet been reported on war as embedded in an international simulation (McRae, 1963)—nor in such computerized models of relations among nations as those developed by Benson (1961), Abt and his associates (1964), or Bremer (1970), for that matter—it is not possible at this time to include an evaluation of programmed work in this area.

Communications

At first glance there seems to be "face validity" in the communications that develop among the nations of a simulation, with the bilateral interchanges often complemented by a one-to-many issuance of messages and conferences among the external decision-makers (EDMs). Credibility is given to this impression by such an occurrence as when the participant positioned to represent the English foreign minister (Lord Grey), in the Hermanns' effort to simulate (M-Run) the events leading into World War I, assembled an international conference of the principal actors. During this meeting, Austria-Hungary was pressured into withdrawing her claims against Serbia (Hermann and Hermann, 1967: 407). Historically, England did call for such an international conference, which subsequently was rejected. The Hermanns (1967: 407-408) concluded, "Thus, an alternative actually considered and subsequently excluded by the historical figures provided the avenue which the simulation participants followed for the resolution of the imposed situation" (correspondence rating: some). It is interesting to note in the less well-matched run (A-Run) that the surrogate nations—Austria, England, France, and Russia—then pursued paths which led to dampening effects, perhaps similar to those which were obtained in the 1908-1909 Bosnian crisis (Hermann and Hermann, 1967: Table 2, 410).

When evidence was examined in a less anecdotal fashion, the validity of communication processes of the simulation was not found to be well substantiated. C. F. Hermann (1969: 175-189) found but little congruence between simulation and reference materials when he checked his hypothesis that "in crisis as compared with non-crisis, the volume of communication between a nation's decision-makers and other international actors, external to the nation, is increased" (C. F. Hermann, 1969: 178). The relation of crisis/noncrisis to the frequency of external communication proved to be significant at the .09 level for a one-tailed Mann-Whitney U-test (1969: Table 31; 188). However, Robert C. North and his colleagues (1963: 164) found that in 1914 "as the crisis developed, decision-makers in the various capitals received rapidly increasing volumes of messages from various parts of Europe." This phenomenon appeared again in the course of the Cuban missile crisis in 1962. Hermann (1969: 181) noted, "The American Secretary of State related that in addition to the adversary and the United Nations, the United States communicated with more than 75 governments in the Cuban missile crisis (Larson, 1963, p. 268)" (correspondence rating: little). This lack of correspondence seems not related to instability of simulation output, inasmuch as Hermann (1967a: note 12) reported an "absence of significant variation between one run and another" on external communication, as well as on three additional variables (out of five) for which a reliability analysis was made.

A somewhat more rigorous comparison of communication processes between simulation and reference materials was presented by Nardin and Cutler (1969; see also above, pp. 284-287) when they related a communication variable (SALIEN) to six other structural characteristics and behavioral processes. In three instances the relationships proved null in both systems; in three other instances, however, the simulation failed to generate the relationships which did appear in the reference system of the early 1960s. Although in this reference system diplomatic exchanges were related to the magnitude of the difference in the gross national product for the two nations, to the nonmilitary exports of one nation of the pair to the other, and to the number of treaties they signed, such relationships were not obtained for homologous variables in the simulation (correspondence rating: little).

Even the modicum of congruence disappeared in examining in further detail the structure of the communication within the simulations. Dina A. Zinnes (1964: 2-6) carefully noted the differences between the representative role of the ambassador in the pre-World War I situation and the policy role of the external decision-maker (EDM) in the Inter-Nation Simulation, making an a priori analysis that would produce important differences in communication effects. The fact that the EDMs in the Brody-Driver runs had much direct interaction with each other, without an "intermediary or buffer," perhaps induced the nations to "behave in a manner comparable to findings in small-group studies, namely, that the hostility between two individuals results in lessened contact between them and that there is a preference for interaction with one's alliance or in-group . . . , relationships [which] do not hold in the 1914 data" (Zinnes, 1966b: 496). The three hypotheses making alternative tests of the relationship in the two sets of materials are presented in Table 8.6 (correspondence rating: incongruent). Bonham's (1967, 1971) experimental simulation of face-to-face negotiations on the post-World War II disarmament negotiations produced the overall effects described by Zinnes. When he intervened by inducing strong disagreement between parties about the relative importance of the inspection versus the reduction-in-arms issues, Bonham (1971: 305) obtained more hostility, as measured by attack made in the course of the simulated negotiations. There were also reductions in the mean number of messages exchanged (1971: Table 3; 306). Bonham (1967: 106) interpreted the matter as follows: "Attempts to reduce the differences of opinion about the salience of the issues may be unsuccessful. Misunderstanding may result and lead to increased hostility. Consequently, the negotiators may tend to withdraw and communicate less with each other." It is interesting to note that in the detailed analyses on the 1955 subcommittee negotiations, using an identical coding scheme, Bonham (1971: 310) also found high amounts of expressed of hostility associated with divergence between the U.S.S.R. and the United States on the importance of reduction in arms versus inspection. It is to be regretted that Bonham could not make comparative analyses of the volume of communications in the reference and simulation materials (correspondence rating: much).

Some years later, Schwartz (1972: 179) confirmed the correspondence ratings of "much" from Zinnes's and Bonham's simulation materials in a systematic appraisal of these outputs using historical reference material. Examining "eight major crises of the nuclear age as examples of crisis decision-making ... Korea (1950), Suez (1956), Lebanon (1958), Quemoy (1958), Berlin (1961), Cuban missile crisis (1962), Tonkin Gulf (1964), Cyprus (1964)," Schwartz (1972: 171, 182) found the same strong negative relationships "between perceptions of threat, unfriendliness, and expressions of hostility, on the one hand, and frequency of interaction," on the other. Though Schwartz's conclusions were drawn from visual inspection of histograms related to the historical data, rather than from statistical analysis, the majority of his historical examples did not contradict the earlier work of Zinnes and Bonham (correspondence rating: some).

These complementary findings by Zinnes, Bonham, and Schwartz with respect to interaction among nations, as reflected in their communication processes, are reminiscent of the earlier finding that decision-makers behave in simulations "remarkably like humans." Our negotiators, be they "ambassadors" (as in Zinnes's work) or "representatives" (as in the Bonham research), behave as though they were members of "face-to-face" decision-making groups (Collins and Guetzkow, 1964). In making recon-

Table 8.6
ZINNES'S FINDINGS ON THE RELATIONSHIP BETWEEN COMMUNICATION INTERACTION AND THE PERCEPTION AND EXPRESSION OF HOSTILITY IN THE BRODY-DRIVER REALIZATIONS OF AN INTER-NATION SIMULATION AND IN 1914 HISTORICAL DATA[a]

Communication Interaction and the Perceptions and Expressions of Hostility as Represented by Spearman Rank Order Correlation Coefficients[b]

Hypotheses:	Simulations[c] (42 pairs of nations possible)			1914 Historical Data (30 pairs of nations possible)			
	pre-nuclear	post-nuclear	sum of three hostility themes	number of messages:		word message volume:	
				total	in crisis	total	in crisis
Hypothesis 11: There is a negative relationship between the *perception of threat* and the frequency of interaction; i.e., the greater the perceived threat, the less the interaction.	-.36 p<.05	-.20	---	-.04	-.03	.04	.01
Hypothesis 12: There is a negative relationship between the *perception of unfriendliness* and the frequency of interaction.	-.56 p<.001	-.41 p<.01	---	-.02	-.03	.04	.11
Hypothesis 13: There is a negative relationship between *x*'s *hostility* to *y* and *y*'s frequency of interaction with *x*.	-.71 p<.001	-.77 p<.001	.07	-.00	-.11	.03	-.04

a. Adapted from Zinnes (1966b: Table IX; 491).
b. The level of significance of the Spearman rank order correlation coefficients above is given only when it was less than either .001 (p<.001), .01 (p<.01), or .05 (p<.05).
c. The pairs of nations were drawn from 16 runs of the simulation, in which 336 high school juniors and seniors served as decision-makers in the 7 nations.

structions of the Inter-Nation Simulation, Zinnes's insight must be taken seriously.

Alliances and Involvement of Force

Because of the important part alliances play in national security within the Inter-Nation Simulation (Guetzkow, 1981b: 59-62), Druckman's ethnocentric evidence is of much relevance. He found that the in-group bias for one's own nation (see above, p. 271) also held, to an extent, for those nations within their alliances and that simultaneously there was depreciation of "out-nations," as is illustrated in Table 8.7 (Druckman, 1968). When alliances shifted in the course of the WINSAFE II simulation (Raser and Crow, 1964), in which Druckman's outputs were gathered, the bias shifted correspondingly. These effects are documented within the general literature of ethnocentrism by Paul C. Rosenblatt (1964) (correspondence rating: much).

Such in-group versus out-group differences are reflected also in the alliance behaviors generated in the Brody-Driver runs (Brody, 1963a). Although it seems that the patterning of communication, as discussed above, does not correspond closely to "realities" of the reference system, the communication net vis-à-vis the bipolar alliances seemed to have simulated somewhat satisfactorily the patterns among those countries existing in the mid-1950s. After Brody (1963a: 725) demonstrated that "there is more interaction within the blocs than between the blocs," using the terminology of Morton Kaplan (1957), he then stated that in the sixteen simulations "there is a tendency for non-nuclear bloc members to communicate with the leader of their bloc rather than with the external nuclear power—the system prior to the spread of nuclear capability is not only bipolar, it is tightly bipolar" (1963a: 731). Presaging developments in the late 1960s and into the 1970s, these simulations (operated during the summer of 1960) then developed a fragmentation of the alliance system with the coming of nuclear proliferation. The schematics presented in Figure 8.3 (Brody, 1963a: Figures 4.3, 4.4; 743-744) highlight the dramatic change which accompanied the experimental introduction of widespread nuclear capability, mirroring in a general way the fragmentation which seemed to be taking place during the 1960s in the alliances of both the East and the West (correspondence rating: some).

The relations of the alignments of nations in the simulations of international relations and in the "realities" of the reference system were explored with some rigor by Nardin and Cutler (1969). There was a close correspondence between alignment and five of the six variables thought to have been homologous, ranging in parallel fashion from strong through

Table 8.7
DRUCKMAN'S ANALYSIS INDICATING ETHNOCENTRISM AT THE END OF TEN REALIZATIONS BY RASER AND CROW OF AN INTER-NATION SIMULATION[a]

Evaluation by Participants of Members of Own Nation, Allies, and Enemies[b]

Ratings By All Decision-Makers	overall evaluation	Mean Ratings of Traits		
		"liking"	"respect"	"strong personality"
of members of own nation	-.44	-.50	-.32	-.21
of allies	+.01	-.02	+.04	-.01
of enemies	+.22	+.28	+.13	+.10

a. Adapted from Druckman (1968: Table 1).
b. Decision-makers were 160 Naval recruits, operating 4 nations in each of 10 runs for Raser and Crow. Data on ratings of all participants as persons were collected at the end of each run. The more negative the mean rating, the more favorable the evaluation. All differences are significant at the .001 level, as tested through analyses of variance.

weak relationships for such pairs of variables as alignment vis-à-vis openness of the regime (strong) and alignment vis-à-vis communication (weak), the latter being in contradiction to the finding by Brody presented immediately preceding (correspondence rating: much). Yet, the relationships between the number of treaties signed and the variables used to characterize the system were simulated with adequacy in only three of the six possible relationships; the three noncongruences were of the kind in which the simulation failed to generate a relationship strong enough to match the operation of the variables in the reference system (correspondence rating: some).

Employing Etzioni's (1975) conceptualization of organizational structure, Forcese (1968, 1976) examined whether alliance cohesion would vary with the level of utilitarian, identive, and coercive power exerted by an allied dominant nation. In the thirteen simulations conducted, each type of power was inspected for its influence on alliance maintenance. He concluded that the level of economic rewards acquired through the coalition ($p < .01$) and its normative, ideological appeal ($p < .01$) significantly related to its cohesion, while the coercion variable did so, but less significantly ($p < .05$; Forcese, 1968: 95). Using NATO-related data, Forcese examined whether a similarly patterned relationship with the three variables existed in the referent system. "Although the operationalizations

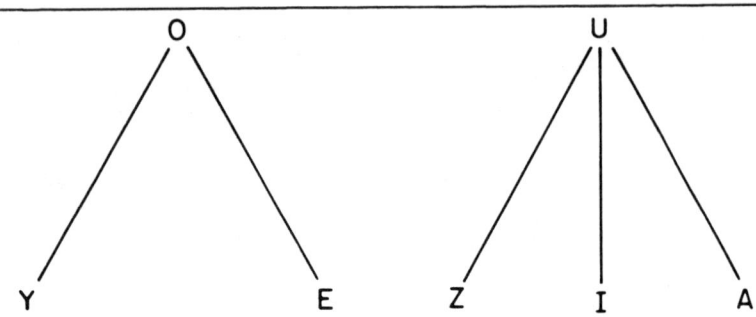

Pre-Spread Inter-Nation Communication

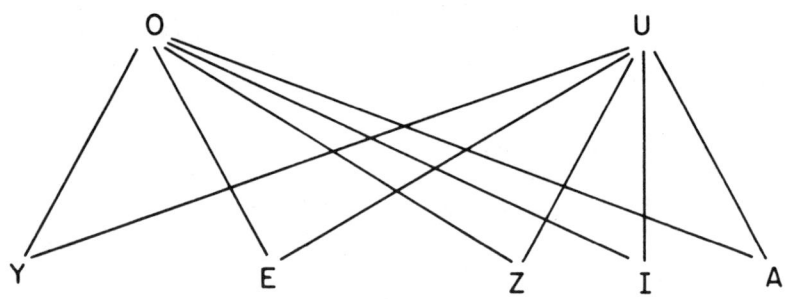

Post-Spread Inter-Nation Communication

Figure 8.3 Richard A. Brody's Conceptualization of Pre-Spread and Post-Spread Inter-Nation Communication

SOURCE: Brody (1963a: Figures 4.3, 4.4; 743-744).
NOTE: Letters represent different nations in the simulation; lines represent modal communication links.

were not altogether satisfactory" (Forcese, 1976: 181), it was clear that the economic benefits derived from alliances were significantly related to their viability ($r[14] = .85$, $p < .05$; correspondence rating: much). Similarly, the identive variable involving ideological symbols correlated significantly with alliance cohesion ($r[14] = .87$, $p < .01$; correspondence rating: much). In the referent system, as in the INS, coercion by a dominant nation tended to have a weaker, albeit significant, relation to coalition maintenance (r[14] = .60, p < .05; Forcese, 1968: 102; correspondence rating: much).

The utilitarian function of coalitions as a determinant of internation cohesion was further examined by Burgess and Robinson's (1969) INS study of Olson's (1965) theory of collective action. Inspecting simulation outputs against Olson and Zeckhauser's (1964) analysis of the behavior of NATO members, they found close correspondences. Coalitions which supplemented individual nations with private benefits as well as collective ones exhibited greater cohesion than those which solely provided collective rewards (p < .001; Burgess and Robinson, 1969: 213; correspondence rating: much). Coalitions lacking this complementarity evidenced greater desire for changes in policies than coalitions which produced both collective and private benefits (χ^2 = 29.34, p < .001; Burgess and Robinson, 1969: 215; correspondence rating: much).

Turning from alliances to consideration of potential uses of violence within the international system, the findings of Nardin and Cutler (1969) on the involvement of force in the simulations are parallel to those found in the reference material they examined. Once again, the correspondences ranged from strong to weak relationships for such pairs of variables as expectation of war vis-à-vis openness of the regime (strong) and the likelihood of war vis-à-vis communication (low) (correspondence rating: much). In fact, the "case" materials generated in the effort to reproduce the events of the summer of 1914 (Hermann and Hermann, 1967) provide grounds for speculation that perhaps the simulation developed by the Hermanns could be "tuned" to produce war. "In the researchers' opinion, if the M-Run simulation [the better matched run, in which an attempt was made to develop homology between the personality characteristics of the historical decision-makers and their counterparts in the simulation] had been continued for another 50-to-100 minutes (one or two more simulated days), war would have been declared along lines similar to the historical situation. This position is confirmed by ten of the fifteen M-Run participants and messengers (66.7 percent) in their debriefing questionnaires" (Hermann and Hermann, 1967: 407; correspondence rating: little).

Less anecdotal is the statistical finding with respect to the involvement of force by Crow and Noel (1977) in their East Algonian Exercise. While there was wide variation in the level of escalation response chosen, almost half of the 384 individuals and more than half of the 96 groups chose the level the authors "judged to represent the historical decision" (1977: 403). They noted that to obtain such congruences in 45 and 57 percent of the cases, respectively, the "validity coefficients would have to be .67 and .75 respectively" (1977: 404; correspondence rating: much).

Interaction Patterns: Cooperation and Conflict

In illustrative data from the "realities" of the reference system, a cooperative phenomenon has been found which seems to correspond in a measure to cooperation patterns in simulations. Hermann (1969: 183) reported that among his decision-makers in the simulation, a search for support was more frequent during crisis; he also noted (1969: 179-180) that the parallel "lesson" was pointed out "a year after the Cuban crisis by an Assistant Secretary of State. 'Even when the decision to employ power is essentially our own ... we find it highly desirable to widen the community of the concerned—to obtain sanction for the necessary "next step" from the broadest practicable segment of the international community' (Cleveland, 1963, p. 645)" (correspondence rating: some).

Bonham's analysis of the timing and contents of concession-making by the United States and the Soviet Union in disarmanent negotiations checked validities of simulation materials against the codings presented by Lloyd Jensen (1963). "The United States tended to make concessions earlier in the round than the Soviet Union" (Bonham, 1971: 311). In the simulation, the "American teams made over 72 percent of their concessions during the *first* half of the simulation, but the Soviet teams made 58 percent of their concessions during the *second* half," a difference statistically significant at the .01 level (1971: 312). But there was little correspondence between the types of concessions reached. Further, Jensen found that the United States and the Soviet Union tended to reciprocate concessions during the twenty-one rounds of the post-World War II disarmament negotiations that he coded. "No relationship was found between American and Soviet [reciprocation in] concession-making ($Rs = -.01$) for the data from all the simulation runs. However, when the control runs were examined separately, the Spearman correlation ($Rs = .55$) was positive and significant" (Bonham, 1967: 47; correspondence rating: some).

Alliances may be used for cooperative purposes, too, as in the development of economic and cultural exchanges. In fact, Chadwick (1966d: 14-15) found both in reference and simulation materials that there were tendencies for economic/cultural and military inter-exchanges to occur simultaneously, the correlations between such agreements being .50** and .26* in the two systems, respectively (correspondence rating: much). When trade per se was examined, Chadwick (1966d: 14-15) found that although there was a very high correlation between imports and exports in the reference system of the mid-1950s, ($r = .93**$), in the Brody-Driver simulation there was no linkage ($r = -.02$; correspondence rating: none). In Chadwick's analysis of the economic/cultural treaties in relation to import and export trade within the simulation and reference systems, there was no correspondence ($r = .04$ and $r = -.09$ versus $r = .79**$ and

Table 8.8

CHADWICK, RUMMEL, AND TANTER: CORRELATIONS AMONG CODED MEASURES OF CONFLICT BEHAVIORS EXHIBITED BY NATIONS IN AN INTER-NATION SIMULATION AND IN 1955-1960 REFERENCE MATERIALS

Correlations Between Conflict Behavior Variables

Conflict Behaviors	Within Inter-Nation Simulation[a] (112 nations)	Within 1955-1960 reference systems[b]	
		1955-1957 (77 nations)	1958-1960 (83 nations)
threats/accusations	.21*	.81	.62
threats/protests	.03	.66	.59
accusations/protests	.03	.69	.64

a. Adapted from Chadwick (1966d: Table 3; 15). Correlations are product-moment coefficients, with no missing figures; 336 participants who served as decision-makers were high school juniors and seniors.
b. Adapted from Tanter (1966: Table 1; 46), in which the 1955-1957 correlations were taken from Rummel (1963). No significance tests are reported.

$r = .70**$, respectively). In the analyses presented by Nardin and Cutler, the trade variable (EXPORT) behaved with little congruence, even though both reference and simulation materials were different from those used by Chadwick. For example, the correlation of .68** found between trade (EXPORT) and treaties (INTAGR) in the reference system was only .02 in the simulation (Nardin and Cutler, 1969: 9; correspondence rating: none).

Correspondences between simulations and "realities" may be examined also with respect to conflict among entities comprising the international system. Chadwick's (1966d) analyses revealed almost no congruence among the measures of conflict, as adapted from the work of Rummel (1963) and Raymond Tanter (1966) for the last half of the 1950s, (see Table 8.8). Nor do the measures of threat and protest yield even low correlations in the simulation ($r = -.10$, $r = .00$) when they are related to economic/cultural treaties which occurred in the reference data ($r = .29*$, $r = .40**$; correspondence rating: none).

In a Chadwick-like analysis of Brody and Driver's simulation materials, Rosenband (1968: 17-19) examined the relationship between systemic features of nations (according to INS programmed relationships) and inter-nation communicative conflicts. When outputs from simulation runs were combined in a single aggregate and compared to findings from the Dimensionality of Nations data for differences in the proportions of nations exhibiting conflict, no correspondence was exhibited ($p < .004$; correspondence rating: none). Though this result was in agreement with Chadwick's conclusion, Rosenband suggested that this may be due to the way the simulation materials were organized for the analysis. Following the examples of Chadwick (1966a) and Elder (1966), Rosenband inspected the INS outputs treating each run as individual histories. "When simulation runs are treated as [such,] the ability to predict to the dependent variable is greatly improved. . . . One-third of the [comparisons] are significant at the .05 level" (1968: 25-27; correspondence rating: some).

However, there was considerable homomorphism in the examination of 1914 reference data in two instances. The Hermanns made a microanalysis of messages, using content analysis categories similar to those used by the Stanford Conflict and Integration Project (1967: Table 3; 411) and found considerable congruence. When a more refined analysis was made of them, using differences between the numbers of hostility and capability statements, the "resulting rank-order correlation (.90) between the 1914 data and that of the M-Run [well-matched] was statistically significant. The correlation for the A-Run [less well-matched] was not significant, however" (1967: 411; correspondence rating: much). Thus, the Hermanns realized experimentally—in a very limited case study—the Stanford hypothesis: "If a state's perception of injury (or frustration, dissatisfaction, hostility, or threat) to itself is 'sufficiently' great, this perception will offset perceptions of insufficient capability, making the perception of capability much less important a factor in a decision to go to war" (Zinnes et al., 1961: 470). The hypothesis has been confirmed again by Chihiro Hosoya (1967) in his analysis of World War II with reference to the Japanese decision-makers in 1941.

Statements made by negotiators from the United States and the Soviet Union during the post-World War II disarmament meetings were coded in comparable ways by Jensen (1963) and by Bonham (1971: 309) for "(a) insecurity about the stability of disarmament, (b) propaganda, and (c) hostility or attacks on the motives of the other side." The frequencies presented in Table 8.9 are rankings "assigned as a result of statistical comparisons of the frequencies by Mann-Whitney U-tests" (Bonham, 1971: 310). Two of the three negotiation processes (insecurity and propaganda) "were replicated successfully by the American teams in the simulation runs," but "the Soviet teams did not replicate [these processes] as successfully" (1971: 310; correspondence rating: some).

In a considerably more elaborate analysis by Zinnes (1966b: 486), which was also based on a content analysis of messages in both simulation and reference systems, much congruence was again found in the effects of alliance systems on perceptions of threats ($z = 5.20$, $p < .001$ versus

Table 8.9
BONHAM'S FINDINGS ON THE RANKINGS AND FREQUENCIES OF EXPRESSIONS OF INSECURITY, PROPAGANDA, AND HOSTILITY FOR TWO NATIONS IN HISTORICAL MATERIALS AND IN SIMULATIONS OF DISARMAMENT NEGOTIATIONS[a]

Expressions of Insecurity, Propaganda, and Hostility[b]

Expressions	in Simulations[c] of Disarmament Negotiations		in Historical Reference Material: 1955 Disarmament Subcommittee	
	"USA"	"USSR"	"USA"	"USSR"
insecurity	high (41)	high (53)	high (65)	low (27)
propaganda	low (18)	low (21)	low (25)	high (92)
hostility	low (16)	low (28)	high (60)	high (83)

a. Adapted from Bonham (1971: Table 6; 310).
b. The rankings of high and low were assigned on the basis of statistical comparisons of the frequencies by Mann-Whitney U-tests; frequencies are given in parentheses following the rankings.
c. Participants in 11 runs were 66 college students, half undergraduate and half graduate.

Table 8.10

ZINNES'S FINDINGS ON HOSTILITY IN THE BRODY-DRIVER REALIZATIONS OF AN INTER-NATION SIMULATION AND IN 1914 HISTORICAL DATA[a]

Relationships between Perceptions of Hostility and Hostile Behaviors as Represented by Spearman Rank Order Correlation Coefficients

Hypotheses	Simulations[b] (42 pairs)	1914 Historical Data[c] (31 pairs)
Hypothesis 4: There is a positive relationship between perceptions of *threat* and perceptions of *unfriendliness*.	.88	.91
Hypothesis 5: There is a positive relationship between x's expression of *hostility* to y and y's perception of *threat*.	.43	.70
Hypothesis 6: There is a positive relationship between x's expression of *hostility* to y and y's perception of *unfriendliness*.	.49	.73
Hypothesis 7: There is a positive relationship between the perception of *threat* and the expression of *hostility*.	.34	.74
Hypothesis 8: There is a positive relationship between the perception of *unfriendliness* and the expression of *hostility*.	.49	.73

a. Adapted from Zinnes (1966b: 487).
b. For each of 16 runs of the simulation from which the pairs were drawn, 336 high school juniors and seniors served as decision-makers in the 7 nations. The simulation results above were statistically significant at the .01 level.
c. Correlations in the historical data were significant at the .001 level.

$U = 22.5$, $p < .001$, respectively) and unfriendliness ($z = 5.40$, $p < .001$ versus $U = 18.0$, $p < .001$, respectively; correspondence ratio: much) as well as hostile behavior ($z = 3.81$, $p < .001$ versus $U = 40.0$, $p < .001$, respectively; correspondence rating: much). Further, Zinnes found considerable congruence in the correlations between perceptions of hostility and hostile behavior, as is summarized in Table 8.10 (correspondence rating: much). These results are confirmed in the Jensen/Bonham comparisons for insecurity and hostility (but not for propaganda) in the disarmament negotiations. For example, "the correlation between American and Soviet hostility for Jensen's data was high, $Rs = .61**$ [and] the hostility relationship was high in the simulation, $Rs = .65**$" (Bonham, 1971: 311; correspondence rating: much).

Summary

The assessment of correspondences between simulations of international relations and "realities" with respect to "relations among nations" as they are generated by the decision-makers and their nations, has been summarized in Table 8.11. In only one of the thirty-three ratings was comparison made with general materials derived from work in the field and laboratory; in all other instances the reference sources involved observations on world affairs, ranging from apt anecdotes through rigorous, systematic analyses. It seems that simulations are not realizing a communication structure which is adequately homomorphic to reference materials, nor do simulation trade activities parallel those found in the international arena. With respect to some activities involving cooperation and conflict, including alliances and the use of force, the correspondences overshadowed the noncorrespondences, whether the interaction was in inter-nation negotiation or at more macro levels. However, the cited research examined only a few of the myriad of relations among nations which have been mentioned as potentially important in world affairs.

INTERNATIONAL PROCESSES SIMULATION

The International Processes Simulation (IPS; Smoker, 1981), developed in a person-machine format at Lancaster and Northwestern Universities, represents a quantum change from the INS by incorporating elements of the latter as well as establishing a program structure which is considerably more complex (Guetzkow, 1981a: 14). For example, Smoker implanted a national and multinational corporate system into the IPS. Citizen groups and nongovernmental organizations were also actively represented by actors in addition to the nation leaders used in the INS. Realized but a few times, Smoker (1981), nevertheless, carried out assessments of the IPS's validity.

"DECISION-MAKERS AND THEIR NATIONS"

Utilizing outputs from twelve of the sixteen two-day runs of the IPS conducted in 1967,[7] Smoker evaluated six national political variables referring to domestic conflict in terms of Rummel's analysis of a

Table 8.11
ASSESSMENTS OF CORRESPONDENCES BETWEEN SIMULATIONS AND "REALITIES" IN INTERNATIONAL RELATIONS REGARDING *RELATIONS AMONG NATIONS*

"Relations Among Nations"	Correspondence with Materials from International Relations				Ratings	
Communications	(S)	Conferences[a] (Hermann & Hermann, 1967)	(I)	Structure (Zinnes, 1966)	(M)	1
	(L)	Volume increases in crisis (Hermann, 1969)	(M)	Salience and Hostility (Bonham, 1971)	(S)	2
	(L)	Saliences (Nardin & Cutler, 1969)	(S)	Frequency of Interaction (Schwartz, 1972)	(L)	2
					(N)	0
					(I)	1
					# =	6
Alliances and Involvement of Forces	(S)	Fragmentation[a] (Brody, 1963)	(M)	Coercive power and alliance cohesion (Forcese, 1976)	(M)	9[b]
	(M)	Alignment (Nardin & Cutler, 1969)	(M)	Public and private benefits (Burgess & Robinson, 1969)	(S)	2
	(S)	Treaties signed in alliances (Nardin & Cutler, 1969)	(M)	Policy changes (Burgess & Robinson, 1969)	(L)	1
	(M)	Utilitarian power and alliance cohesion (Forcese, 1976)	(M)	Expectations of war (Nardin & Cutler, 1969)	(N)	0
	(M)	Identive power and alliance cohesion (Forcese, 1976)	(L)	Armed confrontation[a] (Hermann & Hermann, 1967)	(I)	0
			(M)	Escalation (Crow & Noel, 1977)	# =	12[b]

Table 8.11 (Continued)

"Relations Among Nations"	Correspondence with Materials from International Relations		Ratings
Cooperation and Conflict	(S) Support in crisis[a] (Hermann, 1969)	(M) Hostility (Zinnes, 1966)	
	(S) Concession-making (Bonham, 1967, 1971)	(M) Hostility and capability in crisis (Hermann & Hermann, 1967)	
	(M) Treaties (Chadwick, 1966d)	(S) Insecurity, propaganda, and hostility (Bonham, 1971)	(M) 6
	(N) Trade and treaties (Chadwick, 1966d)		(S) 4
	(N) Trade (Nardin & Cutler, 1969)	(N) Communicative conflict: nations considered as an aggregate (Rosenband, 1968)	(L) 0
	(N) Threats, accusations, protests (Chadwick, 1966d)	(S) Communicative conflict: nations paired, forming composite system (Rosenband, 1968)	(N) 4
			(I) 0
			# = 14
	(M) Perception of external blocs (Zinnes, 1966)	(M) Hostility and perception (Zinnes, 1966)	
		(M) Hostility (Bonham, 1971)	
Correspondence Ratings	(M) "Much"	15	(M) 16[b]
	(S) "Some"	8	(S) 8
	(L) "Little"	3	(L) 3
	(N) "None"	4	(N) 4
	(I) "Incongruent"	1	(I) 1
		# = 31	# = 32[b]

a. Materials involving anecdotes and case illustrations.
b. Includes *correspondence ratings* of the following "General Materials from Field Laboratory": (M) Ingroup v. outgroup[a] (Druckman, 1968, 1965).

Table 8.12

PERCENTAGE DISTRIBUTIONS OF DOMESTIC CONFLICT ACTS IN AN INTERNATIONAL PROCESSES SIMULATION AS CALCULATED BY PAUL SMOKER[a]

Variables	Referent[b] N = 77	IPS N = 72	"Correspondence Rating"[c]
Assassination	6.5	8	"much"
Strikes	8	8	"much"
Guerrilla war	5	3	"much"
Purges	3.5	46	"none"
Riots	52.5	12	"none"
Antigovernment demonstrations	24.5	23	"much"
Total domestic conflict	100	100	

a. Adapted from Smoker (1969d: Table 5).
b. These figures are average percentage distributions taken from Rummel (1963) and Tanter (1966), as used by Smoker (1969d).
c. "Correspondence ratings" were judged according to the following percentage differences: "much" ≤ 2.5%; "some" ≤ 5.0%; "little" ≤ 7.5%; "none" > 7.5%.

1955-1959 reality and Tanter's corresponding study of the 1958-1960 period. A matrix for comparison of these simulation and referent materials is delineated in Table 8.12 below.

A comparison of the percentage distributions of conflict acts suggests that "assassination, strikes, guerilla warfare, and anti-government demonstrations within the total simulation sample are all within the range of tolerance defined by these ... distributions," (Smoker, 1969: 10; correspondence rating: much). Purges and riots, on the other hand, exhibit little congruence to the referent, displaying many more occurrences of the former and far too few of the latter (correspondence rating: none).

Smoker (1969: 10) suggested that a plausible hypothesis for the greater percentage of purges in the simulation is that "all conflict acts are recorded, [whereas] in a reference system" governments may often succeed in suppressing information concerning governmental internal control of the citizens. Pursuing this reasoning, he observed that this control "does not account, however, for the underrepresentation of [IPS] riots" (1969: 10). Smoker concluded by suggesting that this lack of correspondence with the referent may be an area in which future research could concentrate.

Table 8.13
PERCENTAGE DISTRIBUTIONS OF CONFLICT ACTS IN
AN INTERNATIONAL PROCESSES SIMULATION AND A
REFERENT SYSTEM AS CALCULATED BY PAUL SMOKER[a]

Variables	Referent[b] $N = 77$	IPS $N = 72$	"Correspondence Rating"[c]
Antiforeign demonstrations	51	30	"none"
Negative sanctions	11	16	"some"
Severance of diplomatic relations	4	4	"much"
Expulsion or recalling of an ambassador	6	3	"much"
Expulsion or recalling of a lesser official	15	1	"none"
Wars	2.5	9	"little"
Troop movements	8	25	"none"
Mobilizations	2.5	12	"little"
Total foreign conflicts	100	100	

a. Adapted from Smoker (1969d: Table 5).
b. These figures are average percentage distributions taken from Rummel (1963) and Tanter (1966), as used by Smoker (1969d).
c. Rating criteria as in Table 8.12, note c.

"RELATIONS AMONG NATIONS"

Examining the IPS outputs from his 1967 series of twelve runs, Smoker analyzed congruencies between simulated foreign conflict and the 1955-1960 realities evaluated by Rummel (1963) and Tanter (1966). Percentage distributions for eight inter-nation conflict variables in each world are recorded in Table 8.13.

In the foreign conflict area two simulation variables concern formal international diplomacy (the severance of diplomatic relationships and the expulsion or recall of an ambassador) displayed strong congruency with the referent system (correspondence rating: much). A related variable (expulsion or recall of a lesser diplomatic official), however, exhibited no correspondence to the 1955-1960 realities (correspondence rating: none). Possibly the simulation model was not sufficiently sensitive to represent the calibrations of inter-nation political conflict as presented by the distinction between expulsion of ambassadors and expulsion of lesser officials.

A last variable exhibiting strong correspondence between the IPS outputs and the Rummel-Tanter analyses concerned negative sanctioning of nations. The difference between the mean percentage distribution taken from Rummel (1963) and Tanter (1966), and Smoker's outputs was only 5 percent, which is within the stipulated tolerance level (see Table 8.13; correspondence rating: some).

The remaining four foreign conflict variables (wars, mobilizations, troop movements, and antiforeign demonstrations), exhibited weak correspondences between simulation and referent systems for the former two variables (correspondence rating: little and little) and no correspondence for the latter two (correspondence rating: none and none). One pattern emerging from the comparisons of percentage distributions in Table 8.13 is that the former three variables, relating to inter-nation confrontation (wars, mobilizations, and troop movements), "appear to be exaggerated in the simulation. This is consistent with the assumption that the ... more intense forms of conflict are exaggerated by the simulation, while less intense forms [such as the incidence of antiforeign demonstrations] ... are minimized" (Smoker, 1969: 11).

SUMMARY

The assessment of correspondences between the IPS and "realities" indicates that foreign conflict in the simulation is magnified as compared to domestic conflict. In the former area intense conflicts (wars, mobilizations, and troop movements) tend to be more amplified than the less intense forms (antiforeign demonstrations, negative sanctions, the severing of diplomatic relations, and the expelling of foreign diplomats). The "biased mapping of reality in the simulation model" (Smoker, 1969: 11) tends to over emphasize the aggressive "relations among nations" rather than those which occurred between "decision-makers and their nations," as is summarized in Table 8.14. In only three of eight instances of foreign conflict was there homomorphy between the simulation and reality, while on the national level four of six variables exhibited such congruency.[8]

CONCLUSIONS: INS AND IPS

The fragmentary nature of the evidence available for assessing validities in the person-computer simulation of international processes indicates that no firm conclusions about the correspondences between simulation and world "realities" may be drawn at this time. The findings, indicate that

Table 8.14

ASSESSMENTS OF CORRESPONDENCES BETWEEN AN INTERNATIONAL PROCESSES SIMULATION AND "REALITIES" IN INTERNATIONAL RELATIONS

Level	Correspondence with Materials from International Relations			Ratings	
Decision-makers and their nations	(M)	assassinations	(N) purges	(M)	4
	(M)	strikes	(N) riots	(S)	0
	(M)	guerrilla war	(M) antigovernment demonstrations	(L)	0
				(N)	2
				(I)	0
				# =	6
Relations among nations	(N)	antiforeign demonstrations	(N) expulsion or recall of a lesser official	(M)	2
	(S)	negative sanctions		(S)	1
	(M)	severance of diplomatic relations	(L) wars	(L)	2
			(N) troop movements	(N)	3
	(M)	expulsion or recalling ambassadors	(L) mobilization	(I)	0
				# =	8
Correspondence ratings	(M)	"Much"	6		
	(S)	"Some"	1		
	(L)	"Little"	2		
	(N)	"None"	5		
	(I)	"Incongruent"	0		
			# = 14		

further work in simulation development should be guided closely by concurrent validity checks. The results do not signal that work in the simulation of the international relations be abandoned.

When one returns to the broad rubrics of SIP outlined by Guetzkow (1981b), it is gratifying to note that correspondences have been examined within many of the topic areas listed. Considered as a group, researchers straightforwardly interested in the validity problem center their work on intranational processes rather than international processes within the simulation of world affairs; there are almost four entries in Tables 8.3 and 8.5 combined, for every three in Table 8.11.

Eighty-seven entries derived from some thirty-four different studies are summarized in Tables 8.3, 8.5, 8.11, and 8.14. A series of overall summaries of these is given in Table 8.15. About 72 percent of the entries consist of assessments in which the findings from the simulations correspond with "some" or "much" similarity to the findings in the reference materials.

To what extent does the nature of the reference material affect the extent of congruence? Note that over three-quarters of the comparisons were made with materials derived from the "realities" of international relations, rather than from more general materials found in laboratory and field work. As indicated in Table 8.15 (part B), there is less correspondence when materials from the international system are used as the reference data. Is this finding an artifact, inasmuch as work with international materials permits closer scrutiny of the fit between simulation and reference materials than is the case in analyses of intranational materials, which center largely on human components in "general" comparison?

Over three-fourths of the comparisons were made in an articulated fashion, with systematic materials presented for both simulation and reference systems. Although one has less confidence in anecdotal, illustrative materials, it is interesting to note that in the comparisons made to materials from (only) international relations, as exhibited in Table 8.15 (part C), such materials present no more correspondence than do the systematic materials. Is this finding merely a reflection of the authors' deprecatory attitude toward unsystematic material (see above, pp. 255-256), inasmuch as they never allowed an assessment of "much" on the anecdotal, illustrative variety?

There is greater congruence among the materials assembled in assessing the validation related to "decision-makers and their nations" than among entries concerned with "relations among nations," as shown in Table 8.15 (part D). Yet, we are not in a position, now that "some elements of a model have been supported by validity operations," even to "cautiously infer a degree of validity to those related elements which have not," as C. F.

Table 8.15
SUMMARIES OF ASSESSMENTS OF CORRESPONDENCES BETWEEN SIMULATIONS AND "REALITIES" IN INTERNATIONAL RELATIONS

Assessments of Correspondences Between Simulations and "Realities"	Correspondence Ratings					Totals
	"Much"	"Some"	"Little"	"None"	"Incongruent"	
(A) Overall summary of assessments of correspondences from Tables 8.3, 8.5, 8.11, & 8.14	38	24	8	14	3	87
(B) Comparison of correspondences in materials from field and laboratory: international relations:	9 29	3 21	1 7	1 13	1 2	15 72 T = 87
(C) Comparison of correspondences in materials from (only)[a] international relations of anecdotal, illustrative variety: articulated, systematic variety:	0 30	8 13	2 5	0 13	0 2	10 63 T = 73
(D) Comparison of correspondences in materials representing "Decision-makers and their nations" from Tables 8.3, 8.5, & 8.14: "Relations among nations" from Tables 8.11 & 8.14:	20 18	15 9	3 5	7 7	2 1	47 40 T = 87

a. Materials from field and laboratory are *not* included in C.

Hermann (1967b: 225) hoped. The findings to date do not indicate that validity in one part of the model induces validity elsewhere or vice versa. A simulation is more like an "empty world," for therein, as Herbert A. Simon (1965: 73) says, "most things are only weakly connected with most other things." This state of affairs is reflected in the many times a relationship observed in the reference system failed to be generated in the simulation. Chadwick's (1967: 178) hope—that "if one were in possession of simulation and international system materials by which comparisons [of] activity patterns could be made, one could estimate the areas in which simulation theory was relatively insufficient"—seems to be optimistic, given the findings reported above.

Except for the work of Bonham (1967), Chadwick (1966a, 1966b, 1966c, 1966d, 1967), Nardin and Cutler (1969), and Smoker (1981), each entry represents a somewhat isolated relation among two (or, at most, three) variables. This represents a severe limitation on the assessments of the correspondence, given the posture that simulations gain leverage in modeling complex phenomena just because of the way in which they portray complex nets in interrelationships with many interactions among the variables. Could it be that in analyzing the simulation and reference materials we inadvertently imposed an "empty world"? Such hardly seems the case, inasmuch as similar techniques were employed in both analyses, and yet only outputs from the simulations were found so "weakly connected."

Although many of the topics within an encompassing theory of interational relations have been touched upon—perhaps to the tedium of the reader—only the most superficial coverage of attributes was obtained, as has been pointed out again and again in the summary sections of this chapter.

The relative absence of incongruent findings in Table 8.15 (A) suggests that the simulations embody a gamut of "possibilisms" (Sprout and Sprout, 1965: Ch. 5, 192), without generating much nonsense. Even Chadwick (1966d: Figure 1; 17), in his systematic examination of 136 relations stemming from his seventeen variables, rarely obtained an output from the simulation which inverted a finding from the reference system. On reflection, is it for this reason that Noel (1963b) and Guetzkow (1959: esp. 188-190; 1981b) were able to embellish their essays with illustrations of simulation behaviors that seem so credible when a gross, anecdotal comparison is adduced between simulations and verbal theory?

The conclusions about homomorphies of the simulations with the world, summarized above, are subject not only to much basic error, but to differences in intuitive interpretations of the assessments of the correspondences. Recall the tremendous liberties taken in composing the judgments summarized in Tables 8.3, 8.5, 8.11, and 8.14. As was mentioned in the introductory passages of this chapter, little attention was given by the researchers to the problem of reliability of the materials in either the simulations or the world reference materials (but see Smoker, 1981). Nardin and Cutler (1969) and C. F. Hermann (1969) provide the two exceptions (see above, pp. 284-289) with respect to simulations. Zinnes herself (1966b: 494, n. 23) complained that the "1914 data . . . represent only one historical case, and possibly an atypical case since it was a crisis that ended in war." Can one expect valid results if the analyses themselves are based on possibly unreliable materials? Further, the problem of matching variables proved thorny indeed. Chadwick (1966a: 66, n. 29) rightly explains that "the variables defined in INS theory were not provided with empirical indices by INS theorists." Finally, the researches reviewed are most limited in that they are by and large cross-sectional, despite the fact that since simulations are models in operation across time, they are amenable to longitudinal analysis.

The reader examining each of the studies used in this chapter will note how rife are the sources with potential imcomparabilities. As Snyder (1963a: 5) mused some years ago, "the scaling-down process, the sampling of attributes and the use of surrogate processes involves the peril of inadvertent changes in kind when the counterpart of what is 'out there' is constructed 'in here.' " Why can Chadwick and Zinnes both use different reference materials, the one the world of the mid-1950s and the other the pre-1914 world, as checks against the same simulation material, the preproliferation period of the Brody-Driver runs? Is it not startling to find that the same simulation which yielded a patterned analysis for Brody (1963a) produced an almost random-like result for Chadwick (1966a)?

Perhaps the most serious limitation in this chapter's assessments of correspondences between simulations and realities in international relations is found in the almost total, albeit reluctant, reliance upon SIP simulations (i.e., INS and IPS). It is to be regretted that those developing political-military exercises and all-computer simulations have not produced more assessments of the validity of their contributions, so that the homomorphic relations can be compared and contrasted with those exhibited for the Inter-Nation and the International Processes Simulations.

It is within the framework of these shortcomings that one realizes the tentativeness of the overall findings of this review: a preponderance of correspondence, with a proclivity toward errors of omission rather than commission.

ASSESSMENTS OF CORRESPONDENCES DERIVING FROM SIPER

Bremer's (1977) presentation of his all-computer simulation, the Simulated International ProcessER (SIPER), included an examination of its correspondeces with empirical data from a contemporary reality.[9] In this inspection of "decision-makers and their nations" and "relations among nations," algorithms and a completely programmed environment have replaced the surrogates of the INS and IPS. So as also to assess the adequacy of SIPER vis-à-vis an INS person-computer environment, outputs from Raser and Crow's WINSAFE II runs were simultaneously examined by Bremer,[10] along with those from referent systems.

For this series of correspondence ratings it was possible to refine our coding rules for making our judgments of validity (see above, pp. 258-259). Table 8.16 summarizes our coding criteria. A correspondence rating of "much" is given if relationships are statistically significant at the .05 level or better for both the referent and simulation materials. If both the reality and the simulation are significant at the .10 level or better, then the correspondence is designated as "some." "Little" is given if one of two types of materials is significant at least at the .10 level, and the other at the .15 level. If this latter is greater than or equal to .15. then "none" is scored. Nonsignificant relationships are those in which neither set of materials is statistically significant at the .10 level. If the levels of statistical significance of the simulations and referent materials are ratable as "little," "some," or "much," but the relationships are inverse, the set is designated simply as "incongruent."

"DECISION-MAKERS AND THEIR NATIONS"

Three categories of variables (nation conflict, national security, and domestic economy) were analyzed at the level of the nation with respect to population size, the nation's level of economic development, and the level of national decision-makers' accountability to the citizenry (DL, or decision latitude; Bremer, 1977: 139-141).[11] Table 8.17 gives the results of this analysis and the correspondence ratings.[12]

Of the four variables included in the "nation conflict" category, three statistically significant correlations ($p < .10$) occurred with the referent system. The frequency of conspiracy, internal war, and national stability were positively related to the level of accountability (DL) of the incumbent government. Correlations of SIPER outputs for these same variables exhibited no corresponding relationship. The former two variables produced nonsignificant levels (correspondence rating: none and none), while

Table 8.16
CODING CRITERIA FOR CORRESPONDENCE RATINGS OF BREMER'S COMPARISONS OF EIGHTY-FOUR PARTIAL CORRELATION COEFFICIENTS

Rating[a]		Simulation	Referent
"Much"	if	$p \leq .05$	$p \leq .05$
"Some"	if	$p \leq .10$	$p \leq .10$
"Little"	if	$p \leq .10$	$.10 < p \leq .15$
	or	$.10 < p \leq .15$	$p \leq .10$
"None"	if	$p > .15$	$p \leq .10$
	or	$p \leq .10$	$p \leq .15$
Nonsignificant	if	$p > .10$	$p > .10$

a. Simulation and referent materials are judged *"incongruent"* when the direction of the relations are opposite, provided that one type of material is statistically significant at $\leq .10$ while the other is at $\leq .15$.

in the latter there was a significant negative relationship between national stability and accountability (correspondence rating: incongruent).

The four variables concerning the intranational or domestic economy (consumption, absolute growth, growth rate, and investment) exhibited some strong correlations within the referent system. The level of economic development was significantly associated with each variable, except investment, at the .05 level or better. The programmed environment of SIPER also produced weak correlations for investment. National resource consumption was the only variable associated significantly with the level of economic development (-.73***; correspondence rating: much). The two growth-related variables, on the other hand, exhibited virtually no relationship with the level of development in the simulated nations (correspondence ratings: none and none).

The lack of correspondence of SIPER outputs with the empirical data was also evident in the degrees of association between the four domestic economic growth variables and population size. In the referent system, absolute growth and growth rates were significantly related to population size (Table 8.17). Consumption and investment levels, on the other hand, were unrelated to population. SIPER outputs, while demonstrating some analogy with reality for the absolute economic growth and growth rate variables (correspondence ratings: much and some), had no validity in the programmed representations of consumption and investment levels (cor-

Table 8.17
MATRIX OF PARTIAL CORRELATION COEFFICIENTS CALCULATED BY BREMER FOR JUDGING CORRESPONDENCES BETWEEN SIPER AND INS, AND A REFERENT SYSTEM[a]

	Population Size					Level of Development							Accountability (DL)				
	SIPER[b]	Referent	INS			SIPER		Referent		INS			SIPER	Referent		INS	
	r	r	r		Rating	r	Rating	r	r	r	Rating	Rating	r	r	r	r	Rating
	Rating			Rating													
Nation Conflict:																	
turmoil	n.s.	-.09	.05	-.63****	"none"	n.s.	.08	-.11		.28	n.s.	n.s.	.09	-.05	-.17		n.s.
conspiracy	n.s.	-.02	-.14	-.52****	"none"	n.s.	-.10	-.11		.28	n.s.	n.s.	.00	-.32***	-.24*		"little"
internal war	n.s.	.05	-.18	-.03	n.s.	n.s.	.02	-.07		.08	n.s.	n.s.	.03	-.26*	-.32**		"some"
stability	n.s.	.12	.08	.33**	"none"	n.s.	-.09	.13		-.04	n.s.	"incongruent"	-.80****	.28**	-.46****		"incongruent"
International Economy:																	
consumption	"none"	.26**	-.13	.39****	"none"	"much"	-.73****	-.38***		-.18	"none"	n.s.	-.18	-.02	.19		n.s.
growth	"much"	.33***	.87****	.13	"none"	"none"	.09	.62****		.21	"none"	n.s.	.15	.05	.33**		"none"
growth rate	"little"	.24*	.39***	.15	"none"	"none"	.05	-.30**		.15	"none"	n.s.	.08	.09	.21		n.s.
investment	"none"	.44****	.05	.21	n.s.	n.s.	-.17	.21*		-.06	n.s.	n.s.	.03	.07	.25*		n.s.
National Security:																	
force capability	"much"	.50****	.65****	.72****	"much"	"much"	.64****	.61****		.42****	"much"	"none"	.01	-.33***	.18		"none"
defense spending	"much"	.32***	.78****	.88****	"much"	"much"	.74****	.74****		.07	"none"	"incongruent"	.27**	-.29**	-.35***		"much"
defense effort	"incongruent"	-.41****	.36***	.08	"none"	"much"	.74****	.53****		.17	"none"	"none"	.22*	-.44****	-.46***		"much"

a. Table 8.17 includes partial correlation coefficients reported by Bremer (1977: Tables 5.2-5.6).
b. Ns for SIPER, Referent, and INS: 41, 41, 30, respectively.
Significant F-test: *$p < .15$; **$p < .10$; ***$p < .05$; ****$p < .01$.

respondence ratings: none and none). Within the simulation, consumption and investment levels were positively related to population size, though within the referent system there was no such correlation.

Of the sets of intra-nation variables examined, those concerning national security tend to produce the most correspondences with reality. Within the referent system, all three national security variables (force capability, defense spending, and defense effort) were in all but one instance significantly correlated ($p < .05$) with population size, level of development, and accountability (DL). Defense spending slightly deviated from this pattern when associated with accountability, producing a correlation at the .10 level: SIPER outputs, while producing seven significant results ($p < .10$) of a possible nine, exhibit only five such that received correspondence ratings of much." Two simulation outputs were associated in directions opposite to those of the empirical data. Defense spending was incongruent, with the referent system exhibiting positive rather than negative correlations with governmental accountability (correspondence rating: incongruent). The converse held in the incongruent relationship between defense effort and population size (correspondence rating: incongruent).

In his examination of SIPER's validity, Bremer (1977: 179-181) also analyzed the "way members of a system allocated their resources" and the "level of economic exchange between system members" in the simulation outputs and empirical data (see Table 8.18). The percentages of resources devoted to consumption, investment, and defense allocation were analogous in the programmed environment and reality (correspondence ratings: some, some, and much). The average trade proportion evidenced no correspondences between SIPER outputs and referent system data (correspondence ratings: none).

In order to clarify whether the INS does in fact exhibit greater validity than SIPER, Bremer inspected INS outputs from six of the twelve Raser and Crow (1964) WINSAFE II trials involving thirty nations.[13] Examining the same variables used in the SIPER validity research (with the exception of the four variables examining dynamic correspondences), Bremer exhibited results comparable to the all-computer simulation. Approximately one-third of the correspondence ratings indicated congruency with the referent system, with ratings of "much" or "some," while about one-half were rated "none" or "incongruent" (one-sixth of the comparisons displaying nonsignificant results; see Tables 8.17 and 8.18). These findings indicate that the economic and political relationships examined in the INS and SIPER have equally low validity.

Bremer (1977: 186-191, 194-196) used the same outputs displayed in Table 8.18 for analyzing SIPER and INS's congruence with a historical

Table 8.18

COMPARISONS OF ALLOCATIONS AND TRADE
IN SIPER AND INS AS FORMULATED BY BREMER[a,b]

Variable	Rating	SIPER	Referent	INS	Rating
Average percentage of resources devoted to consumption	"some"	84.6%	70.3%	91.2%	"some"
Average investment allocation	"some"	4.5%	18.8%	7.1%	"some"
Average defense allocation	"much"	10.9%	3.7%	3.4%	"much"
Average trade proportion	"none"	7.1%	38.8%	4.6%	"none"

a. Correspondence ratings of "much" were judged if there were roughly 10 or less percentage points difference between the simulation outputs and referent data. "Some" and "little" were judged if the differences were of a magnitude of roughly 20 to 30 percentage points, respectively. Differences of more than 30 percentage points were rated "none." The coding procedure used here for these comparisons is a transformation of the one sketched in Table 8.12, note c. As is indicated below Δ %'s of Table 8.12 were multiplied by 4 to obtain the Δ %'s used here:

	Δ % Table 8.12	Δ % Table 8.18
"much"	⩽ 2.5	⩽ 10
"some"	⩽ 5.	⩽ 20
"little"	⩽ 7.5	⩽ 30
"none"	⩽ 7.5	⩽ 30

b. Adapted from Bremer (1977: Tables 6.2-6.5).

referent system (1960-1969) composed of nine nations: the United Kingdom, Germany, Italy, Norway, Sweden, the United States, Canada, Denmark, and France.

In general, there were better correspondences between the simulations and the historical realities than occurred with comparisons to the contemporary referent, with three of the eight comparisons increasing their congruence. For the SIPER outputs, average trade proportion was judged to have "little" correspondence as opposed to the "none" rating it had previously received (see Table 8.18). INS outputs for two categories, average investment allocation and average trade proportion, also increased their ratings, from "some" and "none" to "much" and "little," respectively.[14]

Bremer's historical analyses of these outputs have not been included in the final assessment of simulation validity for two reasons: (a) We think it is inappropriate to use these simulation outputs twice, as they have already been given correspondence ratings vis-à-vis a contemporary reality; and (b) since SIPER, and the INS outputs, are based on Raser and Crow's (1964, 1969) series of INS runs which were oriented toward exploring deterrence theories in a modern context, we think it may be too great an extrapolation to use these outputs now for comparative historical analysis. In conjunction with these comments we find M. D. Wallace's (1978: 242) criticism that Bremer's "choice of a [historical] spatial-temporal domain was dictated by data availability, a criterion which inevitably generates bias," a powerful reason for not including the historical research in this study of SIP validity.

Exploring dynamic correspondences between SIPER and a referent system,[15] Bremer (1971: 191) inspected two aspects of their "transformation process": "(1) the direction of systemic change (e.g., Are the systems becoming more or less militarized?) and (2) the rate of systemic change (e.g., How rapidly are the systems becoming more or less militarized?)." Analyzing outputs from six simulation periods (assuming one period equals one year of real time) in comparison with data about eight Western nations drawn from the years 1957-1966,[16] he examined trends of four variables: consumption, investment, defense, and trade.[17]

Trends for resource consumption in the contemporary referent system indicated a slight falling off (-.1 percent) during the nine years considered. SIPER outputs were congruent with the reality, also having a tendency to reduce consumption (- 1.7 percent; correspondence rating: much).[18] Allocation of resources for investment displayed diverging results. While the referent indicated increasing allocations at 1 percent, the simulation exhibited a marked tendency for decrease (- 5.9 percent; correspondence rating: incongruent). Inspection of defense allocation trends also produced discrepancies between the two systems. The referent exhibited a declining rate of 1.9 percent per year. In contrast to this, the SIPER systems appeared to be "caught in intense arms races" (Bremer, 1977: 193), having rates of annual increase at the level of 17.5 percent (correspondence rating: none).

With respect to trade in SIPER and the referent, each displayed "an overall increase in the ratio of trade to the total product, although the trend is slight in both cases" (.9 and 1.9 percent, respectively; Bremer, 1977: 193; correspondence rating: much).[19]

"RELATIONS AMONG NATIONS"

In our examination of "decision-makers and their nations," outputs from the intranational component of the all-computer environment were examined. Now we inspect the validity of outputs derived from the inter-nation portion of the SIPER program.

Bremer (1977) investigated three variables concerning relationships of cooperation and conflict among the nations: relative trade, trade magnitude, and diplomatic conflict. These, like the intra-nation variables, were correlated with population size, level of development, and accountability (DL) as found in Table 8.19. The empirical materials exhibited five significant associations ($p < .10$) in the nine tests. The all-computer simulation outputs exhibited only three such significant correlations, of which two were analogous in the referent (correspondence ratings: much and some). There was no correspondence for (a) the three instances in which the simulation failed to produce the corresponding relation found in the referent (correspondence ratings: none, none, and none), and (b) the one instance in which the referent failed to produce the corresponding relation found in the simulation (correspondence rating: none).

SUMMARY

Our judgments concerning the validity of the Simulated International ProcessER's (SIPER) modeling of "decision-makers and their nations" are summarized in Table 8.20. Thirteen of the twenty-seven instances examined coincide with the referent materials. Seven were displayed among the intranational economy variables; the other six significant findings were found among the national security variables. These congruencies contrast with the fourteen analyses exhibiting "little," "none," or "incongruent" ratings. For each of the above two categories of variables (intranational economy and national security), six and five such ratings, respectively, were made. Among the nation conflict variables no validity was found. In overview it is apparent that SIPER lacks considerable correspondence with realities for intranational economy, national security, and nation conflict.

This summation can be refined. SIPER's modeling of dynamic national economic processes was homomorphic to the referent for four of the six comparisons judged. The validity of the simulated national economy diminished when its components (growth, resource consumption, investment) were correlated with population size and the level of national development. In only three of seven instances did we judge congruency with reality.

National security in the all-computer environment also displayed inconsistencies. In five of six comparisons with population size and level of national development, defense-related variables exhibited homomorphism to the referent materials. Yet no congruency was found when these same variables were correlated with the decision latitude of national leaders. Though only relatively few characteristics of decision-makers and their

Table 8.19

A MATRIX OF PARTIAL CORRELATION COEFFICIENTS CALCULATED BY BREMER FOR JUDGING CORRESPONDENCES BETWEEN SIPER AND INS, AND A REFERENT SYSTEM FOR THREE VARIABLES CONCERNING INTERNATIONAL RELATIONSHIPS[a]

	Rating	Population Size				Level of Development					Accountability (DL)			
		SIPER[b] r	Referent r	INS r	Rating	SIPER Rating	r	Referent r	INS r	Rating	SIPER r	Referent r	INS r	Rating
International Activity:														
relative trade	"none"	.01	-.63****	-.06	"none"	"none"	-.29**	.12	-.03	n.s.	-.08	.01	.19	n.s.
trade magnitude	"much"	.50****	.74****	.08	"none"	"none"	-.12	.74****	.07	"none"	.00	.06	.30*	n.s.
diplomatic conflict	n.s.	.06	.12	-.35**	"none"	"some"	.29**	.34****	-.08	"none"	.06	-.26**	-.36**	"some"

a. Table 8.19 includes partial correlation coefficients reported by Bremer (1977: Table 5.5).
b. Ns for SIPER, Referent, and INS are 41, 41, 30, respectively.
Significant F-test: $*p < .15$; $**p < .10$; $***p < .05$; $****p < .01$.

Table 8.20
ASSESSMENT OF CORRESPONDENCES DERIVED FROM BREMER'S ANALYSIS OF SIPER AND INS VALIDITIES

Variables:	Correspondences with Materials from International Relations				Ratings:	
	SIPER Outputs		INS outputs			
I. Decision-Makers and Their Nations						
Intranational conflict			*per population size*			
			(N)	turmoil		
			(N)	conspiracy		
			(N)	stability	(M)	0
		per accountability of national leaders			(S)	1
					(L)	1
					(N)	5
	(N)	conspiracy	(L)	conspiracy	(I)	2
	(N)	internal war	(S)	internal war	# = 9	
	(I)	stability	(I)	stability		
Intranational economy			*dynamic processes*			
	(S)	average resources for consumption	(S)	average resources for consumption		
	(S)	average investment allocation	(S)	average investment allocation		
	(N)	average trade proportion	(N)	average trade proportion		
	(M)	resource consumption trends				
	(I)	investment allocation trends				
	(M)	trade ration			(M)	4
					(S)	4
		per population size			(L)	1
	(N)	resource consumption	(N)	resource consumption	(N)	13
	(M)	absolute growth	(N)	absolute growth	(I)	1
	(L)	growth rate	(N)	growth rate	# = 23	
	(N)	investment				
		per level of development				
	(M)	resource consumption	(N)	resource consumption		
	(N)	absolute growth	(N)	absolute growth		
	(N)	growth rate	(N)	growth rate		
		per accountability of national leaders				
			(N)	growth rate		
National security	(M)	average defense allocation	(M)	average defense allocation		
	(N)	defense allocation trend				
		per population size				
	(M)	force capability	(M)	force capability		
	(M)	defense spending	(M)	defense spending		
	(I)	defense effort	(N)	defense effort	(M)	12
					(S)	0
		per level of development			(L)	0
					(N)	7
	(M)	force capability	(M)	force capability	(I)	2
	(M)	defense spending	(N)	defense spending	# = 21	
	(M)	defense effort	(N)	defense effort		
		per accountability of national leaders				
	(N)	force capability	(N)	force capability		
	(I)	defense spending	(M)	defense spending		
	(N)	defense effort	(M)	defense effort		
Correspondence ratings:	(M)	10	(M)	6	(M)	16
	(S)	2	(S)	3	(S)	5
	(L)	1	(L)	1	(L)	2
	(N)	10	(N)	15	(N)	25
	(I)	4	(I)	1	(I)	5
	# = 27		# = 26		# = 53	

Table 8.20 (Continued)

Variables:	Correspondences with Materials from International Relations				Ratings:		
	SIPER Outputs			INS outputs			
II. Relations Among Nations:							
	per population size						
Inter-nation relationships	(N) relative trade (M) trade magnitude			(N) relative trade (N) trade magnitude (N) diplomatic conflict			
	per level of development						
	(N) relative trade (N) trade magnitude (S) diplomatic conflict			(N) trade magnitude (N) diplomatic conflict			
	per accountability of national leaders						
	(N) diplomatic conflict			(S) diplomatic conflict			
Correspondence ratings:	(M)	1	(M)	0	(M)	1	
	(S)	1	(S)	1	(S)	2	
	(L)	0	(L)	0	(L)	0	
	(N)	4	(N)	5	(N)	9	
	(I)	0	(I)	0	(I)	0	
	# =	6	# =	6	# =	12	
Total correspondence ratings:	SIPER outputs		INS outputs				
	(M)	11	(M)	6	(M)	17	
	(S)	3	(S)	4	(S)	7	
	(L)	1	(L)	1	(L)	2	
	(N)	14	(N)	20	(N)	34	
	(I)	4	(I)	1	(I)	5	
	# =	33	# =	32	# =	65	

nations in SIPER were examined, it is evident that the all-computer formulation of intranational processes (i.e., conflict, economy, and security) tends to lack validity.

Bremer's examination of these SIPER-type variables using INS outputs from six of Raser and Crow's WINSAFE II runs produced results similar to those displayed in the analysis of the all-computer materials. For the variables relating to "decision-makers and their nations," the person-computer simulation materials were judged at levels of validity similar to those of the all-computer outputs ($\chi^2 = .53$, df = 1, n.s.).[20] The few comparisons of "relations among nations" examined exhibited similar results. At least two-thirds of the correspondence ratings were judged to have "little" or lower validity. Thus, for all thirty-three inspections of the variables selected by Bremer, the INS lacks validity at levels coincidental with SIPER. This hypothesis was supported by a chi-square test that indicated no significant difference between the SIPER and INS correspondence levels ($\chi^2 = .51$, df = 1, n.s.).[21]

This weakness was probably not uncovered in earlier INS validity research, since simulators were oriented toward investigating social, psychological, economic, and political variables that did not overlap with these. It is important to note that even in an area (economics) where SIPER was supposedly more rigorously constructed than INS, it exhibited no more validity. Some 22 SIPER and 18 INS comparisons with the referent system concerned economic variables.[22] Of these, 11 such relationships for the all-computer simulation were homomorphic to reality, whereas 11 were not. The all-computer simulation exhibited 5 instances congruent with the referent and 13 that were not. A chi-square test supports the hypothesis that there is no significant difference between SIPER and INS with respect to the validity of their economic model ($\chi^2 = 1.05$, df = 1, n.s.).[23]

Further refinement of this critique is displayed in Table 8.21. Though INS and SIPER have similar weaknesses in their overall representations of the 96 comparisons developed by Bremer, in only 27 did they coincide (see Table 8.22 for a distribution of correspondence ratings). In addition to having few correspondences with reality (for these variables), the models seldom corresponded with each other. In only 6 instances did both models produce correspondence ratings of "much" or "some." The remaining 21 comparisons were judged either "none" (8), "incongruent" (1), or nonsignificant (12). The essence of this observation is that SIPER has not used INS structure to give it (SIPER) validity in the same places as this earlier model (INS).

Slightly over one-quarter of the INS outputs and over one-third of the SIPER outputs exhibited homomorphy to realities. Why should these latter studies produce such poor correspondences when over two-thirds of the former INS assessments exhibited stronger congruencies (Tables 8.3, 8.5, 8.11)? Is it possible that simulation models are "lopsided," having greater validity when examining certain processes as opposed to others? With the exception of Chadwick's (1966b, 1967) and Elder and Pendley's (1981) examination of governmental stability, and Chadwick's (1966b) and Nardin and Cutler's (1969) analyses of international trade (see Tables 8.5 and 8.11), there are no INS assessments for variables that resemble those carried out by Bremer. Those he inspected tended to relate mostly to economic budgetary and demographic matters (Tables 8.17-8.19) not considered by previous simulators, who focused more on analyses of social psychological, sociological, and political variables. It may therefore have been that these areas were unintentionally more carefully scrutinized and improved, while others, such as those emphasized by Bremer, were not. Since these valid aspects of the INS model may be linked to its person-computer format, this may be why they were lost in the all-computer formulation of SIPER. Even in the area of economics, where SIPER was supposedly more refined than INS, the all-computer simulation exhibited no more validity.

Table 8.21

SUMMARY OF COINCIDENTAL CORRESPONDENCE RATINGS FOR SIPER AND INS AS DISPLAYED IN TABLES 8.17-8.19

	"Much"	"Some"	"Little"	"None"	"Incongruent"	n.s.	Totals
Intranational conflict	0	0	0	0	1	6	7
Intranational economy[a]	0	0	0	3	0	4	7
Domestic economic factors[b]	1	2	0	2	0	0	5
National security	3	0	0	1	0	0	4
International relationships	0	0	0	2	0	2	4
Totals	4	2	0	8	1	12	27

a. As displayed in Table 8.17.
b. As displayed in Tables 8.18-8.19.

Table 8.22
PERCENTAGES OF SIMULATION CORRESPONDENCE RATINGS FOR INS, IPS, AND SIPER

		"Much"	"Some"	"Little"	"None"	"Incongruent"	Total Rated Instances	Total Nonsignificant Instances	Total Instances Considered
INS correspondences from varigate sources: Tables 8.3, 8.5, & 8.11	%	44	32	8	12	4	100	0[a]	73
	N	32	23	6	9	3	73		
IPS correspondences: Table 8.14	%	43	7	14	36	0	100	0[a]	14
	N	6	1	2	5	0	14		
INS correspondences from variables selected by Bremer	%	19	12.5	3	62.5	3	100	14	46
	N	6	4	1	20	1	32		
SIPER correspondences from variables selected by Bremer: Tables 8.17-8.19	%	31	10	4	45	10	100	17	50
	N	11	3	2	14	3	33		
Totals	%	36	20	7	32	5	100	31	183
	N	55	31	11	48	7	152		

a. No nonsignificant scores considered.

Table 8.23

BREMER'S CORRESPONDENCE
RATINGS FOR SIPER AND INS[a]

	Good		Fair		Poor	
	N	%	N	%	N	%
SIPER	14	33	10	24	18	43
INS	11	26	15	36	16	38

a. Table is adapted from Bremer (1977: 169).

BREMER'S JUDGMENTS OF SIPER AND INS VALIDITY

Thus far we have inspected the congruence of some 50 instances of SIPER outputs with respect to a contemporary reality and 46 INS instances. These same comparisons were earlier examined by Bremer (1977: 146-170), though in only 42 SIPER and 42 INS inspections did he assess their validity using a standardized coding procedure. Three types of statistics were reported for each comparison.[24] Bremer concluded his examination of SIPER and INS with the results listed in Table 8.23.[25] These now may be used for inspecting the reliability of the coding procedure that used in this chapter for assessing the validity of the same variables (Tables 8.17 and 8.19). Comparing Bremer's analysis of the two simulations with ours, we find that there is no significant difference between either his judgments of SIPER's validity ($\chi^2 = .05$, df = 1, n.s.)[26] or INS's validity ($\chi^2 = .95$, df = 1, n.s.)[27] and our own.

Comparison of the findings from INS and IPS with those from SIPER, as exhibited in Table 8.22, indicate no significant difference between the person-computer simulations' correspondence ratings and those for the all-computer simulation ($\chi^2 = 13.184$, df = 9, n.s.). With this result we reiterate our earlier observation (p. 311) as an overall conclusion about SIP simulation validity research—that there is a preponderance of correspondence, with some proclivity toward errors of omission rather than commission. Using the analogy of the glass of water half full/half empty, it seems appropriate to summarize our findings on validity as being both half "there" and half "not there."

EPILOG

Given the barefoot quality of our assessments of correspondences between outcomes of the simulations and the reference materials, it is easy to realize that our listing of congruences is but a first step in the task of making adequate estimates of the validities involved. In the perspective of a sophisticated philosophical analysis, "the confirmation of scientific hypotheses," by one of Reichenbach's students, in which both Popper and Hanson's seemingly contradictory stances are reconciled within a Bayesian framework, it is reassuring to note that "logically prior to the use of Bayes's theorem some generalizations must have been established through induction and enumeration. These are hypotheses based upon crude inductive generalization, but they constitute the logical starting point. Each of them is rather shaky, owing to the childish quality of the induction by enumeration which supports it, but the more sophisticated inferences that follow can be well founded. As evidence accumulates and further inductions are made, the results become more and more securely established" (Salmon, 1967: 131-132). It is to be hoped that others will join in meeting the exciting challenges posed by our validity problems, moving beyond mere enumeration.

Now that we have apparently entered an era in which the construction and application of simulations is blooming, might this not also be the time to refine methods with which our as yet coarse models might increase in validity? Following completion of the project on Simulated International Processes (see Guetzkow, 1981a), a second project, Computer Simulations for Decision-Making in International Affairs (CSDMIA), commenced at Northwestern University to move in this direction. Through construction of modular simulations, various components of international relations processes can be individually formulated and refined. "Once analyzed, these 'mini-modules' are specified as computer simulation modules operable both independently and within the context of a more comprehensive simulation framework, i.e., Bremer's SIPER" (Guetzkow et al., 1977: 6). Each mini-simulation constitutes a mini-theory; through experimentation each may be individually refined. Will such an effort increase the overall validity of the entire simulation, despite Bremer's difficulty in his utilization of a somewhat comparable strategy in the economic realm of SIPER?

Improvements and extensions of extant simulations, however, depend upon how well our colleagues assume the burdens of validating their work. To date, emphasis among simulation builders has been more upon the venture of model construction, with the scholar working as an artist, rather than upon involvement in checking correspondences between the simulations and their respective reference systems, as is incumbent upon the scholar who works as a social scientist or policy-influencer. This obligation, however, does not belong solely to the simulator. As Morton Gorden (1967) pointed out, the verbal theorist shares in the same obligations. When simulator and verbal theorist ground their work in empirical materials, then they may fruitfully join hands with mathematical and simulation theorists in constructing homomorphic models of the international system which will have fidelity. Then their constructions will represent the world more adequately, as it is now and as it may evolve with simulated alternative futures, unfolding the "realities" of the decades ahead.

NOTES

1. As is often the case when new ideas are introduced, there is much difference of opinion among social scientists concerning what terminological uses are fruitful, as Richard Dawson (1962: 1-15) and Martin Shubik (1964: 70-74) have documented. Zinnes's (1976: 221-224) discussion of Guetzkow's (1959) definition of the concept of simulation is most constructive.
2. In utilizing work by Streufert et al. (1965) concerning the Princeton/Rutgers tactical game (see p. 261), no claim is made that this simulation has the scope or complexity of the other simulations described herein.
3. There is current controversy on how useful levels of significance are in utilizing statistical tests. In this chapter, whenever levels of significance were developed by the scholars whose work is being discussed, they are cited. In lieu of the conventional statistical notation p. we at times use two asterisks (**) to indicate that the test is significant at the .01 level or better; one asterisk (*) indicates that the test is significant somewhere between the .01 and .05 levels. That is to say, the chances of obtaining such a result by pure chance are 1 percent or less for results marked with **, and between 1 and 5 percent for those marked with *, where the assumptions involved in deriving the statistic are applicable. When no levels of significance are mentioned in the text, tables, or figures, none were reported in the original source.
4. β = beta-weight; b = partial regression coefficient; s = standard error of the partial regression coefficient; t = t-value of partial regression coefficient; df = degrees of freedom.
5. Some readers may find this next section on the evaluation of variables comprising national programs more technical than most other parts of the chapter, inasmuch as "through simulation we are able to force ourselves to develop more explicit theory" (Guetzkow, 1966a: 250). Throughout the chapter an effort is made to handle the research being reported without need for the reader to consult the original sources. However, before reading the following sections on national programs involving political, economic, and military variables in INS, some readers may want to acquaint themselves with further substantive details by referring to Guetzkow's (1981b) chapter, where the contents of the equations and programmed assumptions are explicated at greater length. Others may find it useful to gain a methodological orientation to the rigorous style by reading "Some Uses of Mathematics in Simulation Of International Relations" (Guetzkow, 1965c) or "Relating Inter-Nation Simulation Theory with Verbal Theory in International Relations at Three Levels of Analysis" (Chadwick, 1966b).
6. In developing his proposals for modifications in the Inter-Nation Simulation, Chadwick (1966c) used factor analysis and partial correlation techniques to elicit the complex interdependencies existing in the reference material; in this way he wished to assess nonadditive explanatory relations through confluence analysis (Alker, 1966: 639-653). Because of the overall lack of relations among the seventeen variables in

the simulation, Chadwick was unable to apply these more adequate techniques to the outputs of the simulation itself, as he had hoped to do. Hence, they are not discussed in this chapter.

7. The first four runs were used for debugging (Smoker, 1969).

8. Following these earlier analyses of the IPS, Smoker further developed his model, adding more nations to it and integrating a "limits to growth" component into the programmed environment. Rechristened the Global Systems Simulations, it is now being used to explore alternative global futures.

9. Referent system data for nondynamic analysis were drawn from a sample of 41 nations (Bremer, 1977: 145):

United States	Peru	Spain
Canada	Chile	Turkey
West Germany	Ceylon	Soviet Union
Belgium	Thailand	Guatemala
Italy	Japan	Dominican Republic
Sweden	Australia	Colombia
Norway	South Africa	Brazil
Portugal	United Kingdom	Argentina
Greece	Ireland	Israel
Yugoslavia	France	Burma
Mexico	Netherlands	Philippines
Cuba	Switzerland	South Korea
Venezuela	Denmark	New Zealand
Ecuador	Finland	

10. Bremer (1977: 147-148) uses a different method for judging validity from the one used here. We discuss this in our section on Bremer's judgments of SIPER and INS validity.

11. These category titles were taken from subtitles Bremer (1977) uses in his Chapters 5 and 6, which analyze simulation validity.

12. Also included in Table 8.17 are analyses of INS outputs by Bremer. Please do not review these results yet, since they will be discussed later.

13. The six other trials were used by Bremer to set the initial parameters for SIPER.

14. Outputs and correspondence ratings for the eight comparisons of SIPER and INS outputs with a historical referent system are as follows (Bremer, 1977: Tables 6-6 through 6-9):

	Ratings	SIPER	Historical Referent	INS	Rating
Average consumption allocation	some	84.6%	73.7%	91.2%	some
Average investment allocation	some	4.5%	17.1%	7.1%	much
Average defense allocation	much	10.9%	4.1%	3.4%	much

| Average trade allocation | little | 7.1% | 33.5% | 4.6% | little |

The coding procedure used for these ratings is the same as the one outlined in Table 8.18 (note a). Consumption and investment allocation data were drawn from Simon Kuznet (1966: 236-239). Defense allocation data were taken as follows: Nineteenth-century through 1929 data are from Quincy Wright (1965: 666-672); the data through 1969 are from the SIPRI *Yearbook of World Armaments and Disarmaments, 1968-1969* (1970: 194-214). Trade proportion data are from three sources. The nineteenth-century data come from Kuznets (1966: 310-316); twentieth century data were from Karl W. Deutsch and Alexander Eckstein (1961: 275), and the United Nations Statistical Office (1958-1967) *Statistical Yearbook, 1967*.

15. INS outputs were not included by Bremer in this series of ratings, since he judged (1977: 191) that the Raser and Crow "INS systems do not lend themselves to [this] kind of analysis."

16. Data for consumption, investment, trade, and gross national product of Denmark, France, West Germany, Italy, Norway, Sweden, the United Kingdom, and the United States are from the United Nations Statistical Office (1958-1967) *Statistical Yearbook*. Defense expenditure data for these years are from the SIPRI *Yearbook of World Armament and Disarmament, 1968-1969* (1970: 194-214).

17. Data for all nondynamic analyses, both above and below, are from the years 1948-1965. Bremer used three principal sources for this information: Russett et al. (1964), Gurr (1968), and Rummel (1963). See Bremer (1977: 141-143, 181).

18. The coding procedure for judging these four variables is identical to the one used in our appraisal of Smoker's validity study of IPS outputs, with one exception: A rating of "incongruent" is given if the relations are in opposite directions but their absolute values are equal to those rated "much," "some," or "little" (see note a to Table 8.12; Table 8.18). This method was chosen rather than the procedure outlined in Table 8.16, since the latter is appropriate only for comparisons having significance levels (see Tables 8.17 and 8.19) rather than percentage differences. It is regretted that a single coding procedure could not be used, since diverging types of information used in these comparisons of simulation outputs and referent system data prevent this (see Tables 8.8, 8.12, 8.17, and 8.18).

19. Bremer also compared these four dynamic SIPER variables with a historical referent (1860-1960), including seven nations: Denmark, France, Italy, Norway, Sweden, the United Kingdom, and the United States. The SIPER outputs versus the referent data for consumption, investment, defense, and trade trends in resource allocation are as follows: -1.7 versus -2.6, -5.9 versus 6.0, 17.5 versus 22.9, $.9$ versus 4.2, respectively (correspondence ratings: much, incongrent, little, and some, respectively). These ratings, with the exception of that for "trade," are identical to those for the comparisons of SIPER and the contemporary referent system. The validity of the historical trade variable exhibited a slight decrease in congruence vis-à-vis the contemporary system comparison exhibiting a "some" correspondence, rather than maintaining the "much" rating it had previously attained. These judgments of correspondences between SIPER outputs and historical trends, similar to the previous inspections of historical data, are not included in our final assessment of SIP simulation validity (see Wallace, 1978: 242).

20. This chi-square test consists of a 2×2 table. The "much" and "some" categories were combined to form single cells for SIPER and INS ($a = 12$ and $b = 9$,

respectively), as were the "little," "none," and "incongruent" categories (c = 15 and d =17, respectively).

21. For this test, a 2 × 2 table was also constructed. As in note 20, the "much" and "some" categories were combined to form two single cells, i.e., one for SIPER and the other for INS (a = 14 and b = 10, respectively). The "little," "none," and "incongruent" categories also were combined (c = 17 and d = 22, respectively).

22. As listed in Table 8.20, the 22 economic relationships of SIPER were drawn from the following categories of variables: intranational economy (13), national security (5), and inter-nation relationships (4). The 18 INS economic relationships were drawn from the same categories but at different frequencies (i.e., 10, 4, and 4, respectively).

23. This test consists of a 2 × 2 table. As in note 20, the "much" and "some" categories were combined to form a single cell for SIPER and another for INS (a = 10 and b = 5, respectively). The "little," "none," and "incongruent" categories were also combined (c = 12 and d = 12, respectively).

24. "The first... reports the partial correlations... found in each of the three data sets [SIPER, INS, and the referent] the second and third... contain information concerning the goodness-of-fit between the SIPER model and the real world... and the INS and the real world.... [B]oth values reflect the degree of discrepancy between the correlation predicted by the simulation and the correlation observed in the real world sample. The first goodness-of-fit statistic... reflects the size of this discrepancy in terms of standard error units.... The second statistic... is the likelihood that this discrepency is due to sampling error in the real world coefficient.... In order to summarize the goodness-of-fit of the two models, the following correspondence categories [are] used. Good: The discrepancy between the predicted (simulated) correlation and the observed (real) correlation, when transformed into units of standard error, has an absolute value of less than 1.0. If the predicted value is correct, the probability of obtaining a discrepancy larger than this is approximately .30. Fair: The discrepancy between the predicted and observed values, measured in standard error units, has an absolute value between 1.0 and 2.0. The probability of obtaining a discrepancy within this range, if the predicted value were correct, is less than .30 but greater than .05. Poor: The discrepancy between the predicted and observed correlations is greater than ±2.0 units of standard error and has a probability of less than .05 of being obtained if the predicted value were correct" (Bremer 1977).

25. The "much" and "some" categories were combined and assumed to approximate Bremer's "good" category. "little" we equated to his "fair" rating, and "none" and "incongruent" to his "poor" rating. Comparisons we assessed as nonsignificant we did not include in this reliability analysis, since we could not rate them as either Good, Fair, or Poor.

26. This test consists of a 2 × 2 table. Due to an empty cell among the Guetzkow-Valadez ratings representing the "fair" category, it was combined with the "poor" ratings. Thus, with the rows labeled as "good" and "fair-poor," and the columns as "Bremer ratings" and "Guetzkow-Valadez ratings," the table has the following appearance: a = 14, b = 10, c = 28, d = 15.

27. This 2 × 2 table is arranged similarly to the one described in note 26: a = 11, b = 7, c = 3, d = 21.

9
Six Continuing Queries for Global Modelers: A Self-Critique

Harold Guetzkow

Since the formal termination of the project on Simulated International Processes (SIP) in 1972, there have been ample opportunities for retrospection. My original collaborators in designing the Inter-Nation Simulation reviewed its premises early on (Sullivan with Noel, 1972). In 1973 James N. Rosenau challenged a number of us in the wider field of international relations to make self-appraisals of our own work. Conclusions about SIP from these reflective proceedings, instigated in collaboration with G. R. Boynton, then of the National Science Foundation, are found in Rosenau's volume, *In Search of Global Patterns* (Guetzkow, 1976b).[1] In answering Rosenau's query, "How is the IR [International Relations] field better off by virtue of the funds and time invested in your project?" I replied (Guetzkow, 1976b: 101-102):

> In the development of social science it seems imperative that importantly different options be kept open for significant periods of time. Simulation as a vehicle for theory construction has been in existence for less than a quarter century; its alternative in ordinary language theory has been practiced since the days of Herodotus, over ten thousand times longer. Little wonder it is difficult to gain perspective at this time on the outcomes of this project in international relations, inasmuch as its resources have been but a minute fraction of those devoted by legions over many centuries in verbal theory.
> Let me be reckless: the international relations field is "better off" because of the development of the Inter-Nation Simulation (INS), and the International Processes Simulation (IPS), and the Simulated

International ProcessER (SIPER) in the Simulated International Processes (SIP) project. The field now has more adequate understanding of the various formats of this new vehicle for mounting theories in a data-related way. Simulations permit one to tackle immense problems of great complexity, involving large numbers of variables in both foreign affairs and international relations. The modules within the simulations tie relationships among variables into bundles, giving opportunity for the display of interacting processes. Furthermore, the project developed simulations which are data-related, not mere conjectured gadgets. The reconstructions are not without validity. The simulations also permit one to work on alternative formulations, without being data-bound. Nevertheless, we realize that simulation is but one of the array of tools with which we gain "better" coherence as we accumulate knowledge in the field of international affairs.

The international relations field is "better off" because SIP catalyzed development of simulations. By occupying a middling position, attempting to capitalize upon the advantages of both the all-manual simulation and the all-computer simulation, it bridged differences between the two extremes, providing a screen for their mutual growth. There has been fascinating competition among simulators, giving users considerable choice. For example, the political-military exercise now encompasses the non-crisis situation, no longer focusing only upon crisis. On the other hand, in the all-computer arena there has been demonstration that this format need not be thought of as suitable only as a research tool, but that it may also be used interactively in the classroom. The international relations field is "better off" because its all-manual and all-computer simulations have reacted to the shortcomings of person-computer simulations by improving contrasting formats.

The international affairs field is "better off" because the SIP project helped create a readiness to shift from all-manual and person-computer simulations to all-computer simulations. Would we yet be content in all-manual simulation if it had not been for the nudging of the person-computer simulation? Would our courage to go ahead into all-computer simulation now be less had we not had a period within person-computer simulation? Could we have skipped the person-computer phase, going directly from limitations of the manual exercise to the all-computer simulation, given the state of the field at the end of the 1950s? Or was an intermediate form necessary to spur young and old to gain the methodological competences required to work in an all-computer format? A decade and a half later one guesses that had the development of the project not been with magnitude and speed, it would have not helped in creating today's widespread readiness to work with global and modularized simulations.

Harold Guetzkow

But let us now be done with retrospection. The record stands. Although our project did not develop a scope or marshal resources like those in Project LINK (Hickman and Klein, 1979), it is reassuring to know that modeling of first-rank quality is achievable, when the discipline's infrastructure matches the challenge. It is to be hoped that efforts following SIP will be undergirded in a fashion commensurate with the importance of the problems involved in creating world peace.

The decade of the 1970s, following the SIP project, has been a tremendous time for those of us concerned with global modeling in international affairs. Thanks in part to the initiatives of the Club of Rome, world modeling has become an integral part of the intellectual scene throughout the world. It is regretted that our work in Simulated International Processes provided no catalyst for these activities. An incomplete display of global models is presented in Table 9.1.

Being largely system engineers and econometricians, the researchers stimulated by the Club of Rome found their concerns with social and political aspects of the world intractable. By eschewing inclusion of political elements, deliberately truncating their products, they may have gained greater acceptance for their models by policy-makers.

Now there is movement from economic engineering to more inclusive modeling, including sociopolitical components thereof, as documented in detail elsewhere (Ward and Guetzkow, 1979). Given the fact that Hughes (1980) is continuing work in the documentation and development of the Mesarovic-Pestel work (1972), there is prospect for incorporation of sociopolitical processes in their World Integrated Model (WIM). Smoker (1973) has transformed his International Processes Simulation (IPS) into a Global System Simulation (GSS) which includes features of the Forrester-Meadows work on the limits of growth. My energies since 1973 have been engaged with associates in developing competing mini-modules for inclusion in macro-models, such as Bremer's Simulated International ProcessER (Guetzkow, 1974; Guetzkow et al., 1977). Resources more commensurate with the task of upgrading SIPER are being devoted to such work at the Institute for Comparative Social Research at the *Wissenschaftszentrum* in Berlin (Bremer et al., 1979). In the Nations in Conflict model developed by Choucri and North (1975: 256-267), the authors contrasted the outcomes of forecasts against the simulations for their six Great European Powers, 1870-1914. Then they conducted policy experiments in their simulations for one of their countries, Great Britain (1975: 272-276), finding, for example, that alterations in their intensity-of-interactions variables, "either up or down [sic], leads to a *decrease* in the values predicted for colonial area, military expenditures, and alliances"—a counterintuitive finding (1975: 273). Will simulation of Ashley's (1980)

Table 9.1
WORLD GLOBAL MODEL VIA SIMULATIONS

Name of Model and Acronym	Approximate Year of Initiation	Developers	Discipline Source(s)	Central Concepts Utilized
Political-Military Exercise [PME] (Goldhammer & Speiers, 1959)	1955	RAND & Bloomfield	political science	war games & international politics
Inter-Nation Simulation [INS] (Guetzkow, 1959)	1956	Guetzkow and Noel & Sullivan	political science, social psychology	decision-making & political, economic, & military processes
International Processes Simulation [IPS] (Smoker, 1967b, 1967d)	1967	Smoker	political science	national & international politics, economics, & peace and military sciences
Project LINK [LINK] (Hickman, 1975)	1968	Klein & Hickman (and many associates)	economics	national & international economics: economic growth and stability
Simulated International Processer [SIPER] (Bremer, 1970)	1969	Bremer	political science, economics	decision-making per goals and budgets; & national/international political (including arms races) & economic (trace and aid) processes
World 2/World 3 (Forrester, 1971)	1970	Forrester, the Meadows, and Behrens, Naill, Randers, & Zahn	system dynamics	demographic, economic, & ecological systems
Latin American Global Model [Bariloche Model] (Herrera, 1973)	1970	Herrera, Scolnik and Chichilnisky, Gallopin, Hardoy, Mosovich, Oteiza, de Romero Brest, Suarez, & Talavera	mathematics: nonlinear, dynamic optimization	demographic, economic (food & housing), & educational processes per basic needs

Table 9.1 (Continued)

Name of Model and Acronym	Approximate Year of Initiation	Developers	Discipline Source(s)	Central Concepts Utilized
World Integrated Model [WIM] (Mesarovic & Pestel, 1972)	1972	Mesarovic & Pestel and Barsotti, Hughes, Richardson, Shook, & Strauch	mathematics: multilevel hierarchical systems, economics	systems involved in demographics, economics energy, agriculture, materials, & trade
Nations-in-Conflict [NIC] (Choucri, Laird, & Meadows, 1972)	1972	Choucri & North	diplomatic history, political science, economics	military conflict & violence behaviors, geographic & interaction processes, & alliances
UN Global Input/Output Model [GIOM] (Leontief, 1974)	1973	Leontief, Carter, & Petri	economics: input/output analysis	economic growth vis-à-vis input/output analysis
Future of Global Interdependence [FUGI] (Kaya & Suzuki, 1974)	1974	Kaya & Onishi & Suzuki, Ishitani, Ishikawa, Gamou, Yamauchi, Shoji, Tazaki, Imoto, Yamaoka, Aoki, & Yazawa	economics	macroeconomics meshed with input/output analysis
Simulation Model of Political, Economic, & Strategic Interactions [SIMPEST] (Luterbacher, 1974)	1974	Luterbacher and Allan & Imhaff	diplomatic history, political science, mathematics: calculus	political, economic, & strategic interactions among superpowers
World Politics Simulation [WPS] (Bennett, 1975)	1975	Bennett & Alker	diplomatic history, political science, artificial intelligence	goals, strategies, & foreign policy outputs in cybernetic configurations

(Table 9.1 continued p. 336)

Table 9.1 (Continued)

Simulation Format	Aggregations: Regions/Nations/ Economic Sectors	Time Frame for Simulation Runs	Evidential[b] Bases	Project Report
all-person game with control team	none / 2 N / none	very near-term (weeks/months)	contemporary diplomatic history	Bloomfield & Gearin, 1973
person-computer game (FORTRAN)	none / 5 to 9 N / 3 S	mid-term (5 yrs./10 yrs.)	prototypic materials, with some empirical grounding	Guetzkow & Valadez, 1980a, 1980b
person-computer game (FORTRAN)	none / 6 N / 3 S	mid-term (5 yrs./10 yrs.)	partially data-grounded	Smoker, 1970b
all-computer econometric model (specialized software)	25 R / 2 to 10 N/ 20 S per region	near-term (1 yr./3 yrs.)	empirical data banks and special as well as general research studies	Hickman & Klein, 1979
all-computer socio-political-economic model (FORTRAN)	none / 5 to 25 N / 3 S	mid-term (5 yrs./10 yrs.)	partially grounded in research studies and data, as available	Bremer, 1977
all-computer model (DYNAMO)	1 R / no / na[a] nations	far-term (50 yrs.)	partially grounded in research studies and data, as available	Meadows, D. L., et al., 1974
all-computer model (FORTRAN)	4 R / no / 13 S nations	far-term (100 yrs.)	partially grounded in research studies and data, as available	Herrera et al., 1976

(Table 9.1 Continued)

Simulation Format	Aggregations: Regions/Nations/ Economic Sectors	Time Frame for Simulation Runs	Evidential[b] Bases	Project Report
all-computer systems model (specialized software)	12 R / no / 26 S nations	far-term (50 yrs.)	partially grounded in research studies and data, as available	Hughes, 1980
econometric model (TROLL)	none / 6 N / na	far-term (44 yrs.); retrospective	partially grounded in research studies, with special data bank plus coded variables	Choucri & North 1975
all-computer econometric model	15 R / no / 48 S nations	far-term (30 yrs.)	partially grounded in research studies and data, as available	Leontief, Carter, & Petri, 1977
all-computer econometric model	9 to 15 R / na / 14 S	mid-term (10 yrs./15 yrs.)	partially grounded in research studies and data, as available	Kaya & Onishi et al., 1977
all-computer model (Dare-P and MINUIT)	none / 7 actors / none	mid-term (10 yrs./20 yrs.)	partially grounded in research studies and data, as available	Luterbacher, Allan, & Imhoff, 1979
all-computer cybernetic model (PL1)	none / 10 N / none	far-term (70 yrs.); retrospective	historical records, as coded	Bennett, 1979

a. na = not applicable
b. In addition to the use of empirical materials (often from the research of others), there are important intuitive sources of judgments in the construction of all simulations.

important revisions in the Choucri-North model yield as intriguing a set of outcomes, should such be attempted? Most simulations to date have employed the same set of algorithms in representing each entity, changing only parameters as one nation-state is differentiated from the other. In Geneva, Luterbacher and his associates (1979) have developed a completely computerized simulation in which international relations are generated by connecting nation-state actors, including the three superpowers; each actor is internally differentiated from the other by using contrasting algorithms for processes in "an economic and resource sector, an international political sector, and a governmental sector" (1979: 1).

Developments in global modeling were not confined to the North American and Western European continents during the 1970s. Under the leadership of Gvishiani (1978) in the U.S.S.R., Gelovani et al. (1975) and Lapin (1978) have been creatively modifying Forrester's World-2 Model in terms of Marxist-Leninist doctrines. Gvishiani (1978: 102) reports that "if the mechanism of planned distribution of investment was introduced into the model, a global disaster would be avoided." In Asia, the early interests of Seki (1969) in the Inter-Nation Simulation have been followed by the economically oriented all-computer FUGI 3 (Kaya and Onishi, 1977). Rastogi's (1978) all-computer work on the cybernetics of societal systems, although focused on the nation, includes the employment of exogenous components, such as trade and foreign aid. The work of the Bariloche group in developing their Latin American World Model (Herrera et al., 1976) signals that global simulations are being undertaken on all but the African continent. In 1978 the International Institute for Applied Systems Analysis found the time propitious to assemble global modelers for an overall review conference in Vienna (Meadows and Richardson, forthcoming). Do these exciting activities of the 1970s presage solid achievements in the 1980s?

SPECULATION ON SIX CONTINUING QUERIES FOR GLOBAL MODELERS

In writing reviews of the work of other scholars, one sometimes raises queries one is often unable to answer oneself. Such occurred in the development of my review (Guetzkow, 1979) of *Problems of World Modeling* (Deutsch et al., 1977). Directing those probes now to my experiences in our Simulated International Processes project, let me use the "six continuing queries for global modelers" posed in the review as a heuristic template for speculation about work in global modeling during the last two decades of the twentieth century. In examining each of the sets of questions enumerated in the review, comparisons will be made of postures on the issues at the beginning of the SIP project (circa 1956-1958) and the positions taken later (circa 1970-1972). Afterthoughts developed since the close of the SIP project in 1972 will help round off my conjectures.

QUERY 1: MODELING STYLE–HARD OR SOFT?

As we move into the twenty-first century, it may well be that our widespread concern for methodology in the social sciences will be replaced largely by a focus upon substantive modeling per se. The style used in such modeling may vary in its formality.

Those gifted with the pen in all likelihood will continue using the vernacular for their analyses of international affairs in ordinary language, be it Chinese, Russian, or English. Some among us will tend to structure the theoretical work into packets, possibly involving sets of propositions, as was early illustrated in the work of Kaplan (1957). Others will use formal languages to display propositionalized theories, as Ward did (1978: 105-106) in his work on inequality through logicodeductive constructions. Some will represent their formulations in systems of equations, with explanations in the vernacular for those unfamiliar with mathematical shorthand, as was done by Choucri and North (1975). A few will gain greater power using formal mathematical procedures for the derivation of theorems, complete with proofs, as demonstrated by Schrodt (1978: appendix) in his work on the "necessary and sufficient conditions which an arms race must meet in order to preserve an arms distribution meeting a criterion of 'collective security'" (1978: 354). Gradually more and more of us will use computer languages, as office and home study terminals become abundant, for the development of our models in simulation formats.

By the end of the century many will have the diversity of skills to do integrative modeling at most points along this soft-hard continuum, as may be congruent with our mood and the constraints of the substance with which we are working. It is my judgment that there will be a gradual movement over the decades toward harder styles in our work on integrative substantive modeling in international affairs.

In the decades spanned by SIP there was a progression from softer to harder modeling. The work of Herbert Goldhammer and Hans Speier (1959) at RAND in all-person gaming was elaborated throughout the 1960s most thoughtfully by Bloomfield, as the Political-Military Exercise (Bloomfield and Gearin, 1973). The use of a "control" directorate as umpire in the games allowed for embodiment of scholarly "wisdom" in the gaming (Bloomfield and Whaley, 1965: 858, 860, 861).

In the Northwestern project, there was movement from the person-computer format to an all-computer construction. Beginning with verbal formulations, Noel, Sullivan, and I developed the equations and routines as presented in my essay, "Structural Programs and Their Relation to Free Activity in the Inter-Nation Simulation," (Guetzkow, 1963, 1981b). In attempting to replace the "control group" used in all-person gaming with equations embodying domestic processes, hardening took place largely for the intranational processes involved in the global modeling. Yet even within these internal components, many decisions were unprogrammed, handled instead as quasi-exogenous inputs of the decision-makers at the beginning of each run. Interaction among the nations took place freely, without any formal structuring of the relations among the nations. When Smoker developed his International Processes Simulation (IPS), he added further programmed components, some of which were representing interactions among the states, as in his routine on world opinion (Smoker, 1972: 340-341, 354-357; 1981: 126-127).

In constructing an all-computer simulation (SIPER), Bremer even was able to automate hostile activities among the actors. However, in the process of going to more rigorous modeling styles, a number of the structures and processes found in the INS and IPS were simply omitted in SIPER, such as war. On the other hand, in keeping with his theoretical interests, Bremer was able to incorporate such exciting programs as expectations about the behavior of other nations as extrapolated from past behaviors. Overall, in SIP we found ourselves using mixes of soft and hard elements in our model construction, moving over the years toward the more rigorous end of the continuum.

The trend in the field toward hardening is not uninterrupted, as the recent work with scenarios by Cole et al. (1978) indicates. In the context of an examination of some sixteen studies oriented in terms of models of an economic/engineering type, these researchers developed a series of a dozen broadly sketched futures, complete with flow charts (1978: Figures 3-6). Using three world views—the conservative, the reformist, and the radical—they outlined ways in which such orientations would yield contrasting alternative futures, as they simultaneously explored high/low growth vis-à-vis egalitarian/inegalitarian images (1978: Table 3).

Yet, is the increase in rigor obtained by eliminating humans as surrogates worth the loss incurred by foregoing direct inputs of human creativity? One of the unfinished items on the agenda for SIP was the "use of very creative persons as decision makers in the INS . . . especially in the operation of an IPS" (Guetzkow, 1976a: 255). Despite Snyder's expectations that serendipitous findings might be obtained through the use of "simulation as a flexible mode of discovery" (Snyder, 1963a: 11), there were no breakthroughs in theory development in SIP. Had creative members of Mensa, a society of bright ones, been recruited as participants, would Smoker's (1969) findings have been more innovative as they developed an alternative future in his experimental work with IPS?

In sum, it may be wise for global modeling in the decades ahead to continue using a variety of formats for theory construction. Inasmuch as artificial intelligences are yet in embryonic stages of development, it would seem prudent that systematic work using humans in our world simulations, in both all-person and person-machine combinations, be sustained alongside the developments in all-computer modeling. Because verbal formulations in ordinary language seem handmaiden to all types of simulations, it would be unwise to abandon a close interface between the traditional modes of verbal analysis and the formats involved in simulations of international affairs. As Michael Don Ward suggests, perhaps a continuous cycling of efforts from soft to hard to somewhat soft again and then to even harder formulations would be a fruitful way of proceeding in the development of rigorous yet enriched global models in the years ahead.

QUERY 2: WHOLES AND/OR PARTS?

The simulations exercised in Simulated International Processes attempted to exhibit the world as a whole; in many respects the researchers fell short of their goals. Only gross approximations were made in operating our global models. Even as we moved into the 1970s, there were at least three ways in which simulations tended to be truncated: (1) Most important, they failed to cover the full scope of the phenomena; (2) they were partial, including but a few of the entities actually existing in the reference system; and (3) they were foreshortened, operating for limited time periods, rather than continuously, in the long run. The abbreviations were inadvertent but not unnoticed, as research became commensurate with resources available.

Smoker's International Processes Simulation was the most comprehensive construction attempted in SIP. As explained by Valadez and Tygesson (1981: 184-186), it developed extensions of the Inter-Nation Simulation (INS) by including such features as a modest international monetary system, a few multinational corporations, and some publics. The all-computer development by Bremer in his Simulated International ProcessER elaborated important components of INS (Valadez and Tygesson, 1981: 186-190) but also omitted a number of features of the earlier person-computer version, such as the differentiation made by Brody in INS between conventional and nuclear military capabilities.

In the simulations oriented from an economic/engineering perspective, such as those catalyzed by the Club of Rome, there has been avoidance of sociopolitical and military components of the world, with little attention given to representing decision-making processes as integral parts of international affairs (Cole et al., 1973). The exclusions of these phenomena have resulted in serious shortcomings, as has been pointed out elsewhere (Ward and Guetzkow, 1979: 448-450). With the development of scholarly work in such areas as ecology (Sprout and Sprout, 1965; Ophuls, 1977), the sketchiness of the SIP models is highlighted. The intentional omission of geographical components (Guetzkow, 1981b: 55-56) further delimits the wholeness of the work.

There are no apologies for the selectivity of phenomena represented in recent models. Even though the Dutch researchers derived their interest in modeling from work promulgated by the Club of Rome, they confined their interests in Linneman's Model of International Relations in Agriculture (MOIRA; International Institute for Applied Systems Analysis, 1977) to food, omitting other components. By so doing they were able to construct a simulation which involved some 130 nations, with a detailed explication of an equilibrium model of trade flows in food. Likewise, Leontief, Carter, and Petri were able to construct an input/output model involving some 44 sectors of the world economy, without pretending to be concerned about the sociopolitical and military aspects of the New International Economic Order to which their research for the United Nations was addressed (Leontief et al., 1977). Given the ever-limited resources available, such focus on particular components of the overall world system may be advantageous in the long run, as we learn how to construct our global models.

The experience gained in developing the economic global models is worth considering, so that we do not falsely oppose "parts" to "wholes." In the work of the Club of Rome Japanese Committee (see Kaya and Onishi, 1977), FUGI (Future of Global Interdependence) consists of a dynamic national input/output model (GIOM) which drives the macro but static world model (GMEM). In this way, the part provides an engine for the whole. In the evolution of LINK, there was an interlacing of the development of national models, sometimes developed indigenously, with the gradual elaboration of the LINK world system, at first including only trade among the nations, but later encompassing even an international monetary system (Hickman and Klein, 1979: 50-51). In this situation, parts drive components of the whole; the comprehensive programs of the whole drive the nations, as mini-modules.

Although both the INS and IPS permitted some variation in the number of nations interacting, at times including as many as nine, the "whole" world of over 150 nations was represented in but prototypic form. SIPER is being expanded to include twenty-five nations (Bremer et al., 1979). In the earlier version there were but five nations involved in Bremer's runs. The earliest Club of Rome model characterized the whole world as a single entity, but it was followed immediately by a world disaggregated into some ten regions (Mesarovic and Pestel, 1974: 36-41), which later were reduced to four by the Bariloche group (Herrera et al., 1976: 42-43) and then expanded to fifteen by Herrera for the ILO. In eschewing the political, the engineering/economic orientation obviated the need for delineation of nation-states as prime actors in the international scene, thereby precluding concern with decision-making per se.

Although as a simulation each model involves international processes over time, the "whole" may be truncated temporally by foreshortening, as was done in INS when simulating the summer of 1914 (Hermann and Hermann, 1967: 406). In this instance, the INS did not operate for even a full period, thereby bypassing longitudinal features of the programmed components. The Hermanns' adaptation of the INS was made possible by holding constant the longer-run processes, such as the impact of trade, which usually vary from period to period. Then INS became virtually identical in format to the Political-Military Exercise (PME) developed by RAND-MIT, except that the latter, derived from the red-versus-blue duality often imposed by the military in their war games, usually involved but two teams, the U.S.S.R. versus the U.S.A. Concerned largely with short-term crises, the PME operations seldom simulated actions of more than a few months in duration. By contrast, in INS and IPS the simulation periods would span years and decades. Yet when Bremer (1977: Ch. 6) attempted to decide whether a given iteration in SIPER constituted a year or a decade, there was puzzlement. With commendable bravado, the various groups related to the Club of Rome often ran their simulations for projections beyond the end of the century, sometimes even to 2050!

Although the simulations usually are operated as whole systems, even though they are less than entirely comprehensive, the analyses conducted in SIP were considerably more restricted than the outputs themselves. For example, even when large segments of outputs were available in computer printouts, Bremer necessarily restricted himself to but a segment of the panoply of material produced by his complex programs. A similar neglect of much of the output material characterized the failure to utilize the rich outputs from both INS and IPS. This state of affairs prompted the development by Busse (1969) of an archive of protocols from four of the simulations open to all.

Some thirty years ago, in attempting to get handles on the problem of comprehensiveness, the suggestion was made that one might build "islands of theory" and then bridge these conceptual nodes to each other (Guetzkow, 1950). At that time, I asked how "small islands of theory... eventually might be tied together into a more definitive theory-system" (Guetzkow, 1950: 426). Three decades later it seems that the use of simulations for the meshing of component programs is one significant way.

By constructing parts so they may then be articulated into wholes, mini-modules might then be assembled into more comprehensive models. Given the fact that our SIP models were not making gains in validity as we moved from INS to IPS and then to SIPER (Guetzkow and Valadez, 1981b), it seemed already in 1972 that our next move should be to develop mini-simulations which then could be integrated to compose a more comprehensive global model. This formed a basic strategy adopted for our post-SIP project, "Computer Simulations for Decision-Making in International Relations" (Guetzkow, 1974). Such aggregation is now occurring elsewhere, too, as Smoker (1973) incorporates features of World 3 into his second generation of IPS. Yet, a mini-module approach (Guetzkow et al., 1977) seems to need guidance from a macro-model, so there may be articulation of the parts into a whole. Unless one formalizes the conceptual framework one embraces for theorizing about global processes, it is difficult to assemble the components into wholes. Unless one knows something of complementary parts available, there will need to be much reconstruction of the mini-modules as they are assembled. As is argued elsewhere (Ward and Guetzkow, 1979: 452), it is perhaps prudent to work simultaneously from the "bottom up," developing the parts, and from the "top down," developing the wholes, allowing the efforts to converge as the research findings interact.

One of the questions regarding wholes and parts posed earlier (Guetzkow, 1979: 12) asked, "What are fruitful ways of determining the boundaries between and among the subprocesses?" To date the segmentation of materials has been guided by the conceptual fragmentation existing in the field. It may be that the need for building and assembling mini-modules into larger, more comprehensive wholes will provide a heuristic device for decreasing the arbitrariness of the partitioning of the materials. The student of international relations does not have as easy a time of it as do the economists, who are data-bound to national economies as the unit of analysis (Hickman and Klein, 1979: 50-51).

Although the attempt to build an adequate, comprehensive model of the world included social-military-political components as well as components of relevance for those with an engineering/economic orientation, SIP was unable to achieve completeness. It seems important in the years ahead that ventures in modeling continue toward wholeness, even if the world is a weakly connected system and funding patterns for research

Harold Guetzkow 345

dictate less risky development of parts, as illustrated in those severely truncated simulations developed in the 1970s. Reaction to the merciless criticisms made of those bold enough to struggle for comprehensiveness in the past induced prudence in the 1970s. Let us hope such censuring does not discourage entirely efforts in the future to construct alternative models of encompassing scope.

QUERY 3: QUASI-CAUSAL CHARACTERISTICS OF SIMULATIONS: SYNCHRONIZATION OF COMPONENTS AND USE OF STOCHASTIC PROCESSES

The SIP simulations operate across time, even though often the analyses which researchers make of the results utilize but a cross-sectional cut of the cumulative end results. Sometimes the program involves parameters which are varied in a stochastic way, as in SIPER, rather than using strictly deterministic functions. Regardless of these variations, simulations imply causal conceptualization in the theory being formatted, as the model is iterated from run to run. The outputs of one trial become inputs for the succeeding trial. In this way the simulation provides for the representation of hypothesized, dynamic, "causal" processes.

It is easy to be overwhelmed by the amount of material generated in one's simulation, be it of the person-computer or all-computer variety. Thus, Brody utilized the findings on threat perception and bloc cohesion from the fourth period immediately before the acquisition of nuclear capabilities by his smaller nations, and compared these with the outputs obtained long after the intervention, during the twelfth period, neglecting the interstitial materials—even though the variables involved had generated successive outputs used as inputs from iteration to iteration. Given his theoretical interests along with his research/resource constraints, Brody found the before/after comparison sufficient for his purposes. Likewise, for some of his analyses Bremer used but the seventh iteration of his run of twenty trials. Yet no matter how restricted the analysis, the numbers involved represent consequences of the simulation as it has progressed through its exercises. Thus, causal processes have been represented, even when cross-sectional analysis has been made only of segments of the longitudinal series created by the simulation.

Although discontinuities may be programmed into simulations, the work in SIP utilized few such complications, as in the specification of change in office-holding on the occasion of elections and revolutions (Guetzkow, 1981b: 36, 47). Brody introduced a "breakpoint" in his runs through an ex machina realization of nuclear capability. By not specifying the mechanisms involved in the development of the proliferation of nuclears, Brody ruptured the causal processes in his seventeen worlds. Although Choucri and North did not program breakpoints in their simulations of Nations in Conflict (NiC), such appeared over and over again as they used linear regressions to "fit" their 1870-1914 data on the Great European Powers (Choucri and North, 1975).

In working with the interface between human participants and computer programs, Guetzkow (1963: 148; 1981b: 63) noted that the juxtaposition of "biological time," as embodied in real time by the decision-makers with the compressed time of economic processes, created unsolved puzzles in the representation of the causation chains of interest to the researcher. As my two partners in the design of the INS wrote a decade later,

> simulated time may be rushing ahead at a month a minute, but messages are read at the same old speed, and meetings take as long as they do in the international system. Time is truly out of joint in simulation.... But we knew if we brought the time interval down to a period appropriate for the inter-personal relations in the international system, nothing would happen of significance in the domestic system. If one has the equivalent of a National Security Council meeting in the simulation, it may take exactly the same amount of time it does in the real system. But in terms of the domestic system, the equivalent of six months may have passed in ten minutes [Sullivan with Noel, 1972: 116, 120].

It became clear later that asynchrony in processes was inadvertently injected into the all-computer programs, too, as when Bremer represented expectations as changing less rapidly in each iteration than might occur in real-time psychological processes (compared with the iterated trade routines occurring but once each "year"). Could it have been that Bremer's puzzlements in pursuing the real-time equivalents of the length of simulated periods were grounded in the fact that SIPER's "clock" for psychological time as represented in the "artificial intelligence" programs was so different from the "clock" for economic or political processes? He was able to compare the match of periods for one year versus ten years of calendar time (Bremer, 1970: 191-196). This problem of synchronization of components did not surface in the 1970s in the all-computer simulations built in the Forrester-Meadows tradition, perhaps because there was no utilization of humans as surrogates, or of artificial intelligence routines for the representation of decision-making.

The time dynamics involved in the hypothesized interacting causal chains increases the problems involved in the interpretation of simulations. These difficulties are increased when the programs contain time lags among the variables as well as feedbacks.

The problems involved in the simultaneous use of different clocks in a simulation are not avoided, even when using an all-person format, as is illustrated in the runs made with the Political-Military Exercise. Because of the need to speed up plays in order to focus cogently on the problem being simulated, the control team often stipulates a jump from a given moment in time to a few days or even a month later. In the work of Robinson et al. (1969), centering on behavior in international crisis situations, there was an ad hoc "solution" to the problem by considering the psychological reactions in biological time as primary, and the accelerated movement from event to event in the simulation as but stimuli in the laboratory environment. It is ironic that one of the most important features of simulation, its ability to speed up real time, brings a host of problems, despite the seeming ease with which it permits the juxtaposition of different "clocks."

Stochastic elements may be considered as part of the causal representations in simulations. In the person-computer constructions in SIP, probabilities were introduced early in INS, as in the determination of the occurrence of revolutions by random generators. Some social scientists argue that psychological processes involve probabilistic elements in decision-making analogous to those which are demonstrated to occur in sensory processers. Bremer used three such stochastic elements in his program for SIPER: in determining outcomes of revolutions and in the probabilistic variation in the depreciation rates of both basic and force capabilities (Bremer, 1970: 38 and 32-33, respectively).

By using but one "setting" of each randomizing element, it is possible to operate an all-computer simulation as a deterministic program in which the outcomes are identical (barring machine malfunctions) regardless of the number of repetitions. Then, instead of requiring multiple runs of the simulation, one obtains the exact consequence of the input without need for statistical treatment of the findings. Such a procedure reduces costs considerably. The elimination of stochastic components in the program permits one then to develop clear delineations of variations one makes in inputs, allowing one to ferret out the implications of variations in initial conditions, through the use of the traditional "sensitivity" analyses, as discussed in the next query. But what are the theoretical costs and policy distortions involved in assuming that social processes are deterministic?

Given the substantive orientation of the work in SIP, no attention was given to the methodological problems involved in the meshing of short-run, intermediate, and/or long-run processes in our simulations. Our experiences in SIP indicate that the problems of representing causal processes with varying clocks, along with the stochastic elements in our simulations, are not trivial.

QUERY 4: PRECISION REQUIREMENTS FOR VARIABLES AND PARAMETERS: PROTOTYPIC VARIABLES, NONLINEAR FORMULATIONS, AND SENSITIVITY ANALYSES

It is always a challenge to designate variables and parameters numerically as simulations are built and exercised. Inasmuch as one pays dearly for precision in conventional data-collecting, consider the extent to which accuracy is needed in simulation for purposes of conceptual clarity, in handling nonlinear formulations, and in conducting sensitivity analysis. It would seem that rapid, incremental bootstrapping is warranted in the development of data resources.

During the early development of the Inter-Nation Simulation in 1957-1959, few data were available. Deutsch (1960) pleaded for the development of information banks, a dream not realized until the Yale group mounted such an enterprise in the *World Handbook of Political and Social Indicators* (Russett et al., 1964). A simulation differs from more abstract mathematical formulations in requiring numbers for processing outcomes, both for asserting values of the variables themselves and for the designation of the parameters. Although empirically oriented researchers are ever data hungry, the widespread sharing of banks (as through the Inter-University Consortium for Political and Social Research) gives leverage to simulators, since they can ground their numbers in contemporary research.

But even more than supplying numbers per se, the variables themselves need be conceptualized. As Bremer has pointed out, if the concepts are not parallel to the ones used by those who construct the measures, in the long run it will be impossible to obtain measurements for the variables utilized in constructing the simulation. As my partners in designing the INS report, "we used rather conventional categories—economic, cultural, and political—as reference standards in developing the system of interacting variables.... Proceeding as if we had done a complex factor analysis to locate fundamental variables in each domain, we defined what Harold Guetzkow has come to call 'prototypical' variables—basic capability, validator satisfaction, decision latitude, and so on" (Sullivan with Noel, 1972: 122).

The requirement for data characterizing each of the INS nations was circumvented by using fabricated numbers judged to yield approximations of the nations needed in the simulation (Guetzkow, 1963: 105). Some countries were designated as superpowers, others as second-world entities, and yet others as smaller, third-world states. In like manner the parameters involved in representing various processes within the simulation were set as numbers judged to be reasonable, given the researchers overall understanding of the operation of the international system. Thus, for example, in giving estimates of the destructive capability of nuclears, Brody consulted with physical scientists to obtain ballpark numbers (Brody, 1963: 703, n. 2).

As years went on, given our great interest in validation, effort was increasingly devoted in SIP to the development of variables and numbers more congruent with those of the situation being referenced, as is illustrated in Forcese's (1969) efforts to parallel the NATO configuration. Perhaps Crow and Noel's (1977) study comes closest in mimicking the contents of the specific situation they attempted to model, as they developed a scenario for the Mexican American confrontations of 1846. The need to disguise historical situations, as was so imperative in replicating the attempts in 1914 to prevent outright recognition of the beginning of World War I by the participants (Hermann and Hermann, 1967), induced a tendency among researchers to establish intuitively approximate equivalences, as they moved from the reference system to their simulations. Yet, the chronology of events prepared by Hermann and Hermann (1967: Table 2), in their tracking of simulated action during the summer of 1914 among the European Great Powers, yielded intriguing correspondences. An action-by-action display of events was also used by Bennett and Alker (1977: Table 19-2) in their study of the War of the Pacific. Again, subjective equivalences of some persuasiveness were obtained by intuitive means.

The ways SIP researchers hardened the substance of their person-machine simulations stands in stark contrast to ways in which variables and parameters were handled by the control teams in the Political-Military Exercise. The relative crudeness of the numerical outputs in most SIP researches similarly stands in contrast to the greater hardness of the data used a decade later in the Bariloche simulations, given the need for numbers of sufficient precision to be capable of being used in mathematically complex optimization routines. Those working from an engineering/econometric perspective traded off the scope of their simulations by omitting sociopolitical variables, thereby having to work only with harder materials. In dramatic contrast to both PME and INS/IPS, Alker and his associates were pushing ahead with list-processing procedures that enabled their all-computer actors to produce qualitatively new strategies "by concatenating the individual precedents" (Bennett and Alker, 1977: 243-247, 251-255) as they simulated interactions among South American nations during the half-century preceding the War of the Pacific (1880-1883).

Those empirically oriented find the use of prototypic and approximate materials quite unsatisfactory. But were one to wait until the values of all the variables and parameters became available, explorations in theory construction in a simulation format would be much delayed. Inasmuch as the numbers one needs depend on the development of the model itself, the movement away from prototypic variables and merely approximate numbers proves too gradual a process for many who are impatient to get on with the theoretical work.

There was little overt thrust toward conceptual refinement in the development of the work in SIP. Except for the exciting work of Elder and Pendley (1981), which occurred during the midterm of the project's life, the challenge of reformulating the prototypic variables themselves went unmet. In demonstrating that the original formulation of officeholding made by Guetzkow (1981b) worked out to be a representation of "governmental system" rather than "officials in decision-making roles," Elder neatly indicated how the use of reference data might help in the evolution of the conceptualization of the variables themselves, from less prototypic to a formulation more congruent with data. Note how the explicitly normative orientation adopted in the evolution of the Bariloche model induced the selection of "life expectancy at birth" as the dependent variable in the Latin American World Model (Herrera et al., 1976: p. 47), a considerable shift in focus in its conceptual development of the posture assumed earlier in exercises undertaken for the Club of Rome. Yet, as the Guetzkow-Valadez essay demonstrates (1981a), by meeting operational demands imposed by a simulation format, there was inadvertently much conceptual refinement, as contrasted with the less detailed formations required by ordinary language (Alker and Bock, 1972).

In the analysis of simulations, it is customary to check out the sensitivity of the construction to changes in the values of parameters by varying one while others are held constant. Recent developments in the field now permit one to handle such one-variable-at-a-time explorations somewhat expeditiously in all-computer constructions (Scolnik and Talavera, 1978). In working with person-machine formats, however, such one-variable-at-a-time analysis is not feasible, given the high costs of operating group experiments in the laboratory. The notion of checking "packages" of variables at a time, as such might be derived from theoretical interests, seemed a possible alternative. These packages of variations in initial conditions and the settings of the operating parameters were merely another way of conceiving the substance of the research. In the study of collective goods, Burgess and Robinson (1969) probed the "sensitivity" of their OSU version of the INS to changes in the parameters representing the ratio of public to private gains. Because of the potential of interactive effects among the variables—as were clearly obtained in Druckman's analyses of ethnocentrism—on role behaviors among the decision-makers, the variable-by-variable analysis may obscure concomitant sensitivities of a more complex variety. But such analyses demand relative accuracy in the numbers employed, if the revealed sensitivities are to be taken seriously.

When nonlinear functions are involved, the demands for precision in the numbers used become even greater. Sometimes it is wise to avoid complex formulations. Such sophisticated research as Choucri and North (1976: 320) used linear formulations for their Nations-in-Conflict (NiC) modeling, delineating breakpoints by dysjunctions in successive linear approximations as they moved from one time segment to another in analyzing the growth of the Great Powers from 1870 to 1914. In their simulations, the discontinuities (as identified by Chow tests) were disregarded; a single linear equation was used for the hypothesized functions.

The nonlinearities employed in the INS varied from the simple, as in the revolution threshold used in calculating the probability of office-holding (Guetzkow, 1981b: Table 2.1a), to the complex, as in the use of a quadratic, replete with an exponential, in relating validator satisfaction to consumption (Guetzkow, 1981b: 42-43). Yet Elder and Pendley, in their provocative analysis of these economic representations in INS, found they were able to approximate the original curvilinear formulation by a simpler, more parsimonious equation involving the use of a logarithmic formulation (Elder and Pendley, 1981: 80-84). In IPS, Smoker (1981: 118) used a nonlinear representation in his research and development algorithm. The nonlinearities unknowingly introduced by the human participants in the person-computer formats of INS and IPS circumvented the uncomfortable simplicity implied in many of our formulations. In SIPER, Bremer (1981: Figures 5.3-5.6) used decision trees, a form of nonlinearity, in his goal formation routines.

But little was done to meet the challenge posed by Fritsch (1977: 212-213) in his notes on "two kinds of complexity." He urges the exploration of both "system dynamics," according to the contributions of Forrester (1971), and differential topology, as represented in Thom's catastrophe theory. Alker and his colleagues are already exploring nonlinear mechanisms in artificial intelligence, involving self-defined goals as well as "structure-altering" and "cybernetic parameter-altering" foreign policies (Bennett and Alker, 1977: Figure 19.1; 220). These thrusts portend important developments even before the end of the twentieth century.

By using sophisticated mathematical formulations, the system engineers and econometricians of the 1970s placed stringent demands on the adequacy of their data—requirements inadequately met, given the evolving state of data around the world (Stone, 1977). In constructing the UN model of the world economy, Leontief and his associates (1977) had particular difficulty in developing parameters for their input/output matrices, and were sometimes forced to use those obtained from earlier analyses of the American economy. But when developing policy applications for authorities in the Mideast, it was possible for the World Integrated Model team to bootstrap toward greater adequacy since they had access to national data banks for incorporation into their simulation (Hughes et al., 1977).

The preceding discussion permits a bit more insight into the query about the relation of the accuracy with which variables and parameters are conceptualized and then measured to the requirements of simulation as explicitly formulated theory. Perhaps the reconceptualization of the variables themselves is expedited by the use of prototypic variables, as one moves back and forth from simulation to the data base. Is the movement toward less-than-approximate measures of the variables and parameters catalyzed by the construction of simulations generating demands for specific levels of precision, as required by nonlinear formulations? If simulations are to be useful tools in theory development in international relations, it is important to have the courage to employ prototypic and approximate designations of the model's contents, so that the outcomes from the early outputs may then help in molding more adequate simulations.

QUERY 5: MESHING EMPIRICS AND ANALYTICS

In the development of SIP research, there was continuing tension between grounding the work empirically and utilizing the simulation formats for analytical explorations. Sometimes a researcher would emphasize concern for verisimilitude. Other times the theoretician would employ the simulation as a device for speculation, projecting alternative futures. The simulation was sometimes used simultaneously for both purposes and developed a contrasting set of variations—one grounded in empirical materials and its counterpart exhibiting a more hypothetical alternative formulation.

In his work with the INS, Brody (1963a) utilized the simulation for the projection of an alternative future in which nuclear capabilities proliferate globally. Raser and Crow (1969) likewise employed the INS as a heuristic device for their probe of the effects of nuclear invulnerability, again matching their simulation to the international scene of the 1960s. In both these cases the analytics were couched as explorations of possible futures.

Because of close attention given to the matching of a historical and contemporary situation involved in the simulations of Crow and Noel (1977) and Forcese (1968, 1976), concerns for validity became paramount, despite the researchers' concomitant interest in theory. Crow and Noel (1977: 403) appraised the extent to which "decisions taken in the experiment conformed to the decision outcome in the actual historical case," that is, "heavy counter-rebel action," by the Mexicans at the Alamo in 1836. Using NATO-related data, Forcese (1976: 181) checked the "homomorphism of the INS model to the referent system."

In Smoker and Bremer we find a challenging mix of concerns with both empirics and analytics. Smoker's IPS centered on comparison of the classical international system of the nineteenth century with a projected multilevel, multiactor world of the last part of the twentieth century, in parallel to ideas developed later about the transformation of the globe by Modelski (1970), among others. Bremer (1977: Chs. 5, 6) anchored his efforts in the present. Simultaneously, he investigated the effects of political factors on trade pricing policy and the way in which information-processing impinged upon national performance, contrasting status quo with future-oriented artificial intelligence heuristics (1977: Chs. 3, 4). By meshing an analysis of possible alternatives with empirically grounded realizations of their simulations, both Smoker and Bremer gained credibility for their outputs.

By and large the simulations of the 1970s developed from concerns with the world *problematique* were concerned with prediction, in congruence with the professional postures of system engineers and econometricians. Although usually no point predictions were attempted, concerns about trends in the decades ahead occupied these researchers. For example, the Japanese (Kaya and Onishi, 1977) developed FUGI, focusing on their complex interdependencies as related to futures in the Pacific. In building an agricultural model based on the earlier work of Mesarovic and Pestel with the World Integrated Model, Linneman and his colleagues (International Institute for Applied Systems Analysis, 1977), concerned with distributions of food both within nations as well as between the nations, were able to detail their findings for some hundred countries. Yet the use of both World 2/3 and the World Integrated Model by the members of the Club of Rome as "models of doom" produced motivations for alternative futures, even if the simulations themselves were not exercised by their own creators to exhibit such potentials. For example, Bremer (1978) was able to produce a more livable world by introducing into World 3 (Meadows et al., 1974) both endogenous and exogenous technological changes. In an analogous fashion Gelovani and his associates (1975) avoided global disaster by introducing planned investments in World 2 (Meadows et al., 1972).

In the beginning of our work in SIP, "we wished to construct the [INS] simulation so that the unprogrammed behavior could be explained by what went on in the simulation, rather than by what the participants brought to the simulation.... We attempted to make the simulation highly abstract so that the participant would play his role with the information we provided, not with vague notions of how 'X' country might behave" (Sullivan with Noel, 1972: 114). It would be intriguing to abstract even further the person-machine simulation by removing entirely its substantive international contents, as was suggested once by Sullivan (Guetzkow, 1981a: 20) in analogy to the work of Rapoport and Chaman (1965). When one makes comparison of the various models associated with the stream of activity initiated by the Club of Rome, one wonders whether the somewhat standard systems apparatus employed cause the underlying structural characteristics of the models to be fundamentally quite similar. Thus, the intrigue in world modeling is in the analytic development of special algorithms, such as the "bias matrix" in SARUM (Roberts, 1977: 12-13, Table 3, Figure 6), in conjunction with skill in anchoring empirically the variables in appropriate data sets.

SIP researchers deplored our inability to ground our simulations more adequately in evidence obtained from the reference system. Had our interest in alternative potentials been greater, perhaps our use of prototypic variables and crude numbers would have been less deprecated. Inadvertently the researchers had freed themselves and were no longer data-bound. Just as the anthropologists at times seek not to be culture-bound, so simulators can find themselves (this time uncomfortably) in a situation in which they are free of data-binds. Is such freewheeling at times imperative to more creative analytical work?

As the complexities of world models grow, utilizing knowledge obtained from the variety of disciplines, larger teams will be involved in the research with a greater division of labor among the researchers. There will be less opportunity for one person to be completely acquainted with the entire simulation, as the components are developed separately by sub-teams assembled for particular mini-module construction. This conjecture is disconcerting in that it implies that each participant in the research can no longer be expected to have Weberian *verstehen* of the whole, except in a most abstract and incomplete way (Abel, 1953).

The combination of analytics and empirics in SIP thus varies widely from study to study, given the dispositions and interests of the simulators. There seems to have been no pronounced trend in the course of the project toward one orientation versus the other. As data banks became available, the thrust toward anchoring the numbers in contemporary "realities" was reinforced. In a number of cases the ability to tap both domains seems to have been fruitful. Had Smoker's (1969) radical "inverse" perspective, arguing world realities should be built in terms of alternative, projected futures, been feasible, SIP perhaps would have emphasized more analytic, heuristic explorations. The bootstrapping perspective that obtained in SIP, however, resulted in a mesh of analytical ventures rooted in the empirics.

QUERY 6: NORMATIVE CONCERNS FOR POLICY APPLICATIONS

The roots for my persistence in evermore following through on the use of simulations in the study of international relations are found in my hopes that, in the long run, policy-makers will be able to make constructive normative use of the models.

There was little explicit concern in SIP about problems in values at either a meta-level or in the substance of the research itself. Except for the work of Shapiro (1966a) on the influence of moral considerations among the surrogate decision-makers on their policies, as studied through content analysis of messages sent in the INS, no attention was given by the researchers to normative considerations. The cross-cultural work in INS initiated by Solomon (1965) was completed only by Cappello (1972) and Ruge (1969, 1972). Although this comparative effort could have been the occasion for important normative work, no meta-findings were developed by the four groups of experimenters involved in the project, with much loss to all. Only once, as far as I know, has there been an explicit attempt to remodel the Forrester-Meadows work in terms of normative concerns—namely, by the Bariloche group (Herrera et al., 1976), in its development of a Latin American Model in which the simulation was refocused on life expectancy at birth.

In contrast to the elegant way in which goals as ends have been explicitly incorporated by means of a lexicographic decision algorithm by the cognitive mappers in their simulations of policy analysis (Bonham et al., 1976: 130, 141-142), value emphases might be implemented, albeit indirectly, in the Northwestern simulations. For example, it would be possible to change the weightings given the security and consumption components in computing validator satisfaction (VS) in the INS, weighting the one greater than the other instead of simplistically allowing each to be equal. In a regionalized world model built in the style of the early reports to the Club of Rome, the Aid Association for Lutherans explored the prerequisites demanded once desired outcomes are posited, such as reduction in death rates (Kile and Rabehl, 1977b).

Even though SIP involved no explicit work with values per se, its use of the frameworks of others ladened the work with normative consequences, by virtue of its selection of variables and its postulation of relationships among them, as Gvishiani has noted (1978: 98-100). The researchers in

SIP embodied a realpolitik framework within INS, as was demonstrated by Modelski (1970). Smoker redeveloped the INS in terms of Parson's schematizatson (Smoker, 1981), involving subsystems approximating the four basic requirements of a social system, namely "pattern maintenance, adaptation, goal attainment, and integration." Some of us were tempted to incorporate other seminal developments into our model-building, such as the work in ecology by the Sprouts (1965). Had the SIP project continued throughout the 1970s, Wallerstein's (1976) formulations of core versus peripheral states might have been employed, just as Forcese (1968, 1976) used Etzioni's (1975) conceptualizations of power (utilitarian, coercive, and identive). Inasmuch as a global simulation is but an embodiment of thoughts about international affairs by the scholar using a computer format for his theoretical formulations in handling complexity, such implicit biasing of our models is not surprising.

One would speculate that the work of SIP, funded out of Project Michelson (1959-1966) in close interface with a similarity analysis group in the field (at China Lake, California) and out of the Advanced Research Projects Agency (1961-1972) at headquarters (in the Pentagon), would have had policy impact. Milburn (1969: 278) enumerated concrete contributions made by Project Michelson, none of which, however, involved simulations. By the end of the SIP project in 1972 not much interest had been taken by the policy community, either in the U.S. Department of Defense nor in the Department of State, in its outcomes.

Although considerable efforts were made in delivering briefings to various policy groups, there was little attraction to global modeling by soldiers, lawyers, and historians in the government bureaucracies; their backgrounds were not sympathetic to more rigorous and general formulations. Personnel in the Joint War Games Agency (located in the complex surrounding the Office of the Joint Chiefs of Staff in the Pentagon), which operated political-military manual games as well as all-computer simulation models of nuclear exchange, found the SIP work of little immediate relevance. Raser and Crow's work, focusing on the impact of the capacity for delayed response in nuclear confrontations, aroused but one inquiry, as far as I know, from those with opportunity for making policy inputs.

Although the work of SIP was far from adequate, should not its formulations have been placed in competition with the ad hoc, judgmental "wisdom" of less systematic knowledge by our policy-makers? But such experience is not unusual. As was reported in a study, conducted for the National Science Foundation, of mathematical models commissioned by nondefense federal agencies, "on an overall basis, models seem to be used much less frequently than their designers or sponsors intend" (Fromm et al., 1975: 4).

One wonders whether the derivation of funding from the military gave rise to a compensatory reaction in SIP by the researchers to ensure that their work would be basic and fundamental, in keeping with the imperative laid upon us by our initial sponsors in the Air Force and as noted in their commendation of the SIP work as an example of the "contribution basic research has already made and . . . what may be accomplished in the future" (Office of Aerospace Research, 1964: v, 92-93). The fact that the project operated at a major university within the larger framework of an academic program of graduate study and research in international relations (1957-1971) which had concomitant funding from a private foundation, may have provided a context of independence for SIP's researchers. Did the project members thereby lose their sensitivity to the needs of potential users?

The location of SIP at Northwestern should have produced alertness to normative issues. In 1965-1966 our colleagues, Lee F. Anderson and Paul F. Kress, had mounted a series of three conferences on "social scientists and the normative analysis of political life"; even the head of the government unit sponsoring the SIP research participated in these deliberations. In post-project years, two of SIP's central collaborators, Richard Snyder and Charles F. Hermann, were to engage in a challenging proposal for monitoring the normative development of the world system (Snyder et al., 1976), involving the potential use of simulation. Could it have been that despite the post-behavioral revolution during the life of the project itself, there was little impact on its outputs merely because a more adequately articulated social-political-ethical thrust was still in the offing (Paden, 1979)?

Despite the constructive motivations of its researcher, little time or money was devoted in the course of the SIP project to normative concerns. In addition, policy-makers made little use of the simulation, even though the impact of the "models of doom" aroused great interest in the 1970s on the part of the general public. Although simulations are now used casually in many academic situations (Horn, 1977), the college textbooks in elementary international relations are only beginning to instruct future policy-makers concerning the potential value of global models (Ray, 1979: Ch. 7). But then, like Karl Deutsch candidly remarked (1977: 193), "I am very much in favor of having knowledge applied, but first we must produce it."

Our experiences in the project on Simulated International Processes yielded no definitive replies to my six queries. They are *continuing queries,* indeed.

In practice, five of the six queries catalyzed the work in SIP. Overall, there was considerable change in postures as we moved across the years from SIP's beginnings in 1956-1957 to its close in 1971-1972. (1) As the researchers moved from a person-machine format to an all-computer simulation, they were able to add rigor to their formulations; the human "black boxes" were replaced partially by explicit algorithms. (2) Yet, this very move to artificial intelligences decreased the "wholeness" of the construction, inasmuch as the human surrogates in INS played extensively, encompassing phenomena beyond those included in SIPER. (3) The operational features of the simulation, be it person-machine or all-computer, facilitated the use of quasi-causal explanations. (4) As more adequate data became available in the development of SIP, such were employed; the side effects of imprecision became more evident as the move was made from INS to SIPER. (5) Throughout the project, its researchers were attracted to the potentials found in simulations as devices for the creation and analysis of alternatives. (6) SIP formats forced no attention to normative elements involved in global modeling.

It is imperative to note that these queries arose in the course of our work in Simulated International Processes; the project was not designed to address the queries per se. SIP's achievements are in its construction of three simulations: the Inter-Nation Simulation, Smoker's International Processes Simulation, and Bremer's Simulated International ProcessER. The queries will continue to haunt our successors (Valadez and Tygesson, 1981: 195), as they have so consistently troubled me. Perhaps, as we develop a science about our scientific methods (rather than relying solely on a philosophy of science), more definitive guides will emerge—one cannot hope for "answers" to the queries (Guetzkow, 1976: 102-103). Then the queries may help guide new thrusts for future efforts in the simulation of international processes.

NOTE

1. About this time, a young European scholar came to Evanston with censorious tidings (Seidelmann, 1973). My intense conversations with Reimund Seidelmann prepared me for criticisms of an even stronger variety. Francis W. Hoole and Dina A. Zinnes (1976) invited participation at the 1974 national meetings of the International Studies Association in their panel devoted to a survey and critical assessment of four projects in quantitative international politics. This provided occasion (Guetzkow, 1976a, 1981a) for a final revision of the earlier, interim history presented at the 1967 symposium on "The Process of Model-Building in the Behavioral Sciences" (Guetzkow, 1970) at Ohio State University. The Hoole and Zinnes meeting in 1974 also gave Christensen and Butterworth (1976), Thorson (1976), and Bremer (1976) the impetus to present evaluations on SIP's work.

Appendix A: Core Bibliography on Simulated International Processes

Joseph J. Valadez

ABEL, T. (1953) "The operation called verstehen," pp. 677-687 in H. Feigle and M. Broadbeck (eds.) Readings in the Philosophy of Science. Englewood Cliffs, NJ: Prentice-Hall.

ABT, C. C. (1964) "War gaming." International Science and Technology 32 (August): 29-37.

——— and M. GORDEN (1969) "Report on Project TEMPER," pp. 245-262 in D. G. Pruitt and R. C. Snyder (eds.) Theory and Research on the Causes of War. Englewood Cliffs, NJ: Prentice-Hall.

Abt Associates Inc. (1965) "Report of a survey of the state of the art: Social, political, and economic models and simulations." Cambridge, MA: Author. (for the National Commission on Technology, Automation, and Economic Progress, Washington, D.C.)

ACHESON, D. G. (1960) "The President and the Secretary of State," in D. K. Price (ed.) The Secretary of State. Englewood Cliffs, NJ: Prentice-Hall.

ALBERTINI, L. (1953) The Origins of the War of 1914 (I. M. Massy, ed. and trans.). London: Oxford University Press.

*ALGER, C. F. (1963) "Use of the Inter-Nation Simulation in undergraduate teaching," pp. 150-189 in H. Guetzkow et al. (eds.) Simulation in International Relations: Developments for Research and Teaching. Englewood Cliffs, NJ: Prentice-Hall.

——— (1966a) Personal Communicaton. Geneva, Switzerland, November.

——— (1966b) "Interaction and negotiation in a committee of the United Nations General Assembly." Peace Research Society (International) Papers 5: 141-159.

——— (1968a) "Interaction in a committee of the United Nations General Assembly," in J. D. Singer (ed.) Quantitative International Politics: Insights and Evidence. New York: Macmillan (abridged version in Midwest Journal of Political Science 10, 4)

——— (1968b) "International relations, 1: The field," in International Encyclopedia of the Social Sciences. New York: Macmillan.

Author's Note: Asterisked entries are studies involving the Northwestern project on Simulated International Processes.

——— (1978) "Role of people in the future global order." Alternatives 4(2): 233-262.
*ALKER, H. R., Jr. (1965) "The uses of simulation for international relations theory-building: Some reflections and research possibilities." New Haven: Yale University.
——— (1966) "The long road to international relations theory: Problems of statistical non-additivity." World Politics 18: 623-655.
*——— (1968) "Decision-Makers' environments in the Inter-Nation Simulation," pp. 31-58 in W. D. Coplin (ed.) Simulation in the Study of Politics. Chicago: Markham.
*——— (1969) "Highly programmed political-military simulations: Developments in holistic, all-computer models." Presented at a seminar on Simulated International Processes, Industrial College of the Armed Forces, Washington, D.C.
——— (1978) Memo to H. Guetzkow and J. J. Valadez. July.
——— and P. G. BOCK (1972) "Propositions about international relations: Contributions from the *International Encyclopedia of the Social Sciences*," pp. 385-495 in J. A. Robinson (ed.) Political Science Annual: An International Review, Vol. 3. Indianapolis: Bobbs-Merrill.
*ALKER, H. R., Jr., and R. D. BRUNNER (1969) "Simulating international conflict: A comparison of three approaches." International Studies Quarterly 13(1): 70-110.
ALLPORT, G. A. (1958) The Nature of Prejudice. Garden City, NY: Doubleday.
ANGELL, R. C. (1965) "An analysis of trends in international organizations." Peace Research Society (International) Papers, 3: 185-195.
ARBATOV, G. (1973) The War of Ideas in Contemporary International Relations (D. Skvirsky, trans.). Moscow: Progress.
ARGYRIS, C. (1967) Some Causes of Organizational Ineffectiveness Within the Department of State. Washington, DC: Government Printing Office. (for the Center for International Systems Research; DS Publication 8180)
ARON, R. (1967) Peace and War: A Theory of International Relations (R. Howard and A. B. Fox, trans.). Garden City, NY: Doubleday.
ASHLEY, R. K. (1980) The Political Economy of War and Peace. New York: Nichols.
*BAILEY, G. C. (1967) "Utilizing simulation of international behavior in political military affairs: A preliminary analysis." McLean, VA: Human Resources Research, Inc.
BANKS, A. S. and R. B. TEXTOR (1963) A Cross-Polity Survey. Cambridge, MA: MIT Press.
BARBER, J. D. (1966) Power in Committees: An Experiment in the Government Processes. Skokie, IL: Rand McNally.
BASOWITZ, H., H. PERSKY, S. KORCHIN, and R. GRINKER (1955) Anxiety and Stress. New York: McGraw-Hill.
BAVELAS, J. B., A. S. CHAR, and J. A. GUTHRIE (1976) "Reliability and validity of traits measured by Kelly's repertory grid." Canadian Journal of Behavioral Science 8(1): 23-28.
*BEACH, P., R. A. BRODY, and M. J. DRIVER (1962) "Chronologies of the INS-8 series." Evanston, IL: Northwestern University.
BEER, S. (1965) "The world, the flesh, and the metal." Nature 205(4968): 223-231.
——— (1969) "Futures for simulation: Needed advances in the state of the art." Philadelphia: Conference on Simulation in the Social Sciences for Research and Policy.

BENNETT, J. P. (1975) "Foreign policy as maladaptive behavior: Operationalizing some implications." Peace Science Society (International) Papers 25: 85-104.
— — — (1978) "Perpetuating failure: Security practices and system transformation of Southern Pacific transnational politics, 1830-1905." Ph.D. dissertation, Massachusetts Institute of Technology.
— — — and H. A. ALKER, Jr. (1977) "When national security policies bred collective insecurity: The war of the Pacific in a world politics simulation," pp. 215-302 in K. W. Deutsch et al. (eds.) Problems of World Modeling: Political and Social Implications. Cambridge, MA: Ballinger.
BENSON, O. (1961) "A simple diplomatic game," pp. 504-511 in J. N. Rosenau (ed.) International Politics and Foreign Policy. New York: Macmillan.
BERKOWITZ, L. (1962) Aggression: A Social Psychological Analysis. New York: McGraw-Hill.
BLACK, D. (1958) The Theory of Committees and Elections. New York: Cambridge University Press.
BLOCK, J. and H. THOMAS (1955) "Is satisfaction with self a measure of adjustment?" Journal of Abnormal and Social Psychology 51: 254-259.
BLOOMFIELD, L. and N. PADELFORD (1959) "Three experiments in political gaming." American Political Science Review 53: 1105-1115.
— — — and C. J. GEARIN (1973) "Games foreign policy experts play: The political exercise comes of age." Orbis 16(4): 1008-1031.
BLOOMFIELD, L. and B. WHALEY (1965) "The Political-Military Exercise: A progress report." Orbis 8(4): 854-870.
BOGUSLAW, R. (1965) The New Utopians: A Study of System Design and Social Change. Englewood Cliffs, NJ: Prentice-Hall.
— — —, R. H. DAVIS, and E. B. GLICK (1966) "A simulation vehicle for studying national policy formation in a less armed world." Behavioral Science 2(1): 43-61.
*BONHAM, G. M. (1965) "Relations of validator satisfaction to some external perceptions of decision makers." Cambridge, MA: Massachussetts Institute of Technology. (mimeo)
— — — (1967) "Aspects of the validity of two simulations of phenomena in international relations." Ph.D. dissertation, Massachussetts Institute of Technology.
— — — (1970) "A computer simulation of non-crisis information processing by foreign policy decision makers." Berkeley, CA: University of California. (mimeo)
— — — (1971) "Simulating international disarmament negotiations." Journal of Conflict Resolution 15(3): 299-315.
— — —, M. J. SHAPIRO, and G. J. NOZICKA (1976) "A cognitive process model of foreign policy decision-making." Simulation and Games 7(2): 123-152.
BOULDING, K. (1969) "National images and international systems," pp. 422-431 in J. N. Rosenau (ed.) International Politics and Foreign Policy. New York: Macmillan.
*BREMER, S. A. (1970) "National and international systems: A computer simulation." Ph.D. dissertation, Michigan State University.
— — — (1976) "An appraisal of the substantive findings of the Inter-Nation Simulation project," pp. 304-327 in F. W. Hoole and D. A. Zinnes (eds.) Quantitative International Politics: An Appraisal. New York: Praeger.
— — — (1977) Simulated Worlds: A Computer Model of National Decision-Making. Princeton: Princeton University Press.
— — — (1978) "Technological advance and the limits of growth." Berlin: International Institute for Comparative Social Research, Science Center Berlin.

——— (1981) "The Simulated International ProcessER," pp. 135-177 in H. Guetzkow and J. J. Valadez (eds.) Simulated International Processes: Theories and Research in Global Modeling. Beverly Hills, CA: Sage.

*——— and D. S. ROSS (1970) "SIPER Simulated International Processes (Version III." Evanston, IL: Northwestern University.

BREMER, S. A., T. R. CUSACK, B. M. POLLINS, and V. U. WIDMAIER (1979) "Cumulative efforts in sociopolitical global modeling." Berlin: International Institute for Comparative Social Research, Science Center Berlin.

BRIGHT, J. (1968) Technological Forecasting for Industry and Government. New York: Elsevier North-Holland.

BRODBECK, M. (1959) "Models, meanings, and theories," pp. 373-402 in L. Gross (ed.) Symposium on Sociological Theory. New York: Harper & Row.

*BRODY, R. A. (1963a) "Some systemic effects of the spread of nuclear-weapons technology: A study through simulation of a multinuclear future." Journal of Conflict Resolution 7(4): 663-753.

*——— (1963b) "Varieties of simulations in international relations research," in H. Guetzkow et al. (eds.) Simulation in International Relations: Developments in Research and Teaching. Englewood Cliffs, NJ: Prentice-Hall.

*——— (1963c) "The spread of nuclear weapons and alliance stability: The model." Evanston, IL: Northwestern University.

——— (1968) "Deterrence," pp. 130-134 in International Encyclopedia of the Social Sciences, Vol. 4. New York: Macmillan.

——— and A. H. BENHAM (1969) "Nuclear weapons and alliance cohesion," pp. 165-175 in D. G. Pruitt and R. C. Snyder (eds.) Theory and Research on the Causes of War. Englewood Cliffs, NJ: Prentice-Hall.

——— and J. S. MILSTEIN (1967) "Hostile international communication, arms production, and perception of threat: A simulation study. Peace Research Society (International) Papers 7: 15-40.

BROGDEN, M. (1966) "INGOs in perspective." Lancaster, England: Peace Research Centre. (Publication 11-12).

BURGESS, P. (1966) "Nations in alliance: A simulation of international coalition process." Columbus, OH: Mershon Seminar, Ohio State University.

——— and J. A. ROBINSON (1969) "Alliances and the theory of collective action: A simulation of coalition processes." Midwest Journal of Political Science 8(2): 194-218.

BURNS, A. L. (1961) "Military technology and international politics," in Yearbook of World Affairs. London: Stevens and Sons.

BURTON, J. W. (1966) "International relations simulation on the cheap." London: University College.

*BUSSE, W. E. (1969) "The Northwestern Simulation Archives: Man-computer models of international relations." Evanston, IL: Northwestern University.

——— (1981) "The Northwestern Simulation Archives," in H.Guetzkow and J. J. Valadez (eds.) Simulated International Processes: Theories and Research in Global Modeling. Beverly Hills, CA: Sage. (Abstract of Busse, 1969)

CAMPBELL, A. et al. (1960) The American Voter. New York: John Wiley.

*CAMPBELL, D. T. (1967) "Inter-nation simulation as a laboratory for the teaching of theories relevant to international relations." Evanston, IL: Northwestern University.

——— and R. A. LEVINE (1961) "A proposal for cooperative cross-cultural research on ethnocentrism." Journal of Conflict Resolution 5(1): 82-108.

––– (1965) "Propositions about ethnocentrism for social science theories." Working paper for the Cross-Cultural Study of Ethnocentrism, Northwestern University.
CAMUS, A. (1965) The Rebel. New York: Vintage.
Canadian Peace Research Institute (1969) Peace Research Abstracts Journal. Clarkson, Ontario: International Peace Research Association.
CAPPELLO, H. M. (1972) "International tension as a function of reduced communication," p. 39-45, in J. A. Laponce and Paul L. Smoker (eds.) Experimentation and Simulation in Political Science. Toronto: University of Toronto Press.
*CASPARY, W. R. (1962) "The causes of war in INS-8." Evanston, IL: Northwestern University.
*––– (1963) "Simulation studies in inter-nation conflict, Part II: Application." Midwest Sociological Association (April 19): 1-16.
CATTELL, R. B. (1949) "The dimensions of culture patterns by factorization of national character." Journal of Abnormal and Social Psychology 44: 443-469.
––– and R. GORSUCH (1965) "The definition and measurement of national morale and morality." Journal of Social Psychology 67(1): 77-96.
*CHADWICK, R. W. (1966a) "Development in a partial theory of international behavior: A test and extension of Inter-Nation Simulation theory." Ph.D. dissertation, Northwestern University.
*––– (1966b) "Relating Inter-Nation Simulation theory with verbal theory in international relations at three levels of analysis." Evanston, IL: Simulated International Processes project, Northwestern University.
*––– (1966c) "Extending Inter-Nation Simulation theory: An analysis of intra- and international behavior." Evanston, IL: Simulated International Processes project, Northwestern University.
*––– (1966d) "Theory development through simulation: A comparison and analysis of associations among variables in an international system and an Inter-Nation Simulation." Evanston, IL: Simulated International Processes project, Northwestern University.
*––– (1967) "An empirical test of five assumptions in an Inter-Nation Simulation, about national political systems," pp. 177-192 in General Systems: Yearbook for the Society of General Systems Research 12, Ann Arbor, MI: Society for the Advancement of General Systems Theory.
*––– (1969) "An inductive, empirical analysis of intra- and international behavior and aimed at a partial extension of Inter-Nation Simulation theory." Journal of Peace Research 6(3): 193-214.
*––– (1970) "A partial model of national political-economic systems." Journal of Peace Research 7(2): 121-132.
––– (1972) "Theory development through simulation: A comparison and analysis of associations among variables in an international system and an Inter-Nation Simulation." International Studies Quarterly 16(1): 83-127.
*––– and P. L. SMOKER (1966) "Some research problems and proposals for continuing and extending SIP validity operations." Evanston, IL: Northwestern University.
CHERRYHOLMES, C. H. (1966a) "The House of Representatives and foreign affairs: A computer simulation of roll call voting." Ph.D. dissertation, Northwestern University.
––– (1966b) "Some current research on effectiveness of educational implications for alternative strategies." American Behavioral Scientist 10(2): 4-7.
CHOUCRI, N. and R. C. NORTH (1975) Nations in Conflict: National Growth and International Violence. San Francisco: Freeman.

———, M. LAIRD, and D. L. MEADOWS (1972) Resource Scarcity and Foreign Policy: A Simulation Model of International Conflict. Cambridge, MA: Center for International Studies, Massachussetts Institute of Technology.

*CHRISTENSEN, C. (1969) "A user's observation of the Benson model." Evanston, IL: Northwestern University.

——— and R. BUTTERWORTH (1976) "An appraisal of the philosophy of science of the Inter-Nation Simulation project," in F. W. Hoole and D. A. Zinnes (eds.) Quantitative International Politics: An Appraisal. New York: Praeger.

CLEVELAND, H. (1963) "Crisis diplomacy." Foreign Affairs 41: 638-649.

COHEN, A. R. (1953) "The effects of situational structure and individual self-esteem on threat-oriented reactions to power." Ph.D. Dissertation, University of Michigan.

——— (1959) "Situation structure, self-esteem, and threat-oriented reactions to power," in D. Cartwright (ed.) Studies in Social Power. Ann Arbor: University of Michigan Press.

COLBY, K. M. (1963) "Computer simulation of a neurotic process," pp. 165-179 in S. S. Tompkins and S. Messick (eds.) Computer Simulation of Personality. New York: John Wiley.

COLE, H.S.D., C. FREEMAN, M. JAHODA, and K.L.R. PAVITT (1973) Models of Doom: A Critique of "the Limits to Growth." New York: Universe.

COLE, S., J. GERSHUNY, and I. MILES (1978) "Scenarios of world development." Futures 10(1): 3-20.

COLEMAN, J. S., S. BOOCOCK, and E. O. SCHILD [eds.] (1966a) "In Defense of Games." American Behavioral Scientist 10(2).

——— (1966b) "Simulation games and learning behavior." American Behavioral Scientist 10(3).

COLLINS, B. E. and H. GUETZKOW (1964) A Social Psychology of Group Processes for Decision-Making. New York: John Wiley.

COOMBS, C. II (1964) A Theory of Data. New York: John Wiley.

*COPLIN, W. D. (1966) "Inter-nation simulation and contemporary theories of international relations." American Political Science Review 60(3).

——— (1967) "Toward an all-computer simulation of the foreign policy-making forces at the level of general policy trends." Research Memorandum 3 for Center for International Systems Analysis of the U.S. Department of State, Comparative Foreign Policy Systems Program, Wayne State University.

*——— (1968a) "Comparison of State Department and high school runs in the world politics simulation." Detroit: Wayne State University.

——— [ed.] (1968b) Simulation in the Study of Politics. Chicago: Markham.

CRECINE, J. P. (1965) "A computer simulation model of municipal resource allocation." Ph.D. dissertation, Carnegie Institute of Technology.

CROW, W. J. (1963) "A study of strategic doctrines using the Inter-Nation Simulation." Journal of Conflict Resolution 7(3): 580-589.

*——— and R. NOEL (1965) "The valid use of simulation results." La Jolla, CA: Western Behavioral Sciences Institute.

——— (1977) "An experiment in simulated historical decision-making," pp. 385-405 in M. G. Hermann with T. Milburn (eds.) A Psychological Examination of Political Leaders. New York: Macmillan.

CROW, W. J. and J. R. RASER (1964) "A cross cultural simulation study." La Jolla, CA: Western Behavioral Sciences Institute.

CYERT, R. and J. MARCH (1963) A Behavioral Theory of the Firm. Englewood Cliffs, NJ: Prentice-Hall.
DAHL, R. A. (1956) A Preface to Democratic Theory. Chicago: University of Chicago Press.
DAVIS, O. (1967) "Some results related to a mathematical model of policy formation in a democratic society," pp. 14-38 in J. Bernd (ed.) Mathematical Applications in Political Science III. Charlottesville: University of Virginia Press.
——— and M. HINICH (1966) "A mathematical model of policy formation in a democratic society," pp. 175-205 in J. Bernd (ed.) Mathematical Applications in Political Science II. Dallas: Southern Methodist Press.
*DAWSON, R. E. (1962) "Simulation in the' social sciences," pp. 1-15 in H. Guetzkow (ed.) Simulation in Social Science: Readings. Englewood Cliffs, NJ: Prentice-Hall.
DE JOUVENEL, B. [ed.] (1963 and 1965) Futuribles: Studies in Conjecture. Geneva, Switzerland: Droz.
DEUTSCH, K. W. (1960) "Toward an inventory of basic trends and patterns in comparative and international politics." American Political Science Review 65(1): 34-57.
——— (1964) "Integration and the social system: Implications of functional analysis," pp. 179-208 in P. Jacob and J. Toscano (eds.) The Integration of Political Communities. Philadelphia: J. B. Lippincott.
——— (1968) The Analysis of International Relations. Englewood Cliffs, NJ: Prentice-Hall.
*——— (1969) "Simulation of international politics: A provisional assessment." American Political Science Association meeting, New York. (mimeo)
——— and A. ECKSTEIN (1961) National industrialization and the declining share of the international economic sector, 1890-1959." World Politics 13(2).
*DEUTSCH, K. W. and W. D. SENGHASS (1969) "Toward a theory of war and peace: Propositions, simulations and realities." Presented at the meetings of the American Political Science Association, New York, September.
DEUTSCH, K. W., B. FRITSCH, H. JAGUARIBE, and A. MARKOVITTS (1977) Problems of World Modeling: Political and Social Implications. Cambridge, MA: Ballinger.
DEVEREUX, G. (1967) From Anxiety to Method in the Behavioral Sciences. Paris: Mouton.
DOWNS, A. (1957) An Economic Theory of Democracy. New York: Harper & Row.
DRAPER, G. (1966) "Technological, economic, military, and political evaluation routine (TEMPER): An evaluation." Washington, DC: National Military Command Support System Center.
*DRIVER, M. J. (1962) "Conceptual structure and group processes in an Inter-Nation Simulation, Part 1: 'The perception of simulated nations: A multidimensional analysis of social perceptions as affected by situational stress and characteristic levels of cognitive complexity in perceivers.' " Ph.D. dissertation, Princeton University.
*——— (1965) "A structure analysis of aggression, stress, and personality in an Inter-Nation Simulation." Paper 97, Institute for Research in the Behavioral, Economic, and Management Sciences, Herman C. Krannert Graduate School of Industrial Administration, Purdue University.
——— (1966) Personal Communication. November 22.
*——— (1972) "European perceptions of nations: A multidimensional analysis of national points of view." Evanston, IL: Northwestern University.

*——— (1977) "Individual differences as determinants of aggression in the Inter-Nation Simulation," pp. 337-353 in M. G. Hermann with T. Milburn (eds.) A Psychological Examination of Political Leaders. New York: Macmillan.
*DRUCKMAN, D. (1965) "Ethnocentric bias in the Inter-Nation Simulation." M.A. thesis, Northwestern University.
*——— (1968) "Ethnocentrism in the Inter-Nation Simulation." Journal of Conflict Resolution 12 (March): 45-68.
——— and L. LUDWIG (1970) "Consensus on evaluative description of one's own nation, its allies, and its enemies." Journal of Social Psychology 81: 223-234.
DUESENBERRY, J. S., G. FROMM, L. R. KLEIN, and E. KUH [eds.] (1965) The Brookings Quarterly Economic Model of the United States. Skokie, IL: Rand McNally.
DUIJKER, H.C.J. and N. H. FRIJDA (1960) National Character and National Stereotypes. New York: Elsevier North-Holland.
DURKHEIM, E. (1957) Professional Ethics and Civic Morals. London: Routledge & Kegan Paul.
EASTON, D. (1965a) A Framework for Political Analysis. Englewood Cliffs, NJ: Prentice-Hall.
——— (1965b) A Systems Analysis of Political Life. New York: John Wiley.
ECKSTEIN, H. and D. E. APTER [eds.] (1963) Comparative Politics: A Reader. New York: Macmillan.
EDELMAN, M. (1964) The Symbolic Uses of Politics. Urbana: University of Illinois Press.
*ELDER, C. D. (1966) "Some conceptual and statistical problems in the treatment of integrated septem-runs in the Inter-Nation Simulation: A methodological note. Evanston, IL: Northwestern University International Relations Program. (mimeo)
*——— (1969) "Moderately programmed political-military simulations: The world politics simulations' transformation of the Inter-Nation Simulation into a man-machine exercise in an interactive mode." Washington, DC: Industrial College of the Armed Forces.
*——— and R. E. PENDLEY (1966) "Simulation as theory building in the study of international relations." Evanston, IL: Simulated International Processes project, Northwestern University.
——— (1981) "An economic model and government stability: Reconstructing the Inter-Nation Simulation," pp. 65-100 in H. Guetzkow and J. J. Valadez (eds.) Simulated International Processes: Theories and Research in Global Modeling. Beverly Hills, CA: Sage.
EPSTEIN, W. (1975) "Nuclear proliferation in the third world." Journal of International Affairs 29(2): 185-202.
ETZIONI, A. (1965) Political Unification. New York: Holt, Rinehart & Winston.
——— (1975) A Comparative Analysis of Complex Organizations. New York: Macmillan.
*FABRI, D. (1968) "Structural theory of aggression, Galtung." Lancaster, England: Peace Research Centre.
FEIGENBAUM, E. A. and J. FELDMAN [eds.] (1963) Computers and Thought. New York: McGraw-Hill.
FERGUSON, C. K. and H. H. KELLY (1964) "Significant factors in overevaluation of own-group's product." Journal of Abnormal and Social Psychology 69: 223-228.

*FISCHER, R. L. (1969) "The RAND/MIT Political-Military Exercise and international relations theory. Cambridge, MA: Arms Control Project, Center for International Studies, Massachussetts Institute of Technology.
——— (1971) "Das 'Political-Military Exercise' und Theorien internationaler beziehunger," pp. 219-238 in L. Kern and H-D. Ronsch (eds.) Simulation Internationaler Prozesse. Politisch Vierteljahresschrift Sonderheft 3.
*FORCESE, D. (1968) "Power and military alliance cohesion: Thirteen simulation experiments." Ph.D. dissertation, Washington University.
——— (1976) "Research note: The validity of the Inter-Nation Simulation." International Interactions 12: 179-182.
FORRESTER, J. V. (1971) World Dynamics. Cambridge, MA: Wright-Allen.
FOX, W.T.R. and A. B. FOX (1968) "International politics," pp. 50-60 in International Encyclopedia of the Social Sciences, Vol. 8. New York: Macmillan.
FRANK, P. G. [ed.] (1954) The Validation of Scientific Theories. Boston: Beacon.
FRITSCH, B. (1977) "Two kinds of complexity: Within numerical integration and beyond it," in K. W. Deutsch et al. (eds.) Problems of World Modeling: Political and Social Implications. Cambridge, MA: Ballinger.
FROMM, G., W. L. HAMILTON, and D. E. HAMILTON (1975) "Federally supported mathematical models: Survey and analysis." Washington, DC: National Science Foundation.
FUNKENSTEIN, D. H., S. H. KING, and M. E. DROLETTE (1957) Mastery of Stress. Cambridge, MA: Harvard University Press.
GALBRAITH, J. K. (1958) The Affluent Society. New York: Harper & Row.
GALTUNG, J. (1964) "Summit meetings and international relations." Journal of Peace Research 1: 36-54.
——— (1967) "Entropy and the general theory of peace." International Peace Research Association Conference, Stockholm, Sweden.
——— and M. RUGE (1965) "The structure of foreign news." Journal of Peace Research 1: 64-91.
GAMSON, W. A. (1961) "A theory of coalition formation." American Sociological Review 26(3): 373-382.
——— and A. MODIGLIANI (1965) "The carrot and/or the stick: Soviet responses to Western foreign policy 1946-1953." Peace Research Society (International) Papers 3: 47-78.
GELOVANI, V. A. et al. (1975) "Concerning one administrative problem in Forrester's Global Dynamic Model." Proceedings of the USSR Academy of Sciences 220 (Part 3).
General Electric Company (158) TEMPO Project 068—Environmental Factors. Santa Barbara, CA: General Electric, Technical Military Planning Operation.
GEORGE, A. L. (1969) "The 'operational code': A neglected approach to the study of political leaders and decision-making." International Studies Quarterly 13: 190-222.
GIFT, R. E. (1969) "Trading in a threat system: The U.S.-Soviet case." Journal of Conflict Resolution 13(4): 418-437.
*GLEDITSCH, N. P. (1967) "Report on the reliability of the message from coding in international processes simulation." Evanston, IL: Northwestern University.
GOLDHAMMER, H. and H. SPEIER (1959) "Some observations on political gaming." World Politics 12(1): 71-83.
*GOMER, L. C. (1967) "Master list of variables in the simulation of international processes." Evanston, IL: Northwestern University.

*GORDEN, M. (1965) "International relations theory in the TEMPER simulation." Cambridge, MA: Abt Associates Inc.

*——— (1967) "International relations theory in the TEMPER simulation." Evanston, IL: Simulated International Processes project, Northwestern University.

*——— (1968) "Burdens for the designer of a computer simulation of international relations: The case of TEMPER," in D. B. Bobrow (ed.) Proceedings of the Computers and the Policy-Making Community Institute. Englewood Cliffs, NJ: Prentice-Hall.

GOTTHEIL, D. L. (1966) "An approach to a comparison of verbal theories of international relations with Inter-Nation Simulation theory: Examples from Wolfers." Urbana: University of Illinois.

GREGG, P. M. and A. S. BANKS (1965) "Dimensions of political systems: Factor analysis of a cross-polity survey." American Political Science Review 59 (September): 602-614.

*GUETZKOW, H. (1950) "Long-range research in international relations." American Perspective 4(4): 421-440.

*——— (1959) "A use of simulation in the study of inter-nation relations." Behavioral Science 4(3): 183-191.

*——— (1962a) "Inter-nation simulation: An example of a self-organizing system," pp. 72-92 in M. C. Yovits et al. (eds.) Self-Organizing Systems. Washington, DC: Spartan.

*——— (1962b) "Joining field and laboratory work in disaster research," pp. 337-355 in G. W. Baker and D. H. Chapman (eds.) Man and Society in Disaster. New York: Basic Books.

*——— [ed.] (1962c) Simulation in Social Science: Readings. Englewood Cliffs, NJ: Prentice-Hall.

*——— (1963) "Structured programs and their relation to free activity within the Inter-Nation Simulation," pp. 103-149 in H. Guetzkow et al. (eds.) Englewood Cliffs, NJ: Prentice-Hall.

*——— (1964a) "Simulation in international relations," pp. 249-278 in Proceedings of the IBM Scientific Computing Symposium on Simulation Models and Gaming. Yorktown Heights, NY: Thomas J. Watson Research Center.

*——— (1964b) "Toward an acceleration of research in simulating international processes." Evanston, IL: Northwestern University.

*——— (1965a) "General strategy in the incremental development of international processes through PLATO." Evanston, IL: Northwestern University.

*——— (1965b) "Planning research on the utilization of simulation." Evanston, IL: Northwestern University.

*——— (1965c) "Some uses of mathematics in simulation of international relations," pp. 21-40 in J. Bernd (ed.) Mathematical Applications in Political Science. Dallas: Southern Methodist Press.

*——— (1966a) "Simulation in international relations," pp. 249-278 in Proceedings of the IBM Scientific Computing Symposium on Simulation Models and Gaming. White Plains, NY: International Business Machines Corporation.

——— (1966b) "Transcending data-bound methods in the study of politics"; "Comment on Professor Deutsch's paper," pp. 185-191 in J. C. Charlesworth (ed.) A Design for Political Science: Scope, Objectives, and Methods. Philadelphia: American Academy of Political and Social Science.

*——— (1969a) "Prospects for developments in international relations in the 1970s through simulation." Washington, DC: Industrial College of the Armed Forces.

*――― (1969b) "Report on a decade of activity." Evanston, IL: Northwestern University.
*――― (1969c) "Simulations in the consolidation and utilization of knowledge about international relations," pp. 284-300 in D. G. Pruitt and R. C. Snyder (eds.) Theory and Research on the Causes of War. Englewood Cliffs, NJ: Prentice-Hall.
*――― (1969d) "Some correspondences between simulations and 'realities' in international relations," pp. 202-269 in M. A. Kaplan (ed.) New Approaches to International Relations. New York: St. Martin's.
*――― (1970) "A decade of life with the Inter-Nation Simulation," pp. 31-53 in R. M. Stogdill (ed.) The Process of Model-Building in the Behavioral Sciences. New York: Norton.
*――― (1972) "Final report: Simulated International Processes project, Advanced Research Projects Agency, contract SD 260." Evanston, IL: Northwestern University.
――― (1974) "Collaboration in computer simulation for decision-making in international affairs." International Studies Notes 1(1): 8-9.
――― (1976a) "An incomplete history of fifteen short years in Simulating International Processes," pp. 247-258, in F. W. Hoole and D. A. Zinnes (eds.) Quantitative International Politics: An Appraisal. New York: Praeger.
――― (1976b) "Sizing up a study in Simulated International Processes: Roughly hewn surmises for a project autobiography," in J. N. Rosenau (ed.) In Search of Global Patterns. New York: Macmillan.
――― (1979) "Six continuing queries for global modelers in the twenty-first century." Economic Development and Change 28(1): 183-194.
――― (1981a) "Simulated International Processes: An incomplete history," pp. 13-21 in H. Guetzkow and J. J. Valadez (eds.) Simulated International Processes: Theories and Research in Global Modeling. Beverly Hills, CA: Sage.
――― (1981b) "The Inter-Nation Simulation," pp. 23-64 in H. Guetzkow and J. J. Valadez (eds.) Simulated International Processes: Theories and Research in Global Modeling. Beverly Hills, CA: Sage.
――― (1981c) "Six continuing queries for global modelers: A self-critique," pp. 331-358 in H. Guetzkow and J. J. Valadez (eds.) Simulated International Processes: Theories and Research in Global Modeling. Beverly Hills, CA: Sage.
――― and A. E. BOWES (1957) "The development of organizations in a laboratory." Management Science 3: 380-402.
*GUETZKOW, H. and C. CHERRYHOLMES (1966) Inter-Nation Simulation Kit. Chicago: Science Research Associates.
GUETZKOW, H. and W. L. HOLLIST (1976) "Some instructive experiences gained in Simulating International Processes, 1957-1972," pp. 328-346 in F. W. Hoole and D. A. Zinnes (eds.) Quantitative International Politics: An Appraisal. New York: Praeger.
*GUETZKOW, H. and L. JENSEN (1966) "Research activities on Simulated International Processes." Background: Journal of the International Studies Association 9(4): 261-274.
GUETZKOW, H. and J. J. VALADEZ (1981a) "Simulation and 'reality': Validity research," pp. 197-251 in H. Guetzkow and J. J. Valadez (eds.) Simulated International Processes: Theories and Research in Global Modeling. Beverly Hills, CA: Sage.
――― (1981b) "International relations theory: Contributions of Simulated International Processes," pp. 253-330 in H. Guetzkow and J. J. Valadez (eds.) Simulated

International Processes: Theories and Research in Global Modeling. Beverly Hills, CA: Sage.
——— (1981c) Simulated International Processes: Theories and Research in Global Modeling. Beverly Hills, CA: Sage.
*GUETZKOW, H., C. F. HERMANN, and M. G. HERMANN (1964) "Pilot simulation of World War II." China Lake, CA: U.S. Naval Ordnance Test Station.
GUETZKOW, H., W. L. HOLLIST, and M. D. WARD (1977) "Computer simulations for decision-making in international affairs: Moving toward consolidation of research in international relations through empirical analysis and computer simulation." International Peace Research Newsletter 25(3): 5-13.
GUETZKOW, H., P. KOTLER, and R. L. SCHULTZ [eds.] (1972) Simulation in Social and Administrative Science: Overviews and Case-Examples. Englewood Cliffs, NJ: Prentice-Hall.
*GUETZKOW, H., R. A. BRODY, M. J. DRIVER, and P. F. BEACH (1962) "An experiment on the N-country problem through Inter-Nation Simulation," in R. C. Hunt (ed.) Proceedings of the Seminar on International Conflict and Peace. New Haven, CT: Yale University.
*GUETZKOW, H., C. F. ALGER, R. A. BRODY, R. C. NOEL, and R. C. SNYDER (1963) Simulation in International Relations: Developments for Research and Teaching. Englewood Cliffs, NJ: Prentice-Hall.
GULLAHORN, J. R. and J. E. GULLAHORN (1965) "Some computer applications on social science." American Sociological Review 30(3): 353-365.
GURR, T. R. (1968) "A causal model of civil strife: A comparative analysis using new indices." American Political Science Review 62(4): 1104-1124.
——— (1970) Why Men Rebel. Princeton, NJ: Princeton University Press.
GVISHIANI, D. (1978) "Global modelling: Complex analysis of world development." World Marxist Review 21(8): 96-104.
HAAS, E. B. (1964) Beyond the Nation-State: Functionalism and International Organization. Stanford, CA: Stanford University.
HAMBLIN, R. L. (1962) "The dynamics of racial discrimination." Social Problems 10: 103-121.
HARVEY, O. J., D. E. HUNT, and H. M. SCHRODER (1961) Conceptual Systems and Personality Organization. New York: John Wiley.
HEILBRONER, R. L. (1966) Understanding Macro-Economics. Englewood Cliffs, NJ: Prentice-Hall.
HENNESSY, B. C. (1962) "Psycho-cultural studies of national character: Relevance for international relations." Background: Journal of the International Studies Association 6(1-2): 27-49.
*HERMANN, C. F. (1964) "A validity problem: Crisis in simulated foreign policy organizations." Presented at the meetings of the American Political Science Association.
——— (1965) "Crises in foreign policy-making: Simulation of international politics." Ph.D. dissertation, Northwestern University.
——— (1967a) "Threat, time and surprise: A simulation of international crisis." Princeton, NJ: Princeton University.
*——— (1967b) "Validation problems in games and simulations with special reference to models of international politics." Behavioral Science 12(3): 216-231.
——— (1969) Crises in Foreign Policy: An Analysis. Indianapolis: Bobbs-Merrill.
——— (1972) "Threat, time, and surprise: A simulation of international crisis," pp. 187-211 in C. F. Hermann (ed.) International Crises: Insights from Behavioral Research. New York: Macmillan.

*——— and H. GUETZKOW (1962) "Prediction considerations of possible relevance in validating Inter-Nation Simulation." China Lake, CA: U.S. Naval Ordnance Test Station.

*HERMANN, C. F. and M. G. HERMANN (1962) "The potential use of historical data for validation studies of the Inter-Nation Simulation: The outbreak of World War I as an illustration." China Lake, CA: U.S. Naval Ordnance Test Station.

*——— (1963) "Validation studies of the Inter-Nation Simulation." China Lake, CA: U.S. Naval Ordnance Test Station.

*——— (1967) "An attempt to simulate the outbreak of World War I." American Political Science Review 61(2): 400-416.

*——— and R. A. CANTOR (1974) "Counterattack or delay: Characteristics influencing decision-makers' responses to the simulation of an unidentified attack." Journal of Conflict Resolution 18: 75-106.

*HERMANN, M. G. (1965) "Stress, self-esteem and defensiveness in an Inter-Nation Simulation." Ph.D. dissertation, Northwestern University.

*——— (1966) "Testing a model of psychological stress." Journal of Personality 34(3): 381-396.

——— with T. W. MILBURN (1977) A Psychological Examination of Political Leaders. New York: Macmillan.

HERRERA, A. (1973) "Latin American world model: Progress report." Argentina: Fundacion Bariloche.

———, H. D. SCOLNIK, G. CHICHILNISKY, G. C. GALLOPIN, J. E. HARDOY, D. MOSROVICH, E. OTEIZA, G. L. de ROMERO BREST, C. E. SUAREZ, and L. TALAVERA (1976) Catastrophe or New Society? A Latin American World Model. Ottawa: International Development Research.

HICKMAN, B. G. (1975) "Project LINK in 1972: Retrospect and Prospect," pp. 657-669 in G. A. Renton (ed.) Modelling the Economy. London: Heineman Educational for the Social Research Council.

——— and L. R. KLEIN (1979) "A decade of research by Project LINK." Social Science Research Council Items, 33(3-4): 49-56.

*HICKS, B. H. (1965) "Potential use of PLATO for simulation of international processes." Evanston, IL: Northwestern University.

HILSMAN, R. (1959) "The foreign policy consensus: An interim research report." Journal of Conflict Resolution 3: 361-382.

HOCHBERG, H. (1965) "Simulation, models and theories." Developed for the Seminar on Simulation of Human Organizational Systems 1961-63, Office of Naval Research, U.S. Department of Defense. (grant 1228[22])

HOLLIST, W. L. and H. GUETZKOW (1978) "Cumulative research in international relations: Empirical analysis and computer simulation of competetive arms processes," pp. 165-195 in W. L. Hollist (ed.) Exploring Competitive Arms Processes: Applications of Mathematical Modeling and Computer Simulation in Arms Policy Analysis. New York: Marcel Dekker, Inc.

HOLSTI, O. R. (1963) "The quantitative analysis of content," in R. C. North et al. (eds.) Content Analysis: A Handbook with Applications for the Study of International Crisis. Evanston, IL: Northwestern University Press.

——— (1965) "The 1914 case." American Political Science Review 59(2): 365-378.

HOMANS, G. C. (1961) Social Behavior: Its Elementary Forms. New York: Harcourt Brace Jovanovich.

*HOOLE, F. W. (1972) "Societal conditions and political aggression: The examination of selected hypotheses derived from frustration-aggression theory." Bloomington: Indiana University.

——— (1979) "Review of *Simulated Worlds: A Computer Model of National Decision-Making*, by Stuart A. Bremer." American Political Science Review: 1509-1510.
——— and D. A. ZINNES [eds.] (1976) Quantitative International Politics: An Appraisal. New York: Praeger.
HORN, R. E. [ed.] (1977) The Guide to Simulations/Games for Education and Training. Cranford, NJ: Didactic Systems Inc.
HOSOYA, C. (1967) "Japan's decision for war in 1941." Hitotsubashi Journal of Law and Politics 5 (April): 10-19.
HUGHES, B. B. (1977) "General structural description of the World Integrated Model (WIM)." Cleveland: Case Western Reserve University.
——— (1980) World Modeling: The Mesarovic-Pestel World Model in the Context of Its Contemporaries. Lexington, MA: D. C. Heath.
HUGHES, B. B., M. BIRU, A. HUSSEIN, and Y. WILLIAMS (1977) "The use of the world model for policy analysis: Education and labor policy the Midwest." Presented at the annual meeting of the International Studies Association, St. Louis.
HUNT, E. B., J. MARIN, and P. J. STONE (1966) Experiments in Induction. New York: Academic.
Industrial College of the Armed Forces, Simulation and Computer Directorate (1969) World Politics Simulation: Description of the Model. Washington, DC: Author.
International Institute for Applied Systems Analysis (1977) MOIRA: Food and Agricultural Model. Proceedings of the Third IIASA Symposium on Global Modeling, Laxenburg, Austria, September 22-25, 1975.
JANIS, I. L. (1958) Psychological Stress. New York: John Wiley.
JENKINS, R. and J. MACRAE (1967) "Religion, conflict and polarization in Northern Ireland." Peace Research Centre, Lancaster, England, Publication no v-4 (June).
JENSEN, L. (1963) "Soviet-American bargaining behavior in the post-war disarmament negotiations." Journal of Conflict Resolution 7(3): 522-541.
——— (1966a) "American foreign policy elites and the prediction of international events." Peace Research Society (International) Papers 5: 199-209.
*——— (1966b) "United States elites and their perceptions of the determinants of foreign policy behavior." Presented at the meetings of the Midwest Political Science Association.
*——— (1972) "Predicting international events." Peace Research Reviews 4(6): 1-65.
*——— and M. J. WHITE (1966) "Selected abstracts related to the simulation of international military processes." Evanston, IL: Northwestern University.
JERVIS, R. (1977) Perceptions and Misperceptions in International Politics. Princeton, NJ: Princeton University Press.
JONES, S. D. and J.D. SINGER (1972) "Beyond conjecture," in International Politics: Abstracts of Data-Based Research. Itasca, IL: Peacock.
JUNGK, R. (1956) Brighter than 1000 Suns: The Moral and Political History of the Atomic Scientists. Harmondsworth, England: Penguin.
——— and A. J. WEINER (1967) The Year 2000: A Framework for Speculation on the Next Thirty-Three Years. New York: Macmillan.
KAHN, H. (1961) On Thermonuclear War. Princeton, NJ: Princeton University Press.
——— (1965) On Escalation: Metaphors and Scenarios. New York: Praeger.
KAPLAN, A. (1964) The Conduct of Inquiry: Methodology for Behavioral Science. New York: ITT.
KAPLAN, M. A. (1957) System and Process in International Politics. New York: John Wiley.
KARIEL, H. (1968) "Expanding the political present." University of Hawaii, Honolulu.

KATZ, D. and R. L. KAHN (1966) The Social Psychology of Organizations. New York: John Wiley.
KAYA, Y. and A. ONISHI (1977) "Report on Project FUGI: Future of global interdependence." Tokyo: Nippon Institute for Research Advancement.
KAYA, Y. and Y. SUZUKI (1974) "Global constraints and a new vision for development." Technological Forecasting and Social Change 6: 277-297; 371-388.
KELMAN, H. C. [ed.] (1965) International Behavior: A Social-Psychological Analysis. New York: Holt, Rinehart & Winston.
--- (1968) A Time To Speak. San Francisco: Jossey-Bass.
KENNEDY, J. L. (1962) "The systems approach: Organizational development." Human Factors 4(1): 25-52.
KEYNES, J. M. (1936) The General Theory of Employment, Interest, and Money. New York: Harcourt Brace Jovanovich.
KILE, F. and A. RABEHL (1977a) "Evolution of an integrated modeling approach." IEEE Transactions on Systems, Man, and Cybernetics, Washington, D.C., SMC-7(12): 859-863.
--- (1977b) "A value-driven, rationalized world model." Presented at the Fifth IIASA Global Modeling Conference.
KISSINGER, H. A. (1961) The Necessity for Choice: Prospects of American Foreign Policy. New York: Harper & Row.
KLINEBERG, O. (1964) The Human Dimension in International Relations. New York: Holt, Rinehart & Winston.
KOGAN, N. and M. A. WALLACH (1964) Risk Taking. New York: Holt, Rinehart & Winston.
--- (1967) "Risk taking as a function of the situation, the person, and the group," pp. 111-278 in New Directions in Psychology. New York: Holt, Rinehart & Winston.
*KREND, J. A. (1969) "A comparison of Guetzkow-Modelski correspondence ratings." Evanston, IL: Northwestern University.
*--- (1970) "A reconstruction of Oliver Benson's 'Simple Diplomatic Game.'" Evanston, IL: Northwestern University.
*--- (1971) "A documentation of Paul Smoker's IPS." Evanston, IL: Northwestern University.
*--- (1972a) "Computer simulations of international relations as heuristics for social status, action and change." Evanston, IL: Simulated International Processes project, Northwestern University.
*--- (1972b) "War and peace in the international system: Deriving an all-computer heuristic." Presented at the Summer Simulation Conference, San Diego, California.
*KRESS, P. (1966) "On validating simulation: With special attention to the simulation of international politics." Evanston, IL: Northwestern University.
--- (1974) "On validating simulation with special attention to simulation of international politics." International Interactions 1(1): 41-50.
*KRIESBERG, L. (1968) "Aspects of international collective decision-making." Evanston, IL: Northwestern University.
*--- and M. R. LEAVITT (1969) "A simulation of international negotiations with trade-offs in objectives." Evanston, IL: Northwestern University.
KUHN, T. S. (1970) The Structure of Scientific Revolutions. Chicago: University of Chicago Press.
KUZNETS, S. (1966) Modern Economic Growth. New Haven, CT: Yale University Press.

LABARR, D. F. and J. D. SINGER (1976) The Study of International Politics. Santa Barbara, CA: Clio.

LAGERSTROM, R. P. and R. C. NORTH (1969) "An anticipated-gap, mathematical model of international dynamics." Stanford, CA: Institute of Political Studies, Stanford University.

LAPIN, N. I. (1978) "Social indicators in global development models," pp. 79-88 in USSR Academy of Sciences, Institute for Sociological Researches, Sociology and Problems of Social Development. Moscow: Nauka.

LAPONCE, J. A. and P. L. SMOKER [eds.] (1972) Experimentation and Simulation in Political Science. Toronto: University of Toronto Press.

LARSON, D. L. (1963) The "Cuban Crisis" of 1962. Boston: Houghton Mifflin.

LASSWELL, H. D. (1956) The Decision Process. College Park, MD: Bureau of Governmental Research.

——— (1965) "Introduction: The study of political elites," in H. D. Lasswell and D. Lerner (eds.) World Revolutionary Elites. Cambridge, MA: MIT Press.

LAULICHT, J. (1966) "The Vietnam peace game: A simulation study of conflict resolution." Clarkson, Ontario: Canadian Peace Research Institute.

——— (1967) "A Vietnam peace game: Computer-assisted simulation of complex relations in international relations." Computers and Automatism 16(3): 14-18.

LAZARUS, R. S. (1964) "A laboratory approach to the dynamics of psychological stress." American Psychologist 19: 400-411.

——— and R. W. BAKER "Personality and psychological stress: A theoretical and methodological framework." Psychology Newsletter 8: 21-32.

*LEAVITT, M. R. (1967) "A comparison of four war models in man-computer simulations." Evanston, IL: Northwestern University.

*——— (1968a) "Four man-computer war calculation routines: Computer module." Evanston, IL: Northwestern University.

*——— (1968b) "International communications: Computer module." Evanston, IL: Northwestern University.

*——— (1969a) "Partial annotated bibliography on military operations/defense systems simulations." Washington, DC: Industrial College of the Armed Forces.

*——— (1969b) "Transition to the 70s: The development of computer simulation modules for the study of international relations." Evanston, IL: Northwestern University.

*——— (1970a) "Allyl: Description of the model." Evanston, IL: Northwestern University.

*——— (1970b) "A computer simulation of international relations." Madison: University of Wisconsin.

*——— (1970c) "Thoughts on computer simulation of international relations." Presented at the meetings of the American Political Science Association, Los Angeles, September.

*——— (1970d) "Three-man bargaining model: Computer module." Evanston, IL: Northwestern University.

*——— (1971a) "A computer simulation of international alliance behavior." Ph.D. dissertation, Northwestern University.

*——— (1971b) "MULTYP/Multiple typal analysis: A clustering program." Behavioral Science 16(4): 417-418.

*——— (1972) "Markov processes in international crisis: An analytical addendum to 'An event-based simulation of the Taiwan Straits Crises,'" pp. 280-292 in J. A. Laponce and P. L. Smoker (eds.) Experimentation and Simulation in Political Science. Toronto: University of Toronto Press.

*--- and L. KRIESBERG (1968) "Two-man bargaining model: Computer module." Evanston, IL: Northwestern University.
LEBANON, A. (1979) "International studies of the demand for energy." Presented at the International Institute for Applied Systems Analysis, Laxenburg, Austria.
LEONTIEF, W. (1974) "Structure of the world economy." American Economic Review 64(6): 822-834.
---, A. P. CARTER, P. E. PETRI (1977) The Future of the World Economy. New York: Oxford University Press.
LEVENTHAL, H. and S. I. PERLOE (1962) "A relationship between self-esteem and persuasibility." Journal of Abnormal and Social Psychology 64: 385-388.
*LICKLIDER, R. E. (1971) "Simulation and the private nuclear strategies." Simulation and Games 2(2): 163-171.
LISKA, G. (1968) "Foreign aid," pp. 513-521 in the International Encyclopedia of the Social Sciences, Vol. 5. New York: Macmillan.
LOUISE, I. M. (1974) "The generality of cognitive complexity across measures and stimuli." Ph.D. dissertation, Loyola University.
LUTERBACHER, U. (1974) Dimensions Historiques de Modeles Dynamiques de Conflit. Leiden: Sijthoff.
---, P. ALLAN, and A. IMHOFF (1979) "SIMPEST: A Simulation Model of Political, Economic, and Strategic Interactions among Major Powers." Colloque d'Histoire et de Politiques Internationalesseance du 15.12.77.
MACRAE, J. and P. L. SMOKER (1967) "A Vietnam simulation: A report on the Canadian/English Joint Project," in Journal of Peace Research. Groningen, Netherlands: International Peace Research Association.
MACK, R. W. and G. W. BAKER (1961) "The occasion INSTANT: The structure of social responses to unanticipated air raid warnings." Washington, DC: Disaster Research Group of the National Academy of Sciences, National Research Council.
MACK, R. W. and R. C. SNYDER (1957) "The analysis of social conflict: Toward an overview and synthesis." Journal of Conflict Resolution 1: 212-248.
MANDEL, R. (1977) "Research note: Political gaming and foreign policy-making during crises." World Politics 29(4): 610-625.
MARCH, J. G. (1962) "Some recent substantive and methodological developments in theory of organizational decision-making," in A. Ranney (ed.) Essays on the Behavioral Study of Politics. Urbana: University of Illinois Press.
MARSHALL, A. (1895) Principles of Economics. New York: Macmillan.
MARX, K. (1959) Das Capital. New York: Modern Library.
MAYER, A. (1967) The Urgent Future. New York: McGraw-Hill.
McCLINTOCK, C. G., A. A. HARRISON, S. STRAND, and P. GALLO (1963) "Internationalism-isolationism, strategy of the other player, and two-person game behavior." Journal of Abnormal Psychology 67: 631-636.
*McGOWAN, P. J. (1967) "Studies in Inter-Nation Simulation validity." Evanston, IL: Northwestern University.
*--- (1972) "Some external validities of the Inter-Nation simulation." Evanston, IL: Northwestern University. (mimeo)
--- and H. B. SHAPIRO (1973) The Comparative Study of Foreign Policy: A Survey of Scientific Findings. Beverly Hills, CA: Sage.
McPHEE, W. N. (1963) "Note on a campaign simulator," pp. 169-183 in Formal Theories of Mass Behavior. New York: Macmillan.
McRAE, V. V. (1963) "Gaming as a military research procedure," pp. 188-224 in I. de S. Pool (ed.) Social Science Research and National Security. Washington, DC: Smithsonian Institute.

MEADOWS, D. H. and J. M. RICHARDSON, Jr. (forthcoming) Groping in the Dark: Report on the Fifth IIASA Global Modeling Conference.
MEADOWS, D. H., D. L. MEADOWS, J. RANDERS, and W. W. BEHRENS III (1972) The Limits to Growth. New York: Universe.
MEADOWS, D. L., W. W. BEHRENS III, D. H. MEADOWS, R. F. NAILL, J. RANDERS, and E.K.O. ZAHN (1974) Dynamics of Growth in a Finite World. Cambridge, MA: Wright-Allen.
*MEIER, D. L. (1964) "Progress report: Event Simulation Project." Evanston, IL: Simulated International Processes project, Northwestern University.
*――― (1965a) "Progress report: Event Simulation Project." Evanston, IL: Simulated International Processes project, Northwestern University.
*――― (1965b) "Simulation techniques in a 'realistic' policy context." Journal of Human Resources 13(3): 356-371.
――― and A. STICKGOLD (1965) "Progress report: Analysis procedures." St. Louis, MO: Event Simulation Project, Washington University.
MERELMAN, R. (1966) "Learning and legitimacy." American Political Science Review 60: 548-561.
MESAROVIC, M. D. and E. PESTEL (1972) "A goal-seeking and regionalized model for analysis of critical world relationships: The conceptual foundation." Kybernetes Journal 1.
――― (1974) Mankind at the Turning Point: The Second Report to the Club of Rome. New York: Elsevier North-Holland.
*MEYERS, M. L. (1968) "Bibliographic and abstracted sources: An annotated listing of sources which include materials dealing with simulation in the social sciences, especially those concerned with the simulation of international processes." Evanston, IL: Northwestern University.
MILBURN, T. W. (1969) "Intellectual history of a research program," in D. G. Pruitt and R. C. Snyder (eds.) Theory and Research on the Causes of War. Englewood Cliffs, NJ: Prentice-Hall.
MILLS, C. W. (1959) The Sociological Imagination. New York: Oxford University Press.
MILSTEIN, J. S. and W. C. MITCHELL (1968) "Computer simulation of international processes: The Vietnam war and the pre-World War 1 naval race." Cambridge, MA: Sixth North American Peace Research Conference, Peace Research Society (International).
*MODELSKI, G. (1970) "Simulations, realities, and international relations theory." Simulatin and Games 1(2): 111-134.
MORGENTHAU, H. J. (1960) Politics among Nations. New York: Knopf.
――― (1963) "Alliances in theory and practice," pp. 184-212 in A. Wolfers (ed.) Alliance Policy in the Cold War. Baltimore: John Hopkins University Press.
*NARDIN, T. (1965a) "An inquiry into the validity of a simulation of international relations." Evanston, IL: Northwestern University.
*――― (1965b) "Integrative behavior in a simulated international system." Evanston, IL: Northwestern University. (mimeo)
*――― (1967) "Uses of threats in strategic interaction: An experiment in international politics." Ph.D. dissertation, Northwestern University.
*――― (1969) "Reliability and validity of some patterns of international interaction in an Inter-Nation Simulation." Journal of Peace Research 6(19): 2-12.
*――― and N. E. CUTLER (1967) "A seven variable study of the reliability and validation of some patterns of international interaction in the Inter-Nation Simulation." Evanston, IL: Northwestern University.

NAROLL, R. and R. COHEN [eds.] (1968) Handbook of Methodology in Cultural Anthropology. New York: Natural History Press.
NAYLOR, T. H., J. L. BALINTFY, D. S. BURDICK, and K. CHU (1966) Computer Simulation Techniques. New York: John Wiley.
NEUSTADT, R. (1960) Presidential Power. New York: John Wiley.
NEWELL, A. and H. A. SIMON (1963) "GPS: A program that simulates human thought," pp. 279-293 in E. A. Feigenbaum and J. Feldman (eds.) Computers and Thought. New York: McGraw-Hill.
*NOEL, R. C. (1963a) "A simplified political-economic system simulation." Ph.D. dissertation, Northwestern University.
*--- (1963b) "Evolution of the Inter-Nation Simulation," pp. 69-102 in H. Guetzkow et al. (eds.) Simulation in International Relations: Developments for Research and Teaching. Englewood Cliffs, NJ: Prentice-Hall.
*--- (1963c) "Inter-Nation Simulation participants' manual," pp. 43-68 in H. Guetzkow et al. (eds.) Simulation in International Relations: Developments for Research and Teaching. Englewood Cliffs, NJ: Prentice-Hall.
NORTH, R. C. (1962) "Decision-making in crisis: An introduction." Journal of Conflict Resolution 6(3).
--- (1968) "Conflict: Political aspects," pp. 226-231 in the International Encyclopedia of the Social Sciences, Vol. 3. New York: Macmillan.
---, O. R. HOLSTI, M. G. ZANINOVICH, and D. A. ZINNES (1963) Content Analysis: A Handbook with Application for the Study of International Crisis. Evanston, IL: Northwestern University Press.
Office of Aerospace Research, United States Air Force (1964) U.S. Air Force Achievements in Research. Washington, DC: Government Printing Office.
OLSON, M., Jr. (1965) The Logic of Collective Action. Cambridge, MA: Harvard University Press.
--- and R. ZECKHAUSER (1964) "An economic theory of alliances." Santa Monica CA: RAND Corporation. (Paper 2992)
OPHULS, W. (1977) Ecology and the Politics of Scarcity. San Francisco: Freeman.
OPHULS, W. (1977) Ecology and the Politics of Scarcity. San Francisco: Freeman.
ORGANSKI, A.F.K. (1958) World Politics. New York: Knopf.
ORWELL, G. (1949) 1984. New York: Harcourt Brace Jovanovich.
PADEN, J. N. (1979) "Corss-cutting issues and modes of discourse." Evanston, IL: Symposium on Values and Social Science, Department of Political Science, Northwestern University.
PAIGE, G. D. (1977) The Scientific Study of Political Leadership. New York: Free Press.
*PARK, T. W. (1968) "A guide to data sources in international relations: Annotated bibliography with lists of variables." Evanston, IL: Northwestern University.
PARSONS, T. (1951) The Social System. New York: Macmillan.
*PELOWSKI, A. L. (1969a) "International business growth: Computer module." Evanston, IL: Northwestern University.
*--- (1969b) "One approach to simulation module construction in international relations." Evanston, IL: Northwestern University.
--- (1970a) "A global eco-tactic: Population control as a multinational business proposition," pp. 370-392 in L. L. Roos, Jr. (ed.) The Politics of Ecosuicide. New York: Holt, Rinehart & Winston.
*--- (1970b) "National attributes and cross-national business: A combined regression-simulation study." Evanston, IL: Northwestern University.
*--- (1972) "An event-based simulation of the Taiwan Straits Crisis," pp. 259-279 in J. A. Laponce and P. L. Smoker (eds.) Experiment and Simulation in Political Science. Toronto: University of Toronto Press.

PEN, J. (1966) A Primer of International Trade. New York: Vintage.
*PENDLEY, R. E. (1966) "INSCAL: A FORTRAN program for performing the calculations for the Inter-Nation Simulation." Evanston, IL: Northwestern University.
*——— and C. D. ELDER (1970) "An analysis of political constraints in an internation simulation: A critique in terms of contemporary theory and data on the stability of regimes and governments." Evanston, IL: Northwestern University. (mimeo)
PERLMUTTER, H. (1966) "Social architectural problems of the multinational firm." Evanston, IL: Northwestern University. (mimeo)
*PFALTZGRAFF, R. L. (1972a) "Simulation and international relations literature." Medford, MA: Tufts University.
*——— (1972b) "Simulation and international relations theory: A comparison of simulation models and international relations literature." Mimeo. Medford, MA: Tufts University.
*PIRRO, E. B. (1972) "Frustration-aggression: A causal model analysis." Evanston, IL: Northwestern University.
PLATIG, E. R. (1966) International Relations Research: Problems of Evaluation and Advancement. New York: Carnegie Endowment for International Peace.
*POOL, I. de S. (1969) "Comparison of a human game and a computer simulation." Cambridge: Massachussetts Institute of Technology.
——— and A. KESSLER (1965) "The Kaiser, the Tsar and the computer: Information processing in a crisis." American Behavioral Scientist 8: 31-38.
POOL, I. de S., R. P. ABELSON, and S. L. POPKIN (1964) Candidates, Issues, and Strategies. Cambridge, MA: MIT Press.
PRUITT, D. G. (1962) "An analysis of responsiveness between nations." Journal of Conflict Resolution 6(1): 5-18.
*——— (1964) "Some comments on the use of simulation in the study of international relations: A discussion of papers presented by R. A. Brody and L. Solomon at the Symposium in Psychology and International Relations." Washington, DC: Georgetown University. (mimeo)
*——— (1964-1965) "Problem solving in the Department of State: Monograph 2." Denver, CO: Social Science Foundation and Department of International Relations, University of Denver.
PRZEWORSKI, A. and H. TEUNE (1970) The Logic of Comparative Social Inquiry. New York: John Wiley.
RAPOPORT, A. (1966) "Two views of conflict: The cataclysmic and the strategic models," in Proceedings of the International Peace Research Association Inaugural Conference. Assen: Van Gorcum.
——— (1967) "Games which simulate deterrence and disarmament." Peace Research Reviews 1(1): 40-45.
——— and A. M. CHAMAN (1965) Prisoner's Dilemma: A Study in Conflict and Cooperation. Ann Arbor, MI: University of Michigan Press.
RAPOPORT, A. and C. ORCUTT (1962) "Experimental games: A review." Behavioral Sciences 7: 1-38.
*RASER, J. R. (1966) "Personal characteristics of political decision-makers: A literature review." Peace Research Society (International) Papers 5: 161-181.
——— and W. J. CROW (1964) "WINSAFE II: An Inter-Nation Simulation study of deterrence postures embodying capacity to delay response." La Jolla, CA: Western Behavioral Sciences Institute.

――― (1968) "A study of deterrence theories," pp. 389ff. in L. A. Kreisberg (ed.) Social Processes in International Relations. New York: John Wiley.
――― (1969) "A simulation study of deterrence theories," pp. 136-149 in D. G. Pruitt and R. C. Snyder (eds.) Theory and Research on the Causes of War. Englewood Cliffs, NJ: Prentice-Hall.
RASER, J. R., D. T. CAMPBELL, and R. W. CHADWICK (1970) "Gaming and simulation for developing theory relevant to international relations." General Systems 15: 183-204.
RASHEVSKY, N. (1947) Mathematical Theory of Human Relations: An Approach to a Mathematical Biology of Social Phenomena. Bloomington, IN: Principia.
RASTOGI, P. N. (1978) The Behaviour of Societal System. New Dehli: Indian Institute of Advanced Study.
RAY, J. L. (1979) Global Politics. Boston: Houghton Mifflin.
Raytheon Company (1965) TEMPER: Technological, Economic, Military, and Political Evaluation Routine. Bedford, MA: Author.
*REMY, R. C. (1967) "Trade and defense in the IPS–International Processes Simulation–and selected reference systems." Evanston, IL: Northwestern University.
*RENNAGEL, W. C. (1969) "A report on the International Systems Simulation Seminar at O.S.U." Presented to the Simulated International Processes project, Northwestern University.
RICHARDSON, L. F. (1960) Arms and Insecurity. Pittsburgh: Boxwood.
RICHARDSON, L. and E. SOUCAR (1971) "Comparison of cognitive complexity with achievement and adjustment: A convergent discriminant study." Psychological Reports 29(3, part 2): 1087-1090.
ROBERTS, P. C. (1977) "SARUM 76–A global modelling project." Futures 9(1): 3-16.
*ROBINSON, J. A. (1964) "Simulating crisis decision-making." Presented at the joint meetings of the Institute of Management Sciences and the Operations Research Society of America.
*―――, C. F. HERMANN, and M. G. HERMANN (1964) "Studies of crisis decision-making." China Lake, CA: U.S. Naval Ordnance Test Station.
*――― (1969) "Search under crisis in political gaming and simulation," pp. 80-94 in D. G. Pruitt and R. C. Snyder (eds.) Theory and Research on the Causes of War. Englewood Cliffs, NJ: Prentice-Hall.
*ROBINSON, J. A., L. F. ANDERSON, M. G. HERMANN, and R. C. SNYDER (1966) "Teaching with Inter-Nation Simulation and case studies." American Political Science Review 60 (March): 53-65.
ROME, B. K. and S. C. ROME (1966) "Leviathan: An experimental study of large organizations with the aid of computers," pp. 257-311 in R. V. Bowers (ed.) Studies on Behavior in Organizations: A Research Symposium. Athens: University of Georgia Press.
ROSENAU, J. N. (1966) "Pre-theories and theories of foreign-policy," in R. B. Farrell (ed.) Approaches to Comparative and International Politics. Evanston, IL: Northwestern University Press.
――― (1968) "National interest," pp. 34-39 in the International Encyclopedia of the Social Sciences, Vol. II. New York: Macmillan.
*ROSENBAND, L. (1968) "Comparisons between an Inter-Nation Simulation and a real world of 1955." Evanston, IL: Northwestern University.

ROSENBLATT, P. C. (1964) "Origins and effects of group ethnocentrism and nationalism." Journal of Conflict Resolution 8(2): 131-146.
RUGE, M. H. (1969) "Small-power versus big-power perspective on foreign policy: A comparative analysis of behavior in Norwegian-U.S. simulation experiments" pp. 203-213 in Proceedings for the Third IPRA General Conference, Karlovy Vary, Vol. III.
——— (1972) "Image and reality in simulated international systems," pp. 293-314 in J. A. Laponce and P. L. Smoker (eds.) Experimentation and Simulation in Political Science. Toronto: University of Toronto Press.
RUGG, D. S. (1972) Spatial Foundations of Urbanism. Dubuque, IA: Wm. C. Brown.
RUMMEL, R. J. (1963) "Dimensions of conflict behavior within and between nations," pp. 1-50 in General Systems: Yearbook of the Society for General Systems Research, Vol. 8, Ann Arbor, MI: Society for the Advancement of General Systems Theory.
——— (1965) "A social field theory of foreign conflict." Peace Research Society Papers IV, Cracow Conference.
——— (1966a) "The Dimensionality of Nations Project," pp. 109-129 in R. L. Merritt and S. Rokkan (eds.) Comparing Nations: The Use of Quantitative Data in Cross-National Research. New Haven, CT: Yale University Press.
——— (1966b) "A social field theory of foreign conflict behavior." Peace Research Society (International) Papers 4: 131-150.
——— (1968) "The relationship between national attributes and foreign conflict behavior," in J. D. Singer (ed.) Quantitative International Politics: Insights and Evidence. New York: Macmillan.
——— (1972) Dimensions of Nations. Beverly Hills, CA: Sage.
RUNGE, W. A. (1963) "Analysis of the Department of State communications traffic during a politico-military crisis." Menlo Park, CA: Stanford Research Institute.
RUSSETT, B. M. (1968) "Delineating international regions," in J. D. Singer (ed.) Quantitative International Politics: Insights and Indicators. New York: Macmillan.
———, H. R. ALKER, Jr., K. W. DEUTSCH, and H. D. LASSWELL (1964) World Handbook of Political and Social Indicators. New Haven, CT: Yale University Press.
*SAGER, A. M. (1967) "Comparative politics and the national political model of the Inter-Nation Simulation: A test of five hypotheses across four groups of nations." Evanston, IL: Northwestern University.
*——— (1972) "The internal validity of the Inter-Nation Simulation: A comparison of the WINSAFE II and INS-8 simulations." Austin: University of Texas.
SALMON, W. C. (1967) The Foundations of Scientific Inference. Pittsburgh: University of Pittsburgh Press.
SCHANK, R. C. and K. M. COLBY [eds.] (1973) Computer Models of Thought and Language. San Francisco: Freeman.
SCHELLING, T. C. (1963) The Strategy of Conflict. Cambridge, MA: Harvard University Press.
SCHMIDT, H. (1968) "Peace research and politics." Journal of Peace Research 3.
SCHRODER, H. M., M. J. DRIVER, and S. STREUFERT (1967) Human Information Processing. New York: Holt, Rinehart & Winston.
SCHRODT, P. A. (1978) "Statistical problems associated with the Richardson arms race model." Journal of Peace Science 3(2): 159-172.
*SCHWARTZ, D. C. (1966) "Experimental studies in alliance behavior." Evanston, IL: Northwestern University.

*––– (1972) "Decision-making in historical and simulated cases," pp. 167-184 in C. F. Hermann (ed.) International Crises: Insights from Behavioral Research. New York: Macmillan.
SCHWARTZENBERGER, G. (1964) Power Politics. London: Stevens.
SCOLNIK, H and L. TALAVERA (1978) "Mathematical and computational aspects of the construction of self-optimizing dynamic models." Presented at the Sixth Global Modeling Conference, IIASA, October.
SEIDELMANN, R. (1973) Simulation in Internationaler und Auswartige Politik: Die Inter-Nation Simulation (INS) und ihre Verwerbarkeit fuer Analyse und Prognose. Meisenheim an Glan: Verlag Anton Hain; Marburger Abhandlungen zur Politischen Wissenschaft, Vol. 22.
*SEKI, H. (1966) "The use of PLATO in Inter-Nation Simulation." Evanston, IL: Northwestern University.
*––– (1967) "Toward an N-generation model of international process simulation theory." Evanston, IL: Northwestern University.
––– (1969) Foundations of International Systems Theory. Tokyo: University of Tokyo Press.
SELYE, H. (1956) The Stress of Life. New York: McGraw-Hill.
SHAPIRO, M. J. (1966a) "The House and the federal role: A computer simulation of roll call voting." Ph.D. dissertation, Northwestern University.
*––– (1966b) "Cognitive rigidity and moral judgments in an inter-nation simulation." Evanston, IL: Northwestern University.
––– (1969) "Rational political man: A synthesis of economic and social psychological perspectives." American Political Science Review 63: 1106-1119.
*SHERMAN, A. W. (1963) "The social psychology of bilateral negotiations." M.A. thesis, Northwestern University.
SHUBIK, M. [ed.] (1964) Game Theory and Related Approaches to Social Behavior. New York: John Wiley.
––– (1975) Games for Society, Business, and War: Towards a Theory of Gaming. New York: Elsevier North-Holland.
SHURE, G. H. and R. J. MEEKER (1965) "A personality/attitude schedule for use in experimental bargaining studies." Technical Memorandum TM-2543, System Development Corporation, Santa Monica, California.
––– and E. A. HANSFORD (1965) "The effectiveness of pacifist strategies in bargaining games." Journal of Conflict Resolution 9(1): 106-117.
SILVERMAN, I. (1964) "Differential effects of ego threat upon persuasibility for high and low self-esteem subjects." Journal of Abnormal and Social Psychology 69: 567-572.
SIMMEL, G. (1950) The Sociology of Georg Simmel (K. H. Wolf, ed. and trans.). New York: Macmillan.
SIMON, H. A. (1957) Models of Man. New York: John Wiley.
––– (1965) "The architecture of complexity," pp. 63-76 in General Systems: Yearbook of the Society for General Systems Research 10, Ann Arbor, MI: Society for the Advancement of General Systems Theory.
SINGER, J. D. (1958) "Threat-perception and the armament-tension dilemma." Journal of Conflict Resolution 2(1): 90-105.
––– (1961) "The level of analysis problem in international relations." World Politics 14 (October): 77-92.
––– (1965) "Data-making in international relations." Behavioral Science 10(1): 68-80.
––– (1977) "The historical experiment as a research strategy in the study of world politics." Social Science History 2(1): 1-22.

——— and H. HINOMOTO (1965) "Inspecting for weapons production: A modest computer simulation." Journal of Peace Research, International Peace Research Association, Groningen, Netherlands 2(1): 18-38.
SINGER, J. D. et al. (1969) Beyond Conjecture: Data Based Research in International Politics. Itasca, IL: Peacock.
SKINNER, D. D. and R. N. WELLS, Jr. (1965) "Participants' manual: Michigan Inter-Nation Simulation." Ann Arbor, MI: University of Michigan.
SMOKER, P. L. (1965a) "Trade, defence, and the Richardson theory of arms races: A seven nation study." Journal of Peace Research 2: 161-176.
——— (1965b) "A preliminary empirical study of an international integrative subsystem." International Associations 11: 638-646.
*——— (1967a) "The arms race as an open and closed system." Peace Research Society (International) Papers 7: 41-62.
*——— (1967b) "International Processes Simulation: Notes on step-change from Inter-Nation Simulation." Evanston, IL: Northwestern University.
*——— (1967c) "Nation-state escalation and international integration." Journal of Peace Research, International Peace Research Association Groningen, Netherlands 4(1): 60-75.
*——— (1967d) "Report on International Processes Simulation." Evanston, IL: Northwestern University.
*——— (1968a) "International Processes Simulation: A man-computer model." Evanston, IL: Northwestern University.
*——— (1968b) "Analyses of conflict behaviors in an International Processes Simulation and an international system (1955-60)." Evanston, IL: Northwestern University.
*——— (1968c) "An International Processes Simulation, conflict theory and analysis." Evanston, IL: Northwestern University.
*——— (1968d) "Feiereband frustration/aggression theory: Computer module." Lancaster, England: Peace Research Centre.
*——— (1968e) "IPS research and development: Computer module." Lancaster, England: Peace Research Centre.
*——— (1968f) "An International Processes Simulation: Development, usage and partial validation." Ph.D. dissertation, University of Lancaster.
*——— (1968g) "An international processes simulation: Theory and description." Evanston, IL: Northwestern University.
*——— (1968h) "Participant's manual–International Processes Simulation." Evanston, IL: Northwestern University.
*——— (1968i) "Richardson arms race dynamics: Computer module." Lancaster, England: Peace Research Centre.
*——— (1968j) "Tanter/Midlarsky theory of revolution: Computer module." Lancaster, England: Peace Research centre.
*——— (1969a) "Simulation for social anticipation and creation." Evanston, IL: Northwestern University.
*——— (1969b) "A time series analysis of Sino-Indian relations." Journal of Conflict Resolution 13(2): 172-191.
*——— (1969c) "Working electoral theory: Computer module." Lancaster, England: Peace Research Centre.
*——— (1969d) "Social research for social anticipation." American Behavioral Scientist (July-August): 7-13
*——— (1970a) "International Processes Simulation: An evaluation." Presented at the Events Data Conference, Michigan State University, East Lansing.

*--- (1970b) "International relations simulation." Peace Research Reviews 3(6): 1-84.
--- (1970c) "Simulating the human world." Science Journal 6(7): 49-53.
*--- (1972) "International Processes Simulations: A description," pp. 315-365 in J. A. Laponce and P. L. Smoker (eds.) Experimentation and Simulation in Political Science. Toronto: University of Toronto Press.
--- (1973) "Global Systems Simulation: Computer program." Lancaster, England: Lancaster University Programme for Peace and Conflict Research.
--- (1981) "The International Processes Simulation," pp. 101-133 in H. Guetzkow and J. J. Valadez (eds.) Simulated International Processes: Theories and Research in Global Modeling. Beverly Hills, CA: Sage.
*SNYDER, R. C. (1961) "Deterrence, weapons systems, and decision-making. China Lake, CA: U.S. Naval Ordnance Test Station.
--- (1962) "A proposal for a five year grant to the program of Graduate Training and Research in International Relations: Proposal to the Carnegie Corporation of New York." Evanston, IL: Northwestern University.
*--- (1963a) "Some perspectives on the use of experimental techniques in the study of international relations," pp. 1-23 in H. Guetzkow et al. (eds.) Simulation in International Relations: Developments for Research and Teaching. Englewood Cliffs, NJ: Prentice-Hall.
--- (1963b) "Some recent trends in international relations theory and research," in Proceedings of the Conference of the International Political Science Association. Urbana: University of Illinois Press.
--- and G. D. PAIGE (1958) "The United States decision to resist aggression in Korea: The application of an analytical scheme." Administrative Science Quarterly 3: 341-378.
---, C. F. HERMANN, and H. D. LASSWELL (1976) "A global monitoring system: Appraising the effects of government on human dignity." International Studies Quarterly 20(2): 221-260.
SOLOMON, L. N. (1965) "Simulation research in international decision-making," pp. 37-52 in G. Sperrazo (ed.) Psychology and International Relations. Washington, DC: Georgetown University Press.
*SOROOS, M. S. (1971) "Crisis behaviors in the International Processes Simulation and the Berlin Reference System." Raleigh: North Carolina State University.
*--- (1973) "An interpretation of patterns of discrepancies between the International Process Simulation and an international reference system," pp. 1-28 in J. D. Ben-Dak (ed.) The Simulation of Inter-Societal Relations. New York: Gordon and Breach.
*--- (1975) "Patterns of cross-national activities in the international simulation and a real-world reference system," in E. Azar (ed.) International Interactions: A Reader. New York: Gordon and Breach.
SPROUT, H. and M. SPROUT (1965) The Ecological Perspective on Human Affairs: With Special Reference to International Politics. Princeton, NJ: Princeton University Press.
STEINBRUNNER, J. D. (1969) "Relatively unprogrammed political-military simulations: The RAND/MIT Political-Military Exercise and developments for data-based operations." Washington, DC: Industrial College of the Armed Forces.
Stockholm International Peace Research Institute (1970) Yearbook of World Armament and Disarmament 1968-69. New York: Humanities.
STOGDILL, R. M. (1970) "Introduction: The student of model building," pp. 3-13 in R. M. Stogdill (ed.) The Process of Model Building in the Behavioral Sciences. New York: Norton.

STONE, R. (1966) "British economic balances in 1970," pp. 249-282 in Mathematics in the Social Sciences and Other Essays. Cambridge, MA: MIT Press.
––– (1977) "Major accounting problems for a world model," pp. 57-83 in K. W. Deutsch et al. (eds.) Problems of World Modeling. Cambridge, MA: Ballinger.
*STREUFERT, S. (1968) "The components of a simulation of local conflict: An analysis of the tactical and negotiations game." Evanston, IL: Northwestern University.
––––, P. SUEDFELD, and M. J. DRIVER (1965) "Conceptual structure, information search, and information utilization." Journal of Personality and Social Psychology 2(5): 736-740.
STREUFERT, S., M. A. CLARDY, M. J. DRIVER, M. KARLINS, H. M. SCHRODER, and P. SUEDFIELD (1965) "A tactical game for the analysis of complex decision-making in individuals and groups." Psychological Reports 17: 723-727.
SUEDFELD, P. and A. D. RANK (1976) "Revolutionary leaders: Long-term success as a function of changes in conceptual complexity." Journal of Personality and Social Psychology 34(2): 169-178.
SUEDFELD, P. and P. TETLOCK (1977) "Integrative complexity of communications in international crises." Journal of Conflict Resolution 21(1): 169-184.
*SULLIVAN, D. G. (1960) "The concept of power in international relations." Presented at the meetings of the Midwest Political Science Association, Chicago.
*––– (1963) "Towards an inventory of major propositions contained in contemporary textbooks in international relations." Ph.D. dissertation, Northwestern University.
––– with R. C. NOEL (1972) "Inter-Nation Simulation: A review of its premises," pp. 111-124 in M. Inbar and C. S. Stoll (eds.) Simulation and Gaming in Social Science. New York: Macmillan.
SURANSKY, L. (1980) "International relations games and simulations: An evaluation," in R. E. Horn and A. Cleaves (eds.) The Guide to Simulations/Games for Education and Training. Beverly Hills, CA: Sage.
TANTER, R. (1966) "Dimensions of conflict behavior within and between nations, 1958-60." Journal of Conflict Resolution 10(1): 41-64.
––– (1967) "Towards a theory of political development." Midwest Journal of Political Science 11(2): 145-172.
*TARG, H. and T. NARDIN (1966) "The Inter-Nation Simulation as a predictor of contemporary events." Evanston, IL: Northwestern University.
THOMPSON, J. D. and R. W. HAWKES (1962) "Disaster, community organization, and administrative process," pp. 268-300 in G. W. Baker and D. W. Chapman (eds.) Man and Society in Disaster. New York: Basic Books.
THORELLI, H. B. and R. L. GRAVES (1964) International Operations Simulation with Comments on Design and Use of Management Games. New York: Macmillan.
THORSON, S. J. (1976) "The Inter-Nation Simulation project: A methodological appraisal," pp. 284-303 in F. W. Hoole and D. A. Zinnes (eds.) Quantitative International Politics: An Appraisal. New York: Praeger.
TOCHER, K. D. (1963) The Art of Simulation. London: English Universities Press.
TOMKINS, S. S. and S. L. MESSICK [eds.] (1963) Computer Simulation of Personality. New York: John Wiley.
TUCKER, L. R. and S. L. MESSICK (1963) "An individual differences model for multi-dimensional scaling." Psychometrika 28(4): 333-367.
United Nations Statistical Office (1958-1967) Statistical Yearbook. New York: United Nations Publications.

VALADEZ, J. J. (1977) "Comments on R. W. Chadwick's critical analysis of INS theory." Evanston, IL: Northwestern University.
――― (ed.) (1979) Simulated International Processes Project Files. Vol. I: Verbal Theory; Vol. II: Analyses; Vol. III: Models and Methods. Principal investigator, H. Guetzkow. Evanston, IL: Northwestern University Library Archives.
――― (1981a) "Core bibliography on Simulated International Processes," Appendix A in H. Guetzkow and J. J. Valadez (eds.) Simulated International Processes: Theories and Research in Global Modeling. Beverly Hills, CA: Sage.
――― (1981b) "Guide to Northwestern University simulation documents," Appendix B in H. Guetzkow and J. J. Valadez (eds.) Simulated International Processes: Theories and Research in Global Modeling. Beverly Hills, CA: Sage.
――― and G. L. TYGESSON (1981) "Generational development in modeling," pp. 181-196 in H. Guetzkow and J. J. Valadez (eds.) Simulated International Processes: Theories and Research in Global Modeling. Beverly Hills, CA: Sage.
VAN ATTA, R. (1969) "A simulation test of the balance of power." Evanston, IL: Northwestern University.
VERBA, S. (1961) "Assumptions of rationality and non-rationality in models of the international system." World Politics 14: 93-117.
――― (1964) "Simulation, reality, and theory in international relations." World Politics 16(3): 490-519.
*WALBECK, N. V. (1968) "Aspects of international interaction in the referent system and the International Processes Simulation: Cooperation and conflict." Evanston, IL: Northwestern University.
WALLACE, M. D. (1978) "Review of *Simulated Worlds: A Computer Model of National Decision-making*, by Stuart A. Bremer." Canadian Journal of Political Science 11: 241-242.
WALLACH, M. A. and N. KOGAN (1965) "The roles of information, discussion, and consensus in group risk taking." Journal of Experimental Social Psychology 65: 75-86.
WALLERSTEIN, I. (1974) The Modern World-System. New York: Academic.
WARD, M. D. (1978) The Political Economy of Distribution: Equality vs. Inequality. New York: Elsevier.
――― (1979) "Challenges for more adequate global modeling." American Political Science Review 73(4): 1113-1115.
――― and H. GUETZKOW (1979) "Toward integrated global models: From economic engineering to social science modeling." Journal of Policy Modeling 1(3): 445-464.
WASKOW, A. (1968) "Looking forward: 1999. Who plans your future?" New University Thought 6 (Spring): 34-55.
WEBB, E. J., D. T. CAMPBELL, R. D. SCHWARTZ, and L. SECHREST (1966) Unobtrusive Measures: Nonreactive Research in the Social Sciences. Skokie, IL: Rand McNally.
WEEDE, E. (1969) "Conflict behavior of nation-states." Presented at the Midwest Meeting of the Peace Research Society (International), April 17.
WELLS, H. G. (1964) War of the Worlds. New York: Limited Editions.
*WINTER, E. F. (1967) "Perception problems in international relations research." Evanston, IL: Northwestern University.
WINTER, G. (1968) Elements for a Social Ethic. New York: Macmillan.
WOHLSTETTER, R. (1962) Pearl Harbor: Warning and Decision. Stanford, CA: Stanford University Press.

World Politics Simulation: Description of the Model (1969) Washington, DC: Simulation and Computer Directorate, Industrial College of the Armed Forces, USDOD.
*WRIGHT, G. D. (1963) "Inter-group communication and attraction in Inter-Nation Simulation." Ph.D. dissertation, Washington University.
WRIGHT, Q. (1955) The Study of International Relations. Englewood Cliffs, NJ: Prentice-Hall.
――― (1965) A Study of War. Chicago: University of Chicago Press.
YORK, H. (1970) Race to Oblivion: A Participant's View of the Arms Race. New York: Simon & Schuster.
ZELDITCH, M., Jr., and T. K. HOPKINS (1961) "Laboratory experiments with organizations," pp. 464-478 in A. Etzioni (ed.) Complex Organizations: A Sociological Reader. New York: Holt, Rinehart & Winston.
*ZINNES, D. A. (1964) Memorandum: "Support of simulation studies through a parallel historical study." January.
*――― (1966a) "Coalition formation in simulation and international systems." Princeton, NJ: Princeton University Press.
*――― (1966b) "A comparison of hostile behavior of decision-makers in simulated and historical data." World Politics 18(3): 474-502.
――― (1976) Contemporary Research in International Relations: A Perspective and a Critical Appraisal. New York: Macmillan.
―――, R. C. NORTH, and H. E. KOCH (1961) "Capabilities, threat, and outbreak of war," pp. 469-482 in J. A. Rosenau (ed.) International Politics and Foreign Policy. New York: Macmillan.
*ZINNES, D. A., D. E. VAN HOUWELING, and R. H. VAN ATTA (1972) "International system structure and the balance of power propositions: A computer simulation study." Bloomington: Indiana University.

Appendix B: Guide to Northwestern University Simulation Documents

Joseph J. Valadez

This appendix lists seminal papers collected in three volumes at the Northwestern University Library and written under the auspices of Northwestern's Simulated International Processes (SIP) project during 1957-1972. Because these papers grappled with specialized materials of immediate interest to the SIP research unit, they were not appropriate for wide dissemination. Most of them were too rough-cut for publication. These "in-house" materials by and large represent many of the earliest formulations and analyses of the generations of work produced by SIP. Each in its own way represents an event which assisted in the production of the more widely distributed SIP research.

Though for the past two decades these papers have been read by dozens of simulation scholars, there has been complaint about the "relative inaccessibility of many of the studies" (Bremer, 1977: 14). Now that the SIP project has ended and the present summary volume is available, the studies are listed in this appendix for use by all interested persons. It had been my original intention to remedy the inaccessibility of the SIP studies by placing them on microform, but the expense proved prohibitive. It is hoped that this listing will help scholars track down the fugitive SIP essays. Each of the papers appears in the Northwestern volumes as it has in my files, containing "off-the-record" marginal notes.

The three volumes are organized under three broad headings: Verbal Theory, Analyses, and Models and Methods. Each is arranged alphabetically, with no attempt to indicate its relative priority or importance. The latter two volumes consist of two separately bound parts, 1 and 2. This division was made solely to facilitate binding and to increase the portability of each book.

The collection from our project files is a gift to the Northwestern University Library. Not being "circulation copy" but "original," it is restricted to use within the library. Scholars who are unable to visit our facilities are encouraged to write the librarian for a machine copy of desired material.

—Harold Guetzkow
Evanston, Illinois

Volume I: *Verbal Theory*

1. Alker, Hayward R. "The Uses of Simulation for International Relations Theory-Building: Some Reflections and Research Possibilities." New Haven, CT: Yale University, 1965. 6 pp.   1
2. Campbell, Donald T. "Inter-Nation Simulation as a Laboratory for the Teaching of Theories Relevant to International Relations." Evanston, IL: Northwestern University, 1967. 7 pp.   8
3. Caspary, William. "Simulation Studies in Inter-Nation Conflict." Evanston, IL: Northwestern University, 1963. 20 pp.   15
4. Deutsch, Karl W. and Deiter W. Senghass. "Toward a Theory of War and Peace: Propositions, Simulations and Realities." Presented at the meetings of the American Political Science Association, New York, September 1969. 98 pp.   36
5. Elder, Charles D. and Robert E. Pendley. "Simulation as Theory Building in the Study of International Relations." Evanston, IL: Northwestern University, 1970. 29 pp.   135
6. Hermann, Charles F. and Harold Guetzkow. "Prediction Considerations of Possible Relevance in Validating Inter-Nation Simulation." China Lake, CA: U.S. Naval Ordnance Test Station, 1962. 31 pp.   178
7. Hochberg, Herbert. "Simulation Models and Theories." Evanston, IL: Northwestern University, 1963. 34 pp.   209
8. Jensen, Lloyd. "United States Elites and Their Perceptions of the Determinants of Foreign Policy Behavior." Presented at the meetings of the Midwest Political Science Association, 1966. 39 pp.   245
9. Kriesberg, Louis and Michael R. Leavitt. "A Simulation of International Negotiations with Trade-Offs in Objectives." Evanston, IL: Northwestern University, 1969. 33 pp.   284
10. Leavitt, Michael R. "Thoughts on Computer Simulation of International Relations." Presented at the meetings of the American Political Science Association, Los Angeles, September 1970. 21 pp.   317
11. Pruitt, D. G. "Some Comments on the Use of Simulation in the Study of International Relations," Presented at the Symposium in Psychology and International Relations, Georgetown University, June 26-27, 1964. 12 pp.   336
12. Robinson, James A. "Simulating Crisis Decision-Making." Presented at the joint meetings of the Institute of Management Studies and the Operations Research Society of America, 1964. 20 pp.   348
13. ——— and A. Wyner. "Information Storage and Search in an Inter-Nation Simulation." Columbus, Ohio: Ohio State University, May 1965. 35 pp.   368
14. Seki, Hiroharu. "Toward an N-Generation Model of International Process Simulation Theory." Evanston, IL: Northwestern University, 1967. 14 pp.   403

Volume II, *Analyses:*
Part 1

1. Bonham, G. Matthew. "Relations of Validator Satisfaction to Some External Perceptions of Decision Makers." Cambridge, MA: Massachusetts Institute of Technology, 1965. 22 pp.   1
2. Caspary, William. "The Causes of War in INS-8." Evanston, IL: Northwestern University, 1962. 38 pp.   23
3. Coplin, William D. "Comparison of State Department and High School Runs in the World Politics Simulation." Detroit: Wayne State University, 1968. 47 pp.   63

4. Driver, Michael J. "A Structural Analysis of Aggression, Stress, and Personality in an Inter-Nation Simulation." Lafayette, IN: Purdue University, 1965. 102 pp. 110
5. ———. "European Perceptions of Nations: A Multidimensional Analysis of National Points of View." Evanston, IL: Northwestern University, 1972. 40 pp. 218
6. Gottheil, Diane L. "An Approach to a Comparison of Verbal Theories of International Relations with Inter-Nation Simulation Theory: Examples from Wolfers on Alliances." Urbana, IL: University of Illinois, 1966. 40 pp. 260
7. Hermann, Charles F. and Margaret G. Hermann. "Memorandum No. 1 For Project Michelson: Some Relations of Crisis to Selected Decision Processes and Outcome Variables." Studies in Crisis Decision-Making Project. Evanston, IL: Northwestern University, 1964. 24 pp. 300
8. ———. "Memorandum No. 2 For Project Michelson: Some Relations of Crisis to Selected Decision Process and Outcome Variables." Studies in Crisis Decision-Making Project. Evanston, IL: Northwestern University, 1964. 8 pp. 326
9. Hoole, Francis W. "Societal Conditions and Political Aggression: The Examination of Selected Hypotheses Derived from Frustration-Aggression Theory." Bloomington: Indiana University, 1972. 18 pp. 334
10. Krend, Jeffrey A. "A Comparison of Guetzkow-Modelski Correspondence Ratings." Evanston, IL: Northwestern University, 1969. 6 pp. 352
11. McGowan, Patrick J. "Some External Validities of the Inter-Nation Simulation." Evanston, IL: Northwestern University, 1972. 100 pp. 358

Volume II, *Analyses:*
Part 2

1. Nardin, Terry. "Integrative Behavior in a Simulated International System." Evanston, IL: Northwestern University, 1965. 54 pp. 1
2. Pirro, Ellen B. "Frustration-Aggression: A Causal Model Analysis." Evanston, IL: Northwestern University, 1972. 50 pp. 57
3. Pool, Ithiel de Sola. "Comparison of a Human Game and a Computer Simulation." Cambridge, MA: Massachusetts Institute of Technology, 1969. 21 pp. 106
4. Remy, Richard C. "Trade and Defense in the IPS–International Processes Simulation–and Selected Referent Systems." Evanston, IL: Northwestern University, 1967. 47 pp. 127
5. Rosenband, Larry. "Comparison Between an Inter-Nation Simulation and a Real World of 1955." Evanston, IL: Northwestern University, 1968. 30 pp. 174
6. Schwartz, David C. "Experimental Studies in Alliance Behavior." Evanston, IL: Northwestern University, 1966. 19 pp. 332
7. Sherman, Allan William. "The Social Psychology of Bilateral Negotiation." Evanston, IL: Northwestern University, August 1973. 102 pp. 223
8. Shapiro, Michael J. "Cognitive Rigidity and Moral Judgments in an Inter-Nation Simulation." Evanston, IL: Northwestern University, 1963. 17 pp. 350
9. Smoker, Paul L. "International Processes Simulation: An Evaluation." Presented at the Events Data Measurement Conference, University of Michigan, East Lansing, May 1970. 32 pp. 370
10. Soroos, Marvin S. "Crisis Behaviors in the International Processes Simulation and the Berlin Reference System." Raleigh: North Carolina State University, 1971. 32 pp. 411

11. Streufert, Siegfried. "The Components of a Simulation of Local Conflict: An Analysis of the Tactical and Negotiations Game." Evanston, IL: Northwestern University, 1968. 62 pp. 456
12. Targ, Harry R. and Terry Nardin. "The Inter-Nation Simulation as a Predictor of Contemporary Events." Evanston, IL: Northwestern University, 1965. 27 pp. 518

Volume III, *Models and Methods:* Part 1

1. Bailey, George C. "Utilizing Simulation of International Behavior in Political-Military Affairs: A Preliminary Analysis." Human Sciences Research, Inc., April 1967. 30 pp. 1
2. Bonham, C. Matthew. "A Computer Simulation of Non-Crisis Information Processing by Foreign Policy Decision-Makers." Berkeley: University of California, 1970. 30 pp. 38
3. Christensen, Cheryl. "A User's Observation of the Benson Model." Evanston, IL: Northwestern University, 1969. 8 pp. 68
4. Gleditsch, Nils Petter. "Report on the Reliability of the Message from Coding in International Processes Simulation." Evanston, IL: Northwestern University, 1967. 12 pp. 76
5. Gomer, Louise C. "Master List of Variables in the Simulation of International Processes." Evanston, IL: Northwestern University, 1967. 122 pp. 93
6. Krend, Jeffrey A. "Computer Simulations of International Relations as Heuristics for Social Status, Action and Change." Simulated International Processes Project. Evanston, IL: Northwestern University, 1972. 82 pp. 210
7. ———. "A Documentation of Paul Smoker's IPS." Evanston, IL: Northwestern University, 1971. 136 pp. 293

Volume III, *Models and Methods:* Part 2

1. Krend, Jeffrey A. "A Reconstruction of Oliver Benson's Simple Diplomatic Game." Similated International Processes Project. Evanston, IL: Northwestern University, 1970. 69 pp. 1
2. Leavitt, Michael R. "A Comparison of Four War Models in Man-Computer Simulations." Evanston, IL: Northwestern University, 1967. 47 pp. 81
3. ———. "Partial Annotated Bibliography on Military Operations/Defense Systems Simulations." Washington, DC: Industrial College of the Armed Forces, 1969. 18 pp. 155
4. Meyers, Mary Lee. "Bibliographic and Abstracted Sources: An Annotated Listing of Sources Which Include Materials Dealing with Simulation in the Social Sciences, Especially Those Concerned with the Simulation of International Processes." Evanston, IL: Northwestern University, 1968. 23 pp. 173
5. Park, Tong-Whan. "A Guide to Data Sources in International Relations: Annotated Bibliography with Lists of Variables." Evanston, IL: Northwestern University, 1968. 45 pp. 197
6. Pelowski, Allan L. "One Approach to Simulation Module Construction in International Relations." Evanston, IL: Northwestern University, 1969. 28 pp. 242
7. Seki, H. "The Use of PLATO in Inter-Nation Simulation." Evanston, IL: Northwestern University, 1966. 3 pp. 309

8. Smoker, Paul L. "Participant's Manual—International Processes Simulation." Evanston, IL: Northwestern University, 1968. 39 pp. 270
9. Zinnes, Dina A. "Coalition Formation in Simulation and International Systems." Princeton, NJ: Princeton University, 1966. 32 pp. 312

SIP Ph.D. Dissertations

These dissertations are not included in the SIP Northwestern University Library collection. Copies may be obtained through Inter-Library Loan and in many cases through University Microfilms International, Ann Arbor, Michigan.

1. Bremer, Stuart A. "National and International Systems: A Computer Simulation." East Lansing: Michigan State University, 1970. 307 pp.
2. Brody, Richard Alan. "Some Systemic Effects of the Spread of Nuclear Weapons Technology: A Study Through Simulation of a Multi-Nuclear Future." Evanston, IL: Northwestern University, 1963. 192 pp.
3. Chadwick, Richard Waller. "Developments in a Partial Theory of International Behavior: A Test and Extension of Inter-Nation Simulation Theory." Evanston, IL: Northwestern University, 1966. 311 pp.
4. Driver, Michael J. "The Perception of Simulated Nations: A Multidimensional Analysis of Social Perception as Affected by Situational Stress and Characteristic Levels of Cognitive Complexity in Perceivers." Princeton, NJ: Princeton University, 1962. 370 pp.
5. Forcese, Dennis. "Power and Alliance Cohesion." St. Louis: Washington University, 1968. 152 pp.
6. Hermann, Charles Fraser. "Crises in Foreign Policy Making: A Simulation of International Policy." Evanston, IL: Northwestern University, 1965. 321 pp.
7. Hermann, Margaret G. "Stress, Self-Esteem, and Defensiveness in an Inter-Nation Simulation." Evanston, IL: Northwestern University, 1965. 144 pp.
8. Leavitt, Michael R. "A Computer Simulation of International Alliance Behavior." Evanston, IL: Northwestern University, 1971. 299 pp.
9. Nardin, Terry. "Uses of Threats in Strategic Interaction: An Experiment in International Politics." Evanston, IL: Northwestern University, 1967. 190 pp.
10. Noel, Robert C. "A Simplified Political-Economic System Simulation." Evanston, IL: Northwestern University, 1963. 169 pp.
11. Smoker, Paul L. "An International Processes Simulation: Development, Usage, and Partial Validation." Lancaster, England: University of Lancaster, 1968.
12. Soroos, Marvin Stanley. "International Involvement and Foreign Behaviors in the International Processes Simulation and a Real World Reference System." Evanston, IL: Northwestern University, 1972. 195 pp.
13. Sullivan, Dennis G. "Towards an Inventory of Major Propositions Contained in Contemporary Text Books in International Relations." Evanston, IL: Northwestern University, 1963. 390 pp.
14. Targ, Harry Robert. "Impacts of an Elementary School Inter-Nation Simulation on Developing Orientations to International Politics." Evanston, IL: Northwestern University, 1967. 205 pp.
15. Wright, George D. "Inter-Group Communication and Attraction in Inter-Nation Simulation." St. Louis: Washington University, 1963. 148 pp.

Appendix C: The Northwestern Simulation Archives

Walter E. Busse

Social, political, and economic outputs from four SIP simulations, consisting of a variety of paper forms and records, computer printout, and microfilm, are accessible to all qualified researchers who wish to consult them. The simulations include (1) the Richard A. Brody (1963a) and Michael J. Driver (1977) INS runs; (2) the John Raser and Wayman Crow (1964, 1969) WINSAFE II, INS runs; (3) the INS directed by Dorothy Meier and Arthur Stickgold (1965) and investigated later by Terry Nardin (1967, 1969); and (4) Paul Smoker's (1969, 1981) International Processes Simulation. The Simulation Archives are located at the Northwestern University Library in Evanston, (Illinois 60201). A complete listing of the Archives is presented by Walter E. Busse (1969) in "Northwestern Simulation Archives: Man-Computer Models of International Relations," which is available from the Northwestern University Library upon request.

Index

In order to keep the index within bounds, emphasis has been given in the listing to those scholars in international relations whose works have been used in building global models, both in terms of their development of the simulations themselves and in their provision of empirical grounding for the constructions. The indexing of the substantive materials in the book includes references to basic concepts as well as a listing of variables used in constructing the simulations.* Although the index is not comprehensive in its coverage, it is believed that central aspects of the project on Simulated International Processes have been referenced.

Abel, T., 354
Abt, C., 19, 288
accountability, level of, 312
aggression, 203, 213, 217, 235, 236, 246, 261
agreements, 59, 131, 223, 228, 287
aid (AID), 155; seeking of, 262
Alger, C. F., 16, 102, 115, 255, 256, 258
Alker, H. R., Jr., 18, 97, 199-200, 203-244, 249, 349, 350, 351
Allan, P., 338
alliances (ALLY), 161, 182, 201, 219, 224, 227, 228, 229, 236, 245, 246, 248, 292, 293
alternative future world, 224, 228, 235, 236, 238, 245, 249
ambiguity, perceived, 232, 246
Anderson, L. F., 255, 357
Angell, R. C., 104
antiforeign demonstrations, 238, 245, 301, 306
antigovernment demonstrations, 238, 245, 301
Arbatov, G., 299
armament, 54, 59, 290
Aron, R., 146, 199
Ashley, R. K., 333-334
assassination, 304
attitudes, see ambiguity, caution, defensiveness, ethnocentrism, fixity of attitudes, fixity of beliefs, friendli-

ness, militarism, moral rigidity, nationalism, national stereotyping, peacefulness, respect, risk-taking, self-esteem, tension, trust, world opinion
authority, 26, 27, 28, 280

Banks, A. S., 92, 142, 287
basic capability (BC, BCP, TBC), 39, 42, 45, 48, 58, 66, 117, 119, 138, 139, 140, 142, 158, 159, 162, 163, 164, 168, 239, 240, 282, 283, 285, 298, 315, 384
basic resources, 123, 127
Beach, P. F., 268
Beer, S., 256
Benson, O., 13, 192, 288
Bennett, J. P., 349, 351
blocs (OPOW, APOW, FCCUE, EDEP, TAID, NEED), 56-58, 60-61, 150, 156, 167, 218, 229, 245-248, 272, 287-289, 292-295, 298, 299; voting behavior, 201, 223, 228; see also alliances
Bloomfield, L. P., 17, 19, 268, 339
Bock, P. G. and Alker, 197, 199-200, 203-244, 249, 350
Boguslaw, R., 268
Bonham, G. M., 254, 258, 271, 272, 290, 296, 298, 301, 310, 355
Boocock, S., 255

*When a concept or variable is discussed verbally in addition to its formal representation in the simulations and as a focus for statistical analyses of simulation outputs, only the latter two occurrences are indexed. For example, the item "alliances" refers the reader only to pages on which it is formalized in SIP models or when it is a component of theory statistically examined.

Index

Bremer, S. A., 14, 15, 18, 21, 135-177, 182, 186, 188, 189, 190, 191, 192, 193, 194, 195, 196, 198, 200, 201, 239-240, 241-244, 245, 248, 255, 258, 259, 288, 312, 315, 316, 317, 318, 321, 322, 325, 333, 340, 341, 343, 345, 346-347, 348, 351, 353, 354, 358
Brody, R. A., 23, 169, 182, 195, 201, 202, 203, 224-229, 231, 245, 246, 247, 248, 258, 261, 263, 266, 267, 269, 281, 283, 287, 289, 292, 293, 296, 297, 311, 341, 345, 349, 352; et al., 269
Brogden, M., 104
Brunner, R. D., 18
Burgess, P., 182, 201, 202, 221-224, 227-228, 245, 250, 295, 350
Burton, J. W., 20
Busse, W. E., 343
Butterworth, R., 198

Campbell, D. T., 17, 191, 257
Cantor, R. A., 201, 202, 232-234, 246, 247, 248, 250, 251, 261, 262, 276
capacity to delay response, 201, 230, 231, 232, 246, 271
Cappello, H. M., 201, 202, 223, 226, 231, 247, 355
capital investment, 117, 118, 119
Carter, A. P., 342
Caspary, W. R., 201, 202, 229, 247
caution, 230
Chadwick, R. W., 17, 191, 193, 257, 281, 282, 283, 284, 287, 296, 297, 298, 310, 311, 322
Chaman, A. M., 354
Cherryholmes, C. H., 255
Choucri, N., 333, 339, 346, 351
Christensen, C., 198, 358
cognitive complexity, 203, 204, 206, 208, 210, 213, 233, 235, 246, 247, 248, 261, 264, 265, 266, 267, 269
Colby, K. M., 260
Cole, H. S., 193, 340, 342
Coleman, J. S., 255
collective action, 221, 249
communication, 19, 51, 52, 54, 201, 211, 225, 227, 229, 230, 231, 235, 247, 248, 269, 278, 287, 288, 289, 290, 293, 295

concessions, 296
conflict, diplomatic, 238, 239, 318; domestic, 236; see also aggression, antiforeign demonstrations, antiforeign government, assassination, conspiracy, counterattack war, crisis, expulsion of a lessor diplomat, expulsion overall of an ambassador, guerrilla war, hostility, internal war, mobilization, proliferation (nuclear), proliferation (weapons), protest, purges, riots, revolutions, sanctions, severance of diplomatic relations, strikes, surprise attack, threat, troop movement, unidentified attack
consensus, 276, 277
conspiracy, 312
consumer goods, 158, 159, 160, 163, 164
consumer satisfaction, 137, 138, 139, 141, 163, 164, 165, 168, 176, 184, 355
consumption standards (CS), 39, 41, 43, 66, 76, 78, 85, 189, 283
cooperation, 217, 222, 296
Coplin, W. D., 18, 85, 90, 97, 255
corporations, national and multinational, 107, 108, 109, 113, 117, 122, 182, 186, 236, 239, 303, 332
counterattack, 261
crisis, 208, 214, 232, 235, 248, 262, 263, 267, 276, 277, 278, 280, 288, 289, 290, 296; perceived, 205, 207
Crow, W. J., 194, 201, 202, 205-210, 213, 215, 216, 218, 230-235, 246-250, 269, 270, 271, 272, 275, 276, 278, 292, 295, 312, 315-317, 349-353, 356
Cusack, T. R., 194, 333
Cutler, N. E., 268, 287, 289, 292, 295, 297, 310, 311, 322

Davis, O., 96
Dawson, R. E., 17
decision-making, 217-219, 222-223, 241, 277-278; alternatives in, 210-211, 267, 277; in groups, 206-208, 232, 233, 248, 276, 277-280, 282; see also national goals
decision latitude (DL), 34, 35, 44, 47,

86, 84, 123, 128, 142, 143, 144, 156, 158, 239, 281, 287, 288, 312, 318, 348
defense, effort, 315, 318; spending, 239, 315, 317, 318, 329; see also defensiveness, military capability, military response, national security, passive defense
defensiveness, 262
Deutsch, K. W., 13, 102, 139, 199, 338, 348, 357
disarmament insecurity, 298, 301
Driver, M. J., 182, 201-206, 208, 210, 211, 213, 230, 231, 233, 246, 247, 248, 250, 261, 262, 263, 265, 266, 267, 269, 272, 281, 289, 292, 297, 311
Druckman, D., 191, 215-219, 228, 247, 248, 250, 270, 271, 278, 292

economic development, 313, 318
economic prowess, 287
Elder, C. D., 65-100, 127, 128, 176, 193, 281-283, 298, 322, 350, 351
ethnocentrism, 201, 215, 218, 228, 247, 248, 270, 271, 272, 277, 278, 292, 350
Etzioni, A., 154, 219, 246, 293, 356
expansionistic nations, 207, 208, 209
expulsion or recall of a lessor diplomatic official, 305, 306
expulsion or recall of an ambassador, 238, 245, 305

face-to-face negotiation, 290
Feigenbaum, E. A., 260
Feldman, J. 260
Fischer, R. L., 18
fixity of beliefs and attitude, 266
force capability (FC, AF, CF, TFC, FCCUE, FICP, FCP), 43, 44, 45, 46, 47, 48, 58, 117, 119, 123, 124, 138, 139, 141, 143, 152, 154, 156, 158, 159, 160, 163, 164, 167, 168, 171, 172, 233, 234, 239, 240, 241, 283, 298, 352
Forcese, D. P., 201, 202, 219-221, 223, 228, 248, 293, 294, 349, 352, 353, 356
Forrester, J. V., 193, 333, 338, 346, 351, 355

friendliness, intentions, 218, 219; perceived, 209, 213, 217, 222, 223, 226, 235, 272, 290
Fritsch, B., 338, 351, 357
Fromm, G., 357

Galtung, J., 102, 125
Gamson, W. A., 255
Gelovani, V. A., 338, 353
Gift, R. E., 177
Glick, E. B., et al., 268
Goldhammer, H., 13, 337
Gorden, M., 18, 19
growth, absolute, 313; economic (ALGRO, GRO), 148; rate, 313, 318
guerrilla warfare, 220, 245, 304, 338
Gurr, T. R., 143
Gvishiani, D., 338, 355

Haas, E. B., 102, 236
Hamilton, D. E., 357
Hamilton, W. L., 357
helpfulness, 222
Hermann, C. F., 16, 188, 191, 201, 202, 208-213, 232-234, 246-248, 250, 251, 255, 260, 265, 267, 271, 272, 273, 276, 277, 278-280, 288, 289, 295, 296, 298, 310, 311
Hermann, M. G., 188, 191, 201, 202, 208-213, 250-251, 261, 262, 265, 270, 271, 276, 277, 278, 288, 295, 298 et al., 261, 262 (3rd time),276, 277
Herrera, A., 254, 338, 343, 350, 355
Hickman, B. G., 254, 333, 342, 344
historical world, 236, 239, 241, 244, 245
Hochberg, H., 16, 255
Hollist, W. L., 21, 193, 200, 258, 344
Holsti, O. R., 256, 277, 278, 289; et al., 256, 289
Hoole, F. W., 15, 194, 241
Horn, R. E., 357
Hosoya, C., 298
hostility, acts, 201, 213, 225, 230, 245, 247, 248, 276, 284, 289, 290, 298, 300, 301; communications, 152, 154, 162, 168, 169, 172, 190, 298
Hughes, B. B., 333, 352

Index 397

ideological dependency (IDEP), 155, 156
Imhoff, A., 338
information, handling, 264; search, 210, 262, 263, 277; see also communication, message complexity
internal war, 312
international organization, 106, 107, 133, 182, 186, 301
investment allocation, 239, 313, 317, 328

Jaguaribe, H., 338, 351, 357
Jensen, L., 14, 296, 298, 301
Jervis, R., 267
Jones, S. D., 18

Kaplan, M. A., 142, 256, 292, 339
Kaya, Y., 338, 342, 353
Kile, F., 355
Klein, L. R., 254, 332, 342, 344
Klineberg, O., 270
Kotler, P., 17, 258
Krend, J., 260
Kress, P., 16, 255, 357

Lapin, N. I., 338
Laulicht, J., 20
Leavitt, M. R., 14
Leontief, W., 342, 351
Luterbacher, U., 338

MacRae, J., 125, 126
Markovits, A., 338, 357
mass production, 121-122
McGowan, P. J., 199
McRae, V. V., 288
Meadows, D. H., 193, 254, 338, 353
Meadows, D. L., 353
Meier, D. L., 268, 287
Mesarovic, M. D., 193, 333, 343, 353
message complexity, 262
Milburn, T. W., 208, 356
militarism, 206, 209, 213, 233, 246, 247, 248, 269, 270, 317
Milstein, J. S., 169
mobilizations, 238, 306
Modelski, G., 18, 182, 198, 201, 259, 260, 356
Modigliani, A., 255

moral rigidity, 266, 269, 204, 248
Morgenthau, H. J., 102

Nardin, T., 201, 202, 223, 228, 246, 248, 268, 287, 289, 292, 295, 297, 310, 311, 322
national goals, 209, 211, 232
nationalism, 206, 207, 213, 246, 248
nationality, 269, 270, 272
national security (ALSEC, ALSESC), 125-126, 152-154, 156m, 184, 189, 284, 318, 355
national stereotyping, 201
Noel, R. C., 14, 23, 32-33, 50, 201, 202, 205-208, 209, 213, 233, 234, 246, 247, 248, 249, 258, 269, 270, 275-276, 283, 295, 311, 331, 340, 346, 348, 349, 353, 354
non-governmental organization, see international organization
North, R. C., 145, 177, 256, 289, 298, 323, 339, 346, 351
nuclear proliferation, 224-228, 229, 233, 245, 248, 292

office holding, probability of (POH), 25, 29-33, 65, 85-95, 123-125, 128, 142, 184, 203, 239, 281, 282, 350, 351
Onishi, A., 338, 342, 353
Organski, A.F.K., 145

Paden, J. N., 357
Paige, G., 208, 257, 277
passive defense, 129
peaceableness, 217
Pendley, R. E., 65-100, 176, 193, 281-283, 322, 350, 351
perception, see ambiguity, crisis, of hostility, of other nations by decision-makers, strength, threat
perception of other nations by decision-makers, 267-275
Pestel, E., 333, 343, 353
Petri, P. E., 342
Pfaltzgraff, R. L., 18
political stability (ALPOH, POH), 146, 147, 148, 158, 194, 239, 240
Pollins, B. M., 194, 333
population, 313, 318
power, 219-221, 229, 293, 356

private benefits, 222-223, 228, 245
productive resources (TBC), 239; see also basic capability
proliferation, weapons, 201
propaganda, 298
protest, 284, 297-298
Pruitt, D. C., 161, 280
public benefits, 221-223, 228, 245
public opinion, 124, 128
purges, 238, 245, 304

Rapoport, A., 354
Raser, J. R., 20, 191, 194, 201, 202, 210, 215, 216, 218, 223, 230-231, 232, 235, 246, 248, 250, 257, 265, 269, 270, 271, 278, 292, 312, 315, 317, 352, 356
Rastogi, P. N., 338
Ray, J. L., 357
relative trade, 318
research and development, 113, 118, 186
resource consumption, 239, 312-315, 317, 318, 329
respect, 227-228, 248
revolution (pR and pSR), 35-39, 47-49, 123, 124, 143, 156, 157, 158, 159, 184-186, 189, 190, 194, 239, 282
Richardson, J., 338
Richardson, L. F., 125
riots, 238, 245, 304
risk-taking, 206, 208, 246, 248, 265, 276
Roberts, P. C., 354
Robinson, J. A., 182, 201, 202, 208-211, 221-224, 228, 245, 247, 250, 255, 277, 295, 347, 350
Rosenau, J. N., 142, 331
Rosenband, L., 201, 297
Ruge, M. H., 20, 201, 202, 213, 218-219, 223, 228, 248-250, 355
Rummel, R. J., 78, 92, 169, 281, 287, 297, 301, 305, 306
Russett, B. M., 78, 92, 348

sanctions, 190, 238, 306
Schild, E. O., 255
Schrodt, P., 339
Schultz, R. L., 17, 258
Schwartz, D. C., 257, 290

Scolnik, H. D., 350
Seidelmann, R., 358
Seki, H., 20, 338
self-esteem, 232-234, 246, 265
severance of diplomatic relations, 238, 245
Shapiro, M. J., 96, 199, 201, 202, 204, 205, 247, 248, 250, 266, 269, 355
Sherman, A. W., 161, 162
Shubik, M., 254
Simon, H. A., 277, 310
Singer, J. D., 18, 146, 148, 199, 241
Smoker, P. L., 14, 18, 95, 101-133, 182, 186, 189, 191, 193, 194, 196, 198, 200, 201, 235-239, 245, 301, 304, 306, 310, 311, 333, 340, 341, 344, 351, 353, 354, 356, 358
Snyder, R. C., 13, 16, 23, 63, 255, 257, 258, 277, 311, 356, 357
Solomon, L. N., 355
Speier, H., 13, 339
strength, perceived, 230
Stickgold, A., 268, 287
Streufert, S., 261, 263, 266, 267
strikes, 106-114, 189, 238, 245, 304
Sullivan, D. G., 19, 20, 331, 340, 346, 348, 354
support, search for, 211, 296
Suransky, L., 255
surprise attack, 201, 232-234, 248, 261, 262
Suedfeld, P., 262, 263

Tanter, R., 297, 304, 305, 306
Targ, H., 287
tension, 220, 233, 234, 246
Tetlock, P., 262
Textor, R. B., 92, 287
Thomas, H., 262
Thompson, J. D., 277
Thorson, S. J., 198
threat, 201, 209, 220, 225, 226, 227-228, 230, 233, 234, 245, 245, 247, 248, 297, 298
trade (TRADE, IMLIM, EXPRC), 121, 122, 124, 125-126, 131, 155, 159-163, 167, 171-172, 239, 287, 296-297
trade magnitude, 318
treaties, 287, 289, 293, 297; see also agreements

Index

troop movements, 238, 245, 306
trust, 203, 204, 208, 210, 222, 230, 235, 245, 246, 247
Tygesson, G. L., 176, 181, 192, 198, 251, 358

unidentified attack, see surprise attack

validator satisfaction (VS), 29-35, 36-39, 42-45, 49, 57, 66, 69, 76, 80, 85, 86, 95, 125, 127, 128, 129, 140, 143, 184, 189, 239, 281, 283, 348, 355
Verba, S., 254, 258

Wallace, M. D., 194, 317, 329
Wallerstein, I., 356

Ward, M. D., 21, 176, 192, 193-194, 326, 333, 341, 342, 344
wars (POW and WD), 129, 131, 184, 190, 229, 232-234, 236, 238, 287, 288, 301, 306; likelihood of, 222, 223, 229, 230, 232, 234, 295
Weede, E., 169
Whaley, B., 19, 268
world opinion, 124, 126-127, 340
Widmaier, V. U., 194, 333
Wright, G. D., 201, 202, 227, 228, 248
Wright, Q., 142, 257, 329

Zaninovich, M. G., 256, 289
Zinnes, D. A., 15, 19, 114-115, 168, 171, 194, 201, 202, 225, 226, 228, 241, 247, 248, 289, 290, 292, 298, 300, 311, 327, 358

About the Editors

HAROLD GUETZKOW (A.B., University of Chicago, 1936; Ph.D., University of Michigan, 1948) is Fulcher Professor of Decision-Making in the Department of Political Science at the College of Arts and Sciences, Northwestern University. He formerly taught in the Department of Psychology at the University of Michigan (1945-1950) and in the Graduate School of Industrial Administration at Carnegie-Mellon University (1950-1956). He has been a Fellow at the Stanford Center for Advanced Study in the Behavioral Sciences (1956-1957) and Co-Director of the International Relations Program at Northwestern with Professors Richard C. Snyder and Chadwick F. Alger (1957-1971). He is author, co-author, or editor of several books, including *Groups, Leadership and Men; Multiple Loyalties; Simulation in International Relations; A Social Psychology of Group Processes for Decision-Making;* and *Simulation in Social and Administrative Science: Overviews and Case-Examples.* He worked in the Office of the Under-Secretary of the U.S. Department of State during 1969-1970, and in the United Nations Secretariat during 1970-1971. In 1980 he received the Lentz International Peace Research Award.

JOSEPH J. VALADEZ (B.A., Northwestern University, 1971; Ph.D., Richardson Institute, Lancaster University, England, 1978) is Assistant Professor of Community Development in the Human Ecology Faculty of the University of Maryland. He is an interdisciplinary social scientist and formerly taught in the Escuela de Architectura at the Universidad Catolica in Santiago, Chile (1972-1973) and in the Department of Sociology and Anthropology at Simon Fraser University in Canada (1976-1977). His post-doctoral work at Northwestern University (1977-1979) was jointly sponsored by the Fulcher Chair of Decision-Making in International Affairs and the Department of Sociology. He has been a principal investigator for an exploration in southern Patagonia sponsored by UNESCO's Man and the Biosphere Committee for Chile, and has worked with architects and planners in analyzing experimental South American cities. A consultant to the World Bank, he is currently developing nonsurvey techniques for quantitative evaluation of urban shelter projects.